Airman's Guide

4th Edition

Wayne A. Valey
Captain, USAF (Ret.)

STACKPOLE
BOOKS

Copyright © 1997 by Stackpole Books

Published by
STACKPOLE BOOKS
5067 Ritter Road
Mechanicsburg, PA 17055

Illustrations by Jake Schuffert
Cover design by Wendy A. Reynolds

Printed in the United States of America

10   9   8   7   6   5   4   3   2   1

This book is not an official publication of the Department of Defense or Department of the Air Force, nor does its publication in any way imply its endorsement by those agencies.

Library of Congress Cataloging-in-Publication Data

Valey, Wayne A.
　　Airman's guide / Wayne A. Valey.—4th ed.
　　　　p.　　cm.
　　Includes index.
　　ISBN 0-8117-2658-4
　　1. United States. Air Force—Handbooks, manuals, etc.   I. Title.
UG632.43.V34　　1997
358.4'0023'73—dc21　　　　　　　　　　　　　　　　97–5941
　　　　　　　　　　　　　　　　　　　　　　　　　　　　　CIP

Contents

Preface

This fourth edition of *Airman's Guide* includes a wide range of information about current policies and procedures that relate to pursuing a successful career in the U.S. Air Force. It has been prepared for new airmen, airmen-to-be, career airmen, and family members—all of whom will find it a convenient way to stay abreast of regulation changes and other matters.

Airman's Guide was written with two primary purposes in mind: to serve as a convenient personal reference, since most airmen don't have access to a "five-foot shelf" of all the pertinent directives and information that directly affect their careers and their families; and to present in one volume some of the most frequently talked about programs and to discuss them in everyday terms. The guide also includes sources of further information.

Airman's Guide could not have been written without the strong support and input of many interested people, including noncommissioned and commissioned officers (both active-duty and retired), spouses and family members, civil service personnel, public affairs representatives, employees of Air Force–related private associations, and many others. All of them have given generously of their time and their thoughts to help ensure that the book is timely and that it represents current policies and guidance.

The author and the publisher take pride in presenting this fourth edition of *Airman's Guide.* Serving those who serve, we invite your comments for future editions.

Acknowledgments

There has been a wide range of transitions since the release of the third edition of the *Airman's Guide*. Some have been evolutionary changes in internal Air Force programs and policies. Others have been much more far reaching, such as the advances in aerospace, communications, and information technology and the implementation of "major" personnel and budgetary reductions for the U.S. Armed Forces.

Special thanks to those who found time during their busy schedules to contribute information on current topics of interest and to provide thoughts, insight, and feedback on the manuscript: functional managers at HQ USAF; Air Force Public Affairs representatives; the staff of Air University; the staff of the USAF Academy Cadet Library; the Air Force Association; and retired Chief Master Sergeants Robert DeYoung, Bob Rummel, Bob Vadnais, and Lee Elmstedt. Also, my associates at the Department of Veterans Affairs (Mary Kay, M. J., and Chip, in particular); Kathy Glaaser; Anthony, Tonya, and Daniel; and last, but certainly not least, Jane Devlin and Ed Skender from Stackpole Books for their assistance in producing this expanded fourth edition.

Introduction

Enlisting in the U.S. Air Force is like embarking on a journey. It's a brand-new experience, full of opportunity: an opportunity to serve one's country; an opportunity to participate in a team effort with people from all walks of American life; and, in the process, an opportunity to achieve personal goals and fulfillment.

Whether you're a young airman who just recently entered the USAF, a career-minded noncommissioned officer, or a family member, this book is for you. It talks about life on and off duty. It provides information about Air Force policies, programs, and opportunities. It includes examples that illustrate programs. And it answers commonly asked questions. Each chapter also includes references so that you can follow up if more information is required.

The term *airman* is used throughout the book, sometimes in a dual context. It specifically refers to enlisted personnel in grades airman basic through senior airman. It's also used in a universal sense, to denote any military member in the USAF. Similarly, *Airman's Guide,* has been written primarily for those presently serving in the grades of airman basic (pay grade E-1) through technical sergeant (pay grade E-6), and also for those who are looking toward the future in the broader context by pursuing a USAF career in positions that require further increases in grade and responsibility.

Air Force members' understanding of their role, and the part they assume within the organization, increases the longer they are in the service. In fact, it is an ongoing process throughout a career. As members assume positions of increased grade and responsibility, they gain additional insight into how all the programs (pieces of the puzzle, if you wish) fit together. We can see this evolution in personal growth and commitment by comparing new trainees with those who have progressed in their careers.

Initially, new trainees have very little understanding of how the USAF as a whole functions; we might say they see the small picture. Their world revolves around their training instructor. As they progress through training, they are exposed to wider ranges of information. They also learn teamwork and gain experience by performing tasks and communicating with others. By the time they graduate, they have a much fuller understanding of the USAF and the role they are expected to assume.

As personnel progress in their careers, they assume supervisory responsibilities and positions of leadership. They need to be technically competent within their career field and familiar with other aspects such as security and facility management. To meet mission requirements, they must establish rapport with their subordinates, peers, and superiors. They establish contact with their counterparts at other bases to get crossfeed and ideas, and also with those at higher levels of command to get policy and guidance on matters that affect their operations.

Senior personnel have much broader responsibilities. They are ultimately responsible for ensuring that operational requirements are met, as well as maintenance requirements; support requirements ranging from medical to chaplain, finance, personnel, civil engineers, transportation, the base exchange and commissary, community relations, and protocol functions; and a variety of other activities. At headquarters levels, they oversee programs at many bases, ranging from personnel issues to deployment of weapons systems. They operate with other services and other countries. They also coordinate with government representatives and pursue long-range research and development initiatives with private industry.

In the U.S. Air Force there are two commonly used terms—*the big picture* and *the bottom line.* Being able to see the big picture means understanding how individual actions and programs work, how they affect each other, and what they mean collectively. A summary of the big picture, usually in a sentence or two, is the bottom line.

The USAF distributes a large amount of information (more than twenty-five hundred directives) to outline its programs and policies and to keep its personnel informed about the big picture. Much of this information was reviewed during the process of writing this book; for obvious space reasons, however, topics that relate more directly to general career issues, rather than to specific career fields, are discussed. Changes in Air Force policy do occur occasionally and may, in time, modify some of the policies outlined here. When pursuing an action or interest, it's always best to review the current directive. The same applies for career field descriptions and designations, which can be affected by shifts in technology or in force structure.

In several instances, the words of airmen—noncommissioned officers and officers, young and old, past and present—have been used to clarify concepts and programs. These comments help summarize common ideas and beliefs and provide insight to the topics discussed. They also help to stimulate thought, sometimes more effectively than a lengthy narrative would.

The following pages should help you look into the big picture as you embark on a career in the Air Force. As a bottom line, consider the information here as a starting point toward gaining more knowledge and preparing to meet tomorrow's challenges and opportunities, and remember this adage: "Every exit is an entry somewhere else." "Somewhere else" includes continuing your efforts to seek career development information that recognizes group goals and values as well as individual aspirations. At the very least, you will want to consult other experienced Air Force members and referral services, to keep informed through internal information programs and professional readings, and to increase your knowledge through Professional Military Education (PME) courses.

1

A Professional Approach

It [military life] teaches you to be proud and unbending in honest defeat, but humble and gentle in success; not to substitute words for action, not to seek the path of comfort, but to face the stress and spur of difficulty and challenge; to learn to stand up in the storm, but to have compassion for those who fall; to master yourself before you seek to master others; to have a heart that is clean, a goal that is high; to learn to laugh yet never forget how to weep; to reach into the future yet never neglect the past; to be serious yet never to take yourself too seriously; and to be modest so that you will remember the simplicity of true greatness and the open mind of true wisdom.

—Gen. Douglas MacArthur

The subject of professionalism has received much discussion during recent years. It's a broad topic, one that doesn't come with a simple formula. There is, however, common agreement about the importance of certain basic traditions and values and their role in an institutional framework. Gaining a basic understanding of these values today is an important first step toward meeting the challenges of tomorrow.

COMMITMENT: A TWO-WAY STREET

The first step in a professional approach is understanding and accepting responsibility for commitment, leadership, integrity, and loyalty. In general, commitment is an act of pledging, entrusting, or putting something to a purpose. In the U.S. Air Force, a commitment considers the interrelationship of the individual, relationships with others, the mission of the Air Force, and the needs of the nation.

Everyone's Air Force career begins with an oath of enlistment, involving pledges and solemn promises: "I do solemnly swear . . . support and defend the Constitution of the United States . . . bear true faith and allegiance . . . so help me God." In making that oath we undertake a series of commitments. The Air Force itself also undertakes commitments: to provide for the needs, aspirations, and welfare of its members and the security of the nation.

LEADERSHIP AND "FOLLOWERSHIP"

As you pursue your career and assume positions of increased rank and responsibility, your individual commitment will require deeper levels of involvement. As part of the leadership of the Air Force, you will become more entrusted to help assure that members' needs and mission requirements are met. Along with the role of leadership come two other responsibilities: integrity—accepting standards, being honest with yourself and others, and having the courage to do the things that are right; and loyalty—carrying out decisions, once they've been made, to the best of your ability.

Leadership is a well-recognized ingredient for success in any organization. "Followership" is equally important. Robert D. Gaylor, a former chief master sergeant of the Air Force, described some of the responsibilities of followership in a 1979 edition of the *The Inspector General (TIG) Brief.*

> Aristotle, that famous Greek Chief Master Sergeant, once remarked, "One who has not learned to follow can never lead." It might very well be the smartest thing the great philosopher ever said. . . .
>
> Everyone in the Air Force works for someone so we all qualify as followers. Let's ask ourselves the question, "What do I want from my boss?" I can't answer for you but I can answer for myself. See how many of my points you agree with:
> • I want to be treated with respect and human concern. Since those are two-way streets, I have to be respectful to my boss.
> • I don't want preferential treatment but I expect fair and just play. I have to be fair and honest with my boss to earn equality in return.
> • I want work that is meaningful and challenging. I've got to show my boss that I possess the skill and training necessary to do my assigned job.
> • I want enough authority to make decisions and become involved in planning and organizing my work. It's important that I don't abuse and misuse the authority I'm given.
> • I want my boss to communicate, listen, and keep me informed. My responsibility is to keep my boss advised of problems and solutions that I might be aware of and to promote open lines of communication.
> • I want a boss who inspires me—one who can bring out the best in me. I have to display self-discipline and motivation so my

boss will know I'm receptive to instructions and capable of innovation.

• I want a boss who is not impulsive—one who does not act in haste. I have got to show that I can obey rules and standards so I don't place the boss in a compromising position.

One point becomes crystal clear: The relationship between a leader and a follower is a two-way street—a give and take. You cannot be an effective leader or follower unless you do what you can to promote that kind of an agreement.

RESPONSIBILITY AND AUTHORITY
Responsibility and authority increase with grade and experience. Whereas younger airmen go through trainee and worker phases, noncommissioned officers evolve through worker, technician, and supervisor phases. Senior noncommissioned officers, in turn, dedicate less time to technical duties and more to broader leadership and management issues.

Responsibility and authority go hand in hand. Being responsible means accepting and executing duties and instructions in a timely manner with a minimum of supervision. It begins when you point the finger at yourself and not at someone else. Authority is the right to act and command. There are two kinds of authority: legal and earned. Legal authority is provided for in the Uniform Code of Military Justice (UCMJ) as a means of enforcing standards and obedience. Earned authority is the best kind; it's derived from respect, which inspires cooperation.

INITIATIVE AND INVOLVEMENT
> *Someone once said there are three kinds of people in the Air Force—those who make things happen; those who watch things happen; and those who ask, "What happened?"*
>
> —MSgt Daniel J. McKeon

Personal involvement and initiative can affect success in both individual and group goals. Master Sergeant McKeon's remark was made during a career counseling session with a first-term airman. He went on to explain the importance of seeking out relevant information, applying it to a situation, making a decision, and following through to completion. He also provided examples—duty performance, promotion testing, and assignment forecasting—that show how people can get ahead when they are actively involved and how they can stagnate when they assume a passive role. Similar themes concerning involvement and initiative have been emphasized at higher levels, for example, the "make it happen, make it better" philosophy put forth by Gen. Wilbur Creech, former commander of Tactical Air Command.

A POSITIVE ATTITUDE

A positive attitude is a major plus in any walk of life. It's also a primary factor in achieving a professional reputation. People with positive attitudes are usually realistic, optimistic, helpful, and confident without being overbearing. They chalk up a lot of accomplishments and, in general, have a positive effect on the people around them.

In an article entitled "Positive Attitudes," MSgt Julian R. Lucero discussed several observations he had made as a first sergeant in the USAF. He noted three specific ways personnel of all grades can use a positive outlook to enhance productivity and motivation within a work center.

1. Set the example: Be on time, look sharp and have a positive attitude. It's very common for people to reflect the tones, feelings and stresses of their supervisors and contemporaries.

2. Be competent: When people see your ideas and results being recognized, others will begin to follow the example. Everyone likes to be part of a winning team.

3. Develop and use "personal power." It's just as important as positional power. Think of the best supervisor you ever worked for and about his or her leadership style—or better yet, his or her attitude. Was it proud, positive, and professional? What was it that really made you want to respond with a total effort? Have you adopted part of that style to enhance motivation and productivity in your work environment?

STANDARDS

The Air Force emphasizes high standards of performance, conduct, discipline, and appearance. These are important because they affect the overall image and efficiency of the Air Force. Accepting these standards is a direct reflection of personal pride and commitment.

PROBLEM SOLVING

As airmen are promoted to noncommissioned officers and positions of increased responsibility, they become, by definition, part of management and should be oriented more toward problem solving than problem finding. Identifying potential problems is a valuable service, of course, but it is also important to help identify options for resolving them.

You can contribute to problem solving in three ways:

1. Make recommendations for each problem you've found.

2. Think of all the possible impacts your proposals might have. For example, introducing new procedures for the rapid repair of jet engines could reduce

processing times, but it might also result in safety hazards and reduced engine reliability.

3. Help and follow through on any subsequent actions that may be necessary.

CONSTRUCTIVE CRITICISM

> *It is not the critic who counts, nor the man who points out how the strong man stumbled, or where the doer of deeds could have done them better.*
>
> *The credits belong to the man who is actually in the arena, whose vision is marred by dust and sweat and blood, who strives valiantly, who errs and comes up short again and again, who knows great devotion, and spends himself in a worthy cause.*
>
> —Teddy Roosevelt

Criticism is usually the result of frustration with another's performance or opinion. It happens from time to time in all walks of life; not everything goes perfectly 100 percent of the time. At the same time, it's important to remember that comments should be offered in a positive and constructive way. Putting yourself in your supervisor's shoes may help you understand the reasons behind an action or decision. Remember that those in key positions are considering many factors; they're looking at the mission from a big-picture perspective.

Should a situation arise where you disagree with a decision, first discuss it with someone above your pay grade and try to minimize the impact of your disagreement on those you supervise. Point out potential problems and recommend alternative courses of action. Keep the emphasis on *what* is right rather than *who* is right. Once a final decision has been made, support it and press on to other matters of importance.

UNDERSTANDING THE DIRECTIVES

Air Force directives contain a wide range of guidance and information. They provide sound foundations on which to base decisions. When using them, remember to go with the spirit and intent of the directive. Requirements that are critical and must be followed to the letter usually are prefaced by *must* or *will*. They normally address subjects where specific procedures must be followed because of operational necessity, safety considerations, or the control of funds and resources. Passages that begin with *should* or *may* usually imply the best course of action but allow for interpretation and flexibility at local command levels. Always check that directives are current. Policies and procedures are updated regularly, and passages used one year cannot automatically be assumed to be in effect the following year.

SELF-IMPROVEMENT

Self-improvement opportunities, including both Professional Military Education (PME) and off-duty education programs, yield benefits for you and for the Air Force. PME provides valuable experiences for gaining insight into Air Force–related disciplines through formal instruction and interaction with contemporaries. Off-duty education programs provide information in a specialized field of your choice. Active participation in such programs is frequently viewed as an indicator of your commitment to excellence and your potential for future success.

2

Careers and Goals

The people who join the U.S. Air Force come from all parts of the country and all walks of life. They join for a variety of reasons, and they pursue their careers, brief or long, with different goals in mind. This chapter will help you put your finger on some of your own needs and goals. It will also help you develop a plan, a road map, for achieving those goals by the most direct route.

WHO JOINS THE AIR FORCE AND WHY

Each man and woman who joins the USAF is unique. On the surface they seem very different. Their actions, feelings, and values have been affected by their backgrounds and by the people they've met throughout their individual lives. So why have they decided to join the Air Force? To some it's a job, providing the security and income they need to be self-reliant and independent. Others join because it's a well-respected family tradition. To many, it's a way to gain valuable education and training benefits. It's also a way of life—the desire to serve one's country, the camaraderie, the feeling of belonging, the excitement, the travel, the love of aircraft. Sometimes it's the intangible feeling of achievement, success, and self-satisfaction. Overall, the USAF does offer a system where common goals and individual roles are well defined; that kind of stability and order is an important consideration for many people.

Everyone who joins the Air Force—regardless of background, rank, or reason for joining—meets certain standards. Almost all those in the enlisted force are high school graduates (over 99 percent during the past two fiscal years); some have university degrees. For commissioned officers, a college degree is mandatory. These achievements are indicators of future success; they show that a person has persistence, the ability to stay with a program and succeed. In addition, each candidate must meet a range of preset standards before being accepted. After meeting basic educational requirements, prospective airmen undergo a very selective screening process: They take aptitude tests and physical examinations, and they must meet the requirements of a background investigation. They are also put through a screening process in basic military training school or officer training programs to ensure that they have "the right stuff." Failing to meet the criteria at any step along the way can shorten their career.

7

WHAT IS SUCCESS?

According to the dictionary, success is the achievement of something desired, planned, or attempted. But success means different things to different people. Your personal feeling of success will depend on the values and needs that have meaning for you. Here are some examples:

• Job satisfaction: a sense of belonging, challenge, achievement, recognition, and progression.

• Status: an enhanced self-image, position, prestige, or level of responsibility.

• Interpersonal relationships: socializing, spending time with family and friends.

• Personal growth: through education, religion, or other self-improvement efforts.

• Leisure: time to pursue and enjoy travel, sports, and hobbies.

• Material success: attaining some degree of financial independence and security (owning a home, a car, a stereo system, providing your children's education).

Most people would agree that the best way to seek success is through a balanced approach, one that takes all your interests into consideration. There's also a need to think about timing. Obviously, you can't achieve everything at once. It's a building process. And half of the fun in success is enjoying your achievements along the way. As you reflect on what a successful career means to you, jot down some notes. They'll be useful as you move into the next section, which outlines how you can identify the goals that you want to pursue as your stepping-stones to success.

GOALS

The concept of setting goals has been around for quite a while. Socrates once said, "If you don't know which port you're sailing to, any wind is favorable." In this instance, he was talking about charting a course—charting "goals" to get from point A to point B.

Goals, in careers as in sports, are like game plans. They are your road map for achieving results. They help you channel your efforts, they designate what is important and meaningful to you, and they help you to make the best use of your time.

Established goals are the basis for any successful career. The best way to begin is to identify some of them, write them down, and set a preliminary timetable. But remember, this is your first attempt. Just let your mind flow; you can redefine and relist your goals at any time. Also, don't limit goals to the near future. Think a bit farther than your next assignment or the next promotion.

Once you've identified your goals, ask yourself whether they are realistic and achievable. If they're not realistic, they're fantasies. For example, most of us would agree that being a commander of an Air Force submarine isn't exactly realistic. Nor would it be realistic to make the rank of chief master sergeant or colonel in less than five years of active duty. Also ask yourself whether your goals are compatible with the mission of your present organization and, in general, with the mission of the Air Force.

Let's start now:

Immediate Goals (next twelve months)	**Intermediate Goals** (one to five years)	**Long-Range Goals** (five years plus)
————————	————————	————————
————————	————————	————————
————————	————————	————————
————————	————————	————————
————————	————————	————————
————————	————————	————————

The best way to start defining your goals is by making a written list.

Some Ideas If You're Drawing a Blank. More ideas for goals will come to you as you progress through this book. But if you're drawing a blank right now, think about some of the following general themes.

•   Establish a professional reputation in your duty section.
•   Meet or exceed standards of dress and appearance.
•   Get outstanding performance reports.
•   Get a high rating on your next inspection.
•   Be promoted to _____ by _____.
•   Receive an award or decoration for your efforts during this tour.
•   Complete a university degree.
•   Complete a Professional Military Education (PME) course (Airman Leadership School, NCO Academy, Senior NCO Academy).
•   Narrow down the options for your next assignment and apply for it.
•   Spend time with family and friends. Pursue mutual interests for leisure, hobbies, sports, or travel.
•   Develop a financial plan tailored to your needs, either short-term (a new car) or long-term (a home, children's education).

Achieving the Goals You've Set. Now that you've established some goals, let's think about some general guidelines for achieving them. Writing them down was your first major step, because it helped you identify more clearly what you want to achieve. You've taken a step beyond most of your contemporaries—they're still thinking about their careers in general terms and taking things one day at a time.

After putting them on paper, the single most important factor in achieving goals will be your personal commitment to press on and to make progress with each of them. The best way to do that is to look at each goal closely, list all the logical steps you need to take, and then set some dates for completing each step.

For example, let's look at a senior airman who receives notification in January that he will be able to test for promotion to staff sergeant in April. If promotion is one of his goals, he won't be content with just going in to take the test. He will list some logical steps and set some target dates to make sure that the primary goals of promotion is achieved. This airman's road map to success might look something like this:

Promotion to Staff Sergeant:
   1. Review promotion criteria (read the directive): January.
   2. Understand the points system under the Weighted Airman Promotion System (WAPS), compute the factors that are known to me (time-in-service, time-in-grade, awards and decorations, and performance reports): January.
   3. Find out what the promotion cutoff score was in my specialty for the last promotion cycle. This will tell me the approximate score I need on both the Promotion Fitness Examination (PFE) and the Specialty Knowledge Examination (SKT): January.

4. Obtain study materials: January.
5. Study PFE: January–February.
6. Study SKT: February–March.
7. Final review to avoid cramming: late March–early April.
8. Take test: April.

Obstacles to Success. Four main obstacles can prevent you from achieving the goals you've set for yourself:

1. "I never have enough time." This is probably the most common reason for not pursuing goals. If you find yourself using this excuse, take a good look at your daily schedule and see where all the time is going. You can map out your day, hour by hour, or you can look at it in a broader context.

Time at work:	10 hours x 5 days x 52 weeks =	2,600 hours
Time at sleep:	8 hours x 7 days x 52 weeks =	2,912
		5,512
Credit for 30 duty days (annual leave)		–300
		5,212
Credit for 10 duty days (holidays)		–100
		5,112 hours

So, approximately 5,112 hours each year (the equivalent of 213 days) is committed to work and sleep. That's approximately 58 percent of your time. And the other 42 percent (the equivalent of 152 days) is committed to . . . what?

Many will be quick to protest, "But the Air Force is a twenty-four-hour-a-day job." It's a twenty-four-hour-a-day *responsibility,* true, but not many USAF people work twenty-four-hour shifts consistently, day after day. If you've been having problems traceable to a lack of time, take a look at where you're spending it. You'll probably be surprised at how much time you actually have at your disposal.

2. Not keeping your options open can be another obstacle. Many people who join the USAF aren't initially sure if they are going to make the service a career, so they avoid many programs because they're planning to leave after the initial term of service. But plans do change. Most of those who decide to make the Air Force a career make the decision within the final six months.

3. Peer pressure can also have an effect on achieving goals—sometimes good, sometimes not so good. It's important to be able to tell the difference. Friends can exert a major influence on your goals, even when their own goals are different.

4. Last but not least, think about the timing required to achieve your goals and the consequences of what may happen if you get too far off track. Think of

your career as a journey through life. Life offers everyone a certain amount of years. So does an Air Force career, usually thirty at the most. Let's look at a couple of examples that illustrate how poor timing and getting off track can have an adverse effect on a career:

• Airman Jones joined the Air Force. Like his father, he wanted to make it a career. He didn't do well in technical training school and had to retrain into a less desirable career field. He was frustrated and decided to go absent without leave (AWOL). He came back and received nonjudicial punishment, an Article 15, from his commander. As a result, he lost a stripe. Then he got in with the wrong crowd and started using drugs. His commander decided that his behavior was incompatible with Air Force standards. Airman Jones was separated from the USAF on a bad-conduct discharge. In this case, Airman Jones's goals weren't consistent with those of the Air Force; he was too far off track.

• Staff Sergeant Smith was also career-minded; she set her sights on making chief master sergeant. But she never really gave much thought to planning her career; she just took each day as it came. She didn't study for promotion; she didn't make any self-improvement efforts; she didn't know who wrote her performance report. She finally made technical sergeant after eighteen years. Then she started to take a closer look at her career. It took her another four years to make master sergeant, but now it was too late to make chief. She had reached her high year of tenure (twenty-four years for a master sergeant), and now her retirement was mandatory. In this case, Sergeant Smith failed to make chief master sergeant because of the lack of proper timing; she had a general goal in mind, but her overall commitment was too little, too late.

Reviewing and Updating Your Goals. From time to time you'll want to review your goals to see if you're making progress and to add new ones. When is the right time to do this? Any time is fine, really, but there are three occasions that usually stimulate a lot of thought: after you've been selected for promotion; after you've changed jobs or assignments; and in January, when most people are making resolutions for the new year or reviewing their taxes.

Conducting your review annually, in a specific month, is probably best. That way, you'll make sure to take a fresh look at your goals at least once a year. And that's important for planning purposes.

Sometimes the only way to know how far there is to go is to look back and see how far you've come. Right now, you're at the crossroads—of the past, the present, and the future.

3

Who's Who:
Grades, Roles, and
Responsibilities

As of 30 September 1996, the U.S. Air Force was composed of more than 571,500 active-duty airmen, cadets, officers, and civilian personnel, and 274,700 Total Reserve Forces. Their roles and responsibilities are based on their grade and status and on the traditions and standards established and subscribed to by the Air Force community.

THE ENLISTED FORCE STRUCTURE
The Enlisted Force Structure has three tiers, each with specific grades that correspond to levels of training, technical competence, and leadership and management responsibilities.

As members of the profession of arms, all enlisted members are sworn to support and defend the Constitution of the United States and to obey the orders of all officers appointed over them. As enlistees progress from airman basic to senior airman, they acquire the necessary discipline and professional military education and may be appointed candidates for noncommissioned officer (NCO) status by their commanders. Attaining NCO status is a special point in an airman's career. It's recognition that he or she is capable of assuming positions of increased grade, responsibilities for providing leadership through example, and upholding Air Force policies, traditions, and standards.

Within the enlisted ranks, NCOs take precedence over all airmen and other NCOs according to grade and within grade. Within each grade, leadership responsibility rests on the individual who is senior in rank. The specific responsibilities within each tier are described below.

The Airman Tier. The airman tier, also referred to as the trainee-apprentice tier, is the first tier of the Enlisted Force Structure. It consists of the grades airman basic (AB), airman (Amn), airman first class (A1C), and senior airman (SrA). When they enter the USAF, these airmen pursue training programs and develop skills in their specialties. As airmen progress in grade, they

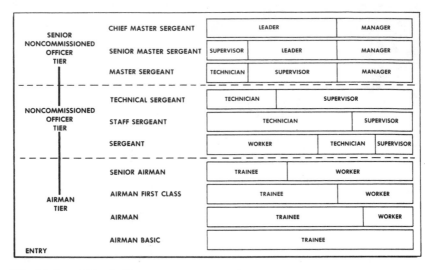

The Enlisted Force Structure

are assigned more responsibilities in their specialties and, at the senior airman level, enter a transition phase to prepare for the second tier and the role of non-commissioned officer. All airmen in the first tier are expected to understand and conform to Air Force standards. As they increase in grade, they develop supervisory and leadership skills and become role models for other airmen.

The Noncommissioned Officer (NCO) Tier. The NCO tier, also referred to as the technical-supervisor tier, includes the grades of sergeant (Sgt), staff sergeant (SSgt), and technical sergeant (TSgt).* The technical and supervisory roles of NCOs increase in scope consistent with their grade and responsibilities. NCOs are responsible for the development of all enlisted personnel under their supervision and must continually strive to ensure that assigned tasks are effectively and efficiently accomplished to meet the needs of the Air Force mission. They have further responsibility for self-development within their specialties through Professional Military Education and off-duty education programs. They establish rapport and maintain open communication with their subordinates, contemporaries, and superiors. They also ensure fair and equitable treatment of personnel and ensure that Air Force standards are met.

The Senior Noncommissioned Officer Tier. The senior noncommissioned officer tier, also referred to as the supervisor-manager tier, includes the

---

* The E-4 sergeant rank was eliminated effective 2 May 1991 as a part of the USAF's manpower drawdown requirements. This change did not affect the status of current E-4 sergeants who attained their rank by 1 May 1991. These personnel will retain the title of sergeant and wear sergeant stripes until they are promoted to staff sergeant.

grades of master sergeant (MSgt), senior master sergeant (SMSgt), and chief master sergeant (CMSgt). Senior NCOs are thoroughly trained in their specialties, and they are also used as leaders and managers with supervisory responsibilities. They are assigned duties commensurate with their skill level and status, for example, as chief of a section or branch, superintendent of a division or unit, or in special circumstances, detachment chief or commandant. They are responsible for developing personnel under their supervision into a cohesive team capable of meeting challenges and effectively accomplishing mission requirements. They provide counsel and guidance to subordinates and provide feedback to commanders and others in their chain of command. They also take the lead in assuring fair and equitable treatment and in achieving, maintaining, and enforcing Air Force standards.

The Life Cycle of Education, Training, and Grade (Rank). The Air Force designated 1992 as the year of training. The outcome of this review created more rigorous training standards for the future and standardized training concepts and procedures. It also aligned skill-level advancement with professional military education (PME) and established career phase points. Along with the changes in the new training program came newly defined terms for the skill levels awarded to enlisted personnel:

• The 3 skill level is referred to as the *apprentice* level. It is awarded to formal technical training school graduates.

• The 5 skill level is referred to as the *journeyman* level. It is awarded when commanders ensure that trainees are at least senior airmen, have been in upgrade training at lease twelve months, have completed the required career development course (CDC) for their Air Force specialties, and have completed all of the training requirements listed in their career field education and training plans (CFETP).

• The 7 skill level is referred to as the *craftsman* level. It is restricted to staff sergeants and above. To be awarded, the airman must be entered into upgrade training and complete eighteen months of on-the-job training, the required 7-level CDC, and all training requirements listed in the CFETP. Trainees are awarded the 7 skill level when they graduate from the craftsman technical training course.

• The 9 skill level is referred to as the *superintendent* level. The new policy restricts the 9 skill level award to senior master sergeants upon graduation from the senior noncommissioned officer academy (SNCOA) for active-duty personnel or completion of the SNCOA correspondence course for AFRES and ANG personnel.

The accompanying illustration shows enlisted education and training paths that coincide with the grades and ranks of USAF enlisted personnel.

Special NCO Positions. The *First Sergeant* plays a vital role in every unit. He or she is a senior noncommissioned officer in the grade of master sergeant, senior master sergeant, or chief master sergeant. First sergeants ensure that

ENLISTED INSIGNIA OF GRADE

AIR FORCE				ARMY	MARINES	NAVY
Old		New				
		(Good until 1 Oct. 99)				

AIR FORCE

Chief Master Sergeant of the Air Force (CMSAF)

Chief Master Sergeant (CMSgt)

First Sergeant (E-9)

Chief Master Sergeant (CMSgt)

First Sergeant (E-9)

Senior Master Sergeant (SMSgt)

First Sergeant

Senior Master Sergeant (SMSgt)

First Sergeant (E-8)

Master Sergeant (MSgt)

First Sergeant (E-7)

Master Sergeant (MSgt)

First Sergeant (E-7)

ARMY

Sergeant Major of the Army (SMA)

Command Sergeant Major (CSM)

Sergeant Major (SGM)

First Sergeant (1SG)

Master Sergeant (MSG)

Platoon Sergeant (PSG) or Sergeant First Class (SFC)

MARINES

Sergeant Major of the Marine Corps (SgtMajMC)

Sergeant Major (SgtMaj)

Master Gunnery Sergeant (MGySgt)

First Sergeant (1stSgt)

Master Sergeant (MSgt)

Gunnery Sergeant (GySgt)

NAVY

Master Chief Petty Officer of the Navy (MCPON)

Master Chief Petty Officer (MCPO) **

Fleet Command Master Chief Petty Officer ***

Senior Chief Petty Officer (SCPO) **

Chief Petty Officer (CPO)

Air Force	Army	Marines	Navy
Technical Sergeant (TSgt)	Staff Sergeant (SSG)	Staff Sergeant (SSgt)	Petty Officer First Class (PO1) **
Staff Sergeant (SSgt)	Sergeant (SGT)	Sergeant (Sgt)	Petty Officer Second Class (PO2) **
Senior Airman (Sr Amn) / Sergeant (Sgt) / Senior Airman/Sergeant	Corporal (CPL) / Specialist 4 (SP4)	Corporal (Cpl)	Petty Officer Third Class (PO3) **
Airman First Class (A1C)	Private First Class (PFC)	Lance Corporal (LCpl)	Seaman (Seaman)
Airman (Amn)	Private E-2 (PV2)	Private First Class (PFC)	Seaman Apprentice (SA)
Airman Basic (AB) (no insignia)	Private E-1 (PV1) (no insignia)	Private (Pvt) (no insignia)	Seaman Recruit (SR)

OFFICER INSIGNIA OF GRADE

AIR FORCE	ARMY	MARINES	NAVY	
General	General	General	Admiral	
Lieutenant General	Lieutenant General	Lieutenant General	Vice Admiral	
Major General	Major General	Major General	Rear Admiral (Upper Half)	
Brigadier General	Brigadier General	Brigadier General	Rear Admiral (Lower Half)	

Captain	Commander	Lieutenant Commander	Lieutenant
Colonel	Lieutenant Colonel	Major	Captain
Colonel	Lieutenant Colonel	Major	Captain
Colonel	Lieutenant Colonel	Major	Captain

OFFICER INSIGNIA OF GRADE

AIR FORCE	ARMY	MARINES	NAVY
First Lieutenant	First Lieutenant	First Lieutenant	Lieutenant Junior Grade
Second Lieutenant	Second Lieutenant	Second Lieutenant	Ensign

SILVER AND BLACK

W-5 Chief Warrant Officer	W-4 Chief Warrant Officer	W-3 Chief Warrant Officer

SILVER AND BLACK

W-2 Chief Warrant Officer	W-1 Warrant Officer

(None)

SCARLET AND SILVER

W-5 Chief Warrant Officer	W-4 Chief Warrant Officer	W-3 Chief Warrant Officer

SCARLET AND GOLD

W-2 Chief Warrant Officer	W-1 Warrant Officer

W-4 Chief Warrant Officer	W-3 Chief Warrant Officer

W-2 Chief Warrant Officer	W-1 Warrant Officer

Note: Grade insignia of 2d lieutenant and major are gold; of other grades in Army, Air Force, and Marine Corps, silver. Naval insignia are gold. The Navy pin-on (collar) insignia are the same as for the other services except that the devices are smaller, and the enamel bands on the warrant officers' bars are navy blue.

assigned personnel are aware of and understand their commander's policies, and they also represent the interests of enlisted personnel to their commanders. They are actively involved in morale, welfare, and career issues that affect members on and off duty. Personnel in these positions frequently interact with other key personnel and agencies on base. As such, they are good points of contact for information, guidance, and assistance.

The *Senior Enlisted Advisor (SEA)* occupies a position at most major installations and at the major commands, numbered air forces, air divisions, direct reporting units, and separate operating agencies. The incumbent, normally a chief master sergeant, has the responsibility of maintaining liaison between the commander and the enlisted force. He or she works closely with other key personnel and staff agencies to ensure that the commander's policies are known and understood, and advises the commander on issues of concern for the enlisted force. SEAs also monitor compliance with Air Force standards, serve on advisory councils, maintain liaison with officials and programs in the local community, and perform other duties related to their positions based on local command needs.

The *Chief Master Sergeant of the Air Force (CMSAF)* is the senior enlisted member of the U.S. Air Force and takes precedence over all enlisted members while serving in the position. The incumbent acts as the personal advisor to the Air Force Chief of Staff and the Secretary of the Air Force on matters concerning the morale, welfare, effective use, and progress of the enlisted force.

CADETS

Cadets of the U.S. Air Force Academy are presidential appointees and are officers in the constitutional sense. They do not have a military rank and neither outrank nor are outranked by enlisted personnel. Cadets are not on active duty, are not saluted by enlisted personnel, and are not placed in supervisory positions over enlisted personnel. However, since they are officers in a constitutional sense, they hold a position below commissioned officers for protocol purposes.

COMMISSIONED OFFICERS

Commissioned officers perform in leadership and management roles and also in specialized and technical fields. For certain USAF positions, a commission is a prerequisite (for example, exercising command authority or other authority as required by law and other statutory provisions, such as the Uniform Code of Military Justice, appropriations acts, and so forth). Officers' responsibilities increase with grade and are based on a three-tier formation: (1) company-grade officers include second lieutenants, first lieutenants, and captains; (2) field-grade officers include majors, lieutenant colonels, and colonels; (3) general officers include brigadier generals, major generals, lieutenant generals, and generals.

CIVILIAN PERSONNEL
Civilian employees constitute approximately one-third of the U.S. Air Force's workforce and perform in a wide range of capacities. Civilian positions are subject to either the General Schedule (GS) or the Federal Wage System (FWS). An act of Congress governs the classification of GS positions, which involve work characterized as professional, scientific, technical, managerial, administrative, or clerical. The annual pay rates for GS positions are the same worldwide and are based on similar positions in private U.S. industry. The FWS governs positions involving trades, crafts, and manual labor. At base level, the focal point for questions about the civilian work force is the Civilian Personnel Office.

FOREIGN NATIONAL EMPLOYEES
As of 30 September 1996, the U.S. Air Force employed more than 6,800 foreign nationals on overseas installations and bases. Foreign nationals are normally used in support roles, as stipulated in Status of Forces Agreements and local laws. At base level, questions regarding their policies or use should be referred through USAF supervisory channels or the host nation's civilian personnel office.

SOURCES OF ADDITIONAL INFORMATION
Air Force Regulation 39-6, *The Enlisted Force Structure.*
Air Force Pamphlet 36-2241, *Promotion Fitness Examination Study Guide.*

4

Organization and Mission

The U.S. Air Force, like the other U.S. armed forces, is organized and operated in the interest of national defense. The basic institutional framework for the armed forces is derived from the Constitution, which places the military under civilian control—under the President, who occupies the position of Commander-in-Chief.

The President delegates authority to the Office of the Secretary of Defense, the Department of Defense, the Office of the Joint Chiefs of Staff, unified and specified commands, and the military departments: the Air Force, the Army, and the Navy (including the Marine Corps, and in times of war, the Coast Guard). In turn, each military department develops and trains its forces to perform the primary functions that support national objectives and policies, and the efforts of the other services.

THE AIR FORCE MISSION

We need a mission that transcends the functions or skills or equipment of any one person, or any single career field, or any one moment in time. We need a mission that unifies all our people, that defines what makes us special, that can inspire, can make sacrifice seem worthwhile. Our mission must be to reach into the air and into space, to control this dimension, to exploit it, to use it to keep Americans alive and free.
—Gen. Merrill A. McPeak, former Chief of Staff
Air University, Maxwell AFB, AL, June 1992

The mission of the U.S. Air Force is to defend the United States through control and exploitation of air and space. Teamed with the Army, Navy, and Marine Corps, the Air Force is prepared to fight and win any war if deterrence fails. In doing this, the Air Force is responsible for providing the following:
• Aircraft and missile forces necessary to prevent or fight a general war.
• Land-based forces needed to establish air superiority, to interdict the enemy, and to provide air support of ground forces in combat.

• The primary aerospace forces for the defense of the United States against air and missile attack.
• The primary airlift capability for use by all the nation's military services.
• Major space research and development support for the Department of Defense.
• Assistance to the National Aeronautics and Space Administration in conducting our nation's space program.

RECENT AIR FORCE RESTRUCTURING INITIATIVES

During 1991 and 1992, the U.S. Air Force underwent its most significant change since its creation in 1947 as a separate military service. Shrinking budgets, technological advances, changed world political environments, and lessons learned from recent armed conflicts were catalysts in the development of a strategic framework designed to ensure that the United States retains the capability to respond to any threat worldwide. As a result, the Air Force restructured with a focus toward streamlining its organizational structure. Unnecessary organizational layers were removed; power and accountability were pushed down the organization; and responsibility and authority were realigned. All levels of the Air Force, from departmental headquarters to base level, were affected by this restructure.

ORGANIZATION

The Air Force mission is planned and carried out at different organizational levels. At the top level, the Department of the Air Force is administered by a civilian Secretary and is supervised by a military Chief of Staff, an Air Force four-star general. Both of these officials are appointed by the President, with the consent of the Senate. The Secretary of the Air Force exercises authority through civilian assistants and the Chief of Staff but retains immediate supervision of activities that involve vital relationships with Congress, the Secretary of Defense, other governmental officials, and the public. The Chief of Staff serves as a member of the Joint Chiefs of Staff and the Armed Forces Policy Council. He also presides over the Air Staff, transmits Air Staff plans and recommendations to the Secretary of the Air Force, and acts as the Secretary's agent in carrying them out. To assist the Secretary and the Chief of Staff, the Secretariat and the Air Staff (also referred to as HQ USAF) establish programs and policies to implement objectives. These, in turn, become mission requirements. The Air Staff operates out of the Pentagon in Washington, D.C., and several other locations. Below the HQ USAF level, there are nine major commands (MAJCOMs), thirty-six field operating agencies (FOAs), and three direct reporting units (DRUs) that, along with their subordinate elements, constitute the field organization that carries out the Air Force mission.

DEPARTMENT OF THE AIR FORCE

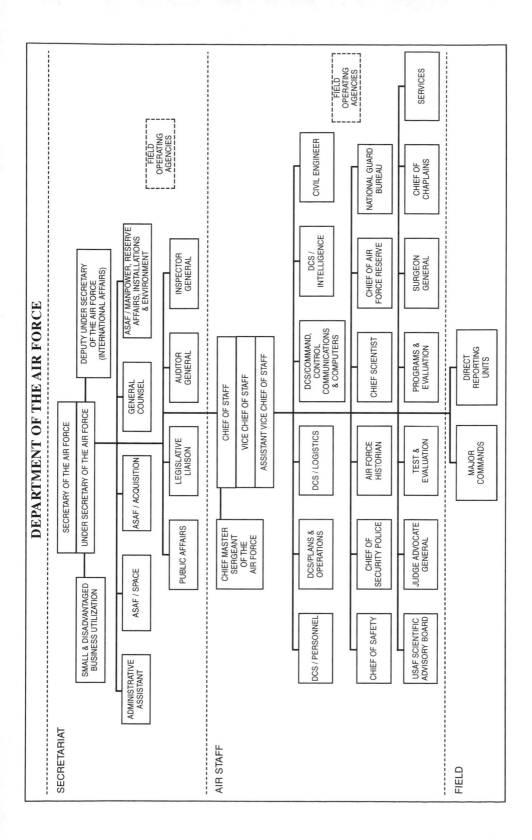

SECRETARIAT

- SECRETARY OF THE AIR FORCE
- UNDER SECRETARY OF THE AIR FORCE
- DEPUTY UNDER SECRETARY OF THE AIR FORCE (INTERNATIONAL AFFAIRS)
- ADMINISTRATIVE ASSISTANT
- SMALL & DISADVANTAGED BUSINESS UTILIZATION
- ASAF / SPACE
- ASAF / ACQUISITION
- ASAF / MANPOWER, RESERVE AFFAIRS, INSTALLATIONS & ENVIRONMENT
- PUBLIC AFFAIRS
- LEGISLATIVE LIAISON
- GENERAL COUNSEL
- AUDITOR GENERAL
- INSPECTOR GENERAL
- FIELD OPERATING AGENCIES

AIR STAFF

- CHIEF OF STAFF
- VICE CHIEF OF STAFF
- ASSISTANT VICE CHIEF OF STAFF
- CHIEF MASTER SERGEANT OF THE AIR FORCE
- DCS / PERSONNEL
- DCS/PLANS & OPERATIONS
- DCS / LOGISTICS
- DCS/COMMAND, CONTROL COMMUNICATIONS & COMPUTERS
- DCS / INTELLIGENCE
- CIVIL ENGINEER
- CHIEF OF SAFETY
- CHIEF OF SECURITY POLICE
- AIR FORCE HISTORIAN
- CHIEF SCIENTIST
- CHIEF OF AIR FORCE RESERVE
- NATIONAL GUARD BUREAU
- USAF SCIENTIFIC ADVISORY BOARD
- JUDGE ADVOCATE GENERAL
- TEST & EVALUATION
- PROGRAMS & EVALUATION
- SURGEON GENERAL
- CHIEF OF CHAPLAINS
- SERVICES
- FIELD OPERATING AGENCIES

FIELD

- MAJOR COMMANDS
- DIRECT REPORTING UNITS

MAJOR COMMANDS (MAJCOMS)

The Major Commands group similar functions together and provide an intermediate level of command between base-level operations and Headquarters USAF. They are organized by function in the United States and by geographical location in overseas areas. Their missions are either operational or support. Operational commands are composed, in whole or in part, of strategic, tactical, space, or defense forces; or of flying forces that directly support such forces. Support commands may provide supplies, weapons systems, support systems, operational support equipment, combat material, maintenance, surface transportation, education and training, or special services to the Air Force and other supported organizations.

Some of the major restructuring changes to the MAJCOM missions that have been undertaken since 1991 include the following:

• Military Airlift Command (MAC), Strategic Air Command (SAC), and Tactical Air Command (TAC) were inactivated, and two new commands, Air Combat Command (ACC) and Air Mobility Command (AMC), were activated. These commands were organized with the realization that airplanes have both tactical and strategic capability and should not be constrained by artificial distinctions. Lessons learned during Desert Storm clearly demonstrated that the line between tactical and strategic airpower had become blurred. During this armed conflict, fighter and attack-designated aircraft that belonged to TAC and bombers that belonged to SAC were employed together against tactical and strategic targets.

• Air Force Systems Command (AFSC) and Air Force Logistics Command (AFLC) merged to become the Air Force Materiel Command (AFMC). This move was, in part, an outcome of the Air Force's commitment to streamline its headquarters organizations. AFMC is now a single organization responsible for fielding and maintaining quality weapons systems. As such, it gives the operational commands a single point of contact for research, development, acquisition, modification, maintenance, and long-term weapons systems support.

• Air Force Communications Command (AFCC) was reclassified from a major command (MAJCOM) to a field operating agency (FOA). As a part of the restructuring effort, the size of AFCC dropped dramatically due to the transfer of field operational communications and computer responsibilities to the new MAJCOMs and agencies they supported.

• Air Education and Training Command (AETC) was formed in July 1993 to combine the missions of the Air Training Command (ATC) and Air University (AU).

As a result of the restructuring initiative, the USAF now has eight MAJCOMs. Their names, roles, and missions are as follows:

• *Air Combat Command (ACC)* is responsible for Continental United States (CONUS) based fighters; bombers; reconnaissance aircraft; command, control, communications, and intelligence platforms; and some theater airlift and

Air Combat Command

Air Mobility Command

Air Force Space Command

Pacific Air Forces

U.S. Air Forces in Europe

Air Education and Training Command

Air Force Materiel Command

Air Force Special Operations Command

Emblems of Major Air Commands

tanker/refueling operations. ACC provides forces directly to unified commands or augments theater forces already deployed to forward locations. ACC was formed in June 1992 from elements of the former MAJCOMs of SAC, TAC, and MAC. Headquarters: Langley AFB, Virginia.

•   *Air Mobility Command (AMC)* is responsible for all intertheater airlift assets and most of the tanker and theater airlift force. AMC was formed in June 1992 from elements of SAC and MAC. The integration of airlift and tankers enables the Air Force to better provide global mobility and reach, thereby enhancing rapid response and the ability to operate with other services and nations. AMC also has single-manager responsibility for tanker/refueling scheduling. Headquarters: Scott AFB, Illinois.

•   *Air Force Space Command (AFSPACECOM)* is both a USAF major command and the USAF's component of the United States Space Command, a unified command of the U.S. armed forces. It is responsible for planning, managing, and operating all assigned space assets; ballistic missile warning and offensive attack; and spacelift/launch and ground control for Department of Defense (DOD) satellite operations. AFSPACECOM also works to ensure close cooperation between research or development activities and operational users of Air Force space programs. Headquarters: Peterson AFB, Colorado.

•   *Pacific Air Forces (PACAF)* is the principal air component of U.S. Pacific Command (PACOM). PACAF's primary mission is to plan, conduct, control, and coordinate offensive and defensive air operations in the Pacific and Asian theaters and in those arctic regions under U.S. control. In performing this mission, PACAF is under the operational control of PACOM. In the administrative and support chain of command, PACAF is responsible to the Air Force Chief of Staff. PACAF's area of responsibility includes Alaska and extends from the west coast of the Americas to the east coast of Africa, and from the Arctic to the Antarctic. Headquarters: Hickam AFB, Hawaii.

•   *United States Air Forces in Europe (USAFE)* conduct, control, and coordinate offensive and defensive air operations in the European theater. Its area of responsibility extends from the United Kingdom to Pakistan. In the operational chain of command, USAFE is a component of the unified U.S. European Command. In the administrative and support chain of command, USAFE is a MAJCOM under the supervision of the Air Force Chief of Staff. The USAFE Commander also serves as the Commander of NATO's Allied Forces, Central Europe. Headquarters: Ramstein Air Base, Germany

•   *Air Education and Training Command (AETC)* is responsible for recruiting, accessing, commissioning, and training USAF enlisted and officer personnel. This includes basic military training, initial and advanced technical training for enlisted and commissioned personnel, and flying training. AETC also conducts and manages the Air Force Recruiting and the Air Force Reserve Officer Training Corps (ROTC) programs, and administers the Community College of the Air Force (CCAF) program. With the integration of Air University (AU) programs into this new MAJCOM, AETC is also responsible for conducting Professional Military Education (PME), graduate education, and professional continuing education programs for commissioned officers and noncommissioned officers. These include the Senior NCO Academy at Gunter AFB, Alabama; the Air War College, the Air Command and Staff College, and the Squadron Officer School for the professional military development of Air Force commissioned officers; the Ira C. Eaker Center for Professional Development; the Air Force Quality Center, which provides quality Air Force education programs and materials, research, and consulting reviews; the Extension Course Institute (ECI), which offers nonresident professional and technical education of Air Force members on active duty, and also publishes and distributes Career Development Courses (CDCs) for an airman's progression through on-the-job training programs; the Air Force Institute of Technology; the Center for Aerospace Doctrine, Research, and Education; the Air University Library; and the Headquarters Civil Air Patrol, a congressionally chartered civilian auxiliary of the Air Force, whose main missions are aerospace education, training, and emergency services. Headquarters: Randolph AFB, Texas.

• *Air Force Materiel Command (AFMC)* researches, develops, tests, acquires, delivers, and logistically supports every Air Force weapons system. It works closely with its customers (the operational commands) to ensure that each has the most capable aircraft, missiles, and support equipment possible. AFMC's involvement is ongoing, from the initial inception of a weapons system on the drawing board to support through its operational life and its final disposition and retirement from use. It operates major product centers, logistics centers, test centers, and laboratories. The command was created in July 1992 from the integration of the Air Force Logistics Command and the Air Force Systems Command. This integration was driven by budget reductions, streamlining of the Air Force, and defense management reforms. The new command emphasizes continuous process improvement and strong partnership with the operational commands and industry. Headquarters: Wright-Patterson AFB, Ohio.

• *Air Force Special Operations Command (AFSOC)* organizes, trains, and equips Air Force Special Operations forces for worldwide deployment and assignment to regional unified commands for conducting unconventional warfare, direct action, special reconnaissance, counterterrorism, foreign internal defense, humanitarian assistance, psychological operations, personnel recovery, and counternarcotics. Headquarters: Hurlburt Field, Florida.

Large installations or Air Force bases are normally assigned to a major command that has a similar overall mission, so you may often hear your base referred to as an "ACC base," a "USAFE base," or an "AMC base," for example.

SUBCOMMANDS AND LOWER LEVELS OF COMMAND
Below the major command level, intermediate levels of command and organization are established to meet mission requirements. They include numbered air

forces, wings, groups, squadrons, and flights. Air divisions (ADs), which were intermediate levels of command between the numbered air forces and wings, were eliminated during 1993 with the restructuring initiative and the decision to delegate more power and authority down to the wing level. This action shortened operational command lines and reduced overhead staff functions.

Numbered air forces (NAFs) were also restructured during 1993 to a strictly operational and warfighting role. With the elimination of support functions, staffing has been reduced by approximately 50 percent. Usually commanded by a two- or three-star general, the remaining NAF staff is dedicated to operational planning and employment of forces for several wings.

Wings are the basic Air Force units for generating and employing combat capability. They may have an operational mission (such as air combat, airlift, or flying training) or a specialized mission such as an intelligence wing. They may also have the responsibility for providing support to a MAJCOM headquarters

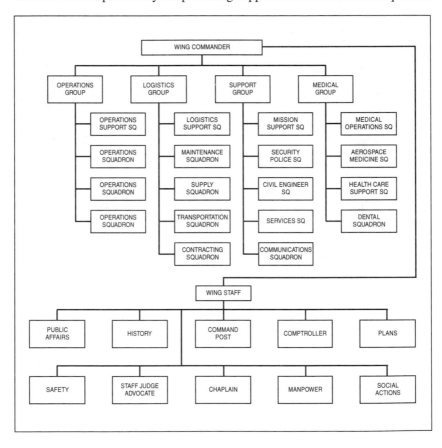

Objective Wing Organization

or geographically separated units. Each wing has a commander who is responsible and accountable for that wing's mission results. A new wing structure, referred to as the objective wing, was designed and implemented to streamline and consolidate responsibilities and move toward clear lines of command. In the majority of cases, the objective wing organization will only have operations, logistics, support, and medical groups assigned. Additional groups, such as security police, civil engineering, and communications, may be added to larger wings. Each of these groups has a commander who is responsible and accountable to the wing commander for mission accomplishment. The Air Force has composite wings that operate more than one kind of aircraft and wings that continue to operate a single type of aircraft. Both may be configured as self-contained units designated for quick air intervention anywhere in the world.

Groups are flexible units composed of two or more squadrons that may have identical, similar, or different missions. Their role may be operational, supporting, or administrative. Groups have numerical designations and usually take the number of the wing to which they are assigned. For example, the groups assigned to the 123 Wing would be designated the 123 Operations Group, the 123 Logistics Group, the 123 Support Group, and so forth.

Squadrons are the basic unit of the Air Force. Each squadron formation is based on either operational commands or the functional grouping of specific tasks and responsibilities (for example, aircrew or missile operations, security police, civil engineering, aircraft maintenance, or transportation).

Detachments are elements of a large unit (squadron, group, or wing) that are geographically separated from the parent unit.

Flights are the lowest unit level in the Air Force. Numerically designated flights exist for small mission elements that need to be incorporated into an organized unit. Alphabetically designated flights are used to group similar functions within a unit. For example, A, B, C, and D flights could be used to designate certain personnel within a Security Police squadron. In turn, those designations could be used to schedule training requirements and periods of duty (day shift, swing shift, mid-shift, and breaks). The term *flight* can also be used to denote a parade formation of two or more squads.

FIELD OPERATING AGENCIES (FOAS)

A field operating agency (FOA) is a subdivision of the Air Force that carries out field activities under the operational control of a USAF functional manager. As a part of the restructuring initiative, HQ USAF redesignated the separate operating agencies (SOAs) as FOAs. This accurately reflects the missions they implement in support of field operations and separates the headquarters management activities and policy-making functions. The USAF has thirty-seven FOAs, whose missions complement but remain separate from those of the major commands.

CAPABILITY	AIRCRAFT
MULTI-ROLE	24 F-16C
NIGHT/UNDER WEATHER ATTACK	12 F-16C (LANTIRN)
LONG RANGE/PRECISION GUIDED MUNITIONS	12 F-15E
AIR SUPERIORITY	24 F-15C
AIR REFUELING	6 KC-135R
SURVEILLANCE/CONTROL	3 E-3A

NOTE 1. THE MISSION OF A WING, SUCH AS THE ONE SHOWN ABOVE, WOULD BE AIR INTERVENTION.

NOTE 2. A COMPOSITE WING TASKED FOR GROUND SUPPORT COULD ALSO INCLUDE A MIX OF A-10s, F-16s, AND AC-130 GUNSHIPS.

NOTE 3. A COMPOSITE WING TASKED FOR SPECIAL OPERATIONS COULD ALSO INCLUDE A MIX OF MH-53J PAVE LOW AND MH-60G PAVE HAWK HELICOPTERS, MC-130 COMBAT TALONS, AND AC-130 GUNSHIPS.

NOTE 4. BOMBERS AND ELECTRONIC SUPPORT AIRCRAFT, SUCH AS THE EF-111 RAVEN, COULD ALSO BE INCLUDED IN COMPOSITE WINGS WHOSE MISSIONS REQUIRE THE SUPPORT OF SUCH AIRCRAFT.

Possible Makeup of a Composite Wing

Air Force Audit Agency (AFAA). Headquartered in Washington, D.C., AFAA provides all levels of Air Force management with independent, objective evaluations of the effectiveness with which they are carrying out managerial responsibilities (operational, financial, and support).

Air Force Base Conversion Agency (AFBCA). Headquartered in Washington, D.C., this new field agency serves as the federal real property disposal agent and provides integrated execution management for Air Force bases in the United States as they are closed under the delegated authorities of the Base Closure and Realignment Act of 1988 and the Defense Base Closure and Realignment Act of 1990. AFBCA works closely with state and local committees, commissions, and special authorities to help develop reuse opportunities that will help minimize adverse economic impacts in communities affected by base closings.

Air Force Center for Environmental Excellence (AFCEE). Headquartered at Brooks AFB, Texas, AFCEE is responsible for providing expertise for environmental compliance and cleanup; management support for military construction programs; and design services for Air Force installations and facilities.

Air Force Civil Engineer Support Agency (AFCESA). Headquartered at Tyndall AFB, Florida, AFCESA is responsible for providing civil engineering technical and professional support to the Air Force. Through seven directorates, the agency provides products and processes that deal with readiness, fire protection, maintenance, systems engineering, communication-computer systems, construction and cost management, and executive services.

Air Force Command, Control, Communications, and Computer Agency (AFCCCCA). Headquartered at Scott AFB, Illinois, AFCCCCA develops and validates command, control, communications, and computer (C^4) architectures, technical standards, requirements, policies, procedures, and solutions. It also ensures the integration and interoperability among Air Force C^4 systems and ensures that policies, procedures, and applications take full advantage of C^4 capabilities to meet future information requirements. The headquarters is composed of four primary functional areas: Plans and Analysis, Systems and Procedures, Interoperability and Technology, and Resources.

Air Force Cost Analysis Agency (AFCAA). Located in Arlington, Virginia, AFCAA is responsible for the development of cost analysis tools, methods, databases, models, and automated systems. These are used in resource allocation and cost management decisions Air Force–wide.

Air Force Doctrine Center (AFDC). Headquartered at Langley AFB, Virginia, AFDC develops and publishes basic and operational-level doctrine for the Air Force, provides Air Force input into joint and multinational doctrine development, and ensures that Air Force doctrine is consistent with policy and joint doctrine. AFDC serves as the coordinating review authority for joint tactics, techniques, and procedures and their development. It also serves as the Air Force's primary source of expertise for military operations other than war doctrine, and strategy development as well as training, education, exercises, and simulations.

Air Force Flight Standards Agency (AFFSA). Headquartered at Washington, D.C., AFFSA manages the interoperability of civil and military airspace and air traffic control systems to ensure worldwide combat and peacetime capabilities.

Air Force Frequency Management Agency (AFFMA). Located at the Pentagon, AFFMA represents the USAF in various national and international forums concerning the use of the radio frequency electromagnetic spectrum.

Air Force Historical Research Agency (AFHRA). Located at Maxwell AFB, Alabama, AFHRA provides facilities for research in Air Force history. The agency furnishes historical and archival services to the Air Force and serves as the principal repository for Air Force historical records. It contains more than 3 million documents relating to the history of the Air Force from its beginning to its present. AFHRA also determines the lineage and honors of the Air Force units and prepares books and other historical works on the Air Force and military aviation. In addition, it serves as an advisor regarding declassification of Air Force records held by the National Archives.

Air Force History Support Office (AFHSO). Headquartered in Washington, D.C., AFHSO performs three primary functions: It researches, writes, and publishes books and other studies on the history of the Air Force; provides historical support through the Air Force historian to HQ USAF; and publishes books to help the Air Force formulate strategy, plans, and doctrine to conduct its operations, educate Air Force students at professional military schools, provide scholars with research and teaching materials, and inform the public about the role of the Air Force in national security.

Air Force Inspection Agency (AFIA). Located at Kirtland AFB, New Mexico, AFIA reports to the Inspector General and is functionally aligned under the Office of the Secretary of the Air Force. Through its four inspection directorates, it assesses Air Force warfighting capabilities and resource management effectiveness. It also makes recommendations for improving USAF mission capabilities and conducts special reviews and inquiries.

Air Force Legal Services Agency (AFLSA). Headquartered at Bolling AFB, D.C., AFLSA provides Air Force–wide legal services in the areas of military justice, patents, claims and tort litigation, general litigation, labor law, preventive law, and legal aid. It conducts post-trial review of court proceedings and ensures proper appellate action. AFLSA also operates and maintains the Judge Advocate General's Department computer research and data management systems.

Air Force Logistics Management Agency (AFLMA). Located at the Gunter Annex to Maxwell AFB, Alabama, AFLMA's mission is to enhance the USAF's readiness and combat capability by conducting studies and developing, analyzing, testing, evaluating, and recommending new or improved concepts, methods, systems, or procedures that result in improving logistics efficiency and effectiveness.

Air Force Management Engineering Agency (AFMEA). Headquartered at Randolph AFB, Texas, AFMEA develops and maintains Air Force manpower standards in order to improve manpower utilization. AFMEA ensures implementation of technical and procedural guidance of the AF Management Engineering Program and supervises its assigned Management Engineering Teams (MET), who use process analysis and work-measurement techniques to make recommendations to improve productivity for Air Force activities.

Air Force Medical Operations Agency (AFMOA). Headquartered at Bolling AFB, D.C., AFMOA supports the Air Force Surgeon General in formulating plans, policies, and programs for the USAF's Medical Service, aerospace medicine, clinical investigations, quality assurance, health promotion, family advocacy, bioenvironmental engineering, military public health, and radioactive material management.

Air Force Medical Support Agency (AFMSA). Headquartered at Brooks AFB, Texas, AFMSA assists the Air Force Surgeon General in developing programs, policies, and practices that relate to Air Force health care in peace and war. To carry out these responsibilities, AFMSA has four divisions: Patient Administration, Health Facilities, Medical Information Systems, and Medical Logistics.

Air Force News Agency (AFNA). Headquartered at Kelly AFB, Texas, AFNA provides a focal point for special information activities of the Air

Force. It has an internal information program that provides news and information to members of the USAF through printed and electronic products such as *Airman Magazine,* the *Air Force Policy Letter,* "Air Force Television News," and "Air Force Radio News." Its external information program provides hometown news items and other releases to public newspapers and to radio and television stations. The agency also provides information and entertainment programming to overseas Department of Defense (DOD) personnel and their families as part of the DOD Armed Forces Radio and Television Service (AFRTS).

Air Force Office of Special Investigations (AFOSI). Headquartered at Bolling AFB, D.C., AFOSI conducts investigations of criminal offenses and fraud, as well as other special investigations as requested by the commander of any Air Force activity. In carrying out its mission, AFOSI acts primarily as a fact-finding agency. It has its own highly trained special agents, who may be Air Force commissioned officers, NCOs, or civilians. In the criminal area, the AFOSI conducts investigation of offenses committed against persons, property, or the Air Force, Usually jurisdiction is limited to the commission of crimes on Air Force installations that involve personnel subject to the Uniform Code of Military Justice. AFOSI is also involved in matters of counterintelligence and investigation instances of espionage, sabotage, treason, and major security violations that involve Air Force people. AFOSI also conducts antiterrorism and personnel protective operations.

Air Force Operations Group (AFOG). Located in Washington, D.C., AFOG maintains a twenty-four-hour watch on all current operations and handles emergency actions through the Air Force Operations Center. It coordinates actions among USAF major commands, other field operating agencies, and direct reporting units in response to taskings from the Joint Chiefs of Staff National Military Command Center (NMCC). AFOG also maintains the USAF portion of the Worldwide Military Command and Control System Intercomputer Network, the Air Force's resources and training system database, and the Joint Uniform Lessons Learned database. Structurally, AFOG is supported by ten Air Staff functional areas: Operations, Plans, Logistics, Manpower and Personnel, Intelligence, Civil Engineering, Security Policy, Information Systems Management, Medical Readiness Division, and Chaplain Resources. The Air Force Reserve and the Air National Guard also provide support to the AFOG.

Air Force Pentagon Communications Agency (AFPCA). Headquartered in Washington, D.C., AFPCA provides command, control, communications, and computer systems and services for the Office of the Secretary of Defense (OSD), the Joint Chiefs of Staff, the National Military Command Center (NMCC), the Secretary of the Air Force, HQ USAF, and other command centers in Washington, D.C. This includes maintaining secure and nonsecure telecommunications switches, eight thousand telephones, and an extensive pager and cellular telephone network.

Air Force Personnel Center (AFPC). Headquartered at Randolph AFB, Texas, AFPC provides personnel operations service and develops programs and policies for the USAF's military and civilian personnel.

Air Force Personnel Operations Agency (ASPOA). Located in Washington, D.C., ASPOA executes several personnel programs; develops and operates officer, enlisted, and civilian models and databases for management information; executes the Air Force Employee Development Program and training budgets; and manages the Air Force Relocation, Employee, and Labor Relations Program.

Air Force Program Executive Office (AFPEO). Located at the Pentagon, AFPEO is composed of six senior officials who each manage a portfolio of major and selected Air Force acquisition programs: Bombers, Missiles, and Trainers; Conventional Strike Systems; Tactical and Airlift Systems; Information Systems; Space Systems; and Command, Control, and Communications Systems.

Air Force Real Estate Agency (AFREA). Located at Bolling AFB, D.C., AFREA works with the Office of the Deputy Assistant Secretary for Installations to acquire, manage, and dispose of real property worldwide for the Air Force.

Air Force Reserve (AFRES). Headquartered at Robins AFB, Georgia, AFRES provides trained units and qualified personnel to augment active-duty forces in time of war or national emergency, or when required to maintain national security. It also performs peacetime missions compatible with training and mobilization readiness requirements.

Air Force Review Boards Agency (AFRBA). Located at the Pentagon, AFRBA manages various military and civilian appellate processes for the Secretary of the Air Force. The agency is composed of the Air Force Board for Correction of Military Records; the Air Force Civilian Appellate Review Agency; and the Air Force Personnel Council, which examines matters such as discharges, physical disability cases, and decorations.

Air Force Safety Center (AFSC). Located at Kirtland AFB, New Mexico, AFSC is responsible for executing Air Force Safety and Nuclear Surety policies, plans, and programs. The center has eight directorates: flight safety; ground safety; weapons and space safety; nuclear surety; system safety and engineering; life sciences; safety education; and computer systems.

Air Force Security Police Agency (AFSPA). Located at Kirtland AFB, New Mexico, AFSPA provides a center of expertise for developing and implementing programs associated with the security of nuclear weapons and weapons systems; law enforcement; airbase defense; antiterrorism; information security; and combat arms marksmanship and training.

Air Force Services Agency (AFSA). Headquartered in San Antonio, Texas, AFSA supports the bases, major commands, and Air Staff by providing technical assistance, fielding new initiatives, developing procedures, and managing selected central support functions to ensure successful services programs.

AFSA also manages Air Force nonappropriated central funds and operates central systems, such as banking, investments, purchasing, data flow, insurance, and benefit programs.

Air Force Studies and Analyses Agency (AFSAA). Located at the Pentagon, AFSAA helps the Secretary of the Air Force, the Air Force Chief of Staff, and other senior staff address issues concerning force structure, resource allocation, weapons systems acquisition and employment, arms reduction proposals, and the effects their analyses have on implementing national security policy.

Air Force Technical Applications Center (AFTAC). Headquartered at Patrick AFB, Florida, AFTAC monitors global compliance with nuclear test ban treaties. The center installs and operates equipment for detection and identification of foreign nuclear weapons tests and determines whether events are produced by humans or nature. AFTAC also conducts research to improve atomic energy detection systems.

Air Intelligence Agency (AIA). Headquartered at Kelly AFB, AIA was formed by integrating the personnel and missions of the former Air Force Intelligence Command, Air Force Intelligence Support Agency, and elements of Air Combat Command. AIA's primary missions are to provide direct intelligence, security, electronic combat, foreign technology, and treaty monitoring support to national decision makers and field air component commanders. This also includes, but is not limited to, the employment of agency assets to support low-intensity conflicts, counterdrug, and special operations.

Air National Guard (ANG). Located at Andrews AFB, Maryland, ANG is responsible for the maintenance, operational, and technical functions essential for combat readiness of the Air National Guard (ANG). ANG units are under the command authority of the governors of the states to which they are assigned. While under control of the states, the ANG provides trained, disciplined, and equipped forces to preserve peace and protect lives and property during disasters, civil disorders, and other emergencies. When ANG units are mobilized for federal service, they are under the direct control of the Air Force.

Air Reserve Personnel Center (ARPC). Located in Denver, Colorado, ARPC provides personnel services and administrative support to members of the Air Force Reserve and the Air National Guard.

Air Weather Service (AWS). Headquartered at Scott AFB, Illinois, AWS provides technical advice, procedures, and systems for weather support systems. Through its subordinate units, it provides centralized weather, climatological, and space support to Air Force and Army operations.

Joint Services Survival, Evasion, Resistance, and Escape (SERE) Agency (JSSA). Headquartered in Fort Belvoir, Virginia, JSSA serves as the Department of Defense's executive agent for Operational Evasion and Escape matters; Code of Conduct and Survival, Evasion, Resistance, and Escape (SERE) training; and the DOD Prisoner of War (POW)/Missing in Action (MIA) program.

DIRECT REPORTING UNITS (DRUS)

A direct reporting unit (DRU) is a subdivision of the Air Force. These units are directly subordinate to HQ USAF, but they are not under the operational control of an HQ USAF functional manager because of their unique mission, legal requirements, or other factors. The USAF has three DRUs: the Air Force District of Washington, the USAF Academy, and the Air Force Operational Test and Evaluation Center.

Air Force Operational Test and Evaluation Center (AFOTEC). Headquartered at Kirtland AFB, New Mexico, AFOTEC is the USAF's independent test agency responsible for operational testing of new or modified weapons systems and components (for example, aircraft, missiles, munitions, space systems, and so forth) that are being developed for Air Force and multiservice use.

United States Air Force Academy (USAFA). Located near Colorado Springs, Colorado, the Academy provides instruction and experience to all cadets, so that they graduate with the knowledge and character essential to leadership and the motivation to become career officers in the Air Force. The cadets receive a broad military education as a foundation for developing leadership and professional officer qualities. This includes the theory and practice of warfare, with particular emphasis on the application and contribution of airpower. The USAFA provides a four-year academic curriculum leading to a bachelor of science degree. Approximately 50 percent of cadets complete majors in the areas of science and engineering, and 40 percent in the social sciences and humanities. In addition to the academic program, USAF cadets participate in rigorous physical education and military training. At the USAFA, cadets learn to appreciate the role of airpower, its capabilities, and limitations; high ideals of individual integrity; a sense of responsibility; and about patriotism, loyalty, honor, dedication, selflessness, and honorable service.

The 11th Wing. Headquartered at Bolling AFB, D.C., the 11th Wing provides administrative and ceremonial support for U.S. Presidential, government, and Air Force activities in the National Capital Region, all fifty states, and more than ninety-six countries. Two of the 11th Wing's more visible elements are the U.S. Air Force Honor Guard and the U.S. Air Force Band.

TOTAL FORCE COMPOSITION

The total force composition is based on military and civilian personnel in the Regular Air Force and those in Air Reserve forces. Air Reserve forces include Air Reserve units and the Air National Guard. As of 30 September 1996, the Air Force's active-duty force contained 388,200 military personnel 183,357 civilian personnel, and 274,755 Reserve forces.

SOURCES OF ADDITIONAL INFORMATION

Air Force Manual 1-1, *Basic Aerospace Doctrine of the United States Air Force.*

5

The Importance of
USAF History

When I want to understand what is happening today or try
to decide what will happen tomorrow, I look back.
— Oliver Wendell Holmes, Jr.

History is the continuing story of life and generations—of families, of affiliated groups, and of nations. Since the beginning of recorded history, the armed forces have played a strong role in society. The U.S. armed forces represent our country's heritage more than those of most other countries because of their ability to be in harmony with the fundamentals and values of the culture that they have served. For over two hundred years, the members of our armed forces have worked together, overcoming obstacles and adversity to achieve their objectives. They have done so in the pursuit of institutional values—in a spirit of cooperation, discipline, loyalty, and selflessness. At an individual level, members have sensed that they were part of something bigger than themselves, something that was tied irrevocably to the destiny of their society. They recognized that they were part of a special team whose continuing role was to "support and defend the Constitution of the United States of America"and to help safeguard and ensure the security of the nation and the free world.

As members of the U.S. Air Force, our understanding of past events that are related to the military and our country can be extremely valuable. Past events can serve as sources of pride; they can also help us to project visions for the future. By analyzing possibilities and choices that once existed, we can determine patterns, analyze trends, and draw conclusions about present-day situations and the consequences of the choices available.

The following pages provide insight into the value of history, information about the goals and mechanics of the Air Force History Program, and agencies that you may visit or contact for further information.

THE AIR FORCE HISTORY PROGRAM

In the Air Force we all have front-row seats to history . . .
it promises to be an exciting, demanding time requiring the
best efforts of each one of us to insure our military capabil-
ity for our nation's deterrent strength and peace.

—Gen. John P. McConnell,
former Chief of Staff, USAF

A sense of history has been a quality of most great men and women, and nowhere has this sense of history been more prevalent than in outstanding military leaders. The value of the Air Force History Program has been clearly stated and strongly supported by Gen. Hap Arnold, the first Chief of Staff of the U.S. Air Force, and has been affirmed in writing by each of his successors.

Many Air Force personnel use history in performing their daily duties. They use it to gather facts for speeches, briefings, background information, and studies, and to obtain facts to justify individual and unit awards. In a dramatic litigation case, the use of Air Force histories resulted in a $50 million saving to the Air Force. While these are all valid applications of history, some even more important uses are frequently overlooked.

1. History serves as a cultural tradition—a shared body of ideas, values, experiences, and common bonds that unite diverse groups.

2. History serves as memory and as a source of personal identity. It keeps alive the experiences, deeds, and ideas of people of the past. By allowing us to view people from the past as heroes and role models, history connects past and future and can help develop character.

3. History promotes a sense of collective immortality. By rooting human beings on a continuum of the human experience, history provides each man and woman with a sense of immortality.

4. An understanding of history can also broaden an individual's outlook and understanding and serve as a means of learning from the collective experience of others. As such, it can provide an added dimension for decision-making processes. The breadth and depth of a person's experience is usually limited by his or her time-in-service and career field, but an understanding of Air Force history can provide an Air Force member with a means of acquiring knowledge of Air Force areas beyond his or her own experience. For example, a high-ranking commander or a senior enlisted advisor frequently has responsibility for a large number of personnel and programs; however, he or she will not always have direct experience in all of the activities where decisions must be made. By reading the history of their organizations or similar organizations (in formats such as general Air Force histories, command histories, Inspector General reports, and special subject studies), leaders can broaden their outlook and develop a basis for action. Although this will not always provide direct answers

to specific questions, it will provide a wider frame of reference that can be used as a sound basis for formulating answers.

History and Its Relationship to Air Force Doctrine. Air Force doctrine is noted in Air Force Manual 1-1, *Basic Aerospace Doctrine of the United States Air Force.* The content outlines the body of enduring principles, the general truths and accepted assumptions that provide guidance and a sense of direction for the most effective way to develop, deploy, and employ airpower.

The fundamental assumptions that constitute doctrine are based to a large degree on historical experience. Experience makes doctrine practical rather than merely theoretical. Without an awareness of what airpower has done (and has not been able to do), Air Force members would have to derive doctrine solely from hypotheses about the capabilities of air forces. By recording and trying to understand Air Force history, we are in a better position to evaluate and to analyze objectively what airpower has done; we can gain a better understanding of what really happened and why. By drawing on lessons learned and changes that have occurred, we can enter into the future with a heightened awareness of the best courses of action.

The History Program at the Unit Level—and Your Role in It. Each organizational level—from shop to branch, squadron, group, wing, numbered air force, major command, direct reporting unit, and separate operating agency —contributes written materials to the Air Force Historical Program. Subjects will cover a unit's broad scope of experience during a specified period of time (e.g., three months, six months, or one year). They usually include, but are not limited to, information about weapons systems performance, inspections, achievements and innovative procedures, problems and the actions undertaken to solve them, significant events such as exercises and deployments, financial data, personnel, and morale and welfare issues.

At the working level (shop or branch), supervisors are asked to provide data about their operations to a unit (usually squadron) focal point who is referred to as the unit historian. He or she, in turn, analyzes the information provided, prepares a typewritten narrative, and forwards it to the base-level historian, who usually works for the wing commander. The base-level historian reviews all of the information and decides what is appropriate for inclusion in the printed history. In some cases, historians may request additional information or copies of documents or photographs that provide further insight. They may also visit duty locations and/or conduct interviews. After this, they write the history of the entire unit or base. They note facts and they draw conclusions to provide a "big picture" perspective.

Following the commander's review and approval, the unit submits its final product to historians at its higher headquarters. Those historians review the materials from their subordinate units for format, accuracy, and trends, and then compile additional histories that are printed and forwarded through channels to HQ USAF. In this way the USAF develops the overall history of the USAF, including special subject studies and the analysis of significant trends. These products are made available to decision makers, researchers, and members of the USAF. Some limitations on distribution may be imposed based on the subject matter and the security classification involved.

In short, this process allows personnel at each level of command to record their experience and also to benefit from the experience of others.

PROJECT WARRIOR

Warrior is the name of a program the Air Force initiated to improve the warfighting spirit and the attitudes of Air Force personnel and to improve their understanding of the theory and practice of war, with particular emphasis on airpower. The program was started in 1982 by Gen. Lew Allen during his tenure as Chief of Staff, USAF, based on his belief that "the continuing study of military history, combat leadership, the principles of war, and particularly the application of air power, is essential for us to meet the challenges that lie ahead." This belief was further supported and endorsed by his successor, USAF Chief of Staff Gen. Charles Gabriel, who summed up the value of Project Warrior: "It challenges us to expand our perspectives and knowledge. It also charges us to remember our final and bottom line; when called upon, our job is to fly and fight and win."

There were three primary reasons that Air Force leaders believed such a program was necessary.

1. During the transition from the draft to the all-volunteer force, there was a growing tendency for some USAF members to view their roles as unrelated to warfighting. Many began to feel their day-to-day responsibilities were "just a job" (e.g., a pilot, a doctor, a computer programmer, or a typist). Thus, there was a need for a program that would help focus attention on the USAF's primary mission and also remind each individual Air Force member of his or her importance to the mission.

2. The renewed attention to the Air Force's true mission emphasized improving our ability as a warfighting force so that we may help to prevent war. At the same time, it recognized that we must be prepared for war if we cannot prevent it. It also stressed the need to be familiar with aerospace history and lessons learned from previous engagements.

3. Project Warrior also recognized the need to fight better with less. USAF weapons systems were becoming more sophisticated and expensive, as were personnel and operating costs. Therefore, there was an increasing need to define future arenas and the roles that we would assume in them. More selective decisions had to be made in the development and acquisition of new weapons systems and in the ways that they would be employed. These needs had to be balanced with national security interests; the knowledge that the military arsenals of our potential foes were growing at a rapid rate; and the emer-

gence of new threats, such as regional conflicts, terrorism, hostage taking, and space-based programs.

To achieve Project Warrior objectives, the Air Force is involved in four courses of action:

1. Placing continued emphasis on the importance of the program's objectives throughout the Air Force by way of articles, news releases, Air Force Now films, and speeches.

2. Exchanging ideas between units through a network of major command and unit Warrior coordinators.

3. Developing resources and making them available for use at all of the bases (e.g., pictorial and static displays and expanded offerings in base libraries).

4. Developing programs that can be used throughout the service (e.g., encouraging annual Air Force anniversary celebrations to relive our history and celebrate our heritage and offering special symposiums and conferences).

To date, these initiatives have provided many positive results. Primary among them is a far more effective combat-ready Air Force and, as a result, a much more secure United States of America.

AVENUES TO USAF HISTORY

There are numerous facilities and programs that you can visit or contact to review displays and exhibits of USAF heritage and historical records. Many exist at base level. Some of the more extensive ones are described here.

The USAF Enlisted Heritage Hall. Established at Gunter AFB, Alabama, in 1984, the Enlisted Heritage Hall has nearly one hundred exhibits, including pictures, replicas, and static displays that provide insight into the development of airpower, trace the USAF's lineage from the U.S. Army to the present, and provide insight into the roles and achievements of enlisted personnel. Special exhibits include the following:

• Pictorial and narrative displays of Corp. Eugene Bullard, the world's first black fighter pilot, who flew missions with the French Flying Corps during World War I.

• Special tributes to enlisted members who participated in World War II, the Korean War, and the Vietnam Conflict.

• A section that notes the heroic actions of five U.S. Army Air Force and USAF personnel who were awarded the Medal of Honor and nineteen enlisted personnel who were awarded the Air Force Cross.

• The Chief Master Sergeants of the Air Force Room, which honors the nine men who have risen to the top of the USAF's enlisted corp.

• The Order of the Sword Room, which provides historical information about the development of this special enlisted tradition and lists the names of those honored by this award.

• The Wall of Achievers, which recognizes former enlisted men and women who later became general officers or well-known figures, including Gen. Larry Welch, former USAF Chief of Staff; Chuck Yeager, test pilot; Charlton Heston, actor; and Johnny Cash, country singer and songwriter.

The Enlisted Heritage Hall has been very well received, and plans are under way for more exhibit space, including room for static aircraft displays. For additional information, contact the Enlisted Heritage Hall Director, Gunter AFB, AL 36114, DSN 446-1110, commercial (205) 279-1110.

The United States Air Force Museum. The official United States Air Force Museum is charged with depicting the history and traditions of the USAF. Located at Wright-Patterson Air Force Base by Dayton, Ohio, it attracts over 1 million visitors each year and is internationally recognized as the oldest and largest military aviation museum in the world.

Approximately two thousand of the museum's fourteen thousand–plus holdings are currently on display. When viewed collectively, they are a dynamic tribute to the ingenuity, technology, and boldness of spirit that lifted men and women to the skies and then into space. The exhibits provide considerable insight into aviation history. The range extends from historic da Vinci designs of helicopters, balloons, and gliders to personal effects of legendary aviators. There are exhibits of props, jets, and space-age vehicles. Aircraft and missiles from eras of World War I, World War II, Korea, and Vietnam are on display, as are experimental and prototype aircraft that were never placed into active service. Tours can be self-guided or by group. The museum also has a good-sized restaurant and a well-stocked shopping center with aviation-related books, souvenirs, and memorabilia.

Behind the scenes, the museum maintains extensive archives for use in maintaining historical data in support of the museum's acquisition, restoration, public-information programs, and exhibits. Included are thousands of books, periodicals, technical manuals, drawings, photographs, test reports, and other aviation-related materials. The holdings are available for reference to qualified researchers and aviation enthusiasts, such as historians, authors, engineers, model builders, patent attorneys, and artists. The museum also has an extensive restoration facility.

One of the lesser-known responsibilities of the museum is the maintenance of a central record of all historic properties Air Force–wide. This record is based on listings of holdings that are submitted annually by Public Affairs offices throughout the Air Force. As a central database, it helps the USAF and the museum ensure the identification and preservation of historic aviation property.

The USAF Museum also acts as a clearinghouse for obtaining historic items for display at USAF bases. The most common items that are requested for display are aircraft and missiles. To spread the limited number of display aircraft equitably, the USAF Museum maintains a register of requests by type, model, series, and date of receipt. An attempt is then made to satisfy these many requests from known USAF excesses in storage, from inventory, from museum duplicates, or by exchanges with private own   onal historic aircraft or other items. If a request can be satisfied   hese sources, it then becomes the responsibility of the requester to move the item to his or her site; perform directed safety inspections and modifications; restore it to display condition; and maintain the item in a condition worthy of the U.S. Air Force.

If you or your base has an item of historic value that you do not need, the museum will assist in relocating it or in its disposition. For more information about museum programs, contact your base's Public Affairs office or write to USAF Museum, Wright-Patterson AFB, OH 45433.

U.S. Air Force Historical Research Center. The USAF Historical Research Center (USAFHRC) is the repository for all Air Force historical documents. A direct reporting unit assigned to the Chief of Staff, U.S. Air Force, it is colocated with the Air University Library in building 1405 at Maxwell AFB in Alabama. The center's collection consists of more than 60 million pages of material relating to the history of the service. It represents the largest and most valuable organized collection of documents on U.S. military aviation anywhere in the world.

The center provides research and reference services for professional military education (PME) students and faculty and visiting researchers. More than 85 percent of the pre-1955 holdings are declassified, and the majority of documents are recorded on 16mm microfilm. Holdings consist largely of unit histories prepared by the major commands, numbered air forces, wings, and other subordinate organizations. These histories provide comprehensive coverage and primary source documentation of Air Force activities since 1942, when President Franklin D. Roosevelt authorized the program.

Special collections, some dating back to the early 1900s, complement the unit histories. Among them are monographs, end-of-tour reports, joint and combined command documents, aircraft record cards, and materials from the U.S. Army, the British Air Ministry, and the German Air Force. The center also houses personal papers of key retired Air Force leaders and a substantial collection of oral history interviews. About six thousand documents and collections are added to the archives annually.

The center is organized as follows into four divisions and two offices:

1. The Reference Division maintains documents and microfilm and assists users.

2. Research Division staff members write books and papers; prepare lineage and honors histories of Air Force units; maintain records of the Air Force seal and flag, emblems, and Air Force organizations; determine aerial victory credits; and perform other research and teaching services for Air University.

3. The Oral History Division conducts interviews, monitors the USAF end-of-tour report program, and provides a training course for oral historians.

4. Members of the Technical Service Division access, catalog, abstract, index, and microfilm documents.

5. The Administration Office staff provides supply, budget, personnel, and security support.

6. Members of the Computer Information Services Office conduct automated data processing and coordinate computer applications for remote terminals throughout the Air Force.

The facility was originally named in honor of the first Air Force historian, Dr. Albert F. Simpson. Although its mission focuses on the past, its most important task is using the lessons of history to help plan for the future.

The Air University Library. The Air University Library (AUL) is the largest library in the Department of Defense and the largest federal library outside Washington, D.C. Located at Maxwell AFB, Alabama, in building 1405, and named Fairchild Library in honor of Air University's first commander, Gen. Muir S. Fairchild, its mission is to provide professionally directed academic and research library and information services to the Air University and the Air Force.

AUL's holdings are well balanced and especially strong in the fields of aeronautics, warfighting, Air Force operations, education, international relations, military sciences, and management. The library houses over 450,000 books and bound periodicals, 2,000 current periodicals, over 115 newspapers, 500,000 military documents, and 900,000 maps and charts.

Over seventy staff members are assigned to the Air University library system. Professional librarians assist in research and information retrieval, and cartographers provide one of the largest map and chart resources in the United States. Of special note is the work undertaken by bibliographers who research specific geographic regions and special subjects and prepare special bibliographies for Air University use. To date, AUL has published over 2,000 special bibliographies. A few examples include *Great Warrior Leaders/Thinkers,* a 322-page book of references for Project Warrior; *Wargaming,* a 105-page reference book; *Falklands/Malvinas Conflict,* a 65-page bibliography; and *China: Military Capabilities,* a 58-page reference book.

AUL also publishes the quarterly *AUL Index to Military Periodicals,* which is distributed throughout the world. The annual edition of the index is over 650 pages and is considered to be one of the most comprehensive indexes to military periodicals in print.

Research conducted by Air University is also monitored by AUL through the publication of the "Air University Abstracts of Research Reports." AUL keeps copies of all published research. For additional information, write to Air University Library, Maxwell AFB, AL 36112.

The USAF Academy Academic Library. The USAF Academy Academic Library, also referred to as the Cadet Library, has holdings that include over 240,000 books, some 124,000 government documents, and 394,000 microfiche and hard copies of report literature. The following are of special note:

- The Special Collections, in room 6A52, the Academy's archives. Historical records, newspaper clippings, phonographs, and a rare-book collection on falconry form the major parts of this collection. Personal items, such as scrapbooks donated by distinguished military personalities, provide fascinating, original sources on Air Force history.
- The Colonel Richard Gimbel Aeronautical Library is adjacent to Special Collections. This very valuable collection comprises over seven thousand books, five thousand prints, and a wide variety of other nonbook materials. Topics in this collection include early rare works that deal with various aspects of man's dream to fly, imaginary flight, science fiction, and early experiments in powered and unpowered flight and ballooning. This collection is open only Monday through Friday from 7:30 A.M. to 4:30 P.M.
- The magazine and journal section contains over two thousand current subscriptions, including popular reading, news, professional journals, military magazines, and foreign-language publications.
- The newspaper section represents various U.S. cities and regions and a number of foreign countries (including daily and Sunday editions of the *London Times* with back issues through the mid-1800s on microfilm).
- The Map and Atlas collection comprises U.S. Geological Survey Quadrangle maps for Colorado, some *National Geographic* maps, and a variety of atlases on different subjects and countries.

Library resources are available to the general public for in-house use. Borrowing privileges are primarily for cadets and military and civilian personnel assigned to the Academy; however, others may be granted special permission on a case-by-case basis.

The library is housed on four floors on the northeast corner of Fairchild Hall, building 2354. For additional information, write to the United States Air Force Academy Academic Library, USAFA, CO 80840.

SOURCES OF ADDITIONAL INFORMATION

Air Force Manual 1-1, *Basic Aerospace Doctrine of the United States Air Force.*

Air Force Pamphlet 36-2241, Volume 1, *Promotion Fitness Examination (PFE) Study Guide.* See the chapter on USAF history for a chronology of the major events, ideas, and people that have shaped the course of Air Force history and traditions.

For general information about your present unit's history or Air Force history, contact your unit's historian, public affairs representative, or Project Warrior monitor. Your base library or overseas Stars and Stripes bookstores can also be good starting points.

6

The Communication Process

I know you think you understand what you thought I said,
but I'm not so sure you understood what I really meant.
                                        —Anonymous

Almost everybody can identify with the message in the opening quote. At one time or another, we've all experienced the frustration of being misunderstood. Sometimes it happens more frequently in the USAF because the nature of business is unique. There's a different sense of urgency—it's airpower and defense, it's technology and tradition. It's also a system where we must be fairly specific, because we can't afford to be misunderstood if we are to successfully meet the needs of the USAF mission. On a personal level, your ability to effectively communicate with other people in the USAF will be a key factor in achieving the goals you've set for yourself.

LISTENING

I like my boss. He listens to me.
                                        —A1C Susan Nobles

Of all the communication processes, listening is probably the most important, yet it usually gets the least emphasis. Stop for a moment and think about some of the conversations you've had recently. Did the other people fully understand what you were trying to say? Did you fully understand what they were trying to say? Instead of tuning in to their message, were you really thinking of what you were going to say next?

In the USAF you'll be exposed to a wide range of forums that will require you to listen to others and to draw conclusions from the information provided —from large-scale briefings to small shop meetings—and also to formal and informal discussions with personnel of all ranks. Your ability to develop your listening skills, especially in positions of increased responsibility, will have an effect on almost every other aspect of your career.

Here are some general guidelines to becoming a better listener:

• Define the type of listening that's required. Ask yourself, "Why am I listening?" If it's a formal briefing that conveys information or requires you to make a decision afterward, your attention must be much more focused than in a casual conversation.

• If possible, try to become familiar with the subject matter beforehand.

• Tune in. Give your undivided attention. Try to eliminate as many distractions as possible—put away newspapers and books, turn off the radio, refrain from taking telephone calls, and so forth.

• Don't be afraid to say, "I don't understand." If the message is unclear, ask questions or ask the other person to rephrase the statement.

• When speaking or asking for information, use everyday language. Don't try to make a simple concept seem deep, mystical, and complex.

• Don't overcommunicate. Sometimes it's possible to say too much. When that happens, your main points will be smothered in all the extra words. As a result, you'll confuse your listener and probably lose him or her.

• Separate fact from fiction. Rumors grow by leaps and bounds as they travel through the grapevine. The best rule of thumb: "If in doubt, check it out."

• Take notes if necessary, especially to record specific times, dates, and places. Key words and phrases are sufficient.

SPEAKING

Your effectiveness and self-confidence as a speaker usually improve over time as you become more familiar with the subject matter and your listeners.

Using the Telephone. The telephone is the primary means that USAF servicemembers use to communicate with other Air Force and DOD staff agencies. In many ways, using it is quite easy—a matter of common sense, courtesy, and organization. However, you should be familiar with several unique aspects of the DOD telecommunications system.

Your starting point for obtaining general USAF telecommunications information is the installation telephone directory. Each base publishes one. Revisions are made annually or as required when major changes occur. Most directories list each on-base agency by title, functional address symbol, and telephone number. Some directories note each agency's building numbers. Other items frequently included are general user information, emergency numbers, quick reference lists for agencies that are frequently contacted, maps for the installation, and DSN numbers.

Each primary Air Force base also has telephone switchboard operators who have been trained to respond to inquiries with courtesy, accuracy, and speed. They provide directory assistance, call routing service, and support for geographically separated units (such as off-base sites) that are assigned to the base on which the operators work.

When using the telephone in your duty station, you should keep two primary thoughts in mind:

1. The USAF telephone lines are for official government business; lengthy matters of a personal nature should not be discussed.

2. The telephone lines are not secure for discussing classified information. Military telecommunications facilities and networks, including both owned and leased telephone circuits, are subject to various types of monitoring (wiretapping, electronic eavesdropping, and so forth) by other nations' armed forces and security agencies. Such agencies do this routinely to collect information with potential intelligence value. Since this can pose serious problems for preserving the national security of the United States, our own forces implement security programs to monitor and safeguard the use of our communications systems. These safeguards include the use of technological innovations. For example, in cases where there is a requirement to discuss classified material over the telephone, special instruments equipped with approved encryption devises (frequently referred to as Automatic Secure Voice Communications [AUTOSEVOCOM] instruments) must be used.

Another safeguard is an ongoing communications-security (COMSEC) education program that provides all personnel with information on the proper ways to use unprotected telecommunications. This program continually reemphasizes the prohibition of intentional, willful discussion of classified information over unsecured telecommunications equipment. It also advises personnel of the ways that classified or sensitive intelligence information may be accidentally compromised (for example, during idle gossip or in cases where individuals may be unaware of the sensitivity of the information being discussed) in areas such as operations, plans, programs, strengths, weaknesses, numbers, equipment, deployment, capabilities, and intentions. This second point is very important. In the hands of well-trained analysts, virtually any information can be of intelligence value in and of itself or when pieced together with other collected information.

Some General Tips for Using the Phone.

1. Answer promptly and speak clearly and slowly.

2. Always identify yourself when answering. The common practice for answering the telephone is to first state your duty section and then your rank and name; for example, "Base Operations, Airman Smith speaking." When calling someone else, you would usually provide the same information but in reverse order; for example, "This is Airman Smith from Base Operations."

3. If you are unsure of who is calling, tactfully request the caller's identity.

4. If the call is for someone who is not available, offer to take a message. Offer your own assistance, too. A lot of incoming calls are for general nonsensitive information that you may be able to provide.

5. Take time to organize your thoughts before you place a call. If necessary, jot down a few key points or notes on the items you need to cover.

6. Time is valuable, so conversations should be as brief and concise as possible. If you plan a lengthy discussion, ask whether the person you called has time to talk.

```
+--------------------------------------------------+
| MEMORANDUM                                       |
|    OF CALL            Previous editions usable    |
| TO:                                              |
|      LT.  SUGGS                                   |
| [X] YOU WERE CALLED BY—  [ ] YOU WERE VISITED BY— |
|     SERGEANT  PEGGY  SENKO                        |
| OF (Organization)                                |
|     THE  PUBLIC  AFFAIRS  OFFICE                  |
| [X] PLEASE PHONE ▶     [ ] FTS     [ ] AUTOVON   |
|          432-5678                                |
| [ ] WILL CALL AGAIN      [ ] IS WAITING TO SEE YOU|
| [ ] RETURNED YOUR CALL   [X] WISHES AN APPOINTMENT|
| MESSAGE                                          |
|    WANTS  TO  DO  AN                              |
|    ARTICLE  ON  YOUR                              |
|    AWARD  FOR  THE  BASE                          |
|    NEWSPAPER. " PLEASE                            |
|    CALL  TODAY."                                  |
| RECEIVED BY          |DATE        |TIME           |
|    SGT  COBOS        |18 APR 97   |0900           |
| 63-110  NSN 7540-00-634-4018  STANDARD FORM 63 (Rev. 8-81)|
|  ★U.S.GPO:1986-0-491-247/20046  Prescribed by GSA |
|                     FPMR (41 CFR) 101—11.6        |
+--------------------------------------------------+
```

Standard Form 63, Memorandum of Call

7. If a commitment is made over the phone to pursue a further course of action, make a brief handwritten memo for the record.

Commercial Toll Call Procedures. Official long-distance calls are placed or received through the base operator. They should be made only when time does not permit the use of any other means of communications (official mail or message traffic).

To make outgoing long-distance calls, you must first obtain authorization from your unit's Telephone Control Officer (TCO). You will need to tell the TCO whom you are calling, the number, and the reason for the call. The TCO will record the information on an Air Force Form 1072, "Authorized Long-Distance Toll Calls" (also referred to as a telephone control log), and will provide you with a government billing number to give the operator.

The same procedure applies to incoming collect calls. Since such calls require expenditures of appropriated funds, they must be approved in advance by the unit TCO. These calls must come in through the base switchboard operator so they can be properly recorded and billed.

The Defense Switched Network (DSN). When Air Force personnel need to call long-distance from base to base, they don't call on commercial phone lines; they call DSN. DSN is the principal long-haul, voice communications network within the Defense Communications System. Through a system of government-owned and leased automatic-switching facilities, DSN provides direct-dialing service worldwide to handle unclassified telecommunications traffic for mission-essential functions such as command and control, operations, intelligence, logistics, and administration. A high-tech digital system, DSN can handle computer, video, and voice communication.

The telephone codes for the DSN system consist of seven-digit numbers. Most base telephone directories include a list of those that are most frequently called. The first three numbers identify the base of organization; the last four numbers identify the extension for a specific agency (e.g., the personnel office or the security police). For example, the DSN number for the U.S. Air Force Academy switchboard operation is 259-3111. 259 is the DSN prefix that identifies the base; 3111 is the extension that connects you with the operator.

The DSN system has an automatic preemption capability for high-precedence calls. This means your call can be cut off if another user has a higher priority call to make. The precedence system is based on four levels of urgency.

1. ROUTINE precedence is reserved for all official communications. This category does not have a preemption capability.

2. PRIORITY precedence is reserved for calls that require prompt completion for national defense and security, for the successful conduct of war, or to safeguard life or property. Normally, PRIORITY will be the highest precedence that may be assigned to administrative matters when speed of handling is of paramount importance. This category can preempt ROUTINE precedence calls.

3. IMMEDIATE precedence is reserved for vital communications that have an immediate operational effect on tactical operations, directly concern safety or rescue operations, or affect the intelligence-community operational role. This category can preempt PRIORITY and ROUTINE precedence calls.

4. FLASH precedence is reserved for telephone calls pertaining to command and control of military forces essential to defense and retaliation, critical intelligence essential to national survival, conduct of diplomatic negotiations critical to the arresting or limiting of hostilities, dissemination of critical civil-alert information essential to national survival, continuity of federal government functions, fulfillment of critical U.S. internal security functions essential to national survival, and catastrophic events of national or international significance. This category can preempt IMMEDIATE, PRIORITY, or ROUTINE precedence calls.

FLASH precedence calls in progress may be preempted by the application of the FLASH OVERRIDE capability. This special capability is available only to the President of the United States; the Secretary of Defense; the Joint Chiefs of Staff; the commanders of unified and specified commands when declaring either Defense Condition One (DEFCON ONE) or Defense Emergency; and the Commander in Chief, North American Aerospace Defense Command (CINCNORAD) when declaring either DEFCON ONE or Air Defense Emergency.

Sometimes the use of telephones is restricted. MINIMIZE is one such program. It is a condition imposed by commanders to control and reduce electrical communications, both message and telephone traffic, during exercises or periods of emergency. MINIMIZE may be imposed Department of Defense–wide, Air Force–wide, command-wide, or for given countries, states, or areas as conditions warrant. MINIMIZE may be imposed on DSN, telephone, data, or teletype systems. One or all systems or services may be minimized as required, by the imposing authority.

The Phonetic Alphabet. In the English alphabet a lot of letters sound similar (B, C, D, E, G, P, T, V, Z). The phonetic alphabet was designed to avoid confusion. With it, you can pronounce isolated letters and spell out words that can be difficult to understand, especially over the telephone and on aircraft radio transmissions.

A	=	Alpha	N	=	November
B	=	Bravo	O	=	Oscar
C	=	Charlie	P	=	Papa
D	=	Delta	Q	=	Quebec
E	=	Echo	R	=	Romeo
F	=	Foxtrot	S	=	Sierra
G	=	Golf	T	=	Tango
H	=	Hotel	U	=	Uniform
I	=	India	V	=	Victor
J	=	Juliet	W	=	Whiskey
K	=	Kilo	X	=	X-ray
L	=	Lima	Y	=	Yankee
M	=	Mike	Z	=	Zulu

Imagine a telephone call between two bases.

"The runway at Robins Air Force Base will close at 2100 hours today."

"Was that Robins Air Force Base or Dobbins Air Force Base?"

Both bases did actually exist, so the confusion could have been real. To clarify, the caller uses the phonetic alphabet: "Robins Air Force Base. R as in Romeo." If he had meant Dobbins, he would have said, "Dobbins Air Force Base. D as in Delta."

Military Times and Dates. In the Air Force, as in the other military services, time of day is referred to on a twenty-four-hour basis. This helps reduce the confusion that can arise under the A.M./P.M. system, where two hours in each day have the same numerical designation. Here are the official military times and their A.M./P.M. equivalents:

0030	=	12:30 A.M.	1230	=	12:30 P.M.
0100	=	1:00 A.M.	1300	=	1:00 P.M.
0130	=	1:30 A.M.	1330	=	1:30 P.M.
0200	=	2:00 A.M.	1400	=	2:00 P.M.
0230	=	2:30 A.M.	1430	=	2:30 P.M.
0300	=	3:00 A.M.	1500	=	3:00 P.M.
0330	=	3:30 A.M.	1530	=	3:30 P.M.
0400	=	4:00 A.M.	1600	=	4:00 P.M.
0430	=	4:30 A.M.	1630	=	4:30 P.M.
0500	=	5:00 A.M.	1700	=	5:00 P.M.
0530	=	5:30 A.M.	1730	=	5:30 P.M.
0600	=	6:00 A.M.	1800	=	6:00 P.M.
0630	=	6:30 A.M.	1830	=	6:30 P.M.
0700	=	7:00 A.M.	1900	=	7:00 P.M.
0730	=	7:30 A.M.	1930	=	7:30 P.M.
0800	=	8:00 A.M.	2000	=	8:00 P.M.
0830	=	8:30 A.M.	2030	=	8:30 P.M.
0900	=	9:00 A.M.	2100	=	9:00 P.M.
0930	=	9:30 A.M.	2130	=	9:30 P.M.
1000	=	10:00 A.M.	2200	=	10:00 P.M.
1030	=	10:30 A.M.	2230	=	10:30 P.M.
1100	=	11:00 A.M.	2300	=	11:00 P.M.
1130	=	11:30 A.M.	2330	=	11:30 P.M.
1200	=	noon	2400	=	midnight

As you can see, military times have four digits; the first two show the hour and the last two show minutes after the hour. For example, 1417 would be 2:17 P.M., 2347 would be 11:47 P.M., and 0007 would be seven minutes after midnight.

Once you're accustomed to it, the military time system becomes very easy to use. And it can be critically important. Imagine you're a pilot running low on fuel. Another pilot is going to meet you at twelve, "up in the air," for in-flight refueling. What happens if he's thinking midnight and you're waiting at noon?

The use of calendar dates is much simpler. The format is day, month, and year: 25 December 1987. Sometimes this is abbreviated to the first three letters of the month, all capitalized, and the last two digits of the year: 25 DEC 87.

Military Briefings. Briefings are conducted to provide information to decision makers at all levels. They can range from informal discussions with your contemporaries in your immediate duty section to formal presentations for senior managers in conference rooms. If you are asked to provide a briefing, your supervisor will usually give you some basic guidance. Then it's a matter of defining the following five aspects:

1. Format: Ask if it will be informal or formal. Analyze your audience, the occasion, and the location. Ask if you will be able to read notes or if you will be required to use special visual aids such as flip charts, view-graph slides, or 35mm slides.

2. Content: Determine how much information is required to explain the subject. Some audiences may not need as many details as others. In Air Force jargon, a "wall-to-wall" briefing is fully comprehensive, and that's OK. But a "horizon-to-horizon" briefing is too long and too much in depth; it usually puts people to sleep.

3. Time: Ask how much time you have for your presentation. It will often be governed by the audience and the location.

4. Questions: Anticipate what questions might be asked, and have answers ready. If you don't know, don't guess. It's always better to say, "I don't know the answer to that question, but I'll find out and get back to you."

5. Practice: Give your briefing a dry run beforehand. Solicit feedback from your supervisor and your peers. Revise any parts that could be more clearly stated. By doing this, you'll feel much more comfortable when you're presenting the final briefing.

"Words for the Wise". In addition to the English language, over the years the U.S. Air Force has developed a vocabulary of its own. It consists of terms for official programs, often abbreviated, and a wide variety of unofficial jargon, phrases, and sayings that are commonly understood by all members.

Acronyms. Terms for programs are often abbreviated and spoken as acronyms. In day-to-day life in the USAF, you may hear something like this: "You'll have to go TDY tomorrow on short notice. I'm short of people because Jones is going PCS, Smith is on OJT, and Doe is AWOL." TDY is short for temporary duty, PCS for permanent change of station, OJT for on-the-job training, and AWOL for absent without leave.

When these terms are used in written correspondence, they are usually spelled out in full the first time, followed by the abbreviation in parentheses; after that, the capitalized abbreviation is used alone. When they are used in conversation, a full description is not always given because they are commonly accepted terms. If you're in doubt about a meaning, it's always best to ask until you learn the language.

Some of the most frequently used acronyms include the following:

AFB	Air Force Base
AFDD	Air Force Doctrine Document
AFI	Air Force Instruction
AFMPC	Air Force Military and Personnel Center
AFPC	Air Force Personnel Center
AFPD	Air Force Policy Document
AFS	Air Force Specialty or Air Force Station
AFSC	Air Force Specialty Code
ALS	Airman Leadership School
ASAP	As Soon as Possible
AWOL	Absent Without Leave
BAQ	Basic Allowance for Quarters
BAS	Basic Allowance for Subsistence
BOP	Base of Preference
BTZ	Below-the-Zone
BX	Base Exchange
C^3I	Command, Control, Communications, and Intelligence
C^4	Command, Control, Communications, and Computer Systems
CAFSC	Control Air Force Specialty Code
CBPO	Consolidated Base Personnel Office
CCAF	Community College of the Air Force
CINC	Commander of a Combatant Command (Commander in Chief)
CMSAF	Chief Master Sergeant of the Air Force
COMPUSEC	Computer Security
COMSEC	Communications Security
CONUS	Continental United States
COT	Consecutive Overseas Tour
DAFSC	Duty Air Force Specialty Code
DEROS	Date Eligible for Return from Overseas
DET or OL	Detachment or Operating Location
DG	Distinguished Graduate
DOD	Department of Defense
DOR	Date of Rank
DOS	Date of Separation
DRU	Direct Reporting Unit
EES	Enlisted Evaluation System
EOT	Equal Opportunity and Treatment
EPR	Enlisted Performance Report
FOA	Field Operating Agency
FY	Fiscal Year
HOR	Home of Record
HQ	Headquarters

IG	Inspector General
MAJCOM	Major Command
MPF	Military Personnel Flight
MWR	Morale, Welfare, and Recreation
NAF	Numbered Air Force
NCO	Noncommissioned Officer
NCOIC	Noncommissioned Officer in Charge
NLT	Not Later Than
OJT	On-the-Job Training
OTS	Officer Training School
PAFSC	Primary Air Force Specialty Code
PCS	Permanent Change of Station
PDS	Permanent Duty Station
PFE	Promotion Fitness Examination
PFW	Performance Feedback Worksheet
PME	Professional Military Education
QAF	Quality Air Force
QI	Quality Improvement
RHIP	Rank Has Its Privileges
SDI	Special Duty Identifier
SGLI	Servicemen's Group Life Insurance
SKT	Specialty Knowledge Test
SOA	Separate Operating Agency
SP	Security Police
SSN	Social Security Number
TDY	Temporary Duty
TIG	Time-in-Grade; The Inspector General
TIS	Time-in-Service
VA	Department of Veterans Affairs
VIP	Very Important Person
WAPS	Weighted Airman Promotion System

Some Common Phrases. The other category of unofficial jargon—phrases and sayings that have common understanding—is much more extensive. Most of them have been around for quite a while and their origins are not always known. They're usually used with a touch of humor and often to communicate a moral or emphasize a point.

Above my pay grade: Up the chain of command, usually in the context of decision making. The captain said, "The decision was made above my pay grade."

Action officer: A servicemember who has the primary responsibility for a particular job or project. Does not have to be a commissioned officer. "Sergeant Wilson was the action officer for the foreign object damage program."

Additional duty: A job or responsibility given to an Air Force member in addition to his or her primary job; for example, budget/resource monitor, supply/equipment custodian, security manager, safety monitor, advisory council member.

Aircraft identification codes: Different types of aircraft are distinguished and referred to through the use of alphabetical prefixes. For example, B stands for Bomber (B-1, B-2, B-52); C stands for Cargo (C-5, C-130, C-141); F stands for Fighter (F-4, F-15, F-16); and T stands for Trainer (T-38, T-43). In some cases, two letters are used to further distinguish the role of an aircraft. For example, the R in SR-71 and TR-1 stands for reconnaissance, and S and T stand for strategic and tactical.

Appropriated funds: The funds that Congress authorizes and sets aside for Department of Defense expenses.

Barracks lawyer: Often used in reference to someone who provides opinions and advice that he is not fully qualified to give. In the majority of cases, he communicates inaccurate information. The first sergeant said, "You were driving a car under the influence of alcohol. I want you to get advice from the base legal office. This is a serious matter; don't seek advice from a barracks lawyer."

Beer bust: A party or celebration. "After doing well on inspection, the base had a beer bust."

Below-the-zone material: Someone whose performance has been outstanding and is worthy of rapid promotion before his or her contemporaries.

Big picture: How individual actions and programs work, how they affect each other, and what they mean collectively. The young airman said, "Chief Master Sergeant Smith has good judgment and a lot of experience. He really understands the big picture."

Bite the bullet: Similar in meaning to "grin and bear it." Often used when telling someone to take responsibility for an action, even if it's unfavorable or controversial.

Bottom line: A summary of a complex situation, usually in a sentence or two. It can be a statement of fact or a recommendation on how to proceed.

Brass: A high-ranking commissioned officer. The sergeant said, "The brass will be visiting our duty section this afternoon."

Brown shoe: Used in reference to military members who have been in the service for many years or to those who take a very firm position on the way standards will be met and duties will be carried out.

Buck: Slang for an E-4 sergeant. Jane told her friends she was promoted to buck.

Busted: To be reduced in rank as a result of nonjudicial punishment (an Article 15) or a court-martial. Airman First Class Doe was busted to airman because he went absent without leave.

By the book: To do an action as outlined in official guidance, such as a regulation. The sergeant said, "We'll do it by the book."

Chief: Short title for chief master sergeant, an E-9, the highest enlisted grade.

Check-six: Term usually used by fighter pilots to mean "check your tail" or "look in back of you." To other personnel, it means make sure all your facts are correct.

CINC: Abbreviation for Commander-in-Chief; pronounced as "sink." Usually refers to the President of the United States or to the commander of a major air command (MAJCOM); e.g., CINCUSAFE means the Commander-in-Chief, United States Air Forces Europe.

Classified: Material that has a security classification of confidential, secret, or top secret. The sergeant said, "We can't discuss this information here; it's classified."

Comm squadron: Commonly accepted term to denote a communications squadron, the unit on base that is responsible for all communications, including telephone, message centers, radar, and air traffic control.

Delta Sierra: Derived from the phonetic alphabet. Means a bad action or deep trouble.

Dependent: By federal law, military dependents are defined as spouses, unmarried children under twenty-one years of age, and children of any age unable to support themselves because of physical or mental handicaps. In some cases, the definition extends to parents dependent on military members for their support, to stepchildren, to adopted children, and so forth. Such status entitles them to be eligible for military benefits, including medical care, commissary privileges, and access to many facilities. Although it is a commonly used term, it is sometimes upsetting to some who are categorized as such.

Distance yourself: Usually means to separate yourself from an unfavorable action or person. The first sergeant said, "Distance yourself from Airman Jones. He's being discharged for using drugs."

Down the tubes: To fail an inspection and get less than a satisfactory rating. "Sergeant Jones's shop went down the tubes; they got an unsatisfactory rating on the inspection."

Drawdown: General term used when discussing the reduction of armed forces units or personnel.

Dream sheet: An Air Force form used by all airmen to list the assignments (bases and geographical locations) they would like to be selected for.

Driver/Jock: Slang for pilot. "Captain Camacho is an F-16 driver" or "Captain Green is an F-4 jock."

Electric jet: Slang for the F-16 tactical fighter jet; referred to as such because of its sophisticated avionics (aviation electronics) systems.

Envelope: Term used by aviators when discussing the testing of new aircraft of determining maximum performance. Pilots talk about "pushing the envelope." They're talking about a two-dimensional concept; the bottom is zero altitude (the ground), the top is maximum altitude, the left is zero speed, and the right is maximum speed. In most cases, pilots try to push the upper right-hand corner of the envelope (altitude and speed). According to the *Collected Journals* of Adm. Rick Hunter, "What everybody tries not to dwell on is that that's where the postage gets canceled, too."

Esprit de corps: Pronounced "espree de core." A spirit of devotion and enthusiasm among members of a group for one another, their group, and its purposes.

Face time: When an Air Force member tries to make personal contact with a supervisor or commander to become recognized for outstanding performance. Many people believe that in building a professional reputation, this recognition is just as important as doing an outstanding job. It helps supervisors link a success (what) with a face (who was personally responsible for the success).

Fall on your sword: Originates from Roman generals who performed badly on the battlefield and threw themselves on their own swords. In modern times, it is identified with servicemembers who, to their own detriment, insist on carrying on with an inappropriate action. The commander said, "I don't think that's the best option; carry on if you like, but don't fall on your sword."

Fast burner: Similar to *below-the-zone material.* People who are well respected, highly capable, and successful. As a result, they are usually selected for rapid promotion and positions of increased responsibility.

FIGMO: Acronym for "Forget it—got my orders." Frequently used by personnel who are being reassigned to another base and use their upcoming move as a reason for avoiding additional work or duties. It's OK in jest, but when carried to an extreme it could be detrimental to your career.

First shirt or First skirt: Slang for first sergeant (male or female).

Fiscal year: A twelve-month period for which an organization plans to use its funds. For federal agencies, the fiscal year starts on 1 October and ends on 30 September.

FOD: Acronym for foreign object damage. Used primarily by aircraft maintenance personnel and aircrews, this term refers to items (buttons, hats, loose tools, and so on) that can damage jet engines and other moving parts.

Full bird: Slang for a colonel, an 0-6. Rank insignia: eagles.

Gig-line: When a shirt or blouse is worn tucked into trousers with a front fly opening, the bottom front edge of the shirt, the outside edge of the belt buckle (when required), and the edge of the fly will align. This alignment is called a *gig-line.* The gig-line is to be straight and neat. The sergeant said, "Your uniform looks a bit sloppy; straighten your gig-line!"

GI party: A mandatory formation to clean up a duty section or a dormitory. It usually involves three or more people and is scheduled by a supervisor, the first sergeant, or the commander.

Gofer: Sounds like "gopher." Used to note someone who perpetually runs errands or coordinates matters—one who will "gofer this, gofer that."

Gung-ho: This term has two meanings. It can be used to denote a person who is unswervingly dedicated and loyal or someone who is foolishly enthusiastic.

Hack: Capable of performing. "Staff Sergeant Jones is one sharp troop. She can hack the mission where others would fail."

Hit the ground running: Refers to talented individuals who are immediately productive; used with respect. The supervisor said, "I'm really pleased with Sergeant Smith's performance. She hit the ground running as soon as she signed in for duty."

Homesteading: When a servicemember tries to stay at one duty location for an extended period of time.

Hot: Very important. The commander said, "This is a hot project; everything else can wait."

Integrity: An important part of building a professional reputation. In the USAF, it denotes a servicemember's strong commitment to honest and sincere support of the mission and all personnel: superiors, peers, and subordinates.

Last four: Last four numbers of your Social Security number. Ensures accurate identification of military members. Most frequently used in the personnel office and the hospital/dental facilities.

Lifer: Primarily used by first-term airmen during the 1960s and early 1970s, before the elimination of the draft and the introduction of the all-volunteer force. It described career airmen who reenlisted after their initial four-year term. A long term of service was perceived as a lifetime commitment; therefore, someone who made that commitment was referred to as a lifer.

Line number: A number given to those who have been selected for promotion. It determines the date a promotion will be effective; the lowest numbers are promoted first.

Long-winded: Someone who speaks at length; tediously long.

Loop (in or out of): To be aware of. "Sergeant Smith was in the loop concerning aircraft takeoff times during the alert."

Loyalty: Faithfulness to those ideals and people that a servicemember is under obligation to defend, support, or be true to. In the USAF, it usually refers to commitment to the mission or to personnel in the chain of command (such as your supervisor or your commander). Not to be confused with blind obedience. The concept of loyalty recognizes that all personnel have a responsibility to respectfully point out errors in judgment or potential problems that may be detrimental to the mission.

Mess hall: The dining hall for enlisted personnel; also referred to as the chow hall.

Mid-shift: Short for midnight shift. The third shift of a normal day, usually from 2330 to 0730.

Military brat: Son or daughter of a military member (although not necessarily a "brat").

Motor pool: The office on base that controls and services all the installation's vehicles (cars, trucks, van, buses). Sometimes it supplies drivers; sometimes vehicles can be checked out and driven by other personnel who possess a government vehicle driver's license. Sergeant Skopp said, "Call the motor pool for a truck so we can move this mobility equipment."

Mustang: Slang term for a commissioned officer who has had prior enlisted service.

Nonappropriated funds: Funds generated by Department of Defense military and civilian personnel and their dependents and used to augment funds appropriated by Congress to provide a comprehensive, morale-building welfare, religious, educational, and recreational program, designed to improve the well-being of military and civilian personnel and their dependents.

Old Man: Sang for the commander, regardless of age. Used respectfully, but never in the commander's presence.

OPR: Acronym for Office of Primary Responsibility. "Security Police is the OPR for issuing identification cards."

Press on: To continue with a job or program. The commander, proud of the squadron's progress in the aircraft maintenance program, said, "You're doing your job well. Press on."

Protocol dictates: Actions accepted as proper and correct in official dealings, such as ceremonies and courtesies. The first sergeant said, "Protocol dictates that the guest of honor will have the seat at the head of the table."

Punching out: To eject from an aircraft during flight.

Rainbow: Term used to describe new airmen at basic training who are still wearing multicolored civilian clothing instead of the green fatigue uniform.

RHIP: Acronym for rank has its privileges.

Short: Used to describe the amount of time before a servicemember departs for another unit on a permanent change of station. Airman Jones said, "I'm leaving for my next base in three days. I'm short."

Sierra Hotel: Derived from phonetic alphabet. Used primarily by aircrew members to describe an exceptionally good or commendable action.

Suspense: A deadline/date for completing an official action.

Swing shift: The second work shift of a normal duty day, usually from 1530 to 2330.

System: As in "the system." Used in relation to specific programs, such as the promotion system, the assignment system, and so forth. Sometimes used as an overgeneralization during periods of frustration. The sergeant said, "I got passed over for promotion for the ninth time. It's the system, you know. It just isn't fair."

Ticket: Slang for a performance report. "Did your supervisor write your ticket yet?"

Top three: The top three enlisted ranks or grades in the USAF: master sergeant, senior master sergeant, and chief master sergeant (E-7, E-8, E-9).

Two-digit midget: Term used by short-timers (see *Short*). Refers to the number of days remaining before a servicemember is reassigned or discharged. Sometimes used in conjunction with the term *wake-up* to denote the final days. The airman said, "I'm a two-digit midget now; ninety-nine days and a wake-up." As their time winds down, some short-timers also go to the extent of counting down the hours, minutes, and seconds.

TWX: Sounds like "Twix." Short term for a message transmitted like a telegraph message. Transit time depends on the priority assigned. Some can be transmitted and received within minutes. The majority are processed as routine and usually received within twenty-four hours.

War stories: Recollections of past events during a person's military career. Most have a humorous twist or convey a moral relevant to a current situation. You can tell that one is coming when someone says, "I remember when... "

Wiring diagram: An organizational chart showing clear vertical and horizontal lines of authority. Often used to show who reports to whom, by function or by person (as in a chain of command chart).

Zulu Time: Greenwich Mean Time, the standard of time used throughout the world. Used by USAF members when they are in different time zones to assure that there are no misunderstandings as to which time is being referenced. Zulu is the phonetic alphabet designation for Z. When Zulu is referred to orally, the whole word is used. For example, if someone in Washington, D.C., was planning a mission with a USAF base in England, he or she might say, "The President's aircraft will arrive at 1800 Zulu." In written communications, Zulu time is designated with a Z attached to the end, as in 1800Z.

WRITING

Want to see a general cry? Stop by when I'm reading some of your writing.

—A major general introducing
the Executive Writing Course

Over the past decade, the USAF has put increasing emphasis on the quality of written communications, for two reasons: Clear and concise information is needed to ensure that mission requirements are understood and met; it also saves time, money, and materials.

Written communications are presented in a wide range of standardized formats, prescribed by intended purpose. Here are some of the most frequently used formats.

• The formal letter (the most common) is usually prepared on official Air Force letterhead. It's used to convey policy, guidance, or information.

• A memorandum for record (also referred to as a memo for record) is prepared to document an action, sequence of events, or reasons why a certain decision was made. It is then filed for later reference.

• A staff summary sheet is prepared on AF Form 1768. It provides senior personnel with a summary of key issues for projects, including potential problems, and offers recommendations on an appropriate course of action. Background information is usually attached.

• Messages are the Air Force's equivalent of a telegraph. They're typed on a

DD Form 173 and then sent to the telecommunications center for transmission to other Air Force bases or to Department of Defense activities.
• Directives, such as regulations, supplements, and operating instructions, provide guidance and policy to Air Force units.
• Performance reports and recommendations for awards and decorations are written on special forms. The way they're written (content, directness, and grammar) can often have a direct effect on a servicemember's career.

Air Force correspondence is expected to be as follows:

1. Factual and accurate, focused directly on an issue (what is right, not who is right).

2. Concise, direct, and grammatically correct. Lots of adjectives and fifty-cent words are discouraged.

3. Timely. A matter that is important should be acted on as soon as possible.

Writing well comes with experience and practice. Start by becoming familiar with the different formats available. Decide on your purpose and choose the appropriate format. Organize an outline that is clear and logical. Support your main points with all the relevant facts. Once you've completed your first draft, take a critical look at it and rewrite where necessary. Ask for feedback from your peers and your supervisor. Make adjustments. Have it typed, proofread it, and have typographical errors corrected. Before you send it out, make sure it has been properly coordinated through your chain of command. This is especially true where the policy expressed is new or introduces any dramatic changes.

SOURCES OF INFORMATION
There are two ways to learn what's happening throughout the Air Force community: official channels and unofficial channels.

Official Channels. Information distributed through official channels originates in different forms at different levels of command. For example, at your base and unit level you will receive information through your chain of command and through personal and group contacts such as meetings and commander's calls. Other official channels are locally produced printed media, such as policy and information letters, base newspapers, and daily or weekly information bulletins.

Each base also has a Publications Library (also referred to as a Master Reference Library), usually maintained by the Base Information Management Division. This is where copies of directives that may not be available in your immediate duty section are kept. You can go there during duty hours to review the directives you're interested in. In some cases, these materials can be checked out for periods up to seventy-two hours. The directives that seem to be in the most demand are those concerning assignments, promotion, and performance reports.

Above the base and unit level, the USAF sends out a variety of information to keep everyone up-to-date on current developments that affect the overall mission and the quality-of-life programs. Audiovisual Services produces films on special subjects, such as safety and disaster preparedness and others on a recurring basis, such as the *Air Force Now* monthly series, which covers current events and programs. Air Force Recurring Periodicals (AFRPs) are also printed and distributed to inform personnel about new policies and ongoing programs. Here are some examples:

AFRP 90-1, *The Inspector General (TIG) Brief*

AFRP 35-1, *Airman* magazine

AFRP 36-1, *Afterburner* (USAF News for Retired Personnel)

AFRP 35-3, *Policy Letter*

Unofficial Channels. Unofficial channels of information are provided by private associations that deal in matters of interest to the armed forces. Many of their contributors are former service personnel. To receive their information, you can either join the organization for an annual fee or look for copies in the base library. Included here are some of the primary organizations that will keep you aware of the major issues affecting the USAF.

1. The *Air Force Association* (AFA) is a professional society committed to peace and freedom through adequate aerospace power. It represents all elements of the Air Force family: military and civilian, officer and enlisted, active and reserve, cadet and veteran, dependent and retiree, civil service and aerospace worker. The AFA publishes *Air Force Magazine* each month. Articles cover a wide range of topics, from historical discussions of airpower to personnel issues and special annual reviews of the military capabilities of U.S. and Russian air forces. A variety of other services and programs are also provided. For additional information contact the Air Force Association, 1501 Lee Highway, Arlington, VA 22209-1198.

2. *The Air Force Times* is printed each week in a newspaper format. It's a very good source of current information about the Air Force in general and policy changes that affect members and their families. Of special note are the printed lists of those promoted to grades E-5 (staff sergeant) and above and the lists of personnel being reassigned from one base to another. For additional information contact *The Air Force Times,* Springfield, VA 22159-0250.

3. The *Air Force Sergeants Association* (AFSA) provides a wide range of information and services for its members (noncommissioned officers, grades E-4 through E-9, active duty, retired, or reserve). Of special note is its commitment to represent members' interests to elected government representatives and to spread the word about new programs and changes in benefits. Most bases have a local chapter organized and operated by those in the surrounding area (active duty and retired, or reserve). For additional information, contact Air Force Sergeants Association, Box 31050, Washington, DC 20031.

4. *Aviation Week and Space Technology* is a periodical covering technical developments in the aviation industry and their applications to the military establishment. Often referred to as *"Aviation Leak"* by the intelligence

community, it provides insight into current research and development projects —sometimes more insight than military planners and strategists would like. For additional information, contact *Aviation Week and Space Technology,* P.O. Box 1505, Neptune, NJ 07754-1505.

EMERGING USE OF COMPUTER SYSTEMS WITHIN THE USAF

Within the past five years, the USAF has significantly increased the number of personal computer systems for the purpose of communicating and conducting official Air Force business. Routine applications (such as word processing, graphics, and spreadsheets) are commonly used in every major office, and there are specialized programs for operations such as finance, personnel, supply, and aircraft maintenance.

There are three primary benefits to using these computer systems:

1. They are more economical compared with previous paper-based systems, which had high costs associated with bulk printing and distribution. One primary example, which reduced costs by almost 75 percent, was the conversion of old Air Force regulations (which were previously printed on paper) to directives and instructions that are now being distributed on CD-ROM, a compact disk that stores large amounts of data for use on computers. ROM stands for read only memory, which means users are not able to alter the text.

2. Computerized databases offer quicker generation and retrieval of information. Their products are also easier to view and maintain, compared with sorting through stacks of paper products in file cabinets, three-ring binders, and base publications libraries.

3. Small mobile computer systems are easy to transport and operate at locations other than a home base, be they small forward operating locations or at major deployment sites.

The extent of computer training that is provided depends on the complexity of the applications identified for use and the program or programs they support. Some staff are provided with formal technical training, whereas others are provided with orientations at their base of assignment.

SOURCES OF ADDITIONAL INFORMATION

Air Force Handbook 37-137, *The Tongue and Quill,* is one of the best desktop references. The content is easy to follow and is balanced with illustrations and practical advice.

Air Force Manual 37-126, *Preparing Official Communications.*

Air Force Pamphlet 36-2241, Volume 1, *Promotion Fitness Examination Study Guide,* chapter 13, Communicating in Today's Air Force. This publication is used for those studying for promotion to the ranks of staff sergeant, technical sergeant, and master sergeant. The content is brief but provides valuable information about the importance of effectively communicating in the USAF.

Consult your base library for Air Force recurring periodicals and USAF-oriented magazines, newspapers, and books.

7

Courtesies and Customs

Courtesies and customs are important aspects of military life. They reinforce and reward common goals, unity, and teamwork. Some have their roots in tradition; others create an environment that fosters mutual respect and commitment to duty. Where customs and courtesies are noted, they are extended to members of other U.S. Armed Forces (Army, Navy, Marines, and Coast Guard) and armed forces of friendly nations.

DUTY, HONOR, COUNTRY
The concept of duty, honor, and country is a recognized code for military professionals in all branches of the U.S. Armed Forces. It places a twenty-four-hour-a-day responsibility on each member for a commitment, undertaken with honor, to put the needs of the country and the mission first, without regard to personal wants and preferences. Acceptance of this responsibility contributes to the continued success of each branch of service and is also critical in maintaining the trust and confidence of the American people.

THE AMERICAN FLAG AND THE NATIONAL ANTHEM
The American flag and the national anthem symbolize the democratic principles of our country. To members of the armed forces, they further symbolize the commitment to uphold those principles and the sacrifices made by their fellow men and women in uniform during America's history. Respect to the flag is shown most frequently during reveille and retreat ceremonies. During the raising and lowering of the flag, those in formation are called to attention and render salutes from the first note of the national anthem or "To the Color" to the last note of music. Those not in formation should face the flag, or the sound of the music if the flag is not visible, and salute. All motor vehicles should stop at the first note of the music, and those inside should sit at attention until the music stops. Personnel indoors are not required to stand or salute during reveille or retreat, or usually when the national anthem is played on the radio, on television, or in movies. It is, however, a commonly expected form of respect to stand at attention when the national anthem is played in the base movie theater.

THE SALUTE
The salute is deeply rooted in military custom and tradition. It binds military members together, regardless of rank, through a greeting based on mutual respect. Salutes are rendered to the American flag, to the President of the United States, to all commissioned and warrant officers of the U.S. Armed Forces, to officers of other friendly foreign nations, and to other officials and dignitaries when deemed appropriate.

Salutes are rendered first by the person junior in grade and are held until returned. Turn your head toward the person being saluted, and raise your right hand smartly until the tip of the forefinger touches either the lower part of your headgear (except for flight caps) or your forehead above and slightly to the right of the right eye. The thumb and fingers are extended and joined, palm to the left, upper arm horizontal, forearm inclined at a forty-five-degree angle, with the hand and wrist straight. To complete the salute, drop the arm to its normal position by the side in one motion, at the same time turning your head and eyes to the front.

While the salute itself is a standard procedure, the circumstances under which it is rendered can vary. General guidelines include the following:
• *Outdoors:* Salutes are exchanged between individual members upon recognition and also rendered to senior personnel in properly marked staff cars and government vehicles. For formations and work details, the person in charge renders the salute. For informal groups not in formation, the first person to see the officer should call the group to attention, and all members of the group should face the officer and salute.
• *Indoors:* Salutes are required for formal reporting situations, such as reporting to a commander. Otherwise, they are not normally required.
• *Other situations:* Salutes are not required when a person is encumbered (arms full) or when approaching an officer from the rear. In these cases an exchange of a verbal greeting is appropriate. In some public situations, salutes may be inappropriate or impractical, for example at religious gatherings or sporting events. In uncertain situations, the best rule of thumb is when in doubt, salute.

MILITARY TITLES
Standard titles are used in addressing and introducing all Air Force members. The following accepted forms of rank/grade designation can be used on their own or in conjunction with the person's last name:

Generals of all grades	**"General"**
Colonels and lieutenant colonels	**"Colonel"**
Majors	**"Major"**
Captains	**"Captain"**

First and second lieutenants	**"Lieutenant"**
Doctors and dentists	**By grade or "Doctor"**
Chaplains	**By grade or "Chaplain"**
Warrant officers	**"Mister" or "Ma'am"**
Chief master sergeants	**By full title or "Chief"**
Senior master sergeants	**By full title or "Sergeant"**
Master Sergeants	**" "**
Technical sergeants	**" "**
Staff sergeants	**" "**
Sergeants	**" "**
Senior Airmen	**By full title or "Airman"**
Airmen first class	**" "**
Airmen	**" "**
Airmen basic	**" "**
Cadets of the Air Force Academy	**"Mister" or "Miss"**

Rank, Recognition, and Respect. Formal procedures for recognition and respect are established to facilitate the conduct of military affairs and aid in maintaining standards of discipline. Most are based on grade and tradition. They include five general practices:

1. Airmen and noncommissioned officers are addressed by their grade. During informal work situations within a duty section, personnel of the same grade sometimes refer to each other by first name, but only by mutual consent.

2. Officers are addressed by their grade or "sir" or "ma'am."

3. When speaking to an officer, you should always rise and remain standing, unless directed otherwise.

4. When a senior officer enters the rooms, the first person who sees the officer should call the group to attention, and all should rise and stand at attention. The exception to this procedure occurs when an officer is already in the room who is equal to or senior to the one entering the room—for example, when a colonel enters a room where another colonel or a general officer is present.

5. Senior members, whether officer or enlisted, are always given the position of honor, which is on the right side. This applies to walking, sitting, or riding in a vehicle. The senior officer enters a vehicle or aircraft last and exits first.

Other forms of mutual respect, based on commonly accepted acts of courtesy and good human relations, are also expected by members of all grades.

Retirees of the Armed Forces. A fall 1995 article in *The Inspector General Brief* titled "Earning the Title for Life," written by Gen. Ronald R. Fogelman, Chief of Staff for the U.S. Air Force, outlined the contributions put forth by Air Force retirees and the special reasons why they should, as a courtesy and a sign of respect and dignity, be addressed by their rank. General Fogelman noted the following:

Our nation's Air Force is composed of active duty members, retirees, reservists, guardsmen, and civilians. All are valued members of the broader Air Force team that defends our nation with ready air and space forces. Each member of our professional team deserves to be treated with respect and courtesy.

More than 620,000 Air Force retirees are still active and valuable contributors to our Air Force. Some now work for the Air Force in civilian positions. Others support education programs, and provide forums for the exchange of ideas which further the goals of airpower. More than one million volunteer to help in our medical facilities, libraries, child development centers, and community activity centers.

The retired officers and noncommissioned officers of all services earned their rank through hard work and determination. They endured hardships, made sacrifices, and often risked their lives in serving our country. Our Air Force retirees laid the foundation for the world's premier air and space force. And they remain eligible for recall to active duty in times of national crisis. In fact, during Desert Shield and Desert Storm, many volunteered to reenter active duty to meet Air Force needs and they served admirably. We owe these dedicated professionals, who have given so much to our nation, the courtesy of using the rank they earned. So it is appropriate to use rank when addressing a retired officer or noncommissioned officer who introduces themselves by rank when coming into the clinic for medical care or calling the Military Personnel Flight for assistance. As a source of habit, I encourage it because it accurately reflects the esteem with which we hold our retirees.

While some may consider this a small thing, it is an important concern for retired Air Force members and it is important to me. Our retirees believe they earned their rank for life and should be addressed accordingly—and I agree with them. So, I urge all Air Force people to realize that military retirees from every service deserve to be called by their military rank. It is rightfully theirs because they earned it—for life.

CEREMONIES

Ceremonies reward excellence, pay respect, and stimulate teamwork, morale, and esprit de corps. Some familiar ceremonies are described here.

Two *flag ceremonies,* reveille and retreat, are conducted at most installations. Reveille (pronounced "rev-uh-lee") signifies the start of the official duty day and is associated with a ceremony for raising the flag. Retreat signifies the end of the official duty day and is a ceremony for formally paying respect to the flag. Times and sizes of troop formations are specified by the base or installation commander.

Drill ceremonies teach the value of teamwork. Although ceremonial in nature, they enhance individual performance on the job and in group situations. Because they promote understanding the need for authority, discipline, and following orders promptly and precisely, these ceremonies help develop personal confidence, military bearing, and assertiveness.

Recognition ceremonies honor individual achievements and important events that happen during a member's career. They can take place in either formal environments (staff meetings, commander's calls, parades, or special social functions such as awards banquets) or informal environments (such as in a work center or a supervisor's office). Examples are awards, decorations, reenlistment, promotion, and retirement.

Military social functions include formal gatherings such as awards banquets, special-occasion functions (such as the anniversary of the Air Force, Christmas, and so forth), Dining-Ins, Dining-Outs, and the Order of the Sword. The Dining-In is a formal dinner for members of a military organization or unit. Ceremony, tradition, and good fellowship abound. Guest speakers are frequently invited, awards may be presented, new and departing personnel may be recognized. Those attending wear the formal Air Force mess dress uniform or the semiformal uniform. The Dining-Out follows the same basic format except that spouses, friends, and civilians may also attend. The Order of the Sword is a special program where noncommissioned officers of a command recognize individuals they hold in high esteem and wish to honor. Those selected for induction are usually honored during a formal ceremony at a Dining-In.

AN EMERGING CUSTOM: THE USAF THUNDERBIRDS

When we think about the customs of the armed forces, we think of traditions that have been established over a period of time. Within the USAF, there's an emerging custom that makes its members' emotions swell in both hearts and minds. The USAF Thunderbirds serve as a source of personal pride and symbolism and inspire esprit de corps, teamwork, self-discipline, and the pursuit of excellence. The U.S. Air Force's official aerial demonstration team, the Thunderbirds, gave their first performance in 1953. Since then the Thunderbirds have traveled throughout the United States and to fifty-two countries around the world. Frequently referred to as America's "Ambassadors in Blue," they have logged over three thousand performances before nearly 225 million people, including members of the USAF, prime ministers, presidents, foreign dignitaries, celebrities, and countless fans.

The most visible part of the Thunderbird team is its aircraft, the General Dynamics F-16 Fighting Falcon, a multirole combat fighter. During a typical performance, the red, white, and blue aircraft perform a variety of graceful, intricate maneuvers, sometimes in formations where their wing tips are separated laterally by only three to five feet.

The Thunderbird team is composed of over 140 personnel. Each member is a volunteer, hand selected from the stacks of special-duty applications. They are chosen because of an ability to perform their jobs to the squadron's exacting standards.

Eleven commissioned officers fill positions in the squadron. These include six demonstration pilots, three support officers (maintenance, executive support, and public affairs), and a logistics officer and a narrator (both of whom must be qualified tactical pilots).

Nearly 130 highly skilled enlisted men and women support the operation in thirty-five different career fields, including maintenance, operations, supply, life support, communications, information management, public affairs, photography, and graphics. It is their job to ensure that the planes are ready for each demonstration and to attend to the myriad of small details that assure the success of every performance.

If you are interested in information about applying for a special-duty assignment with the USAF Thunderbirds, see chapter 16, "How to Get the 'Right' Assignments."

SOURCES OF ADDITIONAL INFORMATION

Air Force Pamphlet 36-2241, Volume 1, *Promotion Fitness Examination (PFE) Study Guide.* See chapter 7, "Standards of Customs and Courtesies."

Consult your supervisor or your unit's first sergeant.

8

Your Uniform and Standards of Appearance

THE NEW AIR FORCE UNIFORM

In January 1993, the Air Force selected a new uniform design from a range of options that were considered during 1991 and 1992. The proposed uniform changes were a subject of considerable debate among both active-duty and retired members. Shortly after becoming the Air Force Chief of Staff in October 1994, Gen. Ronald R. Fogelman modified some of the proposed changes, in part because he was concerned that the uniform debate was detracting attention from other, more important, issues. Following this, he stated that the fifty-five uniform changes and pending changes he announced on 15 March 1995 would be the last major alterations to the uniform during his tenure.

The new uniform has been available to Air Force members since the end of 1994, and began to be issued to basic trainees during the latter part of 1995. The mandatory wear date for the new uniform is projected for 1 October 1999. During the transitional period, both the present and the new uniforms will be authorized for wear.

In terms of changes, the new uniform is sleek. It's made of a polyester and wool blend instead of the 100 percent polyester that has been used since 1976. It's also uncluttered in design and has been stripped of many of the adornments that usually characterize military uniforms (for example, outer patch pockets and name tags). Most of the redesign involves the service dress jacket, with the most eye-catching changes being made to the rank insignia.

For enlisted grades, the new uniform returns to tradition by including the silver star on all enlisted chevrons. The star was removed in the late 1970s to give distinction to NCOs. Since NCO status was not directly connected to rank —for example, senior airman (E-4) and sergeant (E-4) both had the same insignia, with three stripes—the star identified those who had earned NCO standing (the E-4 sergeant did, but the E-4 airman did not). But with NCO status now conferred with the rank of staff sergeant, differentiation based on adding or deleting the silver star was no longer needed. A new design feature

73

was selected to provide more recognition of the special trust and responsibility placed with the top three enlisted grades: All three ranks will have five stripes down, with one stripe on top for master sergeants, two stripes on top for senior master sergeants, and three stripes on top for chief master sergeants. This distinguishes the top three enlisted ranks and standardizes Air Force rank with that of the Army and the Marine Corps. The deadline for wearing the new enlisted stripes has been set for 1 October 1997.

The following sections describe Air Force uniforms currently in use. Distinctions are made for the service dress uniform (which is being phased out in 1999) and the new service dress uniform (which may be worn now and will be required beginning 1 October 1999).

THE CURRENT AIR FORCE UNIFORM

Air Force Instruction 36-2903, *Dress and Personal Appearance of Air Force Personnel,* contains a description of each item of the military uniform and the way it should be worn. The Air Force Uniform Board, in conjunction with personnel experts, monitors uniform design with periodic reviews. Changes are implemented when required to meet the needs of the entire force or those of specific career fields. Special consideration is given to ensure that uniforms present a neat, dignified appearance that is plain, not too ornate, and distinctively Air Force. Other important factors include functional use, military image, cleanliness, and safety.

The type of uniforms that may be worn is often determined by the nature of duties performed or by a specific occasion.

1. Service, fatigue, and standardized functional uniforms for men and women include service dress uniforms, long- and short-sleeved blue shirts, long- and short-sleeved blue blouses, men's blue service trousers, women's blue service skirts and slacks, maternity service uniforms, fatigue uniforms, maternity fatigue uniforms, camouflage fatigue uniforms, white food-service uniforms, and white hospital-service uniforms.

2. Pullover sweaters and outer garments include blue pullover sweaters, lightweight blue jackets, all-weather coats, raincoats, overcoats, and headgear.

3. Organizational clothing and equipment items are issued to meet unique work requirements. Functional clothing items, designed for specific duties, include parkas, protective footwear, coveralls, and specialized flight clothing. Distinctive uniforms and items are issued for members of certain organizations while they are performing distinctive duties; for example, USAF Honor Guard uniforms, USAF Band uniforms, and Security Police uniforms.

4. Dress uniforms for men and women include black mess dress uniforms, blue mess dress uniforms, black formal dress uniforms, blue formal dress uniforms, semiformal dress uniforms, and black, white, or blue ceremonial dress uniforms.

Men's New Service Dress Uniform (Enlisted)

Notes:

1. Place highly polished US insignia halfway up the seam, resting on but not over it. Bottom of insignia is horizontal with the ground.

2. Aeronautical badges are mandatory. Others are optional. Center aeronautical, occupational, or miscellaneous badge $1/2$ inch above the top row of ribbons. Center additional badge $1/2$ inch above first one. Wear highly polished badges only.

3. Center ribbons resting on but not over edge of welt pocket. Wear three or four in a row. Wear all or some.

4. Center duty or miscellaneous badge $1\frac{1}{2}$ inches below top of welt pocket and centered, and/or on right side centered between arm seam and lapel, with bottom edge of badge parallel to top of welt pocket. EXCEPTION: Missile and missile maintenance badges are worn $1\frac{1}{2}$ inches below top of welt pocket and centered. Wear highly polished badges only.

5. Center new 4-inch sleeve chevron halfway between shoulder seam and elbow bent at 90-degree angle.

Men's Service Dress Uniform

Notes:

1. (Mandatory) Place highly polished US insignia halfway up the seam, resting on but not over it. Bottom of insignia is horizontal with the ground; officer and enlisted wear US insignia without circle.

2. Aeronautical and chaplain badges are mandatory. Others are optional. Center aeronautical, occupational, or miscellaneous badge 1/2 inch above the top row of ribbons. Center additional badge 1/2 inch above first one. Wear highly polished badges only.

3. Center ribbons resting on but not over edge of pocket. Wear three or four in a row. Wear all or some.

4. Center duty or miscellaneous badge on lower portion of left pocket between left and right edges and bottom of flap and pocket, and/or on right pocket between left and right edges and bottom of flap and pocket. EXCEPTION: Missile and missile maintenance badges are worn on left pocket. Wear highly polished badges only.

5. Airmen center 4-inch sleeve chevron halfway between shoulder seam and elbow bent at 90-degree angle. Wear the current or new style rank insignia.

6. Center name tag resting on but not over edge of pocket, between left and right edges.

Women's New Service Dress Uniform (Enlisted)

Notes:

1. Place highly polished US insignia halfway up the seam, resting on but not over it. Bottom of insignia is horizontal with the ground.

2. Aeronautical badges are mandatory. Others are optional. Center aeronautical, occupational, or miscellaneous badge $^1/_2$ inch above the top row of ribbons. Center additional badge $^1/_2$ inch above first one. Wear highly polished badges only.

3. Center ribbons resting on but not over edge of welt pocket. Wear three or four in a row. Wear all or some.

4. Center duty or miscellaneous badge $1^1/_2$ inches below top of welt pocket and centered, and/or on right side centered between arm seam and lapel, with bottom edge of badge parallel to top of welt pocket. *EXCEPTION:* Missile and missile maintenance badges may be worn $1^1/_2$ inches below top of welt pocket and centered. Wear highly polished badges only.

5. Center new $3^1/_2$- or 4-inch sleeve chevron halfway between shoulder seam and elbow bent at 90-degree angle.

Women's Service Dress Uniform

Notes:

1. Place highly polished US insignia halfway up the seam, resting on but not over it. Bottom of insignia is horizontal with the ground; both officers and enlisted wear US without circle.

2. Aeronautical and chaplain badges are mandatory. Others are optional. Center aeronautical, occupational, or miscellaneous badge $1/2$ inch above the top row of ribbons. Center additional badge $1/2$ inch above first one.

3. Center ribbons on left side between lapel and arm seam, 1 to 3 inches higher than top button, horizontal with ground. Bottom of ribbons will be even with the bottom of name tag. Wear all or some.

4. Center name tag on right side between lapel and arm seam, 1 to 3 inches higher than top button.

5. Center duty or miscellaneous badge $1/2$ inch above name tag. Airman: Center 3-, 3 $1/2$-, or 4-inch sleeve chevron halfway between shoulder seam and elbow when bent at 90-degree angle. Wear current or new style rank insignia.

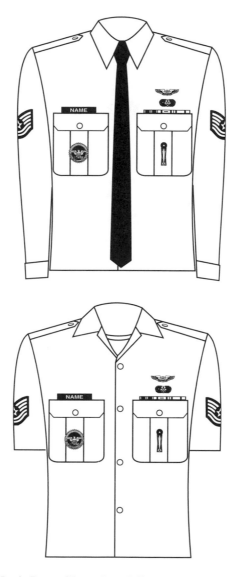

Men's Long-Sleeved and Short-Sleeved Shirt

Notes:

1. Aeronautical and chaplain badges are mandatory. Others are optional. Center aeronautical, occupational, or miscellaneous badge $1/2$ inch above ribbons or pocket if not wearing ribbons. Center additional badge $1/2$ inch above the first one. Wear satin finish or highly polished badges.

2. Center ribbons resting on but not over edge of pocket between the left and right edges. Wear all, some, or none.

3. Center duty or miscellaneous badge on lower portion of left pocket between left and right edges and bottom of flap and pocket, and/or on right pocket between left and right edges and bottom of flap and pocket. EXCEPTION: Missile and missile maintenance badges are worn on left pocket.

4. (Optional) Center tie tack or tie clasp (Air Force coat of arms, grade insignia, or wing and star) between bottom edge of knot and bottom tip of tie.

5. Center name tag on but not over edge of pocket.

6. Officers place shoulder mark insignia as close as possible to shoulder seam. Airmen center 3-inch or $3 1/2$-inch sleeve chevron halfway between shoulder seam and elbow bent at 90-degree angle on the long-sleeved shirt, or halfway between shoulder seam and bottom edge of sleeve on the short-sleeved shirt. Senior noncommissioned officers (SNCO) wear shoulder mark insignia or chevrons. Wear the current or new style rank insignia.

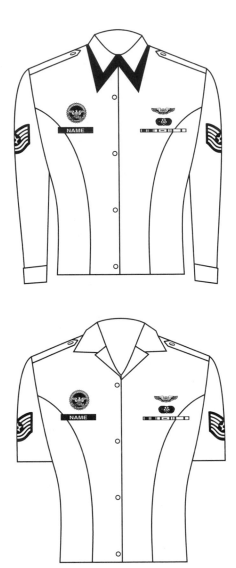

Women's Long-Sleeved and Short-Sleeved Blouse

Notes:

1. Aeronautical and chaplain badges are mandatory. Others are optional. Center aeronautical, occupational, or miscellaneous badge $^1/_2$ inch above the ribbons. When not wearing ribbons, center badge parallel to the name tag. Center additional badge $^1/_2$ inch above first one. Wear satin finish or highly polished badges.

2. Center ribbons on left side parallel with ground. Align bottom of the ribbons with the bottom of the name tag. Wear all, some, or none.

3. (Mandatory for major generals and below.) Pointed Collar: Center name tag on right side, even with to $1^1/_2$ inches higher or lower than the first exposed button. Rounded Collar: Center name tag on right side $1^1/_2$ to $2^1/_2$ inches below bottom of the tab, parallel with ground.

4. Center duty or miscellaneous badge $^1/_2$ inch above name tag. Wear satin finish or highly polished badges. Airmen: Center 3- or 3 $^1/_2$-inch sleeve chevron halfway between shoulder seam and elbow when bent at 90-degree angle on the long-sleeved shirt, and halfway between shoulder seam and bottom edge of sleeve on the short-sleeved shirt. Senior NCOs wear shoulder mark insignia or chevrons. Wear the current or new style rank insignia.

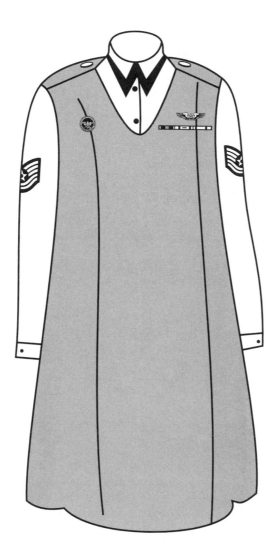

Maternity Service Dress Uniform (Jumper)

Notes:

1. Aeronautical and chaplain badges are mandatory. Others are optional. Center aeronautical, occupational, or miscellaneous badge $1/2$ inch above the ribbons. Center additional badge $1/2$ inch above first one. Wear highly polished badges only.

2. Pointed Collar: Center ribbons on left side even with to $1^{1}/2$ inches high or lower than, the first exposed button. Rounded Collar: Center ribbons on left side $1^{1}/2$ to $2^{1}/2$ inches below bottom of the tab, parallel with ground. Wear all or some.

3. Center duty or miscellaneous badge on right side with bottom edge of badge parallel to bottom edge of ribbons. Wear highly polished badges only.

4. Airmen: Center 3- or 3 $1/2$-inch sleeve chevron halfway between shoulder seam and elbow bent at 90-degree angle. Senior NCOs wear chevrons only. Wear the current or new style rank insignia.

5. *Name tag is not worn.*

Women's Long-Sleeved and Short-Sleeved Maternity Blouse

Notes:

1. Aeronautical and chaplain badges are mandatory. Others are optional. Center aeronautical, occupation, or miscellaneous badge $1/2$ inch above the ribbons. When not wearing ribbons, center parallel to the name tag. Center additional badge $1/2$ inch above first one. Wear satin finish or highly polished badges.

2. Center name tag on left side, horizontal with ground. Bottom of the ribbons is even with bottom of name tag. Wear all, some, or none.

3. Pointed Collar: Center name tag on right side even with to $1^1/2$ inches higher or lower than, the first exposed button. Rounded Collar: Center name tag on right side $1^1/2$ to $2^1/2$ inches below bottom of the tab, parallel with ground.

4. Center duty or miscellaneous badge $1/2$ inch above name tag. Wear satin finish or highly polished badges.

5. Airmen: Center 3- or 3 $1/2$-inch sleeve chevron halfway between sleeve and elbow bent at 90-degree angle on the long-sleeved shirt, and halfway between the shoulder seam and bottom of the sleeve on the short-sleeved shirt. Senior NCOs wear shoulder mark insignia or chevrons. Wear the current or new style rank insignia.

Men's and Women's Battle Dress Uniform

Notes:

1. Aeronautical and chaplain badges are mandatory. Others are optional. Center subdued embroidered badge (aeronautical, occupational, or miscellaneous) $^1/_2$ inch above US AIR FORCE tape. Center additional badge $^1/_2$ inch above the first badge. A third badge (miscellaneous) may be worn on lower portion of left pocket between left and right edges and bottom of flap and bottom of pocket. *NOTE:* Missile and missile maintenance badges are worn in this location.

2. Center US AIR FORCE tape immediately above left breast pocket. Center name tape immediately above right breast pocket. Cut off or fold tapes to match pocket width. Maternity: Place in same relative position.

3. (Commanders' discretion) Center emblems (subdued and/or full color) on lower portion of pocket between left and right edges and bottom of flap and pocket. Center emblem over right pocket $^1/_2$ inch above name tape. When wearing a badge on an emblem designated area, do not wear the emblem. Maternity: Place in same relative position. *NOTE:* Personnel attached to Army units may wear associate unit patch, only while attached to unit.

4. Airmen: Center 3-, 3 $^1/_2$-, or 4-inch (women) or 4-inch (men) sleeve chevron halfway between shoulder seam and elbow when bent at 90-degree angle. Wear either the current or new style rank insignia.

5. NAME/USAF tapes are mandatory on 1 Oct 97. Do not wear the Aircrew Style Name Patch beyond 30 Sept 97.

Men's New Semiformal Dress Uniform

Notes:

1. Place highly polished US insignia halfway up the seam, resting on but not over it. Bottom of insignia is horizontal with the ground.

2. Aeronautical and chaplain badges are mandatory. Others are optional. Center aeronautical, occupational, or miscellaneous badge ¹/₂ inch above the top row of ribbons. Center additional badge ¹/₂ inch above first one. Wear highly polished badges only.

3. Center ribbons resting on but not over edge of welt pocket. Wear three or four in a row. Wear all or some.

4. Center duty or miscellaneous badge 1/¹/₂ inches below top of welt pocket and centered, and/or on right side centered between arm seam and lapel, with bottom edge of badge parallel to top of welt pocket. *EXCEPTION:* Missile and missile maintenance badges are worn 1¹/₂ inches below top of welt pocket and centered. Wear highly polished badges only.

5. Center new 4-inch sleeve chevron halfway between shoulder seam and elbow bent at 90-degree angle.

Women's New Semiformal Dress Uniform

Notes:

1. Place US insignia halfway up the seam, resting on but not over it. Bottom of insignia is horizontal with the ground.

2. Center ribbons resting on but not over edge of welt pocket and between left and right edges. Wear three or four in a row. Wear all or some.

3. Aeronautical and chaplain badges are mandatory. Others are optional. Center aeronautical, occupational, or miscellaneous badge $1/2$ inch above top row of ribbons. Center additional badge $1/2$ inch above first one. Wear highly polished badges only.

4. Center duty or miscellaneous badge $1 1/2$ inches below top of welt pocket and/or on the right side centered between arm seam and lapel, with bottom edge of badge parallel with top of welt pocket. *EXCEPTION:* Missile and missile maintenance badges may be worn in this location. Wear highly polished badges only.

5. Center new $3 1/2$- or 4-inch sleeve chevron halfway between shoulder seam and elbow bent at 90-degree angle.

Men's Semiformal Dress Uniform

Notes:
1. (Mandatory) Place highly polished US insignia halfway up the seam, resting on but not over it. Bottom of insignia is horizontal with the ground; office and enlisted wear US insignia without circle.
2. Aeronautical and chaplain badges are mandatory. Others are optional. Center aeronautical, occupational, or miscellaneous badge 1/2 inch above the top row of ribbons. Center additional badge 1/2 inch above first one. Wear highly polished badges only.
3. Center ribbons resting on but not over edge of pocket. Wear three or four in a row. Wear all or some.
4. Center duty or miscellaneous badge on lower portion of left pocket between left and right edges and bottom of flap and pocket, and/or on right pocket between left and right edges and bottom of flap and pocket. *EXCEPTION:* Missile and missile maintenance badges are worn on left pocket. Wear highly polished badges only.
5. Airmen center 4-inch sleeve chevron halfway between shoulder seam and elbow bent at 90-degree angle. Wear the current or new style rank insignia.
6. Center name tag resting on but not over edge of pocket, between left and right edges.

Women's Semiformal Dress Uniform

Notes:

1. Place highly polished US insignia halfway up the seam, resting on but not over it. Bottom of insignia is horizontal with the ground; both officers and enlisted wear US without circle.

2. Aeronautical and chaplain badges are mandatory. Others are optional. Center aeronautical, occupational, or miscellaneous badge $1/2$ inch above the top row of ribbons. Center additional badge $1/2$ inch above first one.

3. Center ribbons on left side between lapel and arm seam, 1 to 3 inches higher than top button, horizontal with ground. Bottom of ribbons will be even with the bottom of name tag. Wear all or some.

4. Center name tag on right side between lapel and arm seam, 1 to 3 inches higher than top button.

5. Center duty or miscellaneous badge $1/2$ inch above name tag. Airmen: Center 3-, 3 $1/2$-, or 4-inch sleeve chevron halfway between shoulder seam and elbow when bent at 90-degree angle. Wear current or new style rank insignia.

Men's Mess Dress Uniform

Notes:

1.   Aeronautical and chaplain badges are mandatory. Others are optional. Center aeronautical, occupational, or miscellaneous badge $1/2$ inch above top row of medals or when not authorized medals, midway between shoulder and top button. Wear either highly polished or satin finished badges, cuff links or studs. Wear cuff links and studs as a set. Do not mix highly polished or satin finish.

2.   (Mandatory) Center miniature medals between lapel and arm seam and midway between top shoulder seam and top button of jacket.

3.   (Optional) Center duty or miscellaneous badge $1/2$ inch below bottom row of medals or comparable position when no medals are authorized, and/or on top right side in same relative position as those badges worn on left.

4.   (Mandatory) Airmen: Center 4-inch sleeve chevron (either aluminum color on blue background or new style rank insignia) halfway between shoulder seam and elbow bent at 90-degree angle.

Women's Mess Dress Uniform

Notes:

1 and 2.   Aeronautical and chaplain badges are mandatory. Others are optional. Center aeronautical, occupational, or miscellaneous badge $1/2$ inch above top row of medals or when not authorized medals, midway between shoulder and top button. Wear second badge above first badge when authorized. Wear satin finish or highly polished badges. Do not mix highly polished or satin finish.

3.   Center miniature medals between lapel and arm seam and midway between top of shoulder seam and top button of jacket. Airmen: Center 3-, $3 1/2$-, or 4-inch sleeve chevron (either aluminum color on blue background or new style rank insignia) halfway between shoulder seam and elbow bent at 90-degree angle.

5.   Center duty or miscellaneous badge on top right side in same relative position as those badges worn on left.

Hospital White Uniform

Notes:

1. Center name tag on the right side of the shirt with bottom edge parallel to the top of the left breast pocket or on the same relative position if no pocket.

2. Wear metal rank insignia 1-inch up from collar bottom.

3. (Optional) Center metal certification badge or cloth certification patch $^1/_2$ inch above name tag.

4. Aeronautical badges are mandatory, others are optional. Center the metal Air Force occupational badge $^1/_2$ inch above the left breast pocket or same relative position if no pocket.

5. (Commanders' discretion) Center metal or cloth MAJCOM or subordinate unit emblem $^1/_2$ inch above name tag.

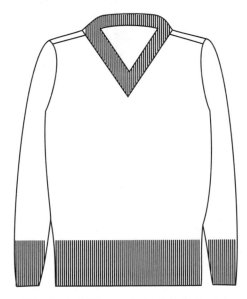

Men's and Women's Pullover Sweater

Notes:

1. Officers and senior NCOs wear shoulder mark grade insignia. All other enlisted members wear metal collar insignia centered horizontally on the epaulet with bottom of insignia placed 1 inch from shoulder seam.

ACQUISITION OF AIR FORCE UNIFORMS

Air Force uniforms and articles that are mandatory for wear are issued to all Air Force members when they enter the service. After that, replacement and optional items are purchased by individual members at Army and Air Force Exchange Service (AAFES) outlets and at Military Clothing Sales Stores (MCSS). Functional and distinctive clothing equipment items, when authorized for wear as outlined in Table of Allowances (TA) 016, are issued through supply channels.

WEAR OF THE AIR FORCE UNIFORM

The Air Force uniform is worn with pride, and each member is responsible for presenting a neat and clean military image. Items other than those provided for in AFI 36-2903 are not to be worn. Uniforms may be worn to off-base establishments for short trips. This policy, however, may be subject to local conditions such as in overseas areas where host nation sensitivities may be affected. In some cases, civilian clothing allowances may be authorized.

WEAR OF AWARDS AND DECORATIONS

Air Force members may wear regular or miniature medals and ribbons for awards and decorations they have received. When worn, they are arranged in order of precedence. The medal or ribbon with the highest precedence is worn nearest the lapel on the top row. Medals are primarily displayed on dress uniforms. Ribbons are displayed on the service dress uniform and on long- and short-sleeved blue shirts and blouses. They are not worn on outer garments such as raincoats, topcoats, overcoats, sweaters, or lightweight blue jackets.

WEAR OF INSIGNIA, BADGES, AND DEVICES

Grade insignia is worn by all Air Force members except those in Basic Military Training School or Officer Training School and agents of the Office of Special Investigations (OSI), unless otherwise directed. There are four types, designed for various uniforms: metal collar insignia, subdued cloth insignia, blue and silver cloth insignia, and formal dress insignia with silver-colored chevrons embroidered on a blue background. In the first sergeant career field, master sergeant selectees and above wear the silver, diamond-shaped device in conjunction with their grade insignia.

Lapel insignia identify the wearer as a member of the U.S. Air Force. Everyone, officers and enlisted, wears the same design (highly polished silver-colored "US" letters $7/16$ inch high) on his or her service dress coat. The bottom of the insignia is aligned halfway up the seam of the collar, resting on but not over, and horizontal with, the ground. Lapel insignia is often referred to as brass.

The standard Air Force name tag is laminated ultramarine blue plastic, $3^3/16$ inches long and $5/8$ inch wide. Names (last names only) are engraved in block style in white letters usually $1/4$ inch in size. Letters may be smaller if necessary to accommodate longer names.

Badges and specialty insignia may be worn on service, fatigue, and dress uniforms. Placement locations are specified and may not be changed unless authorized by the Chief of Staff, USAF. Examples include the following:

• *Aerospace Badges:* Astronaut, Pilot, Navigator or Observer, Flight Surgeon, Flight Nurse, Officer Aircrew Member, Enlisted Aircrew Member, and Parachutist.

• *Noncombatant Designation Badges and Insignia:* Physician, Dentist, Nurse, Biomedical Scientist, Judge Advocate, Chaplain, Air Force Academy Permanent Professor, and Medical Service Corps.

• *Special Service Identification Badges:* Presidential Service, Vice Presidential Service, Office of the Secretary of Defense, Joint Chiefs of Staff, and Army Staff Identification.

• *Duty Identification Badges:* Combat Crewmember, Security Policy, Air Training Command (ATC) Instructor, Air Force Recruiting Service, Fire Protection, Junior AFROTC Instructor, Air Force Reserve Recruiting Service, and Defense Language Institute (DLI) Instructor.

• *Air Force Specialty Qualification Badges:* Air Traffic Controller, Aircraft Maintenance/Munitions, Explosive Ordnance Disposal, Missile, Security Policy Qualification, Space, Weapons Controller, Information Management, Communications-Electronics Maintenance, Medical Technician, Meteorologist, and Supply-Fuels.

• *Other Badges:* Combat Infantry, Army Medical, Army Air Assault, Distinguished International Shooter, USAF Distinguished Rifleman, USAF Excellence-in-Competition Rifleman, USAF Bronze Excellence-in-Competition Rifleman, USAF Distinguished Pistol Shot, USAF Distinguished-in-Competition Pistol Shot, USAF Bronze Excellence-in-Competition Pistol Shot, and Military Societies of the United States.

RESTRICTIONS ON WEAR OF THE UNIFORM AND INSIGNIA

Air Force members may not wear the uniform, or any part, in situations that are counter to the interests of the United States or the U.S. Air Force, including the following:

1. A meeting of, or sponsored by, an organization, association, movement, or group that the Attorney General of the United States has named as totalitarian, fascist, communist, or subversive; that advocates acts of force or violence to deny others their rights under the Constitution; or that seeks to change the U.S. government by unconstitutional means.

2. Activities such as public speeches, interviews, picket lines, marches, rallies, or any public demonstration not approved by the Air Force. To do so could imply the Air Force's sanction of the cause for which the demonstration or activity is conducted.

3. When furthering private employment or commercial interests, if official sponsorship might be inferred.

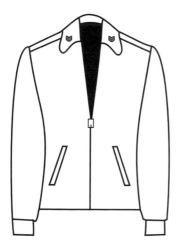

LIGHTWEIGHT BLUE JACKET
(Cotton/Polyester Poplin)

LIGHTWEIGHT BLUE JACKET
(Polyester/Wool Gabardine)

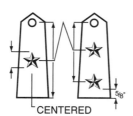

CENTERED

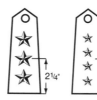

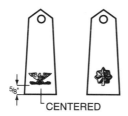

CENTERED

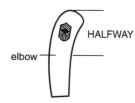

elbow

HALFWAY

CENTERED

Men's Lightweight Blue Jackets

Notes:

1. Enlisted personnel wear standard 4-inch chevrons on sleeves or metal collar insignia.
2. Officers wear regular metal grade insignia on epaulets.

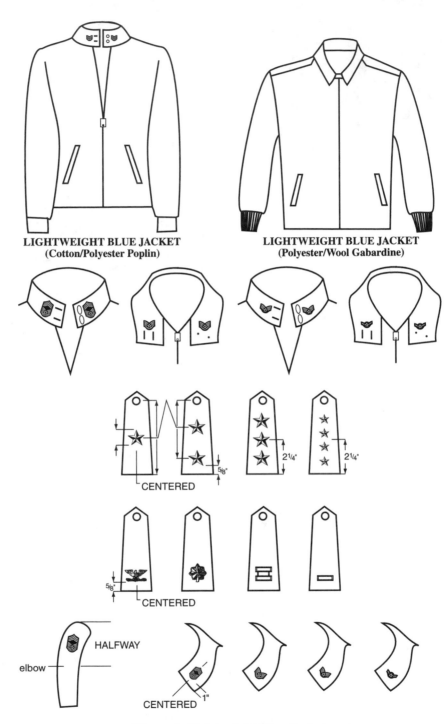

LIGHTWEIGHT BLUE JACKET
(Cotton/Polyester Poplin)

LIGHTWEIGHT BLUE JACKET
(Polyester/Wool Gabardine)

CENTERED

5/8"

2¼"

2¼"

5/8"

CENTERED

elbow

HALFWAY

CENTERED

1"

Women's Lightweight Blue Jackets

Notes:
1. Enlisted personnel wear standard 3- or 4-inch chevrons on sleeves or metal collar insignia.
2. Officers wear miniature metal grade insignia on epaulets.

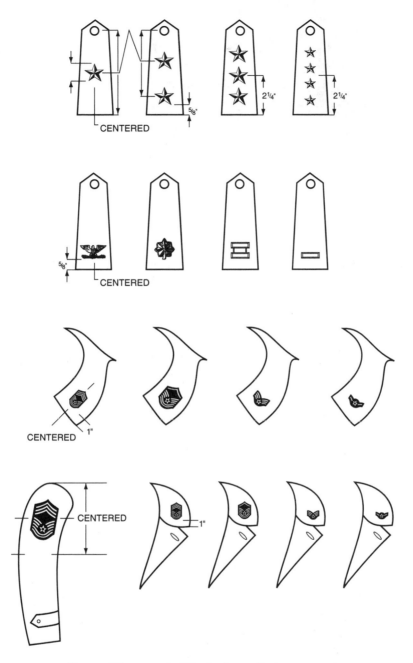

Proper Placement of Insignia on Outergarments

Notes:

1. Full-Length Outergarments and Light Weight Blue Jacket. Officers center regular size metal rank insignia 5/8 inch from end of epaulet or on collar if no epaulet. Enlisted personnel wear 3-, 3 1/2- or 4-inch (women) and 4-inch (men) sleeve chevron on sleeves or metal rank insignia on collar. Wear metal rank insignia centered 1-inch up from bottom collar, and parallel to outer edge. Wear either the current or new style rank insignia. *NOTE:* Sleeve chevrons are not worn on the raincoat so as not to compromise its watertight integrity.

2. Pullover Sweater: Officers and senior NCOs wear shoulder mark rank insignia. All other enlisted members wear metal rank insignia. Center horizontally on the epaulet with bottom of insignia 1 inch from shoulder seam. Wear the current or new style rank insignia.

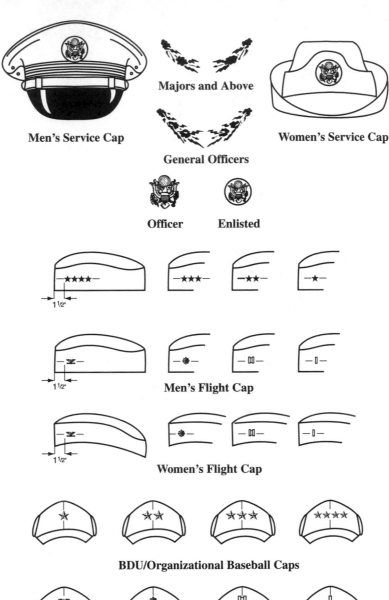

Men's Service Cap

Majors and Above

General Officers

Officer   Enlisted

Women's Service Cap

1 1/2"

1 1/2"   **Men's Flight Cap**

1 1/2"   **Women's Flight Cap**

BDU/Organizational Baseball Caps

Men's and Women's Headgear

Notes:

　　1.　Officers wear regular size metal grade insignia.

　　2.　Wear the regular size cloth or subdued metal grade insignia on the camouflage pattern BDU cap. MAJ-COM commanders may authorize wear of the bright nonsubdued grade insignia by officers on BDU caps while in garrison. *NOTE:* Chaplains may wear chaplains' insignia centered $1/2$ inch above visor of BDU cap.

　　3.　Grade will be centered vertically and horizontally.

　　4.　Officers wear service cap insignia without circle on service cap; enlisted wear service cap insignia with circle.

Presidential Service Badge

Vice-Presidential Service Badge

Office of the Secretary of Defense Badge

Joint Chiefs of Staff Badge

**Permanent Professor
USAF Academy Badge**

Special Service Identification Badges

COMMAND PILOT SENIOR PILOT PILOT

MASTER NAVIGATOR
OR MASTER
AIRCRAFT OBSERVER

SENIOR NAVIGATOR
OR SENIOR
AIRCRAFT OBSERVER

NAVIGATOR OR
AIRCRAFT OBSERVER

CHIEF FLIGHT
SURGEON

SENIOR FLIGHT
SURGEON

FLIGHT SURGEON

CHIEF FLIGHT
NURSE

SENIOR
FLIGHT NURSE

FLIGHT NURSE

MASTER
AIRCREW MEMBER

SENIOR OFFICER
AIRCREW MEMBER

OFFICER
AIRCREW MEMBER

CHIEF
AIRCREW MEMBER

SENIOR
AIRCREW MEMBER

AIRMAN
AIRCREW MEMBER

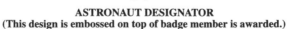

ASTRONAUT DESIGNATOR
(This design is embossed on top of badge member is awarded.)

Aeronautical Badges

Specialty Identification Badges.

MASTER PARACHUTIST   **SENIOR PARACHUTIST**   **PARACHUTIST**

MASTER MISSILE   **SENIOR MISSILE**   **MISSILE**

COMBAT CREW MEMBER

RECRUITING SERVICE   **ATC INSTRUCTOR
INSIGNIA**   **SECURITY POLICE
BADGE**

Duty Identification Badges

USAF
DISTINGUISHED
RIFLEMAN

USAF
EXCELLENCE-IN-
COMPETITION RIFLEMAN

USAF BRONZE
EXCELLENCE-IN-
COMPETITION RIFLEMAN

USAF
DISTINGUISHED
PISTOL SHOT

USAF
EXCELLENCE-IN-
COMPETITION
PISTOL SHOT

USAF BRONZE
EXCELLENCE-IN-
COMPETITION
PISTOL SHOT

Marksmanship Badges

4. When engaged in off-duty civilian employment.

5. When doing so would discredit the armed forces.

6. Any public meeting, demonstration, march, rally, or interview if the purpose may be to advocate, express, or approve opposition to the U.S. Armed Forces.

Air Force members are also prohibited from wearing combinations of uniforms not prescribed in AFI 36-2903 and from wearing or mixing distinctive uniform items (grade insignia, cap devices, badges, insignia, and so forth) with civilian clothing.

Personnel outside of the military are also affected. Any person within the jurisdiction of the United States who, without authority, wears a uniform or distinctive part of a uniform of the armed forces in an attempt to pose as a military member is subject to penalties as outlined in Title 18 U.S.C. 702.

PERSONAL GROOMING

Standards of appearance include four elements: neatness, cleanliness, safety, and military image. Military image is subjective, not always easy to outline in definitive terms, but it is a major consideration because it instills public confidence in the military. This is why standards were established for the most common appearance issues. These standards specify military members' responsibility for maintaining an "acceptable military image" and their right, within limits, to express individuality through their appearance.

General Requirements. Uniforms should be kept in a good state of repair. Shoes should be shined and in a good state of repair. Ribbons should be clean and should be replaced when they become frayed, worn, or faded. All buttons should be buttoned and pocket contents should be concealed from view, except for pens and pencils in the compartment of the left pocket on the fatigue uniform. Visible ornaments may not be worn, except for watches, rings (a maximum of three), and a wrist bracelet less than 1 inch wide if it is neat, conservative, and does not pose a safety hazard. Conservative sunglasses and photosensitive eyeglasses may be worn.

Hair must be clean, well groomed, and neat. If dyed, it must look natural. It must not contain excessive amounts of grooming aids, be worn in an extreme or fad style, or violate safety requirements. The hair must not touch the eyebrows when groomed or protrude below the front band of properly worn headgear (except for women's berets or flight caps). Wigs and hairpieces must conform to the same standards required for natural hair, be of good quality, and fit properly. They must not be worn in aircraft, flightline, or in-flight operations. Hair nets must be worn if required for safety. They must be cotton or synthetic, a conservative solid color similar to the individual's hair color, and strong enough to support and control hair. They must contain no metal fasteners.

Standards for Men. Hairstyles must be tapered on both sides and at the back, both with and without headgear, no more than $1/4$ inch thick at the termination point. A block cut is permitted as long as a tapered appearance is kept. Hair may not touch the ears. Only closely cut or shaved hair on the back of the neck may touch the collar. Overall, the hair must not exceed $1\,1/4$ inches in bulk, regardless of length. It must not have any visible foreign items attached to it. Beards must not be worn except for health reasons when authorized by a commander on the advice of a medical officer. Mustaches may be worn but must not extend downward beyond the lipline of the upper lip or sideways beyond a vertical line drawn upward from the corner of the mouth. These restrictions do not apply to personnel with a shaving waiver. Sideburns, when worn, must be neatly trimmed and tapered in the same manner as the haircut. They must be straight and of an even width (not flared) and end in a clean-shaven horizontal line, not below the lowest part of the exterior ear opening. These restrictions do not apply to personnel with a shaving waiver.

Standards for Women. Hairstyles must present a feminine appearance. Plain and conservative pins, combs, and barrettes similar to the individual's hair color may be worn to keep the hair in place. The hair must not be longer than the bottom edge of the shirt collar at the back of the neck, exceed 3 inches in bulk, or prevent proper wear of headgear. Cosmetics may be worn as long as they are conservative and in good taste. Nail polish may be worn when it is uniform, conservative in color, and in good taste. It must not, however, contain any ornamèntation.

AIR FORCE WEIGHT AND FITNESS PROGRAMS

The Air Force is concerned about the weight and fitness of its members for two primary reasons: First, the American public and its elected representatives form opinions about the Air Force based on the appearance of its members. If military personnel look out of shape, perception of the service's effectiveness will not be good. Second, obesity can pose dangerous health risks—heart problems, strokes, diabetes—that are detrimental to the individual Air Force member and to their physical ability to perform military tasks during both peacetime and war.

Air Force Instruction 40-502, *The Weight Management Program (WMP),* establishes body fat percentage standards for active-duty Air National Guard (ANG), and reserve forces personnel. It defines body fat management as an individual responsibility and lists maximum allowable body fat percentages by age and height. Personnel who exceed these standards are entered into the WMP, which is a positive rehabilitative program designed to encourage behavior modification and weight loss through education, counseling, and command and supervisory emphasis.

Air Force Instruction 40-501, *The Air Force Fitness Program,* establishes the goal of improving the health and fitness of all Air Force members and to increase total force readiness. The objectives of the Air Force Fitness Program are as follows:
- To motivate members to participate in regular physical conditioning programs to improve health and fitness as well as overall performance.
- To provide safe and valid assessments of each member's fitness level.
- To provide safe conditioning and rehabilitative programs for members to improve health and fitness.
- To encourage members to adopt lifestyles that promote health and fitness.

The Air Force recognizes fitness as an individual responsibility. To assure that members have an opportunity to achieve the appropriate levels of fitness, installation commanders are responsible for providing facilities, equipment, and funds to conduct fitness programs. They also appoint an installation fitness program trainer to develop and monitor installation fitness programs.

SOURCES OF ADDITIONAL INFORMATION

Air Force Instruction 36-2903, *Dress and Personal Appearance of Air Force Personnel.*

Air Force Instruction 40-501, *The Air Force Fitness Program.*

Air Force Instruction 40-502, *The Weight Management Program.*

Consult your supervisor or your unit's first sergeant.

9

Initial and
Follow-on Assignments

Reassignments to new duty stations, including overseas stations, are routine and frequent events that affect all military members and their dependents. The reassignment process begins when personnel channels officially notify you of your selection for a permanent change of station (PCS). You will receive printed copies of PCS orders that will confirm the unit and location to which you are being reassigned and the date that you must be there. The military personnel flight from your present base will arrange your outprocessing needs, and personnel from your next base will provide you with information to help your transfer go smoothly.

INTRO AND SPONSOR PROGRAMS
In years gone by, it wasn't unusual for airmen arriving at a base to have had no previous contact with anyone in their new duty section. With the introduction of the sponsor and the INTRO programs, this has changed.

INTRO is short for the Individual Newcomer Treatment and Orientation Program. Under this program, a unit is told of a newcomer's arrival and a sponsor is appointed to help the newcomer settle in. Advance information about the new duty station is provided to the newcomer by a commander's letter, a sponsor's letter, and the INTRO welcome kit. The program also offers orientation to the local mission and environment.

Sponsor programs were designed to provide new personnel with information before their arrival, and then to help them settle in. Sponsors are from the next unit of assignment, preferably the immediate duty section, at the shop or branch level. In most cases, personnel of similar grade and status are assigned as sponsors (airmen for airmen, NCOs for NCOs, singles for singles, married personnel for married personnel, and so on). For senior personnel, sponsors may be the commander or person they are replacing.

Sponsors provide information about the mission of the organization, the military member's duty section, family needs (housing, schools, and base facilities), and any special aspects about the surrounding community (especially if it is an overseas area). Sometimes base brochures outline topics of common interest.

If the assignment is to an overseas duty location, sponsors should always provide additional information: available services, differences in electrical current, the size of quarters on and off base (especially if they are small), and the availability of parts and service facilities for American automobiles.

ARRIVING AT A NEW LOCATION

At duty locations in the United States, new personnel usually arrive by commercial transportation or private vehicle. If possible, try to make prior arrangements to have your sponsor meet you or make reservations for temporary lodging. If prior arrangements have not been made, the base billeting office can advise you on temporary lodging. Usually it will have information for in-processing of new personnel. At most overseas locations, new personnel and their families are met at an air terminal by a base representative who arranges transportation to a central point on base, where sponsors help them obtain temporary quarters and instructions for in-processing.

In-Processing. In-processing consists of reporting in to the orderly room of your new unit of assignment, your duty section, and the Military Personnel Flight (MPF). At the MPF, you will turn in most of the official records you brought with you and will be scheduled for a variety of appointments based on your grade and sometimes your career field.

One of the appointments will be a newcomer's orientation, a meeting that provides information for new arrivals, including spouses if they wish. It covers the unit's mission and areas of common interest, including housing, educational opportunities, and base facilities and programs. In overseas areas, other topics such as driving, travel, and host nation sensitivities may be included. Personnel then visit other locations on base, depending on their individual needs, collecting travel allowances, obtaining housing, arranging delivery of household goods, registering a vehicle on base, meeting training schedules, and so forth.

Getting Permanent Living Quarters. Three primary categories of permanent living quarters are available, and members are assigned based on marital status (married or single), grade, and number of dependents.

• Rooms in dormitories, previously referred to as barracks, are assigned to single and unaccompanied personnel by their unit of assignment or a Central Dormitory Management Office (CDMO).

• Base housing, when available, is assigned to accompanied members on a priority system, based primarily on the date of arrival and the number of bedrooms needed for dependents.

• Off-base quarters are obtained by accompanied or unaccompanied personnel when on-base quarters are not available. They are usually rented from private owners, or can be purchased if a member prefers.

Anyone renting off-base property should be sure to read the rental agreement carefully. It will specify the period of your lease and may include special provisions. If standard contracts are offered by the base housing office, they should be used. They usually contain a standard military release clause that will enable you to move out early if you are offered base housing.

Also, take time to complete an accurate inventory of the rental property. Note the condition of the house or the apartment itself (condition of paint, windows, fences, doors, any damage such as scratches or chips) and the condition of any items not permanently fixed (appliances, curtains, carpets). By doing this you reduce the possibility of being charged for damage that was not your fault. Some housing offices have standard forms for this purpose.

Finally, when you are moving out, be sure to provide formal written notice to the landlord or agent and to do so as early as possible, although the amount of notice you are required to give should be specified in your contract.

Obtaining Private Transportation. Whatever mode of transportation you choose (car, motorcycle, or bicycle), be sure it is safe and reliable. Sometimes bargains work out satisfactorily. When they don't, the outcome can be a real source of frustration, affecting both your health and your bank account.

REPORTING FOR DUTY

Reporting for duty includes becoming familiar with your new unit's mission, the personnel assigned, and the role you will be expected to assume. When you arrive, the focal point is usually a unit orderly room. Here, newcomers are processed in and introduced to key personnel such as the supervisor, the first sergeant, and the commander. Afterward, individual or group meetings provide insight into the unit's specific mission and how it complements the base or installation mission, any special policies or procedures, and some information about where you will work and what or whom you will be responsible for (or to). Then you will go to your immediate duty section (a branch, shop, or office), where you will meet the supervisors, peers, and subordinates you will work with. Duty assignments based on each individual's grade and experience are determined, and work schedules are established.

Supervisory Positions. Experienced airmen may be placed in supervisory positions. These positions carry a wide range of responsibilities and are subject to much discussion. What do these roles encompass? In the words of CMSgt Donald L. Neiworth, being in a supervisory position means "understanding and being actively involved and committed to the Air Force mission, providing leadership through example, and taking care of your people."

"Understanding the mission . . ." Initial information about the mission and your area of responsibility comes from discussions with key personnel and members of the duty section. These will usually emphasize known and projected mission requirements, projects that have been done well, and those that require attention. You'll also get information from directives that outline pro-

gram requirements, inspection reports, self-inspection programs, manning documents, and reports that note observations made during staff assistance visits from higher headquarters and other base-level agencies (such as safety, training, budget, audit, and security functions).

"Providing leadership through example . . ." Many books have been written on the subject of leadership and its importance in achieving results and making good things happen. In the USAF, supervisors provide the leadership to appropriately influence and direct people in order to accomplish the mission. The traits of successful leaders include loyalty, integrity, commitment, initiative, decisiveness, and selflessness (not placing individual comfort before the mission or the people). The most effective style is tailored to the mission, the people, and the environment. The functions of a leader include developing professional relationships, setting goals and standards, providing technical competence, maintaining channels of communication, motivating people, and identifying problems that affect job performance. An in-depth discussion of this subject is provided in Air Force Pamphlet 35-49, *Air Force Leadership.*

"Taking care of your people . . ." Successful supervisors must be sensitive to subordinates' motivational levels and needs if they are to have a positive effect on their performance and job satisfaction. No set of rules can anticipate or cover all the elements of motivating the people who work for you, nor is a textbook solution always the best one. In general, Air Force personnel perform at higher motivational levels when they feel as follows:

• They are an important part of the unit.

• A supervisor takes a personal interest in them as an individual and encourages them to use their initiative and accept additional responsibilities.

• Their grade and AFSC are fairly matched to the job they're doing.

• They have the opportunity for advancement in skill levels, positions of increased responsibility, professional military education, and promotion.

• Work activities and tasks are sensibly organized and decisions are well thought out, correct, and not constantly changing.

• Standards are applied on a consistent basis without bias, and discipline is fair and just (it's OK for it to be "hard" as long as it's fair).

• The base or installation is a good place to work and live.

RESOURCE MANAGEMENT: FUNDS, EQUIPMENT, AND SUPPLIES

At base level, the requirements for funds, supplies, and equipment are managed by two functions: the Budget Office, a branch of the Accounting and Finance Office; and Supply. Funds for official programs are based on known and projected requirements. They are controlled by cost center managers and resource advisors on a daily, quarterly, and annual basis every financial calendar (fiscal) year, which runs from the first day of October to the last day of the following September. They, in turn, work closely with supervisors, commanders, and personnel from the Budget Office. Training classes are held periodically for those responsible for managing funds. Information and guidance are also outlined in Air Force Pamphlet, AFPAM 65-605, *Resource Manager's Handbook.*

Supplies are obtained from Base Supply, according to the local procedures and those outlined in Air Force Regulation 67-23, *Standard Base Supply Customer's Guide.* Some are stocked by Base Supply; others must be ordered. Future requirements can often be determined by past usage rates and other known indicators, such as upcoming exercises and deployments.

Equipment requirements are controlled by the Air Force Equipment Management System, which enables the Air Force to determine needs, authorizations, accountability, and the types and quantities of equipment required to accomplish specified missions. It also provides a database for budgeting and purchasing programs. At the local level, equipment account custodians in each unit or organization identify needs, order items, and are responsible for accounting for each piece of property. They work with personnel from the base's Equipment Management Office. Orders are made on equipment allowance documents that prescribe the items and quantities required for assigned missions and functions. This system provides organizations with a ready reference to equipment selected for Air Force use. It also encourages uniformity of equipment for similar functions, for example, machine shops, print shops, and administrative offices. Procedures are outlined in Air Force Regulation 67-23, *Standard Base Supply Customer's Guide.* Orientation classes are also conducted for equipment custodians.

FACILITIES

The physical appearance of a duty section and the way it is maintained often reflect the efficient, professional, and confident spirit of an organization and its personnel. Efforts to provide the best working conditions should always be made with due consideration to the job at hand, the efficient arrangement of personnel and equipment, and safety features, lighting, and temperature controls.

Improvements require careful planning and the support of supervisors and commanders. They are also dependent on available funds and the approval of other base agencies, such as the safety office and the base civil engineer. Improvements originate in three primary ways:

1. The construction of new facilities is usually planned at least two fiscal years in advance under the Military Construction Program (MCP).

2. Major renovation of existing facilities is normally programmed at least one year in advance. Approval depends on the availability of funds in the base's Operations and Maintenance (O&M) fund.

3. Self-help programs, involving the personnel assigned to the unit, can improve the quality of life in the work environment. Projects might include improving existing operations, enhancing the appearance of a facility, or correcting deficiencies not previously undertaken because of a lack of funds or manpower. To get the best results, do more than just turn the troops loose with materials and paint.

Any facility-improvement project should be carefully thought out and developed into a complete and well-harmonized plan. The plan should do the following:

- List goals: what specifically is to be done.
- List priorities: separate needs, which come first, from wants, which come second, and set tentative target dates for completion.
- Consider the means: self-help, renovation, or new construction.
- Consider funding sources and how your project will compete with other command and local priorities.
- Obtain supervisory and command support.

Smaller in-shop projects do not require major undertakings or releases of funds; there are two that can have an immediate and positive effect on your environment. Put on a coat of fresh paint. Choose good color schemes; if more than one color is used, they should harmonize. And take a look at the way things are displayed on the walls. Bulletin boards can reduce a cluttered appearance. Take down items suspended by masking tape, thumbtacks, or nails; frames can add a touch of class.

Office Layout and Work Flow. Careful consideration to the placement of furniture and equipment will enhance the flow of work, eliminate duplication of effort, and reduce processing times. Work should progress through its production cycle with the minimum of backtracking. Preferably it should flow in a straight line, a circle, an L, a U, or some other regular shape. If more than one floor is involved, this should also be taken into consideration.

Review available options by making some rough sketches on paper; it's a lot easier than moving heavy items around. Sketches should be drawn to scale; consider fixed objects such as doors, windows, posts or pillars, electrical outlets, telephone lines, and so forth. Before you make any major changes, consult all interested parties—functions that have joint use of the space, supervisors, and safety office personnel—as well as civil engineers for modifications beyond moving furniture and equipment.

Security Requirements. Responsibilities for security are shared by everyone in the USAF. The USAF Information Security Program is a system of administrative policies and procedures designed to identify, control, and protect certain types of information from unauthorized disclosure. The Security Police have the overall responsibility for managing this program. They, in turn, are supported by security managers who have been appointed in all units and staff agencies.

At the working level, all members should know how to control, secure, and account for classified materials; assure the adequacy of storage facilities, work areas, and operating procedures; acquire appropriate security clearances for assigned personnel; and provide a continuing security education awareness program.

Specific program information and requirements are outlined in Air Force Policy Directive 31-4, *Information Security,* and Air Force Instruction 31-401,

Managing the Information Security Program. Additional information may be prescribed at local and major command levels based on the needs of specific career fields and duty locations.

PROCEDURAL CHANGES
Changes are sometimes necessary to streamline procedures and enhance the efficiency of an operation. Sometimes rapid changes are needed because of safety or funding considerations. To be effective, a change should be well thought out in advance. It should improve an existing condition and provide a benefit. It should be explained to those affected and implemented gradually. This will help facilitate acceptance and reduce resistance.

ADDITIONAL DUTIES
Additional duties are those assigned to personnel in addition to the primary duties of their Air Force specialty. They include positions such as equipment or supply custodian, safety representative, historian, unit public affairs representative, training manager, suggestion monitor, resource advisor or cost center manager, advisory council member, security manager, and unit career advisor. These duties place increased demands on a supervisor's time, but they also provide many benefits. They can broaden your overall understanding about other Air Force programs and prepare you for increased responsibility. Supervisors and commanders are aware of the importance of these programs and frequently comment on them in performance reports.

THINKING ABOUT THE FUTURE
The best time to think about future assignments is two or three months after you arrive at your new base. Future promotions and assignments are based on performance and the breadth and depth of experience within an Air Force specialty. Getting that kind of experience is not always possible if you remain at one location.

Declining productivity curves and stagnation factors are also associated with staying in one position for too long. With time, each job becomes more routine and it is difficult to remain creative, innovative, and energetic. When that happens, your productivity curve starts heading downward. Those who were there when you arrived will usually depart before you. New supervisors may not be aware of the full extent of previous achievements. If someone makes a suggestion for improving a policy or procedure, and you hear yourself saying, "But we've always done it that way," stagnation has set in.

There are two ways to broaden your experience. One is to seek a change in duty positions at the same location. The other is to seek reassignment to another base or installation by updating your Air Force Form 392, "Airman Assignment Preference Statement." This form communicates your intentions to career managers through the personnel system. When completing it, be sure to consult Air Force Instruction 36-2110, *Assignments,* and select choices that are relevant to Air Force needs at bases or locations that require your Air Force specialty.

SOURCES OF ADDITIONAL INFORMATION
For questions about duty section requirements, consult your supervisor, first sergeant, or commander.

For questions about the duty location, arrival, and initial in-processing requirements, consult your sponsor or the unit INTRO monitor. For specific programs, consult the agencies and directives referred to in this chapter.

10

Career Progression Routes

Your career progression will depend on the efforts you make to develop or improve proficiency in your Air Force Specialty (AFS). This chapter will explain the Air Force Military Personnel Classification System and the criteria for the award of different skill levels. It will also tell you what kind of jobs the Air Force offers and the ways to apply for retraining.

THE AIR FORCE MILITARY PERSONNEL CLASSIFICATION SYSTEM

The classification system identifies the duties for all positions essential to accomplishing the mission of the U.S. Air Force. It is also used to accurately identify the abilities of each individual and match them to the qualifications of the position. These positions are functionally grouped into Air Force Specialties (AFSs) based on skills and qualifications.

Air Force Specialty Codes. Each AFS has a title, a specialty description, and a code number known as an Air Force Specialty Code (AFSC). The specialty codes can be referred to in three different ways:

1. A Primary Air Force Specialty Code (PAFSC) shows which specialty an airman is most qualified in. It is used because some airmen are qualified to perform in more than one specialty (for example, as a medic and as an information management specialist).

2. A Duty Air Force Specialty Code (DAFSC) is used to link an airman to a specific authorized manning document position that he or she is assigned to. It does not necessarily correspond with the airman's qualification level.

3. A Control Air Force Specialty Code (CAFSC) is used to make assignments; it ensures an equitable distribution of airmen by grade and skill level against established manning requirements, and it also helps identify and control training requirements.

The Evolution of Air Force Specialty Codes. On 1 November 1993, Air Force Specialty Codes were converted to a new alphanumeric formula. The new AFSCs were designed to match the restructured Air Force and to align career fields that became fragmented over the years. Many of the older original AFSCs were established in, and have been in place since, 1951, when the Air

Force adopted many of the old Army military occupational specialty (MOS) codes. The new system was designed to accommodate a smaller force. By removing some AFSCs and combining others, it reduced the number of narrowly trained specialists and relied more on generalists who can be assigned to a broader range of duties and career-broadening opportunities.

Figuring Out the New Codes.

- The first digit of the new enlisted AFSCs shows the career grouping.
- The second character is a letter that identifies the career field.
- The third character shows a career field subdivision.
- The fourth character marks the airman's level of qualification:

1	helper
3	apprentice
5	journeyman
7	craftsman
9	superintendent
0	chief enlisted manager

- The fifth character notes the airman's specialty.

The following is an example of AFSC 1A572, which is used to classify one of the levels of the Airborne Radar Systems Craftsman career field.

Career Grouping	Career Field	Career Field Subdivision	Skill Level	Specific AFSC
1	A	5	7	2
Operations	Aircrew Operations	Airborne Systems	Craftsman	Radar

Proficiency Skill Levels. Proficiency skill levels are awarded as codes for Air Force Specialties (AFSs), Special Duty Identifiers (SDIs), and Chief Enlisted Managers (CEMs). They come at intervals during airmen's careers based on their grade, time requirements, performance within their career field, completion of training requirements, and supervisor's recommendation. Generally, it works this way:

1. The 1 skill level designates initial entry into an Air Force specialty.

2. The 3 skill level is awarded to those who qualify as bypass specialists, complete a formal technical training course, or complete 3-level upgrade training on the job.

3. The 5 skill level is awarded for satisfactorily performing on 5-level upgrade training and passing 5-level career development courses. Most airmen who complete a formal technical training course are entered into 5-level training at their first permanent duty station.

4. The 7 skill level is awarded for satisfactorily performing on 7-level upgrade training and passing the 7-level career development course for the appropriate specialty. Those promoted to the grade of staff sergeant are entered into upgrade training for the 7 level.

5. The 9 skill level is awarded to master sergeants and senior master sergeants who are satisfactorily performing in their AFSCs. In some cases, completion of the Senior NCO Academy is a prerequisite for the award of the 9 level.

6. The Chief Enlisted Manager (CEM) codes identify all chief master sergeant positions in the airman classification structure. These codes are awarded to chief master sergeants (or selectees) who already possess a 9-level AFSC. These codes identify personnel who, through extensive experience and training, have demonstrated the leadership and management ability to effectively control a wide range of programs and activity.

7. Special Duty Identifiers (SDIs) are awarded based on satisfactory performance and the date entered into the special duty.

THE AIRMAN CLASSIFICATION STRUCTURE:
"WHERE THE JOBS ARE"

Job opportunities within the enlisted force of the Air Force are categorized under nine career groupings, which are further broken down into several hundred subdivisions. The accompanying chart lists the Air Force specialty descriptions and special duty identifiers (SDIs) with their respective codes. Following this chart are listings of present Special Experience Identifiers (SEIs), Reporting Identifiers, and Air Force Specialty Code Prefixes.

Enlisted Force Specialty Descriptions and Special Duty Identifiers. The following is a list of titles of specialty descriptions and special duty identifiers, along with their AFSCs or codes.

Title	AFSC
Aeromedical	4F0X1
Aerospace Control and Warning Systems	1C5X1
Aerospace Ground Equipment (AGE)	2A6X2
Aerospace Maintenance	2A5X1
Aerospace Maintenance (Superintendent)	2A590
Aerospace Physiology	4M0X1
Aerospace Propulsion	2A6X1
Air Traffic Control	1C1X1
Air Traffic Control Radar	2E0X1
Air Transportation	2T2X1
Airborne Command and Control Communications Equipment	1A5X2

Airborne Command and Control Mission Electronics Systems (Superintendent)	1A590
Airborne Command Post Communications Equipment	2A1X6
Airborne Communications Systems	1A3X1
Airborne Computer Systems	1A5X1
Airborne Radar Systems	1A5X3
Airborne Warning and Control Radar	2A1X4
Aircraft Armament Systems	2W1X1
Aircraft Avionics (Superintendent)	2A490
Aircraft Communication and Navigation Systems	2A4X2
Aircraft Control and Warning Radar	2E062
Aircraft Electrical And Environmental Systems	2A6X6
Aircraft Fabrication (Superintendent)	2A790
Aircraft Fuel Systems	2A6X4
Aircraft Guidance and Control	2A4X1
Aircraft Loadmaster	1A2X1
Aircraft Metals Technology	2A7X1
Aircraft Pneudraulic Systems	2A6X5
Aircraft Structural Maintenance	2A7X3
Aircraft Systems (Superintendent)	2A690
Aircrew Egress Systems	2A6X3
Aircrew Life Support	1T1X1
Airfield Management	1C0X1
Automatic Tracking Radar	2E0X3
Avionics Guidance and Control Systems	2A1X2
Avionics Sensors Maintenance	2A1X1
Avionics Support Equipment	2A1X5
Avionics Test Station and Components	2A0X1
B-1 and B-2 Avionics Systems	2A5X3
Bioenvironmental Engineering	4B0X1
Biomedical Equipment	4A2X1
Bomb-Navigation Systems	2A2X1
Cardiopulmonary Laboratory	4H0X1
Chaplain Service Support	5R0X1
Combat Arms Training and Maintenance	3P1X1
Combat Control	1C2X1
Command and Control	1C3X1
Communication and Navigation Systems	2A1X3
Communications Antenna Systems	2E6X1
Communications Cable and Antenna Systems (Superintendent)	2E690
Communications Cable Systems	2E6X2
Communications Systems (Superintendent)	2E190
Communications-Computer Systems (Superintendent)	2E690

Communications-Computer Systems Control	3C2X1
Communications-Computer Systems Operations	3C0X1
Communications-Computer Systems Planning and Implementation	3C3X1
Communications-Computer Systems Programming	3C0X2
Contracting	6C0X1
Conventional Avionics (Superintendent)	2A190
Correctional Custody Supervisor	8J000
Courier	8P000
Cryptologic Linguist	1N3X
Cryptologic Linguist (Superintendent)	1N390
Cytotechnology	4T0X3
Defense Attache Specialist	8P100
Dental Assistant	4Y0X1
Dental Laboratory	4Y1X1
Diet Therapy	4D0X1
Disaster Preparedness	3E9X1
Education and Training	3S2X1
Electrical (Superintendent)	3E090
Electrical Power Production	3E0X2
Electrical Systems	3E0X1
Electromagnetic Spectrum Management	3C1X2
Electronic Computer and Switching Systems	2E2X1
Electronic Signals Intelligence Exploitation	1N5X1
Electronic System Security Assessment	1N6X1
Electronic Warfare Systems	2A2X2
Electronic Warfare/Offensive Avionic (Superintendent)	2A290
Engineering	3E5X1
Explosive Ordnance Disposal	3E8X1
F-15/F-111 Avionic Systems	2A3X1
F-16 Avionic Systems	2A3X2
Fabrication and Parachute	2A7X4
Family Support Center (Superintendent)	8C000
Financial Analysis	6F1X1
Financial Management	6F0X1
Financial Management and Services (Superintendent/Craftsman)	6F0X0
Financial Services	6F0X2
Fire Protection	3E7X1
First Sergeant	8F000
Flight Engineer	1A1X1
Force Management	3E6X1
Fuels	2F0X1
General Purpose Vehicle and Body Maintenance (Craftsman)	2T470
General Purpose Vehicle Maintenance	2T4X1

Ground Radar (Superintendent)	2E090
Ground Radar Communications	2E1X3
Health Services Management	4A0X1
Heating, Ventilation, Air Conditioning, and Refrigeration	3E1X1
Helicopter Maintenance	2A5X2
Histopathology	4T0X2
Historian	3H0X1
ICBM NCO Code Controller	8S200
Imagery Interpreter	1N1X1
Imagery Production	3V1X1
Imagery Systems Maintenance	2E5X1
In-Flight Passenger Service Specialist	8A000
In-Flight Refueling	1A0X1
Information Management	3A0X1
Instrumentation and Telemetry Systems	2E8X1
Intelligence Operations	1N0X1
Intelligence Operations and Targeting (Superintendent)	1N090
Inventory Management	2S0X1
Law Enforcement	3P0X2
Linguist Debriefer/Interrogator	8D000
Liquid Fuel Systems Maintenance	3E4X2
Logistics Plans	2G0X1
Maintenance Data Systems Analysis	2R0X1
Maintenance Scheduling	2R1X1
Manpower Management	3U0X1
Marine (Superintendent)	2B090
Marine Engine	2B0X2
Materiel Storage and Distribution	2S013
Medical Laboratory	4T0X1
Medical Laboratory (Superintendent)	4T090
Medical Materiel	4A1X1
Medical Service	4N0X1
Medical Service (Superintendent)	4N090
Mental Health Service	4C0X1
Meteorological and Navigation Systems	2E1X2
Military Training Instructor	8B000
Missile and Space Facilities	2M0X3
Missile and Space Systems Electronic Maintenance	2M0X1
Missile and Space Systems Maintenance	2M0X2
Missile and Space Systems Maintenance (Superintendent)	2M090
Missile Control Communications Systems	2E7X2
Missile Facility Manager	8S000
Morale, Welfare, Recreation, and Services	3M0X1

Munitions Systems	2W0X1
Nondestructive Inspection	2A7X2
Nuclear Medicine	4R0X2
Nuclear Weapons	2W2X1
Occupational Therapy	4J0X1
Operations Resource Management	1C0X2
Optometry	4V0X1
Orthotic	4U0X1
Paralegal	5J0X1
Pararescue	1T2X1
Patient	9P000
Pavements and Construction Equipment	3E2X1
Personnel	3S0X1
Personnel (Superintendent)	3S090
Personnel System Management (PSM)	3S0X2
Pest Management	3E4X3
Pharmacy	4P0X1
Physical Therapy	4J0X2
Postal	8M000
Precision Measurement Equipment Laboratory	2P0X1
Premier Band	3N2X1
Printing Management	3R0X1
Professional Military Education Instructor	8T000
Public Affairs	3N0X1
Public Affairs (Superintendent)	3N090
Public Health	4E0X1
Radio and Television Broadcasting	3N0X2
Radio Communications Systems	3C1X1
Radiologic	4R0X1
Radiologic (Superintendent)	4R090
Recruiter	8R000
Regional Band	3N1X1
Research and Development Technician	8E000
Safety	1S0X1
Satellite and Wideband Communications Equipment	2E1X1
Seaman	2B0X1
Secure Communications Systems	2E3X1
Security	3P0X1
Security (Superintendent)	3P090
Sensor Operator	8S100
Signals Intelligence Analysis	1N4X1
Signals Intelligence Production	1N2X1
Social Actions	3S1X1

Space Systems	2E4X1
Space Systems Operations	1C6X1
Special Investigations	7S0X1
Special Purpose Vehicle and Equipment Maintenance	2T3X1
Special Purpose Vehicle and Equipment Maintenance (Craftsman)	2T370
Special Vehicle Maintenance	2T3X2
Still Photographic	3V0X2
Structural	3E3X1
Subsistence Operations	3K0X1
Supply Management (Superintendent)	2S0X2
Supply Systems Analysis	2S0X2
Surgical Service	4N1X1
Survival Training	1T0X1
Tactical Air Command and Control	1C4X1
Tactical Aircraft (Superintendent)	2A390
Tactical Aircraft Maintenance	2A3X3
Target Intelligence	1N0X2
Telephone and Data Circuitry Equipment	2E7X3
Telephone Communications Systems (Superintendent)	2E790
Telephone Switching	2E7X1
Television and Intrusion Detection Systems	2E1X4
Traffic Management	2T0X1
United States Air Force Honor Guard	8G000
Utilities Systems	3E4X1
Utilities Systems (Superintendent)	3E490
Vehicle Body Maintenance	2T4X2
Vehicle Maintenance (Superintendent)	2T390
Vehicle Maintenance Control and Analysis	2T3X3
Vehicle Operations/Dispatcher	2T1X1
Visual Information	3V0X1
Visual Information Production-Documentation	3V0X3
Visual Information Services	3V090
Weather	1W0X1

Special Experience Identifiers (SEIs). Special Experience Identifiers (SEIs) identify special experience and training that are not otherwise identified by AFSC or other codes within the personnel data system (PDS). These codes do the following: identify experience or training that is critical to individuals and the jobs they perform when no other identification is appropriate or available. They permit rapid identification of a resource already qualified to meet unique circumstances, contingency requirements, or management needs, and provide a means to track individuals and identify positions requiring or providing unique experience or training that otherwise would be lost. SEIs are tied to the assignment process and are used to better distribute personnel and optimize the job-and-person match as much as possible.

Most SEI codes are composed of three numeric characters, although three alphanumeric characters can be used for some AFSCs when authorized to do so by the Air Intelligence Agency (AIA). The individual characters within these codes have no specific meaning. Most SEIs are authorized for award with specific AFSCs; some are authorized with any AFSC. The SEIs are functionally grouped by category, such as Civil Engineering, Contracting, Communications, Communications-Electronics, Weather, Security, Medical, Aircraft Maintenance and Weapons Systems (such as Engines and Avionics), Missiles and Space Operations, and Command and Control Systems.

Attachment 42 of Air Force Manual 36-2108 contains a full listing of each SEI Code, a title, and explanation/designation criteria that tell which AFSC they can be awarded for. The following list includes some of the most commonly awarded SEIs.

SEI Code	Title
002	Defense Intelligence College (DIG) Graduate
004	Orderly Room/Unit Administration
009	Wholesale Logistics Experience
010	Space Systems Operations
014	AFOSI Technical Services
031	Crime Prevention/Resources Protection
032	Budget Experience
039	Aviation Fuels Monitor
040	Aviation Fuels Accounting
045	Tactical Air Control System Direct Air Support Center or Air Support Operations Center (TACS DASC/ASOC)
046	Tactical Air Control System Airborne Battlefield Command and Control Center (TACS)
048	Joint Operations Planning System Automated Data Processing (JOPS ADP) User
053	Ground Control Approach
056	Control Tower
057	Seismic Technique
058	Atmospheric Research Equipment
064	Combat Crew Training
065	Central Flight Instructor Course
073	KC-135 Boom Operator
084	Aircraft Flight Test

087	M-60 Machine Gun
090	Airlift Control Element
091	Fitness and Recreation
092	Air Force Quality Advisor
093	Air Force Quality Facilitator
095	Operational Test and Evaluation (OT & E)
153	Contract Administration
167	Satellite Systems Technician
187	National Military Command Center Communications-Electronics Systems Maintenance
239	Combat Crew Communications
256	Airborne Command Post
297	Personnel Control Team (PCT) Member
301	Air National Guard Readiness Center (ANGRC)
304	Military News Editor
305	NCO Preparatory Course Instructor
306	Special Operations Force
310	Patrol Dog—Drug Detection
313	Information Management (IM) Systems
321	Security Police Investigator
326	Red Horse Experience
327	Air Base Ground Defense
328	Air Base Survivability
332	Photojournalist
348	Safety Education Program
350	Airspace Management
370	Patrol Dog—Explosive Detection
372	Additional Duty Social Actions NCO
475	Substance Abuse Certification
485	Independent Duty Dental Laboratory Technician
501	A-10
503	KC-10
506	F-117
510	U-2
513	AC-130H/U, Spectre Gunship
514	HC-130
521	F-4G (Wild Weasel)
522	F/RF-4
527	F-111A/E
533	F-15
535	F-16
545	C-5
546	C-17

547	C-12
550	C-141
569	E-3A/B (AWACS)
596	B-2
677	Air Force Satellite Communications Systems
809	Missile Electronic Equipment Maintenance
836	Munitions Inspector
900	Combat Airspace Manager
916	Strategic Defense Radar Systems Evaluator
927	Ballistic Missile Early Warning System (BMEWS)— Mechanical
928	Ballistic Missile Early Warning System (BMEWS)— Phased Array
942	484L Presidential Aircraft Support System
970	Special Tactics
979	Space Defense Operations Center (SPADOC)
986	Sea Launched Ballistic Missile (SLBM) Phased-Array Warning System (PAVE PAWS)
990	Space Surveillance Center
991	Air Force Space Operations Center
992	Space Command Center
993	Global Positioning System
994	Deep Space Tracking System
996	Defense Support Program/Satellite Control Network

Reporting Identifiers.

Identifier	Title
9A000	Airman Awaiting Retraining (Disqualified for Reasons beyond Control)
9A100	Airman Awaiting Retraining (Disqualified for Reasons within Control)
9A200	Airman Awaiting Discharge, Separation, or Retirement
9C000	Chief Master Sergeant of the Air Force
9E000	Senior Enlisted Advisor
9G000	Airman Aide
9J000	Prisoner
9L000	Interpreter/Translator
9P000	Patient

9S000	Systems Repair Technician
9S100	Scientific Measurements Technician
9S200	Applied Sciences Technician
9T000	Basic Airman
9T100	Officer Trainee
9T200	Precadet Assignee
9U000	Airman Ineligible for Local Utilization
9U100	Unallotted Airman Authorization

Air Force Specialty Code Prefixes.

Prefix	Title
A	Development Craftsman
B	B-2 Personnel
C	Flying Crew Chief
G	Automated Systems Programming Craftsman
J	Parachutist
K	Aircrew Instructor
Q	Aircrew Standardization/Flight Examiner
T	Technical Training
V	Automated Functional Applications Analyst/Monitor
X	Aircrew

RETRAINING OPPORTUNITIES

Airmen may retrain from one career field to another on either a voluntary or selective basis. The voluntary method is preferred because Air Force requirements and individual career goals are satisfied at the same time. The selective method is used primarily when there is a shortage of personnel in a specific career field and a surplus in another; personnel are then "selected" to retrain. Shortages frequently occur when a new weapons system becomes operational, when airmen become disqualified or are not able to work in their present career field, and during the normal process of separations, discharges, and retirements.

In most cases, first-term airmen are not eligible to retrain until they have completed a specified period of their first enlistment. Four-year enlistees must complete a minimum of thirty-six months before applying for retraining. Six-year enlistees must complete a minimum of sixty months. Once they are eligible, most airmen who wish to retrain in another career field apply under the

CAREERS (Career Airman Reenlistment Reservation System) program. Second-term and career airmen can also ask to retrain into another field. Here, too, approval depends largely on the manning levels in the present and prospective fields. Periodically, airmen from overmanned skills are sought by the Air Force Personnel Center (AFPC) to retrain voluntarily into skills with shortages. If voluntary goals are not met, then selective retraining is initiated.

The best way to find out about current retraining opportunities is to see your unit career advisor or the base career advisor. You can also stop by the Military Personnel Flight (MPF) and visit the customer service branch or the classification and training unit. They regularly receive from AFPC the USAF Retraining Advisory, an up-to-date list of all AFSCs showing retraining requirements and overage conditions.

SOURCES OF ADDITIONAL INFORMATION

Air Force Instruction 36-2108, *Airman Classification.*

Air Force Instruction 36-2626, *Airman Retraining Program.*

Consult your unit career advisor or the base career advisor. When discussing career fields you are interested in, be sure to read current duty descriptions. Career fields are redesignated and renumbered from time to time based on new weapons systems and the needs of the Air Force.

The list of current Air Force Specialty Codes is always changing. New systems are coming on line, old systems are being retired, and new organizational structures are evolving. For the current list of AFSCs, consult the Classification and Training section at your Military Personnel Flight (MPF).

11

Training and Education

The road to success is always under construction.
—TSgt Donald N. Craig,
Chief, Unit Training Branch

Whether you pursue a career in the U.S. Air Force or venture out into the civilian community, training and education will play a major rule in determining your future. It has often been said that who we are today is a result of our preparation in the past. Within the USAF, there are many avenues to training, education, and experience—some on-duty, some off-duty. Some airmen decide not to take full advantage of these programs because they will be leaving the USAF to pursue their education. This may be wise if your goals are highly specialized. But in most cases, it's more advantageous and economical to continue your education while in the Air Force.

ENLISTED EDUCATION AND TRAINING

Enlisted Education and Training (E&T) prepares airmen to perform their jobs within the Air Force and an assigned Air Force specialty (AFS). Its goals are to develop military professional skills through professional military education (PME) and to qualify and upgrade airmen in each skill level of an AFS. These goals are achieved by pursuing a mix of formal (classroom) and informal (on-the-job) training.

Formal Training Program. Generally, formal training is provided in one of three ways:

1. Air Education and Training Command (AETC) operated *Technical Training Centers (TTCs)* to teach airmen and noncommissioned officers basic skills needed in their specialties. Some courses are short, from four to six weeks; others are six or eight months. Attendance is in-residence, usually after basic training or when retraining is approved. At graduation, personnel are usually awarded a 3 skill level designation and then reassigned to a permanent duty station.

2. Specialized formal training is also provided to experienced personnel, who usually have a 5 skill level or higher. There are formal in-resident Air

Education and Training Command (AETC) courses, special factory training by a contractor (for example, General Dynamics or McDonnel Douglas), or special training by AETC mobile training teams at the operating unit's location. Information about these programs is outlined in Air Force Catalog 36-2223, *USAF Formal Schools Catalog.*

3. *Field Training Detachment (FTD) courses* are on-site training conducted at base level. These courses use a combination of classroom lectures and hands-on work with equipment. They are primarily for aircraft maintenance personnel and are principally used when there is a change of weapons systems on the base.

On-the-Job Training Programs. On-the-job training, most frequently referred to by the familiar acronym OJT, is the most economical way to train personnel. The first phase of the Air Force dual-channel OJT is career knowledge training, which uses guided study of career development courses (CDCs). CDCs are printed texts for each Air Force specialty, written by noncommissioned officers who have broad experience within the specialty. Other reference materials may also be used for specific subjects. In the second phase, job qualification training, trainees, working under the supervision of a trainer, gain hands-on experience in a work environment.

Air Force Form 623, "On-the-Job Training Record," is used to determine an individual's qualifications, identify training needs, and document progress. One is maintained for each airman in grades airman basic through technical sergeant, and for master sergeant through chief master sergeant if they are in a retraining status. In appearance, it looks like a file folder, with fasteners to hold status updates. One of the most important documents in the OJT training record is an Air Force publication known as the Specialty Training Standard (STS). Each specialty has one; it outlines what a trainee is expected to be able to do for that particular job. Once inserted in the training record, the STS is called a job qualification standard (JQS) and is used to record training completed for each task.

To ensure the effectiveness of OJT programs, specific responsibilities have been established. Commanders have the overall responsibility for effective programs. To assist them, the Military Personnel Flight (MPF) has an OJT manager who plans, organizes, and directs the overall program for the base. The base OJT manager works closely with OJT managers from each unit (usually at the squadron level). In turn, unit OJT managers advise their immediate commanders and work closely with supervisors, trainers, and trainees. Supervisors select qualified trainers who plan, conduct, and evaluate training. Each trainee is responsible for learning the required skills and attaining appropriate proficiency levels.

The overall success of an OJT program is usually traceable to a concerted team effort. Each individual charged with a responsibility is actively involved and committed. Collectively, all recognize that quality training programs will have a positive effect on quality of work and ultimately on their unit's mission.

ENLISTED EDUCATION AND TRAINING PATH

EDUCATION AND TNG REQUIREMENTS		AVG SEW-ON TIME

- BASIC MILITARY TRAINING SCHOOL

 6 MONTHS

- APPRENTICE TECH SCHOOL = 3 SKILL LEVEL

 16 MONTHS

- UPGRADE TO JOURNEYMAN = 5 SKILL LEVEL

 36 MONTHS

  - 6 MONTHS DUTY POSITION/APPRENTICE IS REQUIRED
    BEFORE ENTERING JOURNEYMAN TRAINING
  - MINIMUM 12 MONTHS ON-THE-JOB TRAINING (OJT)
  - COMPLETE APPROPRIATE CDC IF/WHEN AVAILABLE
  - SRA SEW-ON
  - (INTERIM: ALL OF ABOVE)

- AIRMAN LEADERSHIP SCHOOL (ALS)

   7.5 YEARS AVERAGE

  - MUST BE A SRA WITH 48 MONTHS TIME IN SERVICE,
    OR BE A SSGT SELECTEE
  - RESIDENT GRADUATION IS A PREREQUISITE FOR
    SSGT SEW-ON

- UPGRADE TO CRAFTSMAN = 7 SKILL LEVEL

   12.5 YEARS AVERAGE

  - MINIMUM RANK OF SSGT
  - 18 MONTHS OJT
  - FORMAL ADVANCED SKILL TRAINING
    (TECHNICAL SCHOOL)
  - (INTERIM: UNTIL 7 LEVEL SCHOOLS ARE AVAILABLE,
    MINIMUM RANK OF SSGT WITH 18 MONTHS OJT)
  - MUST BE 7 LEVEL TO SEW ON TSGT

- NONCOMMISSIONED OFFICER ACADEMY (NCOA)

   16 YEARS AVERAGE

  - MUST BE A TSGT OR TSGT SELECTEE*
  - RESIDENT GRADUATION IS A PREREQUISITE FOR
    MSGT SEW ON

- USAF SENIOR NCO ACADEMY (SNCOA)

   19.2 YEARS AVERAGE

  - MUST BE A SMSGT OR SMSGT SELECTEE*
  - RESIDENT GRADUATION IS A PREREQUISITE FOR
    CMSGT SEW ON

- UPGRADE TO SUPERINTENDENT = 9 SKILL LEVEL

   21.5 YEARS AVERAGE

  - MINIMUM RANK OF SMSGT
  - MUST BE A RESIDENT SNCOA GRADUATE*
  - (INTERIM: AT SMSGT SEW-ON)

 * ACTIVE DUTY ONLY

PROFESSIONAL MILITARY EDUCATION (PME)

Professional Military Education (PME) is provided to members of the enlisted force based on grade, time-in-service, and supervisory duties. Enlisted PME attempts to broaden enlisted members' perspectives beyond the skills of their Air Force Specialties in order to increase their knowledge of military studies, communication skills, quality force issues, leadership, and supervisory techniques. The in-resident enlisted PME program consists of three courses, each designed for personnel with a particular grade and experience level.

The USAF Airman Leadership School (ALS) prepares senior airmen (SrA) to assume supervisory duties. The four-week course offers instruction and practice in leadership and followership, written and oral communication skills, and military citizenship in the Air Force. Students learn to appreciate their role as military supervisors and how they contribute to the overall goals and mission of the Air Force. The major commands establish selection procedures to ensure that SrA who have the growth potential and ability to become effective leaders and supervisors attend this course. This entry-level enlisted PME program is available to SrA after reaching forty-eight months of total active federal military service (TAFMS) or after being selected for promotion to staff sergeant (SSgt). Graduates of the ALS are authorized to wear the NCO PME Ribbon.

The Noncommissioned Officers Academy (NCOA) is a six-week course to further broaden the leadership and management skills of staff sergeants and technical sergeants. As in ALS, the major commands establish selection procedures. Graduates earn the right to wear the NCO PME Ribbon. They who have graduated from ALS courses are authorized to add a bronze oak leaf cluster to the basic ribbon. NCOA completion is required before assuming the grade of master sergeant (MSgt).

The Senior Noncommissioned Officers Academy (SNCOA) is the highest level of PME available to NCOs. This seven-week course is conducted by Air University at the Gunter Annex of Maxwell AFB, Alabama. This course provides the education necessary for senior NCOs to become more effective leaders and managers during peacetime, as well as times of crisis or conflict. The course includes communicative skills, international relations, national objectives, employment of military force in achieving Air Force objectives, the Air Force role in force application, management, and the effective use of human resources. The course also looks at the individual and the work environment, management concepts and theories, analytical decision making, managerial styles, methods of improving workers' performance, and the application of Quality Air Force (QAF) principles. Each year the Air Force Personnel Center (AFPC) identifies master sergeants and senior master sergeant selectees to attend the course. Chief master sergeants (CMSgt) and CMSgt selectees may also volunteer to attend. Graduates earn the right to wear the NCO PME Ribbon and clusters, when appropriate. SNCOA completion is required before assuming the grade of chief master sergeant.

Although some PME requirements may be fulfilled by correspondence, in-residence attendance is more desirable. There are fewer distractions and the learning experience is much more complete because of the formal presentations, feedback, and interaction with other attendees. There is a lot of competition for these courses; the key to being selected is to know and meet the selection criteria in Air Force Instruction 36-2301, *Professional Military Education.* It is also wise to let the decision makers—your supervisors, first sergeant, senior enlisted advisor, and commander—know that you really want to attend in-residence.

You can obtain more information about enrolling in a PME correspondence course by contacting the base education office. Enrolling early in your career will broaden your professional knowledge. It is also a positive step that shows initiative. Many successful supervisors view such enrollment as an indication that a person has taken a deeper level of interest in his or her USAF career.

OFF-DUTY EDUCATION PROGRAMS

Off-duty education services are provided worldwide to all personnel, and usually to dependents also. The focal point on each base is the base education center. These centers also support smaller geographically separated units within their areas of responsibility. The staff usually includes an education services officer, education specialists, guidance counselors, and in some cases, registrars representing colleges and universities. The primary programs include the following:

• *Extension Course Institute (ECI)* voluntary nonresident study courses are offered in three major categories—Career Development Courses (CDCs), Professional Military Education (PME), and specialized courses. Airmen often order CDCs through the education center so that they can get current materials to study for promotion or to pursue an interest in another Air Force Specialty.

• *The Community College of the Air Force (CCAF)* program provides a way for enlisted members to earn an associate in applied science degree in one of more than seventy fields. Each field is directly related to Air Force Specialties in five career areas: aircraft and missile maintenance, electronics and telecommunications, management and logistics, medical, and public and support services. CCAF is accredited by the Commission on Colleges of the Southern Association of Colleges and Schools. Course credits may be gained through an evaluation of military experience, by completing military courses (technical training schools, PME, OJT), or by completing civilian education programs. This program is a big plus for many airmen because they find that half of their degree requirements can be satisfied by military training they have already completed.

• *Off-duty classes* are offered on base and in surrounding communities by over four hundred accredited colleges and universities. Courses cover a very wide spectrum, leading to a range of degrees: technical certificates, associate degrees (two years), bachelor of arts or science (four years), and graduate degrees including master's and doctorate programs. In overseas areas, U.S. institutions provide services under contract. Participation in host-nation institutions is also possible. At some locations, courses are provided throughout the day to accommodate personnel on different work shifts.

• *College credit by examination* is available through two programs: the College-Level Examination Program (CLEP), and the Defense Activity for Non-Traditional Education Support (DANTES). Up to sixty hours of college credit may be obtained through these tests, and there is no charge for military personnel.

• *Admissions examinations* for undergraduates can sometimes be scheduled for the American College Testing (ACT) Assessment Program and the Scholastic Aptitude Test (SAT). Graduate admissions tests include the Graduate Record Examinations (GRE), the Graduate Management Admissions Test (GMAT), and the Law School Admissions Test (LSAT).

• *The Bootstrap Program* allows airmen who are within four months to one year of completing a college degree to finish the degree at a college or university. When these requests are approved, the airman is placed in a permissive temporary duty (TDY) status. When the degree work is completed, the airman incurs an active-duty service commitment equal to three times the length of the TDY.

• *Education centers* also serve as focal points for information on airman commissioning programs. These are described in chapter 17, "Commissioning Opportunities."

Funding Off-Duty Education. While most of the services provided by the education office are furnished at no expense to the military member, there are instances where fees and charges apply, primarily to cover tuition expenses for courses offered by colleges and universities. Several programs provide funding assistance for those who qualify.

The Air Force Tuition Assistance (TA) Program. The Air Force Tuition Assistance Program represents the Air Force's commitment to the professional and personal development of its members. Under it, the Air Force will pay 75 percent of the tuition fee for all active-duty military personnel, except for those entitled to benefits under the old GI Bill. This is a very popular program. The cost of books and supplies and other fees are not included, however. To receive tuition assistance, obtain an Air Force Form 1227, "Authority for Tuition Assistance—Education Services Program," from the education office. After you fill it out, you and your supervisor must sign the form; return it to the education office before the end of the course registration period.

Veterans Assistance. There are three different veterans education assistance programs. The program you qualify for depends on the date that you entered active military service.

The *Vietnam-Era GI Bill,* also referred to as "the old GI Bill," applies to those who came on active duty prior to 1 January 1977. Under this program, the full cost of the tuition fee could be paid. Entitlement to these benefits expired on 31 December 1989. However, one of the provisions of the Montgomery GI Bill (also referred to as "the new GI Bill") is a conversion feature that applies only to Vietnam-Era GI Bill eligibles who were on active duty on 19 October 1984 and had served for three consecutive years starting on 1 July 1985. This conversion process, in most cases, provides a greater monthly benefit over a reduced period of time, especially for those who never used any of their old GI Bill entitlements. Under some circumstances, such as a disability or prisoner of war or missing in action (POW/MIA) status, the time limits for using entitlements may be extended.

The *Veteran Educational Assistance Program (VEAP)* was established in 1977 as a replacement for the Vietnam-Era GI Bill. Participation under this program was optional For every dollar invested by a military member, the government contributed $2. This program was canceled on 1 April 1987. The cancellation stops enrollment of new personnel but does not affect entitlements to members who had previously participated.

The *Montgomery GI Bill (MGIB)* affects those who entered active duty after 30 June 1985. Enrollment is voluntary. This program, like VEAP, is a pay reduction program. When a servicemember's pay is reduced by $100 for twelve consecutive months, the Department of Veterans Affairs (VA) adds $13,375 for a total of $14,575. You can use these benefits while you are in the service after two years of continuous active-duty service. MGIB benefits expire ten years after separation or retirement.

Scholarships, student loans, and *partial grants* are often available from federal, state, and private sources, based on individual circumstances including financial need, academic success, and veteran's survivor and dependent status. For specific information about the options in your area, contact your base education center.

SUCCEEDING IN ADULT EDUCATION
Most airmen are successful in adult education programs; they attain B grades or higher. There aren't many failures. Unlike high school, attendance isn't mandatory; those who don't want to participate don't have to. Those who do attend learn more efficiently because they have stronger practical reasons for enrolling. Their motivation is self-initiated. They're setting their own goals and preparing for the future. Some attend to become more fully qualified in their present job. Some have decided to broaden into another career. Others enjoy the educational environment and the opportunity to gain knowledge and mix with people who share similar interests. Whatever the reason, they all have one thing in common: They're there because they want to be.

They also bring practical experience to the classroom. Most have had a break from the educational process, and they know that life is much more than textbooks. This provides a frame of reference for the information they are being taught. They know what's important and how they intend to use it.

Right now you're at the crossroads of the past, the present, and the future. Past is past, but the future depends on the present. If you're even vaguely interested in pursuing your education, the best thing to do is to go to the education center. Take a look at what they have to offer. Talk to a counselor, registrar, or education specialist. Enroll in a course that will be interesting but not overwhelming. After you've made a start, move at your own speed in a direction of your choice. Most airmen agree that the first step is the hardest one. After that, it's all downhill. Momentum seems to build with interest in the subject matter, interaction with other students, and the anticipation of completing degree requirements.

One word of caution: Always remember that your value to the Air Force is based primarily on how well you perform in your *present* job. You do want to broaden your horizons, but you don't want to ignore your regular duty performance.

SOURCES OF ADDITIONAL INFORMATION

Air Force Catalog 36-2223, *USAF Formal Schools.*

Air Force Instruction 36-2201, *Developing, Managing, and Conducting Training.*

Air Force Instruction 36-2301, *Professional Military Education.*

Air Force Instruction 36-2306, *The Education Services Program.*

Air Force Pamphlet 36-2241, Volume 1, *Promotion Fitness Examination Study Guide.*

Air Force Policy Directive 36-22, *Military Training.*

12

Performance Reports

THE ENLISTED EVALUATION SYSTEM (EES)

The Enlisted Evaluation System used by the U.S. Air Force today was first implemented on 1 May 1989. Today's EES is the result of enlisted and officer concerns about the prior Airman Performance Report (APR), which the Air Force had used for over twenty years to evaluate enlisted duty performance.

There are four terms used in this chapter that you should be familiar with: *ratee, rater, indorser,* and *evaluators.* A *ratee* is the servicemember who is being rated on an enlisted performance report or a performance feedback worksheet. A *rater* is a person who writes enlisted performance reports or performance feedback worksheets. The rater is usually the ratee's immediate supervisor (E-4 and above). An *indorser* is usually the rater's rater or another person in the ratee's chain of command. Raters and indorsers are referred to as *evaluators.*

The Airman Performance Report (APR) Study Group. The present EES resulted from an APR Study Group chartered by the Air Force Chief of Staff in 1987. The Study Group was made up of selected representatives of all aerospace functional areas. Its task was to identify and document the problems with the then-current APR, identify solutions, and make recommendations for improvement. The study effort included surveys of nearly seven thousand enlisted, senior enlisted, and officer personnel.

The APR Study documented a number of major problem areas, including: a need for more feedback to airmen on job expectations and performance; a difficulty in identifying top performing enlisted personnel because of inflation of numerical ratings, indorsement levels, and narrative comments; and assorted disconnects with the goals of the Weighted Airman Promotion System (WAPS) which guided promotions to E-6, E-7, and E-8. The Study Group's principal recommendations formed the basis of the revised EES implemented by the Chief of Staff in 1989.

Major Changes under the Revised Enlisted Evaluation System (EES). The current EES includes the following features:
• Formal feedback sessions are mandatory for technical sergeants and below and highly encouraged for master sergeants and above.

• Enlisted Performance Reports (EPRs) are no longer required for most airmen basic, airmen, and airmen first class with less than twenty months' total active federal military service (TAFMS).

• EPR indorsements for technical sergeants and below are capped at the rater's rater.

• The highest final voluntary indorsement on EPSs for master sergeants through chief master sergeants is the senior rater (usually the wing commander or equivalent).

• The first field-grade officer in the rating chain may close out the ERP.

• A new regulation was issued to outline the changes in policy and to prescribe new forms with revised rating scales.

Benefits for Air Force Members. The current EES offers three benefits for Air Force members:

1. The performance feedback program increases communication at all levels. Ratees know what their supervisors expect, what their own strengths and weaknesses are, and how to improve.

2. The involvement of senior NCOs and others who are in the immediate supervisory chain is increased. Raters are closer to their ratees and will have direct knowledge of duty performance.

3. The job of producing evaluation reports is made easier with fewer and simpler forms, fewer evaluators, and less need to send reports with justification to higher headquarters. This, in turn, gives supervisors more time to work on their unit's mission.

THE PERFORMANCE FEEDBACK PROGRAM

Performance feedback is a formal written communication between the ratee and the rater about the ratee's responsibilities and duty performance. It consists of the rater filling out a simple, handwritten form followed by a face-to-face discussion between the rater and the ratee. The original copy of the form is given to the ratee. Raters may keep copies of the form for their own records, for future feedback sessions, and for preparation of performance reports.

The rater must provide performance feedback. He or she is usually responsible for the total job effort and is in the best position to observe the ratee's duty performance on a day-to-day basis. Raters normally have the knowledge and experience necessary to discuss the Air Force's expectations regarding general military factors and the opportunities for maintaining proficiency in one's Air Force Specialty (AFS).

Performance feedback is mandatory for the grades of technical sergeant (TSgt) and below. It is optional, but strongly encouraged, for the grades of master sergeant (MSgt) through chief master sergeant (CMSgt).

Scheduling Performance Feedback Sessions. Performance feedback sessions are scheduled at periodic intervals.

WHEN TO PREPARE PFWs

R U L E	A	B	C
	If the ratee is	and	then a feedback session is required and must be conducted.
1	a TSgt or below	has not had an initial feedback session with the current rater	within 60 days of the date supervision began.
2	an AB, Amn, or AIC (with less than 20 months' TAFMS)	has had an initial feedback session with the current rater	every 180 days or until the rater writes an EPR.
3	an AB, Amn, or A1C (with 20 or more months' TAFMS) or a SrA through TSgt	has had an initial feedback session with the current rater	midway between the time supervision began and the planned EPR closeout date (notes 1 and 2).
4	a TSgt or below	has had an EPR written without a change of rater	within 60 days after completing the EPR (note 3).
5	an AB through CMSgt	requests a feedback session	within 30 days of the request if at least 60 days have passed since the last feedback session.
6	an AB through CMSgt	the rater determines there is a need for a feedback session	as the rater determines.

NOTES:
1. If the ratee is due an annual EPR and the period of supervision is less than 150 days, the rater conducts the feedback session not later than 45 days before the projected EPR closeout date.
2. If the ratee is getting a change of rating official (CRO) EPR, the rater tries to hold a feedback session even within 45 days of the EPR closeout date. ·
3. Do not conduct a feedback session if the ratee has had a feedback session within 60 days.

• Initial feedback sessions should be held within 60 days after a ratee is assigned a rating official. The new rater should use this session with the ratee to clearly define his or her performance expectations for the upcoming period.
• Follow-up feedback sessions are due approximately 180 days after the initial feedback session. At this time, the rater should discuss performance during the past period of supervision and provide direction and expectations for the future. Follow-up sessions are also provided within 30 days after the completion of an EPR, during which the rater should discuss the performance recorded on the EPR and provide direction and expectations for the new rating period.
• Midcourse feedback sessions for airmen who receive EPRs should be held midway between the date supervision began and the projected EPR closeout date. Such a session will focus on how well the ratee is performing and meeting the expectations and direction established in the initial feedback session. The purpose is to provide the ratee a performance progress report and the opportunity to improve that performance, if necessary, before the EPR is written.

These sessions are scheduled based on the following criteria, as noted in Air Force Instruction 36-2403, *The Enlisted Evaluation System.*

Performance Feedback Worksheets (PFW). Two formats are used to record performance feedback:
•   AF Form 931, "Airman Performance Feedback Worksheet," is used when the ratee is in the grade of airman basic through senior airman.
•   AF Form 932, "NCO Performance Feedback Worksheet," is used when the ratee is in the grade of sergeant through chief master sergeant.

The accompanying illustrations are copies of the forms used for performance feedback. Section III differs between the forms because personnel are evaluated in different areas as they assume positions of increased grade and responsibility.

Section I is for the ratee's name, grade, and unit of assignment.

Section II is for noting the ratee's primary duties. In most cases, the ratee is responsible for more duties than can be listed in this section; the rater should list those that are most important.

Section III lists the behavior and performance factors required of the ratee. Each subheading on the form lists areas that the rater must evaluate and score by placing an X at the point on the scale that accurately identifies the ratee's behavior. Marks to the far left mean that the ratee needs to work harder in those areas, while marks to the far right mean the ratee is performing well in those areas and needs to either maintain the current level of performance or improve slightly.

Section IV is a space for the rater's handwritten comments. It begins on the front of the form and is continued on the reverse. The rater should comment on the duties listed in Section II, as well as on the servicemember's other significant duties and responsibilities that may not be listed. Supervisors should provide factual, helpful performance and behavior feedback so that ratees will know where improvement is necessary.

The PFW is not an official record of performance; it is a private communication between the rater and the ratee. In preparing the PFW, the rater prepares and signs it in his or her own handwriting. Typing the form using word-processing equipment is prohibited.

The PFW is designed to assist the ratee in improving his or her performance. As such, the ratee may use the form as he or she chooses. The rater who prepares the PFW may keep a copy of the worksheet for personal use to assist in preparing the next EPR, if applicable, and subsequent feedback sessions. However, the PFW may not be shown to any other individual or used in any personnel actions unless the ratee first introduces it or unless the ratee alleges that the rater did not hold a required feedback session.

Raters should conduct feedback sessions face-to-face. Telephone sessions are conducted only in unusual circumstances, such as when there is a geographical separation and a trip for a face-to-face session is not practical.

Since the rater may not introduce the PFW in any proceedings unless the ratee introduces it first, a feedback session that includes discussion of

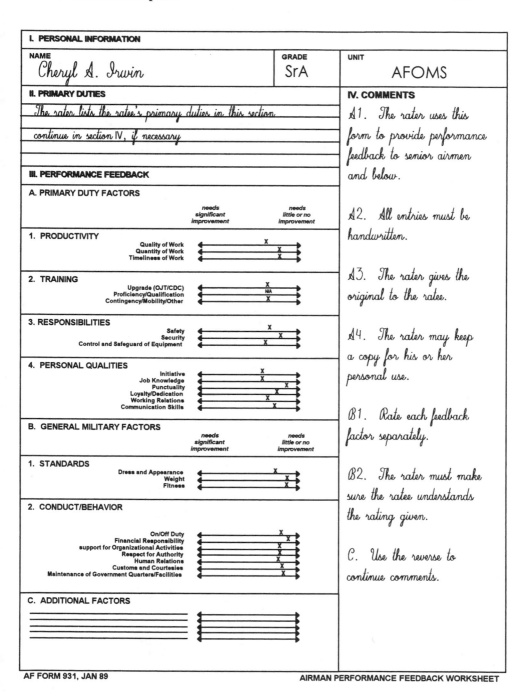

I. PERSONAL INFORMATION

NAME	GRADE	UNIT
Cheryl A. Irwin	SrA	AFOMS

II. PRIMARY DUTIES

The rater lists the ratee's primary duties in this section

continue in section IV, if necessary

III. PERFORMANCE FEEDBACK

A. PRIMARY DUTY FACTORS

	needs significant improvement	needs little or no improvement

1. PRODUCTIVITY
- Quality of Work — X
- Quantity of Work — X
- Timeliness of Work — X

2. TRAINING
- Upgrade (OJT/CDC) — X
- Proficiency/Qualification — N/A
- Contingency/Mobility/Other — X

3. RESPONSIBILITIES
- Safety — X
- Security — X
- Control and Safeguard of Equipment — X

4. PERSONAL QUALITIES
- Initiative — X
- Job Knowledge — X
- Punctuality — X
- Loyalty/Dedication — X
- Working Relations — X
- Communication Skills — X

B. GENERAL MILITARY FACTORS

	needs significant improvement	needs little or no improvement

1. STANDARDS
- Dress and Appearance — X
- Weight — X
- Fitness — X

2. CONDUCT/BEHAVIOR
- On/Off Duty — X
- Financial Responsibility — X
- support for Organizational Activities — X
- Respect for Authority — X
- Human Relations — X
- Customs and Courtesies — X
- Maintenance of Government Quarters/Facilities — X

C. ADDITIONAL FACTORS

IV. COMMENTS

A1. The rater uses this form to provide performance feedback to senior airmen and below.

A2. All entries must be handwritten.

A3. The rater gives the original to the ratee.

A4. The rater may keep a copy for his or her personal use.

B1. Rate each feedback factor separately.

B2. The rater must make sure the ratee understands the rating given.

C. Use the reverse to continue comments.

AF FORM 931, JAN 89   AIRMAN PERFORMANCE FEEDBACK WORKSHEET

AF Form 931, Airman Performance Feedback Worksheet (PFW) (Front).

I. PERSONAL INFORMATION		
NAME *Steven W. Bennett*	**GRADE** SSgt	**UNIT** AFOMS

II. PRIMARY DUTIES	IV. COMMENTS
The rater lists the ratee's primary duties in this section.	*A. The rater uses this form to provide performance feedback to NCOs. All entries must be handwritten.*
continue in section IV, if necessary	

III. PERFORMANCE FEEDBACK	needs significant Improvement	needs little or no Improvement

A. JOB PERFORMANCE

	needs significant improvement	needs little or no improvement
Quality of Work		X
Quantity of Work		X
Timeliness of Work		X
Practices/Enforces Safety		X
Practices/Enforces Security		X
Controls and Safeguards Equipment		X
Problem Solving		X
Self-Sufficiency		X

B. The original is given to the ratee at the end of the feedback session. The rater may keep a copy for his or her personal use, but cannot show the completed form to anyone except the ratee.

B. CONDUCT/BEHAVIOR

	needs significant improvement	needs little or no improvement
On/Off Duty		X
Financial Responsibility		X
Support for Organizational Activities		X
Respect for Authority		X
Human Relations		X
Customs and Courtesies		X
Maintenance of Government Quarters/Facilities		X

C. TRAINING

	needs significant improvement	needs little or no improvement
PME		N/A
Upgrade (OJT/CDC)		N/A
Proficiency/Qualification		X
Contingency/Mobility/Other		X

C. Each performance feedback factor should be rated separately.

D. SUPERVISORY/MANAGEMENT SKILLS

	needs significant improvement	needs little or no improvement
Leads/Motivates Subordinates		X
Sets and Enforces Work Standards		X
Maintains Discipline		X
Evaluates Subordinates Fairly and Consistently		X
Plans, Directs, and Organizes Work		X
Coordination/Work Relations		X

E. COMMUNICATION SKILLS

	needs significant improvement	needs little or no improvement
Listening		X
Writing		X
Speaking		X

D. Continue comments on reverse

F. PROFESSIONAL QUALITIES

	needs significant improvement	needs little or no improvement
Exhibits Loyalty, Discipline, Dedication, Honesty, and Integrity		X
Adheres to and Enforces Air Force Standards		X
Accepts Personal Responsibility		X

E. Rater's signature required on reverse. Also, date the form as of the date of the feedback session

G. ADDITIONAL FACTORS

AF FORM 932, JAN 89   NCO PERFORMANCE FEEDBACK WORKSHEET

AF Form 932, NCO Performance Feedback Worksheet (PFW) (Front).

STRENGTHS, SUGGESTED GOALS, AND ADDITIONAL COMMENTS

Use the reverse of the AF Form 931, Airman Performance Feedback Worksheet and the AF Form 932, NCO Performance Feedback Worksheet to continue entries from the frontside.

The PFW is not the official record of performance. It is private between the rater and ratee.

RATER SIGNATURE	DATE
Rita J. James	1 Jul 95

AF FORM 932, JAN 89 (Reverse)

Air Force Form 931 and 932 (Reverse).

performance, behavior, or conduct that may result in further administrative or judicial action should be recorded on other appropriate forms (e.g., AF Form 174, "Record of Individual Counseling").

Performance Feedback Sessions. To prepare for a feedback session, the rater needs to do the following:

1. *Select a time and place.* Sessions should be scheduled in advance so that the rater and the ratee have sufficient preparation time. The place selected should provide a relaxed atmosphere so that both parties can talk comfortably. It should be properly lit, ventilated, and relatively free from distractions and interruptions. The amount of time allowed for a session may vary depending on the needs of the rater and the ratee and the depth of topics to be discussed. As a general rule, sessions will usually be thirty to sixty minutes in duration.

2. *Set an agenda.* This includes a basic outline of topics and the sequence in which they will be discussed.

3. *Plan to discuss strengths and accomplishments* as well as areas that need improvement.

4. *Anticipate pitfalls and plan to avoid them.* When providing feedback, the role of the rater should be that of a coach or a helper, not one of a critic or a superior who has no faults. Some of the pitfalls that the rater should be aware of and try to avoid are as follows:

• A reluctance to provide or receive feedback.
• Inadequate planning.
• Personal bias or stereotyping.
• Focusing on the person instead of the behavior.
• Drawing or jumping to conclusions based on limited observations or poor recall.
• Rating performance as outstanding when it is not.
• Telling an individual that he or she is the "best" when the individual is not.
• Giving favorable ratings to an individual who is well liked or unfavorable ratings to an individual who is not.
• Loss of emotional control.

5. *Prepare the feedback form,* except for the rater's signature and the date, prior to the session.

During the feedback session, the rater should do the following:

1. *Open in a friendly, relaxed manner.* Be sincere and brief and explain the purpose of the session. The approach should be based on accepted standards and the needs of the Air Force. Seek ideas and opinions from the ratee.

2. *Be a good listener.* Pay full attention to what is being said, and if necessary, rephrase your statements or ask direct questions to clarify areas that are ambiguous. It is also important to be attuned to nonverbal communication, such as eye contact, posture, head nods, and facial expressions.

3. *Consider referrals to agencies that can provide "specialized" assistance,*

if potential problems surface during the session that are beyond the scope of performance feedback. For example, assistance is available from chaplains (religious, marital, personal), medical personnel (physical, mental, CHAP), the Family Support Center, Family Services, the AF Aid Society, the legal office, EOT (equal opportunity and treatment) programs, and the American Red Cross.

4. *Keep the discussion positive and on track.* Give feedback in a manner that communicates acceptance of the ratee as a worthwhile person. Avoid loaded terms that may produce emotional reactions and heightened defenses.

5. *Summarize.* Before the session ends, the rater should take a few moments to review and summarize the key items discussed and to reinforce the goals for the next observation period. A good method of summarizing is to ask the ratee for comments on the discussion to make sure that he or she understands the results of the session. It is important to end on a positive, encouraging, and forward-looking note. One way to do so is to briefly discuss a road map of goals and priorities that the ratee can use for achieving future successes.

6. *In closing, sign and date the performance feedback worksheet and give the original copy to the ratee.*

Program Controls and Responsibilities. A variety of responsibilities are assigned at different levels to assure that the spirit and intent of the performance feedback program are met.

The Military Personnel Flight (MPF) provides PFW notices to raters and ratees. It also provides the unit with a list of airmen who do not receive EPRs but are due a scheduled feedback session.

Unit commanders administer the performance feedback program for their personnel. In doing so, they periodically canvass raters and ratees to ensure that feedback is being accomplished; review the signed PFW notices on airmen who did not receive EPRs; and consider disciplining and removing from supervisory positions raters who fail to conduct documented feedback sessions.

Each rater's rater is responsible for being familiar with the subordinate's duty performance; periodically querying subordinates to ensure that raters are accomplishing feedback sessions; conducting performance feedback sessions when a subordinate rater is not available because of unusual circumstances or when assuming the subordinate rater's responsibilities; and signing the PFW notice and returning it for the unit commander's review in cases where a ratee does not receive EPRs.

The rater prepares, schedules, and conducts feedback sessions; plans sessions to avoid conflicts with TDY, leave, change of raters, and so forth; provides realistic, uninflated feedback to help the ratee improve duty performance and behavior; conducts feedback to help the ratee improve duty performance and behavior; conducts feedback sessions within thirty days of a ratee's request (*Note:* Raters are not required to conduct more than one documented feedback session per sixty-day period; however, they may do so at their discretion); signs the PFW notice on airmen who do not receive EPRs, and returns it to the unit for review by the commander, who destroys the PFW notice after he or she determines that the feedback session has taken place.

The ratee notifies the rater and, if necessary, the rater's rater when a required feedback session does not take place; and may request additional feedback sessions.

ENLISTED PERFORMANCE REPORTS (EPR)

In the majority of cases, Enlisted Performance Reports are prepared for ratees who have twenty or more months of total active federal military service (TAFMS) and have not had a report for at least a year. HQ USAF or a commander can order an EPR in eleven other instances, primarily in cases where there is a change of rater, unsatisfactory performance or conduct, a discharge action, or interruptions in supervision caused by a change of duty status (e.g., extended temporary duty, missing in action, permanent change of station).

The Enlisted Performance Report is probably the single most important document in your personnel record. The EPR provides the Air Force with information on your duty performance and your potential for increased responsibility. When used with other information, it provides a basis for selective retention, promotions, assignments, and retraining.

Three standard forms are prescribed for recording performance:

•   AF Form 910, "Enlisted Performance Report (AB thru TSGT)" is used for technical sergeant, staff sergeant, sergeant, senior airman, airman first class, airman, and airman basic.

•   AF Form 911, "Senior Enlisted Performance Report (MSGT thru CMSGT)" is used for master sergeant, senior master sergeant, and chief master sergeant.

•   AF Form 77, "Supplemental Evaluation Sheet," is used as a letter of evaluation (LOE), continuation sheet for referral reports, commander's comments or an additional evaluator's indorsement, and Air Force advisor reviews. The same form is used for all grades.

See accompanying illustrations of the forms used. You will see that some sections in the Enlisted Performance Reports (Forms 910 and 911) differ; personnel are evaluated in different areas as they assume positions of increased grade and responsibility.

How a Performance Report Is Prepared. When a performance report is due, the Military Personnel Flight (MPF) sends a computer product (commonly referred to as an EPR notice or an EPR shell) to the member's unit of assignment (usually a squadron orderly room). The unit's EPR monitor establishes a suspense (a deadline) for a completed report to be turned in and then forwards the computer product to the rater. For technical sergeants and below, these notices are first routed through the unit's first sergeant. The rater is encouraged to review this notice with the ratee to ensure that all the information is accurate. The rater then completes the form.

I. RATEE IDENTIFICATION DATA *(Read AFR 39-62 carefully before completing any item)*

1. NAME *(Last, First, Middle Initial)*		2. SSN	3. GRADE	4. DAFSC
JAMES, AMBER J.		000-00-0000	TSGT	3A071

5. ORGANIZATION, COMMAND, AND LOCATION	6a. PAS CODE	6b. SRID
Air Force Occupational Measurement Squadron (AETC), Randolph AFB TX	RJOBR549	XOXO

7. PERIOD OF REPORT	8. NO. DAYS SUPERVISION	9. REASON FOR REPORT
From: 31 Jul 93 Thru: 14 May 94	289	Annual

II. JOB DESCRIPTION

1. DUTY TITLE

Air Force Manager, PFE Study Guide

2. KEY DUTIES, TASKS, AND RESPONSIBILITIES

Confine duties to space allocated in this section. Enter a clear description of the ratee's duties. The description should make clear the nature of the ratee's tasks, the degree of assignment selectivity involved, and the number of people supervised. Dollar value of projects managed and the level of responsibility should also be included. Avoid jargon and acronyms that obscure rather than clarify meaning. Include prior and additional duties during the reporting period if they influence the ratings and comments. Do not include classified information.

III. EVALUATION OF PERFORMANCE

1. HOW WELL DOES RATEE PERFORM ASSIGNED DUTIES? *(Consider quality, quantity, and timeliness of duties performed)*

☐ Inefficient. An unprofessional performer.	☐ Good performer. Performs routine duties satisfactorily.	☐ Excellent performer. Consistently produces high quality work.	☐ The exception. Absolutely superior in all areas.

2. HOW MUCH DOES RATEE KNOW ABOUT PRIMARY DUTIES? *(Consider whether ratee has technical expertise and is able to apply the knowledge)*

☐ Does not have the basic knowledge necessary to perform duties.	☐ Has adequate technical knowledge to satisfactorily perform duties.	☐ Extensive knowledge of all primary duties and related positions.	☐ Excels in knowledge of all related positions. Mastered all duties.

3. HOW WELL DOES RATEE COMPLY WITH STANDARDS? *(Consider dress and appearance, weight and fitness, customs, and courtesies)*

☐ Fails to meet minimum standards.	☐ Meets Air Force standards.	☐ Sets the example for others to follow.	☐ Exemplifies top military standards.

4. HOW IS RATEE'S CONDUCT ON/OFF DUTY? *(Consider financial responsibility, respect for authority, support for organizational activities, and maintenance of government facilities)*

☐ Unacceptable.	☐ Acceptable.	☐ Sets the example for others.	☐ Exemplifies the standard of conduct.

5. HOW WELL DOES RATEE SUPERVISE/LEAD? *(Consider how well member sets and enforces standards, displays initiative and self-confidence, provides guidance and feedback, and fosters teamwork)*

☐ Ineffective.	☐ Effective. Obtains satisfactory results.	☐ Highly effective.	☐ Exceptionally effective leader.

6. HOW WELL DOES RATEE COMPLY WITH INDIVIDUAL TRAINING REQUIREMENTS? *(Consider upgrade training, professional military education, proficiency/qualification, and contingency)*

☐ Does not comply with minimum training requirements.	☐ Complies with most training requirements.	☐ Complies with all training requirements.	☐ Consistently exceeds all training requirements.

7. HOW WELL DOES RATEE COMMUNICATE WITH OTHERS? *(Consider ratee's verbal and written skills)*

☐ Unable to express thoughts clearly. Lacks organization.	☐ Organizes and expresses thoughts satisfactorily.	☐ Consistently able to organize and express ideas clearly and concisely.	☐ Highly skilled writer and communicator.

AF FORM 910, JAN 93 *(EF 16FEB93)*   PREVIOUS EDITIONS ARE OBSOLETE.   ENLISTED PERFORMANCE REPORT (AB thru TSGT)

AF Form 910, Enlisted Performance Report

IV. PROMOTION RECOMMENDATION *(Compare this ratee with others of the same grade and AFS)*

RECOMMENDATION	NOT RECOMMENDED	NOT RECOMMENDED AT THIS TIME	CONSIDER	READY	IMMEDIATE PROMOTION
RATER'S RECOMMENDATION	1	2	3	4	5
INDORSER'S RECOMMENDATION	1	2	3	4	5

V. RATER'S COMMENTS

- Use comments sections to provide additional information about the ratee's performance
- Bullet statements and phrases must be used
- Rater comments are required. All evaluators must limit their comments to the space allocated unless the report contains referral ratings
- Comments must be compatible with ratings in Section III and IV
- Comments paragraph 4-9 prohibits will not be included
- If the rater is a single evaluator, enter "This Section Not Used" in sections VI and VII

I certify that performance feedback was accomplished consistent with the direction in AFR 39-62 *(if not accomplished, state the reason).*

NAME, GRADE, BRANCH OF SERVICE, ORGANIZATION COMMAND, & LOCATION	DUTY TITLE		DATE
MEGEAN L. BENNETT, CMSgt, USAF AF Occupational Measurement Squadron (AETC) Randolph AFB TX	Chief, Information Management Element		20 May 94
	SSN 000-00-0000	SIGNATURE *Megean L. Bennett*	

VI. INDORSER'S COMMENTS   CONCUR   NONCONCUR

- The indorser uses this section to support his or her rating decisions
- When the indorser disagrees (marks nonconcur) with the rater, he or she must provide one or more reasons for disagreeing. The indorser's comments should not repeat what the rater stated, but provide new information

NAME, GRADE, BRANCH OF SERVICE, ORGANIZATION COMMAND, & LOCATION	DUTY TITLE		DATE
HERBERT E. SOTO, Capt, USAF AF Occupational Measurement Squadron (AETC) Randolph AFB TX	Superintendent, Professional Development Flight		21 May 94
	SSN 000-00-0000	SIGNATURE	

INSTRUCTIONS

Reports written by a senior rater or the Chief Master Sergeant of the Air Force (CMSAF) will not be indorsed.

Reports written by colonels or civilians (GM-15 or higher) do not require an indorser; however, indorsement is permitted unless prohibited by the Instruction above.

When the rater's rater is not at least a MSgt or civilian (GS-07 or higher), the indorser is the next official in the rating chain serving in the grade of MSgt or higher, or a civilian in the grade of GS-07 or higher.

When the final evaluator (rater or indorser) is not an Air Force officer or a DAF civilian, an Air Force advisor review is required.

VII. COMMANDER'S REVIEW

	CONCUR		NONCONCUR *(Attach AF Form 77)*	SIGNATURE

AF FORM 910, JAN 93 *(EF)* *(REVERSE)*

AF Form 910, Enlisted Performance Report (Reverse).

I. RATEE IDENTIFICATION DATA *(Read AFR 39-62 carefully before completing any item)*

NAME *(Last, First, Middle Initial)*		2. SSN	3. GRADE	4. DAFSC
HERBERT, ERIC S.		000-00-0000	CMSGT	3A0X1

5. ORGANIZATION, COMMAND, AND LOCATION	6a. PAS CODE	6b. SRID
Air Force Occupational Measurement Squadron (AETC), Randolph AFB TX	RJOBR549	XOXO

7. PERIOD OF REPORT	8. NO. DAYS SUPERVISION	9. REASON FOR REPORT
From: 18 Apr 94 Thru: 18 Apr 95	365	Annual

II. JOB DESCRIPTION

1. DUTY TITLE

Superintendent, Occupational Analysis

2. KEY DUTIES, TASKS, AND RESPONSIBILITIES

Confine duties to space allocated in this section. Enter a clear description of the ratee's tasks, the degree of assignment should make clear the nature of the ratee's tasks, the degree of assignment selectivity involved, and the number of people supervised. Dollar value of projects managed and the level of responsibility should also be included. Avoid jargon and acronyms that obsure rather than clarify meaning. Include prior and additional duties during the reporting period if they influence the rating and comments. Do not included classified information.

III. EVALUATION OF PERFORMANCE

1. DUTY PERFORMANCE   *(Consider quality, quantity, and timeliness of duties performed)*

☐ Inefficient. An unprofessional performer.	☐ Good performer. Performs routine duties satisfactorily.	☐ Excellent performer. Consistently produces high quality work.	☐ The exception. Absolutely superior in all areas.

2. JOB KNOWLEDGE   *(Consider whether ratee has technical expertise and is able to apply the knowledge)*

☐ Lacking. Needs considerable improvement.	☐ Sufficient. Gets job accomplished.	☐ Extensive knowledge of all primary duties and related positions.	☐ Excels in knowledge of all related positions. Mastered all duties.

3. LEADERSHIP   *(Consider whether ratee motivates peers or subordinates, maintains discipline, sets and enforces standards, evaluates subordinates fairly and consistently, plans and organizes work, and fosters teamwork)*

☐ Ineffective.	☐ Gets satisfactory results.	☐ Highly effective leader.	☐ Exceptionally effective leader.

4. MANAGERIAL SKILLS   *(Consider how well member uses time and resources)*

☐ Ineffective.	☐ Manages resources in a satisfactory manner.	☐ Skillful and competent.	☐ Dynamic, capitalizes on all opportunities.

5. JUDGMENT   *(Consider how well ratee evaluates situations and reaches logical conclusions)*

☐ Poor.	☐ Sound.	☐ Emphasizes logic and decision making.	☐ Highly respected and skilled.

6. PROFESSIONAL QUALITIES   *(Consider ratee's dedication and preservation of traditional military values - integrity and loyalty)*

☐ Unprofessional, unreliable.	☐ Meets expectations.	☐ Sets an example for others to follow.	☐ Epitomizes the Air Force professional.

7. COMMUNICATION SKILLS   *(Consider ratee's ability to organize and express ideas)*

☐ Unable to communicate effectively.	☐ Organizes and expresses thoughts satisfactorily.	☐ Organizes and expresses ideas clearly and concisely.	☐ Highly skilled writer and communicator.

AF FORM 911, JAN 93 *(EF 16FEB93)*   PREVIOUS EDITIONS ARE OBSOLETE.   SENIOR ENLISTED PERFORMANCE REPORT
(MSGT thru CMSGT)

AF Form 911, Senior Enlisted Report.

IV. PROMOTION RECOMMENDATION *(Compare this ratee with others of the same grade and AFS. For CMSgts, this is a recommendation for increased responsibilities.)*

RECOMMENDATION	NOT RECOMMENDED	NOT RECOMMENDED AT THIS TIME	CONSIDER	READY	IMMEDIATE PROMOTION
RATER'S RECOMMENDATION	1	2	3	4	5
RATER'S RATER'S RECOMMENDATION	1	2	3	4	5

V. RATER'S COMMENTS

- Use comments sections to provided additional information about the ratee's performance
- Bullet statements and phrases must be used
- Rater comments are required. All evaluations must limit their comments to the space allotted unless the report contains referral ratings
- Comments must be compatible with ratings in sections III and IV
- Comments paragraph 4-9 prohibits will not be included
- If the rater is a single evaluator, enter "This Section Not Used" in sections VI and VII

NAME, GRADE, BRANCH OF SERVICE, ORGANIZATION COMMAND, & LOCATION	DUTY TITLE	DATE
MICHELLE L. MITCHELL, Capt, USAF AF Occupational Measurement Squadron (AETC) Randolph AFB TX	Commander, Professional Development Flight	23 Apr 95
	SSN 000-00-0000	SIGNATURE *Michelle L. Mitchell*

VI. RATER'S RATER'S COMMENTS   CONCUR   NONCONCUR

- The rater's rater's comments should not repeat what the rater stated, but should provide new information about the ratee's performance
- When an evaluator disagrees (marks the nonconcur block) with a previous evaluator, he or she must provide one or more reasons for disagreeing

NAME, GRADE, BRANCH OF SERVICE, ORGANIZATION COMMAND, & LOCATION	DUTY TITLE	DATE
NICK MALDONADO, Colonel, USAF AF Occupational Measurement Squadron (AETC) Randolph AFB TX	Commander	24 Apr 95
	SSN 000-00-0000	SIGNATURE *Nick Maldonado*

VII. INDORSER'S COMMENTS   CONCUR   NONCONCUR

- The indorser must be at least a major (Navy lieutenant commander) or civilian (at least a GS-12 or similar grade)
- The final evaluator (indorser completes section VIII)
- The indorser cannot be higher in the rating chain than the senior rater

NAME, GRADE, BRANCH OF SERVICE, ORGANIZATION, COMMAND & LOCATION	DUTY TITLE	DATE
CARRIE C. DYES, BGEN, USAF HQ Air Education and Training Command (AETC) Randolph AFB TX	Director of Technical Training	26 Apr 95
	SSN 000-00-0000	SIGNATURE *Carrie C. Dyes*

VIII. FINAL EVALUATOR'S POSITION		IX. TIME-IN-GRADE ELIGIBLE (N/A for CMSgt or CMSgt selectee)	X. COMMANDER'S REVIEW	
A	SENIOR RATER			
B	SENIOR RATER'S DEPUTY		CONCUR	NONCONCUR *(Attach AF Form 77)*
C	INTERMEDIATE LEVEL	YES	SIGNATURE	
D	LOWER LEVEL	NO		

AF FORM 911, JAN 93 *(EF) (REVERSE)*

AF Form 911, Senior Enlisted Report (Reverse).

Sections I–V

Section I: "Ratee Identification Data." All information for this section is provided on the computer product (the EPR notice or shell).

Section II: "Job Description." The duty title used should be the one noted on the EPR notice. Since the personnel data system has space limitations, the duty titles on some EPR notices may be abbreviated. These computer abbreviations may be used, but if the entries are not clear they should be spelled out. Under "Key Duties, Tasks, and Responsibilities," a clear description of the ratee's duties should be entered. The description should note the nature of the tasks the ratee performs, the degree of assignment selectivity involved, the scope and level of responsibility, dollar value of projects managed, number of people supervised, and so forth. Additional duties during the reporting period may also be included if they influence the ratings and comments. Jargon and acronyms that obscure rather than clarify the meaning should be avoided.

Section III: "Evaluation of Performance." In this section, the ratee's performance is assessed in seven categories. The rater completes this section by placing an X in the rating block that most accurately describes the ratee's performance. Each subsequent evaluator must carefully review the report to make sure that the ratings accurately describe the ratee's performance and that the comments are compatible with and support the ratings. Reports may be returned for reconsideration; however, any adjustments must be the decision of the evaluator concerned. Subsequent evaluators may disagree with ratings given and either upgrade or downgrade any performance factor rating by placing their initials in the rating block they believe most accurately describes the ratee's performance.

Section IV: "Promotion Recommendation." When completing or reviewing this section, each evaluator must carefully consider the ratee's performance and how it compares with the performance of others in the same grade and Air Force Specialty. The Weighted Airman Promotion System (WAPS) uses this information to determine the airman's performance score during the promotion selection process. As such, evaluators must carefully select the promotion recommendation block that best describes the ratee, so that airmen with strong performance records are not rated the same as average or weak performers. In assessing performance, the rater places an X in the "Rater's Recommendation" block that most accurately describes his or her assessment of the ratee's promotional potential.

Since two separate EPR forms are used (one for AB through TSgt and another for MSgt through CMSgt), the terminology for the second promotion recommendation official is different. On the AF Form 910, "Enlisted Performance Report (AB thru TSFT)," the indorser places an X in the "Indorser's Recommendation" block that accurately describes his or her assessment of the ratee's promotion potential. On the AF Form 911, "Senior Enlisted Performance Report (MSgt thru CMSgt)," the rater's rater places an X in the "Rater's Rater's

Recommendation" block that accurately describes his or her assessment of the ratee's promotion potential.

Section V: "Rater's Comments." The rater uses this section to provide additional information in narrative form about the ratee's performance. Short "bullet" statements and phrases must be used. Overall, the comments must be compatible with the ratings recorded in Sections III and IV. Certain items are considered inappropriate and must *not* be considered in the evaluation process or included in the comments of any evaluator. Examples include the following:

• Charges preferred, investigations, reviews by boards of evaluation or inquiry, or any actions related to the ratee that have not been finalized as of the EPRs closeout date. Fact from other sources, however, may be included.

• Actions against the ratee that resulted in acquittal or in failure to successfully implement an intended personnel action.

• Statements, testimonies, or data obtained by or presented to boards that are confidential under Air Force Instruction 91-204, *Investigating and Reporting U.S. Air Force Mishaps.*

• Actions that the ratee takes outside the normal chain of command through procedures that represent guaranteed rights of appeal such as the Inspector General, the Air Force Board for Correction of Military Records, and Congressional Inquiries.

• Recommendations for decorations such as ribbons or medals authorized for wear on the Air Force uniform. *Note:* Nominations for honors or awards such as Outstanding NCO of the Quarter and other recognition programs may be mentioned.

• The ratee's race, ethnic origin, gender, age, or creed, where such references could be interpreted as reflecting favorably or unfavorable on the ratee. However, the pronouns *he, she, him, her, his,* or *hers,* may be used.

• Temporary or permanent disqualification under Air Force Instruction 36-2104, *Nuclear Weapons Personnel Reliability Program.* References to the ratee's behavior that resulted in the action may be included.

• Any score data on the WAPS score notice or the senior NCO promotion score notice (e.g., board score and test scores).

• Substance Abuse Reorientation and Treatment (SART) Program. Evaluators should focus on the ratee's behavior, conduct, or performance rather than participation in the SART program.

• Previous reports. Evaluators may consider, but must not comment on, previous reports when making a promotion recommendation and when recommending CMSgts for increased responsibilities.

• Article 15 and actions taken under Article 15, including the use of the term *Article 15* or any mention of punishment imposed under this authority. The behavior that led to the punishment may be described.

• Family activities or the ratee's marital status. Do not consider or include in the EPR information (either negative or positive) regarding the employment, education, or volunteer service activities (on or off the military installation) of the ratee's family. Do not reflect favorably or adversely on the ratee based solely on the ratee's marital status.

• Incidents that occurred before the EPR's reporting period. unless they add significant information that the previous evaluators did not know.

• Events that occurred after the report's closeout date.

• Matrices, fact sheets, career briefs, background sheets, and other such documents.

• Promotion recommendations.

Performance Feedback Block. Following completion of the rater's comments, the performance feedback block is completed. If feedback was required during the EPR's period, but was not accomplished, the rater must give one or more reasons in the space provided. If there is no entry in this block, the rater is stating that he or she has complied with the performance feedback requirements. After this, data on the rater is typed in. The rater then ensures that all of the appropriate rater's evaluation blocks are marked with an X, signs the form, and forwards it to the next evaluating official.

Sections VI–IX

Section VI on AF Form 910 and Sections VI and VII on AF Form 911 are completed by additional evaluating officials, sometimes referred to as the rater's rater and the indorser. Air Force Instruction 36,2403, *Enlisted Evaluation System,* establishes guidelines for indorsements based on the grade of the person being rated.

If the ratee is a CMSgt, SMSgt, or MSgt, the indorser must be an officer serving in the grade of at least a major (or equivalent) or a civilian (at least a GS-12 or similar grade).

If the ratee is a TSgt, SSgt, Sgt, SrA, A1C, Amn, or AB, the indorser must be the rater's rater. When the rater's rater is not at least a MSgt or a GS-7 civilian, the indorser is the next official in the rating chain serving in the grade of MSgt or higher, or a civilian in the grade of GS-7 or higher. For example, if Airman Jones (the ratee) worked for Sergeant Smith (the rater) who, in turn, worked for Technical Sergeant Doe (the rater's rater), Technical Sergeant Doe would not be able to indorse the EPR. It would have to be indorsed by someone in their chain of command who was more senior in grade. In this case, it would probably be Technical Sergeant Doe's rater or supervisor.

In cases where the indorser is not an Air Force officer, NCO, or civilian (for example, in joint, combined, Allied, and other activities outside the Department of the Air Force), an Air Force advisor review is required. Those assigned to this duty are responsible for clarifying the meaning of reports and making sure that they are properly prepared in terms of Air Force procedures and rating policy. While these advisors cannot change any statement or rating on an EPR, they may provide comments about the EPR's content on an AF Form 77, "Supplemental Evaluation Sheet," which is processed and filed with the completed EPR.

Section VI: "Rater's Rater's Comments" (AF Form 911, "Senior Enlisted Performance Report, MSgt thru CMSgt"). This section is used to support the rating decisions of the rater's rater. If the rater's rater agrees with the rater, the concur block is marked and comments that provide new information are added. If the rater's rater disagrees with any of the ratings assigned by the rater, the nonconcur block is marked and one or more specific reasons that provide facts about the disagreement must be included. After this, data on the rater's rater is typed in. The rater's rater ensures that all of his or her appropriate evaluation blocks are marked with an X, signs the form, and forwards it to the next indorsing official. *Note:* In cases when a unit commander is junior in grade to the rater's rater, the commander must review the report before the rater's rater signs it. If the rater's rater is the final evaluator, the indorser block is annotated "This Section Not Used."

Section VI: "Indorser's Comments" (AF Form 910, "Enlisted Performance Report, AB thru TSgt"). The indorser on the AF Form 910 uses this section to comment on the ratee's performance. If the indorser disagrees with any of the ratings assigned by the rater, he or she marks the nonconcur block and must include one or more specific reasons for disagreeing. *Note:* In cases where a unit commander is junior in grade to the indorser, the commander must review the report before the indorser signs it.

Section VII: "Indorser's Comments" (AF Form 911, "Senior Enlisted Performance Report, MSgt thru CMSgt"). This additional level of indorsement is used, in part, to help those who use AF Form 911 to make personnel decisions. It also provides the rating chain with another opportunity to differentiate further between individuals with similar performance records. It is reserved for those whose performance is clearly above that of others in the organization and who merit immediate promotion. If the indorser agrees with the rater, he or she marks the concur block and adds comments that provide new information, adding more meaning to the EPR. If the indorser disagrees with any of the ratings assigned by the previous evaluators, he or she marks the nonconcur block and must include one or more specific reasons for disagreeing. *Note:* In cases where a unit commander is junior in grade to the indorser, the commander must review the report before the indorser signs it.

Section VII, "Commander's Review" (AF Form 910) and Section IX, "Commander's Review" (AF Form 911). The commander's review is to exercise influence over the quality of reports sent to file and to ensure that reports do not contain exaggerations or unrealistic ratings. It also provides an opportunity to pass information to evaluators for their consideration prior to finalizing the report. In cases where the commander agrees with the report, he or she marks the concur block, signs in the space provided, and does not add any further comments. In cases where the commander disagrees with the report, he or she should discuss the disagreement with previous evaluators, mark the nonconcur block if the disagreement is not resolved, sign in the space provided, initial the block(s) that accurately describes the ratee's performance or promotion recommendation, and provide comments on an AF Form 77, "Supplemental Evaluation Sheet," giving one or more specific reasons for disagreeing.

Section VIII: "Final Evaluator's Position and Senior Rater Identification (SRID) Code" (AF Form 911 only). The final evaluator completes this section by marking the appropriate block for position and enters the ratee's senior rater identification number.

• Block A is used when the senior rater is the final evaluator.

• Block B is used when the senior rater's deputy is the final evaluator. These evaluators usually occupy positions directly under the senior rater (e.g., vice wing commander, group commanders, and division chiefs in headquarters above the wing level.).

• Block C is used for the intermediate level positions that fall below the senior rater's deputy but above the lower level (e.g., squadron commanders, division chiefs in the wing, and branch chiefs within the wing levels).

• Block D is used for lower level positions below the intermediate level (e.g., detachment commanders, unit commanders, and branch chiefs within the wing levels).

Upon completion of the form, it is returned to the unit EPR monitor, who clears the suspense and assures that it is submitted to the Military Personnel Flight (MPF).

Other Considerations. Enlisted Performance Reports, attachments to reports, referral letters, or indorsements to a referral letter should never contain classified information. If an entry would result in the release of classified material, the word *classified* must be used in place of the entry.

All marks (Xs) and signatures must be made only in black or dark blue ink. Most organizations prefer black, as other colors do not reproduce well on office copiers.

Referral reports must be referred to the person being rated during the evaluation process. According to Air Force Instruction 36-2403, a referral report is one that contains either of the following:

• A rating in the far left block of any performance factor in AF Form 910 or 911, Section III.

• A rating of 1, an unsatisfactory performer not recommended for promotion in AF Forms 910 and 911, Section IV.

When an EPR is referred, it is given to the ratee with a standard cover letter containing processing instructions. The ratee then has an opportunity to provide additional information to the next evaluators and indorsers and comment on the items that caused the report to be a referral. Subsequent evaluators may or may not concur with the previous evaluator's assessments. After this, the EPR resumes normal processing and is returned to the Military Personnel Flight, where it is filed in the ratee's official personnel records with all attachments and comments. In-depth information about the processing of referral reports is noted in Air Force Instruction 36-2403.

WHEN YOU PREPARE REPORTS

You can think about performance reports from two perspectives: the ones written on you and the ones you write on airmen you supervise. When you are doing the writing, make sure you know the difference between a poor EPR and a good one.

Poorly Written Reports. Poorly prepared performance reports can have an adverse effect on people's promotions and assignments. What makes a poor EPR? There are three common problem areas, all related to the written comments on the reverse side of the form:

1. *The contents are weak.* Facts and *specific* achievements are in short supply. Statements are much too general and are routinely filled with flowery adjectives. Some raters compile a report by extracting general statements from previous reports they've written—often referred to as the cut and paste method. They feel that if it was accepted before, it probably will be again.

2. *The writing itself is poor.* Sentences are long and rambling. Imprecise words are used. For example, saying someone is "aware of" or "accepts" a responsibility can leave doubt about whether the individual actively pursues or supports the responsibility. Or, raters may say that an airman has "ability" or "capability," but they may not say *how* or *to what extent* an airman uses it. Undefined abbreviations can confuse someone from another career field (for example, a promotion board member from another Air Force Specialty).

3. *Insufficient quality-control procedures are used.* Some raters have low standards: "It's just another piece of paper." Some supervisors don't return poor products for rework, either because they don't want to offend the writer or because they're behind and don't want the report to be late. Some reports have obvious errors and omissions, for example, not mentioning a specific achievement or award. By all means watch out for typographical errors, which detract from the overall effectiveness of the report. Sometimes they can even damage the credibility of the person being discussed. For example, imagine an NCO who "works programs with command impact with *out* [should be *our*] maintenance contemporaries at the major command level.

Well-Written Reports. Having high marks on the front side of the report is where the rating starts. In today's Air Force a great number of airmen get good ratings—a commendable achievement. At the same time, it's important to look closely at the written comments on the reverse side. What's said there will have the greatest overall impact, especially for placement in key positions and promotions to the senior grades.

To provide a well-written and comprehensive report, the first thing you need to do is organize your information. Start by reflecting on the individual's duty description, but do not simply recopy it. Tell how the individual performed and cite specific examples to support your views. Think about personnel (supported or supervised), special projects, innovative techniques, plans, inspection results, aircraft, deployments and exercises, weapons, equipment (acquired or operated), sorties, and resources (value in dollar amounts). Define the scope of

DECORATIONS, AWARDS, AND SERVICE MEDALS

USAF AND DEPARTMENT OF DEFENSE MILITARY DECORATIONS

Medal of Honor (Air Force)

Air Force Cross

Defense Distinguished Service Medal

Distinguished Service Medal (Air Force)

Silver Star

Defense Superior Service Medal

Legion of Merit

Distinguished Flying Cross

Airman's Medal

Bronze Star Medal

Purple Heart

Defense Meritorious Service Medal

Meritorious Service Medal

Air Medal

**Air Force
Commendation
Medal**

**Joint Service
Commendation
Medal**

**Joint Service
Achievement
Medal**

**Air Force
Achievement
Medal**

USAF AND DEPARTMENT OF DEFENSE UNIT AWARDS

Presidential Unit Citation (Air Force)

Joint Meritorious Unit Award

AF Outstanding Unit Award

AF Organizational Excellence Award

USAF ACHIEVEMENT AWARDS

Prisoner of War Medal

Combat Readiness Medal

Good Conduct Medal (Air Force)

Good Conduct Medal (Army)

**Outstanding
Airman of the Year
Ribbon**

**Air Force
Recognition
Ribbon**

**Air Force
Overseas Ribbon
(short tour)**

**Air Force
Overseas Ribbon
(long tour)**

**Air Force
Longevity Service
Award Ribbon**

**Air Reserve Forces
Meritorious Service Medal**

**NCO Professional
Military Education Graduate
Ribbon**

**USAF Basic Military Training
Honor Graduate
Ribbon**

**Small Arms
Expert Marksmanship
Ribbon**

**Air Force Training
Ribbon**

**National
Defense Service
Medal**

**Armed Forces
Expeditionary
Medal**

**Antarctica
Service Medal**

**Vietnam
Service Medal**

**Southwest Asia
Service Medal**

**Humanitarian
Service Medal**

**Military
Outstanding
Volunteer
Service Medal**

**Armed Forces
Reserve Medal**

**United Nations
Medal**

**Multinational
Force and
Observers Medal**

**Republic of
Vietnam
Campaign Medal**

**Kuwait
Liberation Medal
(Kingdom of *Saudi Arabia*)**

**Kuwait
Liberation Medal
(Government of *Kuwait*)**

the programs implemented and the positive effect on the Air Force mission.

Use direct quotes: The Inspector General stated, "Management of this function was the best observed in the command during the most recent two-year period." Numbers provide depth to your descriptions: "She was responsible for a $2.3 million annual budget." "During January and February, his crew processed sixteen J-79 jet engines and obtained a 97 percent utilization rate."

List exercises and deployments the individual supported: name, location, and level (unit, wing, major command, or joint service). For example, "Sergeant Jones was personally selected to support OPERATION VALIANT, a joint exercise that involved forces from six allied nations." Note any new procedures or innovative techniques the individual developed that have potential for use at other locations. "Sergeant Smith designed a fuel-saving device for use on the ZX aircraft. Its use was approved by headquarters and its implementation resulted in savings of $4.1 million annually at six other bases."

Describe positive aspects of the individual's performance that deserve special note. Some themes you may wish to expand on include the following:

Ability to perform (under pressure or competitive conditions)
Appearance and image
Communicative skills (writing and speaking)
Dependability (reliability and integrity)
Initiative and willingness to accept responsibility
Instructing or training (ability to convey complex tasks)
Judgment and common sense (ability to make sound decisions)
Leadership (sets the example for others to follow)
Loyalty (to mission, commander, peers, subordinates)
Organizational ability (attention to detail)
Self-confidence and pride in work
Tact and diplomacy
Team player (inspires respect and confidence in others)
Technical expertise and competence in career field

If you note recommended improvement areas, clearly specify whether references are to serious deficiencies, faults, bad habits, or occasional tendencies. Indicate what progress, if any, has occurred before preparing the report: "This subject has been discussed with him and a marked improvement noted." Comment on any special training or courses of instruction that the ratee completed or actively participated in. Indicate whether participation was in-residence or by correspondence. Also note off-duty education such as college courses or the Community College of the Air Force. Emphasize progress being made, not merely enrollment in a course. These comments reflect initiative and are viewed very favorably, especially by promotion boards selecting personnel for senior grades.

If applicable, comment on the manner in which the ratee discharges his or her on-the-job (OJT) training responsibilities, whether as an OJT supervisor, trainer, or trainee.

Recommendation for suggested assignments should be consistent with the individual's AFSC, experience, and performance; it should also be timed appropriately, based on the person's grade. This section is especially important for staff sergeants and above because their records are often reviewed at new duty locations; it could determine whether they are selected to be a shop chief, branch chief, or policy maker at an intermediate headquarters or a major command. This section is also used to recommend personnel for specific special-duty assignments: "Sergeant Doe is exceptionally well qualified to serve as a military training instruction (MTI)."

The Writing Phase. After you have gathered all the information, it's time to move into the writing phase. The goal is to put together an accurate, factual, and effective product. One of the recommended ways to do this is to use the "decorated cake approach." The "cake" consists of *specific* facts, achievements, and comments about the ratee. "Icing" consists of commonly used "one-liners" with lots of adjectives and adverbs. Too much "icing" can do more harm than good. When you write the report, make the cake first, then apply the icing. You can also look at it from another angle: Eliminate the icing and see how much cake is left.

Your first draft might look something like this:

> SSgt Marvel is an outstanding noncommissioned officer and maintenance specialist whose organization, planning, and steadfastness during critical situations have been a key factor in the accomplishment of the squadron mission. Regardless of the tasking, his performance has been consistently superior. This NCO has had a significant impact on all areas of the unit from unit administration to daily maintenance. He completed a staff study that identified deficiencies in aircrew scheduling. He has consistently increased effectiveness and significantly improved overall unit operation. SSgt Marvel always strives to improve his professional qualities and recently completed 40 percent of the off-duty education requirements for a bachelor's degree.

Now here it is without the icing:

> SSgt Marvel completed a staff study that identified deficiencies in aircrew scheduling and recently completed 40 percent of the off-duty education requirements for a bachelor's degree.

Here's a rule of thumb: If you can change the person's duty title (for example, from aircraft maintenance specialist to medic) and the report still makes sense, it probably needs to be rewritten.

PLANNING AHEAD: FOUR FINAL TIPS

1. Always know when your next report is due. If you write reports on other airmen, you should know when theirs are due too.

2. Keep track of accomplishments—yours and theirs. When the time for a report comes, your supervisor may ask for input, and you may want to ask the airmen you supervise for input. A short handwritten note, including items like primary achievements, additional duties, educational accomplishments, off-duty activities, complimentary reports, or special recognition, is sufficient.

3. Take time to write. Get your thoughts on paper, then revise, edit, and rewrite until you are pleased with the product. As a general rule, you should spend as much time on someone else's report as you would like your rater to spend on yours. You should also allow processing time for temporary duty assignments, leave, and indorsements.

4. Submit reports on time. This keeps everyone in the rating chain happy. Late reports can be an administrative headache and a source of embarrassment to the unit concerned. In extreme cases, they can result in missed or unwarranted promotions.

SOURCES OF ADDITIONAL INFORMATION

Air Force Instruction 36-2403, *The Enlisted Evaluation System.* This directive establishes Air Force policy for enlisted personnel who are on active duty in the USAF and for enlisted personnel in the USAF Reserve (USAFR). It applies to all major commands (MAJCOM), field operating agencies (FOA), direct reporting units (DRU), and other activities of the Air Force. It does not apply to the Air National Guard. It tells how to implement the spirit and intent of the enlisted evaluation programs and includes guidance about new forms and rating criteria.

Personnel in your immediate chain of command (your supervisor and your unit's EPR monitor, first sergeant, and commander) can provide the best information about submission times and levels of indorsements.

The customer service branch of the Military Personnel Flight (MPF) can provide answers to routine questions and, if necessary, will refer you to the EPR section within the MPF.

13

Awards, Decorations, and Recognition Program

Let him who has won the palm bear it.

—Latin proverb

Awards and decorations programs were developed to recognize and reward individuals and organizations for outstanding performance. The commonly accepted term *recognition programs* is sometimes used to refer to programs that technically are awards programs. Both have a similar goal: to provide sincere and timely recognition, which fosters morale, incentive, and esprit de corps. They also have a positive influence on career decisions and retention. In the Air Force, as in the civilian community, a large element of job satisfaction and the desire to reenlist or stay with the company comes with the acknowledgment of a job well done. When people feel their efforts are not fully appreciated, they may consider leaving to seek fulfillment in another role.

DECORATIONS PROGRAMS
A decoration is a formal recognition for personal excellence, such as acts of exceptional bravery, outstanding achievement, or meritorious service. Award of a decoration requires an individual nomination and subsequent approval by designated levels of authority within the Department of Defense or the Department of the Air Force. The types of decorations and their eligibility criteria are listed in Air Force Instruction 36-2803, *The Air Force Awards and Decorations Program.*

U.S. Military Decorations. U.S. military decorations include the Medal of Honor (MH), the Air Force Cross (AFC), the Defense Distinguished Service Medal (DDSM), the Distinguished Service Medal (DSM), the Silver Star (SS), the Defense Superior Service Medal (DSSM), the Legion of Merit (LM), the Distinguished Flying Cross (DFC), the Airman's Medal (AmnM), the Bronze Star Medal (BSM), the Purple Heart (PH), the Defense Meritorious Service Medal (DMSM), the Meritorious Service Medal (MSM), the Air Medal (AM), the Aerial Achievement Medal (AAM), the Joint Service Commendation

156

Medal (JSCM), the Air Force Commendation Medal (AFCM), the Joint Service Achievement Medal (JSAM), and the Air Force Achievement Medal (AFAM). The most frequently awarded are the following:

1. The *Meritorious Service Medal (MSM)* is awarded for outstanding noncombat meritorious achievement or service to the United States. It has distinction above and beyond the Air Force Commendation Medal. Nominations are prepared on one side of a sheet of bond paper, typewritten and single-spaced. Emphasis is placed on awarding this decoration to outstanding field-grade officers and senior noncommissioned officers. Under enlisted promotion score systems, each MSM is valued at five points.

2. The *Air Force Commendation Medal (AFCM)* is awarded for outstanding achievement or meritorious service rendered specifically on behalf of the Air Force, acts of courage, and sustained meritorious performance. Awards are restricted to achievements and services that are clearly outstanding and unmistakably exceptional when compared with similar achievements and accomplishments of personnel of like rank and responsibilities. Nominations may be prepared on Air Force Form 642, "AF Achievement Medal and AF Commendation Medal Justification." This form allows room for seven primary job accomplishments and five other accomplishments (special projects, additional duties, and so on). Each entry allows for one concise and factual sentence. Emphasis is placed on awarding this decoration to outstanding company-grade officers and airmen whose achievements and service meet the prescribed standards. Under enlisted promotion score systems, each AFCM is valued at three points.

3. The *Air Force Achievement Medal (AFAM)* is awarded for outstanding achievement and meritorious service rendered specifically on behalf of the Air Force and for acts of courage that do not meet the requirements for award of the Air Force Commendation Medal. In instances where many people are affiliated with an exceptionally successful program, project, or mission, the AFAM is awarded to those few whose contributions clearly stand out from the others and who have contributed most to the success of the program. Emphasis is placed on awarding this decoration to outstanding junior officers and airmen whose achievements and service meet the prescribed standards. Under enlisted promotion score systems, each AFAM is valued at one point.

These nominations originate with a members' supervisor and are forwarded for review and approval through command channels. All decorations can be awarded to an individual more than once. Usually, they are obtained in sequence as an airman increases in grade and positions of responsibility (the AFAM first, the AFCM second, and the MSM third).

There are three keys to obtaining these decorations: outstanding performance; a well-written nomination that is specific and factual; and the support of the nominee's supervisor and commander. This third point can't be overemphasized. I remember a young sergeant (E-4) who was disappointed because an Air Force Commendation Medal nomination was not favorably considered. The supervisor felt that an Air Force Achievement Medal was more appropriate and could be approved, but the sergeant said, "If I can't get the Commendation Medal, I don't want any." On the next promotion cycle, he missed staff sergeant (E-5) by less than one point. Had he been awarded the Achievement Medal, he would have been promoted.

Foreign Decorations. Congressional authority was given to U.S. Armed Forces personnel to accept decorations proffered by friendly foreign governments in recognition of service performed during the following periods:

> World War II: 7 December 1941 through 24 July 1948
> Berlin Airlift: 26 June 1948 through 20 September 1951
> Korean Operation: 27 June 1950 through 27 July 1955
> Vietnam Hostilities: 1 March 1961 through 28 March 1974

Official acceptance of other foreign decorations is subject to approval on a case-by-case basis. Approval authority has been delegated to the Deputy Chiefs of Staff for Personnel in major commands, FOAs and DRUs.

U.S. Nonmilitary Decorations. U.S. nonmilitary decorations are awarded by the President, the Department of Defense, and the Department of the Air Force. Military personnel are eligible to receive the National Security Medal, for distinguished achievement or outstanding contribution on or after 26 July 1947 in the field of intelligence relating to the national security; and the Presidential Medal of Freedom, for an exceptionally meritorious contribution to the security of national security interests of the United States, world peace, or cultural or other significant public or private endeavors.

AWARDS PROGRAMS
Awards are formal recognition given to a specific group or persons. They fall into several major categories.

Service Awards. U.S. service awards recognize active military service personnel or reserve members who have faithfully and honorably served their country during periods of war, national emergency, or in specific military operations. Common examples are the National Defense Service Medal, the Vietnam Service Medal, and the Armed Forces Expeditionary Medal (for operations such as Beirut, Grenada, and Libya) and the Southwest Asia Service Medal.

The Southwest Asia Service Medal has been authorized to those servicemembers who served in the Persian Gulf area in operations Desert Shield and Desert Storm from 2 August 1990 to 30 November 1995. The medal is suspended from a sand-colored ribbon with red, white, blue, green, and black stripes incorporating the colors of the United States and of the Gulf area. The obverse of the medal depicts the desert and the sea with tank, armored personnel carrier, helicopter, ship, and aircraft in recognition of joint service participation. The reverse depicts an upraised sword entwined with a palm frond, symbolizing military might and preparedness in defense of peace.

☐ AIR FORCE ACHIEVEMENT MEDAL ☐ AIR FORCE COMMENDATION MEDAL **JUSTIFICATION**	DATE 1 Jul 97	

1. NAME (Last, First, MI) DOE, JOHN R.	2. GRADE SSgt	3. SSN 000-00-0000

4. DUTY TITLES(S) AND INCLUSIVE PERIOD

NCOIC, Awards and Decorations   (Use multiple titles if held during period of recommendation)

5. JUSTIFICATION (Use a short "Bullet" statement for each accomplishment. *Minimize description - emphasize results.* Use only as many bullets as required. *Additional space below the dotted lines may be used for Air Force Commendation Medal Justification only.*)

a. PRIMARY JOB ACCOMPLISHMENTS:

(1)   Designed a new system that has raised average on-time percentage rates from less than 30% to over 95%.

(2)   Reduced the average number of recommendations for decorations returned for administrative correction from 18 to less than 3 per month.

(3)   Not only met but ensured all suspenses for AFI 36-2805, *Special Trophies and Awards* nominees were sent to higher headquarters before the required suspenses.

(4)   Initiated a new system that ensures all approved decorations are updated in a manner that totally prevents the need for supplementary consideration for promotion under WAPS.

(5)

(6)   FOR ALL RECOMMENDING OFFICIALS: Please note the justifying statements are short, concise, and factual statements that are devoid of "flowery" phrases and "Atta-Boys." There are five items under "Primary Job Accomplishments" available for justification of the new
(7)   Air Force Achievement Medal (AFAM) and seven for the Air Force Commendation Medal (AFCM). Under "Other Accomplishments" there are three items available for the AFAM and five for the AFCM.

b. OTHER ACCOMPLISHMENTS: *(Special projects, additional duties, etc.)*

(1)

(2)

(3)

(4)

(5)

6. NAME, GRADE AND TITLE OF INITIATOR JOSEPHINE D. SMITH, CMSgt, USAF NCOIC, Military Personnel Flight	7. SIGNATURE *Josephine D. Smith*

AF FORM 642   PREVIOUS EDITION WILL BE USED.
MAR 85

AFAM amd AFCM Justification (AF Form 642).

Non-U.S. service awards that have been accorded presidential acceptance and are authorized for wear by eligible personnel include the United Nations Service Medal (UNSM) and the United Nations Medal (UNM), the Republic of Vietnam Campaign Medal, and the two Kuwait Liberation Medals (KLM). Of the latter, the first KLM has been awarded by the Kingdom of Saudi Arabia for direct participation in Operation Desert Storm between 17 January 1991 and 28 February 1991. The second KLM has been awarded by the Government of Kuwait for service between 2 August 1990 and 31 August 1993.

Unit Awards. Unit awards are presented to U.S. military units that distinguish themselves during peacetime or in action against hostile forces or armed enemies of the United States.

1. The *Presidential Unit Citation (PUC)* is awarded for extraordinary heroism in action against an armed enemy on or after 7 December 1947.

2. The *Joint Meritorious Unit Award (JMUA)* is awarded in the name of the Secretary of Defense to Joint Activities of the Department of Defense for meritorious achievement or service, superior to that normally expected, during combat with an armed enemy of the United States, during a declared national emergency, or under extraordinary circumstances that involved the national interest.

3. The *Air Force Outstanding Unit Award (AFOUA)* is awarded for exceptionally meritorious service or exceptionally outstanding achievement that clearly sets a unit above and apart from similar units. It is primarily awarded to wing-level units and below.

4. The *Air Force Organizational Excellence Award (AFOEA)* is similar to the AFOUA but is awarded to higher-level unnumbered organizations such as major command headquarters, separate operating agencies, and direct reporting units.

The acceptance of foreign service awards is no longer authorized (U.S. service awards are not tendered to foreign military personnel); however, awards that were previously authorized and accepted may be worn. The most prevalent of these worn today include the Republic of Korea Presidential Unit Citation, the Philippine Republic Presidential Unit Citation (Disaster Relief Operations—1972), the Vietnam Presidential Unit Citation, the Republic of Vietnam Gallantry Cross Unit Citation, and the Republic of Vietnam Civil Actions Unit Citation.

Army and Navy unit decorations are similar to those for the Air Force. Members of cited Air Force units and other persons who, while Army and Navy members, received unit decorations that they are entitled to wear permanently may wear the appropriate award devices on the Air Force uniform.

Achievement Awards. Achievement awards recognize specific types of achievements made while serving on active duty in the Air Force or as members of the Air Reserve forces. To be eligible, an individual must meet the criteria for each award, and service for the entire period of the award must be honorable. Air Force achievement awards include the following:

> Prisoner of War Medal (POWM)
> Combat Readiness Medal (CRM)
> Air Force Good Conduct Medal (AFGCM)
> Good Conduct Medal (GCM)
> Outstanding Airman of the Year Ribbon (OAYR)
> Air Force Recognition Ribbon (AFRR)
> Air Force Overseas Service Ribbon (AFOSR)
> Air Force Longevity Service Award (AFLSA)
> Air Reserve Forces Meritorious Service Award (ARFMSA)
> NCO Professional Military Education Graduate Ribbon (NCOPMEGR)
> USAF Basic Military Training (BMT) Honor Graduate Ribbon
>   (BMTHGR)
> Small Arms Expert Marksmanship Ribbon (SAEMR)
> Air Force Training Ribbon (AFTR)

Special Trophies and Awards. The Air Force as well as some private organizations have established programs that recognize individual contributions and achievements based on grade and level of responsibility. They also recognize units of comparable status (wing, base, squadron) and achievements in established programs (for example, safety, personnel, supply, and fuels).

Nominations are made primarily by a written narrative that notes significant achievements during the period of the award. At the Air Force level, one individual or unit is selected for the top award. However, the nominating process provides recognition for many deserving people along the way.

One example of how a program works is the annual Air Force Outstanding Information Management Awards Program. Over a dozen awards are established. One category is for junior enlisted personnel assigned to the base Information Management Division. This means that there's an opportunity for more than one hundred people to be selected as the "best junior enlisted information manager on base," and that a dozen of them will be selected by their major command (Air Combat Command, Air Mobility Command, and so on) as the "best junior enlisted information manager in the command." Command winners are then forwarded to the HQ USAF level, where a "best junior enlisted information manager in the USAF" is selected. Those selected have significant comments for their next performance reports. In most cases, they also receive presentations such as letters of appreciation, certificates, or plaques.

These programs are supported very strongly by supervisors and commanders at all levels, and publicity about them is circulated periodically.

Air Force Instruction 36-2805, *Special Trophies and Awards,* describes the special trophies and awards programs sponsored by the USAF and by private organizations that seek Air Force participation. This directive notes the criteria, policies, and procedures for applying for the following special trophies and awards programs that are monitored by the Air Force Personnel Center:

> Team of the Year Award
> Veterans of Foreign Wars Armed Forces Award
> Institute of Navigation Awards
> Air Force Association Aerospace Awards
> General and Mrs. Jerome F. O'Malley Award
> Verne Orr Award
> USAF First Sergeant of the Year Award
> Pitsenbarger Award
> Vanguard Award
> Joan Orr Air Force Wife of the Year Award
> 12 Outstanding Airmen of the Year Award
> Elder Statesman of Aviation Award
> Wright Brothers Memorial Trophy
> Ten Outstanding Young Americans
> Lance P. Sijan USAF Leadership Award
> GEICO Military Service Awards
> Field of Aeronautics Awards

The directive also provides extensive lists for two other categories of awards and trophies:

1. A list of special functional area trophies and awards set up by other Air Force directives (for example, Information Management Awards, Maintenance Awards, Security Police Awards). The names and numbers of these directives, as well as the name of the monitoring activity, are listed for additional information.

2. A list of special trophies and awards set up by Air Force and private organizations that are not governed by a specific Air Force directive, including lists of agencies to which nominations should be sent.

Unit Level Awards and Recognition Program. Air Force Instruction 36-2805, *Special Trophies and Awards,* also provides commanders with the authority to establish recognition programs and awards for personnel in their organizations. The programs available depend on the mission of the unit and the creativity of assigned personnel. They include commonly accepted day-to-day initiatives and local competitions based on grade and categories.

Day-to-Day Initiatives. Day-to-day initiatives from Air Force supervisors can include personal messages, oral or handwritten, that tell an individual or group that a job was done well, or formal letters or certificates of commendation giving credit to an individual or a group for a specific accomplishment.

Another way to give public recognition is to submit ideas for articles and photographs about the achievement to the editor of the base newspaper. The focal point for the base newspaper is the Public Affairs Office; staff there are accustomed to providing guidance for newsworthy ideas.

Special Recognition Programs. Special recognition programs are developed locally in three primary categories:

1. Grade: such as the airman, noncommissioned officer, or senior noncommissioned officer of the month, quarter, and year.

2. Career area: such as crew chief of the month, maintenance person of the month, personnel specialist of the quarter.

3. In support of a special program: such as the Air Force Suggestion Program or the Foreign Object Damage (FOD) program.

The intervals at which each program is offered usually depend on the number of personnel assigned. A maintenance squadron with more than three hundred airmen would probably initiate an airman of the month program; a maintenance squadron with only fourteen senior noncommissioned officers would probably initiate a senior noncommissioned officer of the quarter or year program.

Methods of selection vary from unit to unit, depending on the nature of the award. Written nominations are required at some locations; most units convene local selection boards. In general, boards are less time-consuming and a better forum for considering a variety of factors. Under this system, each nominee personally appears before a board of five or six noncommissioned officers and a chairperson, usually a senior noncommissioned officer or a commissioned officer. The board usually convenes in a squadron conference room. Nominees are scheduled at fifteen- or twenty-minute intervals.

When nominees report in, their appearance, military bearing, and communications skills are noted. They are asked about subjects such as current events, Air Force mission and organization, Air Force policies and programs, leadership and management, self-improvement efforts, and community involvement. After each one leaves, members of the board assign scores based on the nominee's presentation and responses. (The chairperson usually votes only in case of a tie.) The board recommends the nominee with the highest score to the commander, who notifies the individual of his or her selection. Those selected receive a letter of notification and congratulations. Tangible awards are certificates or plaques, three-day passes, and in some cases special activities (such as incentive rides in high-performance aircraft). These awards are frequently noted in performance reports and can have a favorable influence on promotion and job placement decisions.

Sometimes the thought of meeting a selection board can be a bit nerve-racking, but it is a fair process that gives everyone an equal chance to compete. It helps to steer clear of written nominations, because polished writing styles often result in the selection of deserving but lesser qualified nominees.

Meeting a board can also be a very special experience. It gives you an opportunity to interact with senior personnel and to learn more about the Air Force and about yourself. Also, nomination itself can be a source of personal satisfaction. As one airman put it, "I don't really care if I win or not. I'm just glad that my supervisor thought enough of my performance to recommend me for the competition."

Other Forms of Recognition. Other forms of recognition include special service identification badges (such as the Presidential Service Badge, the Vice Presidential Service Badge, the Combat Crewmember Badge, the Office of the Secretary of Defense Identification Badge, and the Joint Chiefs of Staff Identification Badge), lapel buttons, and special devices such as ribbon bars, clasps, arrowheads, stars, and clusters.

SOURCES OF ADDITIONAL INFORMATION

Air Force Instruction 36-2903, *Dress and Personal Appearance of Air Force Personnel,* concerning the display and wear of ribbons, medals, badges, and devices on the Air Force uniform.

Air Force Instruction 36-2805, *Special Trophies and Awards.*

Air Force Instruction 36-2803, *The Air Force Awards and Decorations Program.*

See chapter 8, "Your Uniform and Standards of Appearance," for wear of awards and decorations.

At the unit level, the best points of contact are your supervisor, the unit awards and decorations monitor, and your first sergeant.

At the base level, contact the Customer Service Section of the Military Personnel Flight.

14

The Inspector General
and the Inspection System

Two little letters—IG—solicit undivided attention from almost every Air Force member, from young airmen to seasoned noncommissioned officers to four-star generals.

IG stands for Inspector General and is commonly used to refer to those responsible for implementing the USAF inspection system. Their purpose and role are frequently misunderstood, but with some insight into their reason for being and the ways they draw their conclusions, you can use their visits as positive stepping-stones in your career.

Historically, the IGs have been viewed as the guys in the black hats. They went out and found problems. An inspectee was either right (in compliance with the regulation) or wrong (not in compliance)—there wasn't very much middle ground. Careers could be seriously affected by the stroke of a pen. Even today war stories circulate about the general who removed people from his staff and wanted them "off base by sundown" (meaning permanent reassignment) because of comments made by a visiting IG team.

As the Air Force moved into the 1960s and the IG role became more defined, this perspective changed. First, the emphasis shifted from compliance to management: Visiting inspectors placed more emphasis on the need to meet the intent of the directives. This approach had a positive effect on those inspected, for it made them participants, involved in the inspection process, rather than unwilling victims. Standards were still high and expected to be met, but now members' ideas were actively solicited in an effort to improve overall readiness, efficiency, and quality of life.

From this stage, the approach evolved still further and now includes follow-up and trend analysis. This ensures that problems are monitored until they are corrected, and also provides a way to identify potential problems that may be occurring at more than one location so that corrective action can be taken before adverse conditions develop.

The inspection system was designed to give the Secretary of the Air Force, the Chief of Staff USAF, and MAJCOM, SOA, and NAF commanders feedback and information on the state of USAF readiness and on the efficiency and effectiveness of units, functions, programs, and guidance. The system uses a two-pronged approach: first, to find problems and help fix them; and second, to stimulate and reward excellence. Policies, procedures, and responsibilities are set by the Inspector General at HQ USAF and those in similar positions appointed by MAJCOMS, SOAs, and NAFs who conduct inspections of subordinate units.

Types of inspections and reviews vary, based on the nature of each command's requirements. Some of the most common are the following:

1. *Operational Readiness Inspection (ORI).* The most direct measure of a unit's warfighting readiness is through an ORI. All units with a wartime mission are evaluated on their ability to conduct combat operations in wartime. These evaluations assess how well a unit can prepare, deploy, and employ forces, as well as survive and operate in a combat environment.

2. *Quality Air Force Assessment (QAFA).* These inspections are designed to assess the process used by inspected activities to complete their mission. The QAFA includes an inspection of a unit's leadership and management, as shown

"A bunch of guys from the IG team dropped by to see you, but I told them to come back tomorrow because you were napping."

in mission and functional area performance, installation support, people programs, service to customers, and compliance with directives. Inspectors examine these processes using Quality Air Force criteria with the intent of identifying those broad areas that may need improvement. QAFAs are the most common type of inspection. Usually conducted by MAJCOM inspection teams, QAFAs may be scheduled in conjunction with other inspections, such as ORIs.

3. *Nuclear Surety Inspection (NSI)*. NSIs assess compliance with procedures for the handling and employment of nuclear weapons. Because of the critical nature of nuclear weapons programs, these inspections can pose the most difficult tests for the activity inspected. Unsatisfactory performance in any nuclear surety area may result in an overall unsatisfactory unit rating, regardless of the ratings earned in other areas.

4. *Health Service Assessment (HSA)*. HSAs are designed to evaluate medical readiness and management of the health-care system. The focus is on performance rather than compliance and is designed to provide a broad look at medical treatment facility operation.

5. *Management Review*. Management reviews are not inspections; they are reviews that are conducted to provide senior leadership with information concerning topics with Air Force–wide significance. There are two categories of review: functional, such as contingency contracting, aircraft engine oil analysis, USAF regional nuclear weapons maintenance, and unfavorable information files (UIFs); and acquisition, such as aircraft battle damage repair, realignment of space launch operations from Air Force Material Command to Air Force Space Command, and initial operational test and evaluation. Ratings are not given for these reviews. Recommended solutions may be included in written reports; however, the program or process owner is responsible for developing the method that will best correct problems that are identified.

When inspections are conducted, observations and findings must be based on facts that can be validated for accuracy. These facts are usually documented in a formal written report that outlines the finding, the impact, the cause, and a recommendation. The effectiveness and efficiency of a program are then measured, using a rating system.

RATING SYSTEMS
Five standard ratings categories are used throughout the USAF by the Inspector General:

1. *Outstanding.* Far exceeds mission requirements. Procedures and activities are carried out in a far superior manner. Resources and programs are very efficiently managed and are of exceptional merit. Few, if any, deficiencies exist.

2. *Excellent.* Exceeds mission requirements. Procedures and activities are carried out in a superior manner. Resources and programs are very efficiently managed, relatively free of discrepancies.

3. *Satisfactory.* Meets mission requirements. Procedures and activities are carried out in an effective and competent manner. Resources and programs are

efficiently managed. Minor deficiencies may exist but do not impede or limit mission accomplishment.

4. *Marginal.* Does not meet some mission requirements. Procedures and activities are not carried out in an efficient manner. Resources and programs are not efficiently managed. Deficiencies exist that impede or limit mission accomplishment.

5. *Unsatisfactory.* Does not meet mission requirements. Procedures and activities are not carried out in an adequate manner. Resources and programs are not adequately managed. Significant deficiencies exist that preclude or seriously limit mission accomplishment.

The criteria used to decide which rating to give are not quite as easy to define. There are many considerations. At a basic level, criteria are developed by each major command, based on its mission directives, theater concept of operations, and special contingency plans. Criteria are performance-oriented toward results, quality, and effectiveness of programs, and are designed to highlight innovative leadership or management actions that have a positive effect on the mission. From this, you should remember one main point: Depending on the type of inspection being conducted, the criteria used to decide the rating may fluctuate from one major command to another.

When the MAJCOMs develop their criteria, they try to balance subjective (what they think) and objective (what they see) assessments. This helps assure that standards are consistent, not superficially tough or unrealistically easy. It also helps eliminate ratings that are inaccurate or undeserved (too high or too low).

Stop to think about criteria and ratings. What rating do you think most accurately describes your operation? Put yourself in the inspector's shoes, look at your own operation, and ask yourself two questions: How is the operation being run compared with others at similar units? If in doubt, should I use a higher or lower rating? Most MAJCOM commanders have a policy for such doubts, and they leave the final decision to the inspectors on the scene. But they do emphasize one point: If you're thinking of giving a higher rating, ask yourself, "Will the person or unit be satisfied with what they're doing and continue that way, or if I go lower, will they be more motivated and have a higher level of interest to correct the problems noted?"

AN INSIDE LOOK AT INSPECTOR GENERAL TEAMS

Organization. Most Inspector General teams are assigned to the staff of a major air command, for example, Air Combat Command (AAC), Air Mobility Command (AMC), U.S. Air Force in Europe (USAF), and so on. The size of the team, in manpower positions, usually is based on the size and scope of the MAJCOM's mission. The Inspector General position is usually filled by an experienced colonel or general officer who reports directly to the MAJCOM commander. The IG staff is composed of an administration branch, a plans and scheduling branch, a trends and analysis branch, and inspection branches for each primary functional area, such as operations, maintenance, communications, and support.

Selecting Individual Inspectors. Prospective inspection team members are identified by past performance and the breadth and depth of their experience in their career fields. Other key factors include integrity, judgment, and ability to communicate both orally and in writing. Tours of duty last for two to three years.

Where do they come from? Generally, inspectors come from either key positions on the MAJCOM's headquarters staff or bases assigned to the MAJCOM. Recently, others from field units are being brought in to augment the team. Training for inspectors depends on their status. Those permanently assigned to an IG team attend an in-residence inspectors' school at the Air Force Inspection Agency (AFIA). Augmentees are assigned a sponsor, usually an inspector for the same functional area, and are then given specific instructions for the areas that they will be evaluating.

If an inspector's performance is substandard—which doesn't happen very often—the individual's role as an inspector stops abruptly. Permanent inspectors may be reassigned to other jobs or even other bases; augmentees who don't meet expectations won't be asked back for future inspections.

Preinspection Planning. The IG team's Plans and Scheduling Branch establishes a tentative inspection schedule, usually six to twelve months in advance. It is then cleared through the commander and the other staff agencies to avoid conflicts with other events, such as major operational taskings or joint exercises.

Then inspectors are notified and preinspection planning begins. The amount of preparation usually depends on the type of inspection. For example, an Operational Readiness Inspection will be more compliance oriented and less preparation will be required. If the inspection is geared primarily toward leadership and management, the preparation will be much more extensive.

Usually there will be a team meeting to define the purpose of the inspection, the unit's primary mission, and any special subjects for inspection, such as exercises and scenarios. Then inspectors will start to do their homework about their specific functional area: operations, logistics, support, and so forth. They'll start by reviewing the unit's previous IG report, staff assistance reports, and a range of computerized analysis reports. They'll talk with members of the functional staff and also the Auditor and the Office of Special Investigations (OSI) on matters of fraud, waste, and abuse. Then they'll look at details about the unit, such as key personnel and how long they've been in their position, organizational charts, host-tenant support agreements, and present manning levels (including how many people are authorized and how many are assigned).

After the inspectors have a feel for your mission, they'll prepare their own inspection schedule: where they plan to go, who they intend to see, and what they want to look at. They'll review all the appropriate directives, manuals, supplements, and policy letters. Then they'll review their checklist and inspection guides and, if necessary, make additions for any unique aspects of the primary mission of the unit being inspected.

After this, the team members turn their attention to matters of administration and logistics: how they get from their base to yours. Usually a project officer will be in touch with a point of contact at the inspected unit. Transportation and billeting arrangements will be confirmed, and security clearances will be validated. Back at the IG's base, special orders will be printed, uniform requirements will be determined, and the members of the IG team will be notified of the time, date, and place to meet for departure to your unit.

The Day Is Here. The IG team arrives at your base and is met by your commander and key staff members. Everything they do from here on out will go according to a predetermined schedule. Almost every base has one. It's called "the IG Reception Plan." It covers everything from arranging transportation and rooms to providing administrative support such as typing and printing.

The In-Brief. Immediately after their arrival, the IG team and key personnel from your unit proceed to a central location, usually the base theater, for the in-brief. The team chief briefs the purpose of the inspection, the functional areas and any special-interest items that will be evaluated, rating criteria, and when and where the final outbrief (the team's findings) will take place. Your commander then presents your unit's mission briefing and an overview of any unique factors that affect the operation of your base. On average, these in-briefs last about one hour.

The Inspection Begins. After the in-brief, inspectors meet with the representatives from your squadron or staff agency (usually your immediate commander, OIC, or NCOIC). Together, they return to your unit and discuss your programs in general and any potential problems that have arisen from increased taskings, personnel shortages, budget constraints, and the like. Next comes the "walk-around"—time for the inspector to see all the facilities and meet you and the personnel in your duty section. This is an important aspect of the inspection; make it favorable—you'll never get a second chance to make a first impression. After this initial walk-through, the inspector will thank the escort and provide him or her with a tentative schedule. The inspector will then spend the majority of his or her time at the working level, in each duty section, with the respective branch or shop chief.

The inspectors have seen shops like yours at other bases. They're very familiar with your operation. They understand your language. They review programs and procedures. They use checklists. They take notes. They ask a multitude of questions about your career field and your operation—training, security, budget, safety, equipment, and supplies. They monitor customs and courtesies, dress and appearance, and care of government vehicles. They take more notes. They ask, "Why do you do this?" and "Why do you do that?" They ask to see your self-inspection notebook. There seems to be no end of things they're interested in. And they're still taking notes . . .

The Team Meeting. At the end of your duty day, the inspector leaves your duty section and goes to a team meeting for a "how goes it" session. This session has two purposes: to give the team chief insight into the status of each functional area; and to allow inspectors to pass along crossfeed information to inspectors of other areas.

Information provided to the team chief is usually very brief. Comments range from "an outstanding operation" to "OK" to "I think we have several major problems here that we should discuss after the meeting." Based on these comments, the team chief discusses each major area with your commander and asks for assistance in gaining further insight or information.

The Write-up. After all facts have been gathered, all the inspectors conduct a thorough review and a validation process to ensure that all the facts are accurate and their observations were correct. They do this by discussing each point with the inspectee, reviewing appropriate directives, and, when necessary, calling the policy makers at headquarters to ensure that their interpretations do not conflict.

Now the writing phase begins. A standard format is used. Major points, both positive and negative, are noted. When deciding what to include, the inspector asks himself or herself either "What's the impact?" or "So what?" If an item has no significant adverse impact, it's usually left out of the report. This lets managers concentrate on major issues. Listing trivia makes for cumbersome reading and may detract from the overall credibility of the report.

The inspector submits his or her report for review, usually to four other people—the functional area chief, the reports monitor, the inspection monitor, and the team chief—each of whom may ask questions about the validity of each finding and performs an editing function to ensure that each sentence will not be misunderstood or misinterpreted. They also check grammar, spelling, and punctuation. Typewritten drafts are prepared. Another review is conducted. If approved, the report is prepared in final form. Then it's reviewed again by each person in the review chain. If approved, it's ready for printing.

The Outbrief. After the report has been finalized, the focus of attention shifts to the outbrief. Each inspector prepares a brief narrative summary for his or her area. As in the report, subratings are given for each shop or branch and an overall rating for each division or unit. Photographs (usually 35mm color slides) that were taken during the inspection are reviewed, and about a half a dozen from each area are selected for the outbrief. All summaries are reviewed, edited, and approved by the team chief, and a final script is typed.

The next morning the outbrief is presented orally at a central location, usually the base theater. The size of the audience is governed by the level of security classification and the "need to know." When the outbrief is unclassified or For Official Use Only, the maximum number of base personnel are encouraged to attend. The team chief begins by covering the purpose of the inspection and the rating system. Then, sticking to the script, the team chief discusses each area.

For highly commendable areas (rated outstanding or excellent), the team chief recognizes those who deserve the credit. For example, "Within the Jet Engine Shop, we found that Technical Sergeant Jones's exemplary leadership and initiative were the primary factors in reducing the wing's foreign object damage rate and maintaining a virtually error-free operation. We believe that three of his programs have exceptional merit and have potential for adoption at other bases in our command. Overall, the Jet Engine Shop was rated outstanding." As the team chief is reading this segment, slides will be projected on the screen: One displays the rating; others show Technical Sergeant Jones and his crew at work in their duty section.

For areas that were rated less than satisfactory (either marginal or unsatisfactory), the team chief will discuss functions only, not the names of the personnel responsible. The emphasis will be on the program that needs attention and the impact if the trend is allowed to continue—for example, maintenance malpractices that can affect the flying mission, an unsafe work environment, misuse of government funds, or the potential for a security compromise because of weak administrative procedures.

At the close of the outbrief, the team chief will give an overall rating for the unit or base. The inspected unit's commander will usually then make a few comments. Usually, he or she will thank the team for their efforts and an in-depth assessment that left no stone unturned. (Almost everyone in the audience will identify with this comment.) The commander will express appreciation to those who have worked long and hard and to those who have been recognized for their outstanding programs. Also, the commander will say that where problems were identified, follow-up actions will be taken to correct them. In cases where a unit does exceptionally well, the MAJCOM commander or his or her designated representative (usually the MAJCOM vice commander or the numbered air force commander, a two- or three-star general) may attend to comment on findings and add appreciation for a job well done.

After the IG Team Departs. Printed copies of the inspection report are released to the unit and are sent to other units in the command, where they will be reviewed to see if similar problems exist or if programs of exceptional merit can be adopted for local use.

Back at the inspected units, those responsible for programs that did well are being congratulated; they're patting themselves on the backs and planning celebrations. The programs that did not do so well are beginning to receive a lot of interest from different levels of command. A complete review will be conducted, actions will be planned, and completion dates will be established.

After the inspectors return to their home base, they formally brief their functional staff counterparts at the MAJCOM headquarters. Sometimes they discuss changes in policy, such as the rewording of a directive to clarify procedures. After this, a formal presentation, similar to the outbrief, is given to the MAJCOM commander, who will draw conclusions based on his or her experience and ask for specific corrective actions or periodic updates of major deficiencies.

After debriefing, it's primarily a matter of follow-up and analysis. The inspectors, in conjunction with the functional staff, will review the adequacy of corrective actions taken by the inspected unit. The trends and analysis branch will conduct a review to determine whether problems are occurring at more than one location. If a trend is found, they will look for causes and try to provide background information to the personnel responsible for managing these programs. The inspection cycle is then complete.

HOW TO SURVIVE AN INSPECTOR GENERAL TEAM'S VISIT

Now that you understand the purpose of Inspector General teams, the rating systems they use, and how a typical visit is planned and conducted, it's time to start developing your own plan. Here are some things to think about.

The best way to prepare is to be ready at all times. Ratings usually have a direct relationship to a unit's daily effort. Outstanding operations are built over a period of time, not two weeks before the inspection.

Be on the same wave length as your supervisor and your commander. Develop a full understanding of your current programs and responsibilities and their importance to your unit's mission.

Actively seek out new ideas to improve your operations. Think about more efficient ways of doing things. Streamline procedures to enhance mission responsiveness or customer service. Take advantage of new technology. Look for actions that are cost-effective without loss of quality. Remember that you get a satisfactory rating by meeting mission requirements. To get a higher rating, you need to exceed mission requirements.

Use a self-inspection system to check yourself, and be honest. Carefully review your checklists if you've marked everything "yes, yes, yes, OK, OK, OK." This will indicate one of three things: your program is indeed outstanding; your checklists are out of date; or someone is "pencil-whipping" the answers. If you fall into category 2 or 3, you should back up and regroup. Remember, the inspectors have experience in your career field; they won't be easily misled. When they do find adverse trends, they usually look harder and deeper. They will find problems where they exist. If you find problems that are beyond your ability to fix, talk to your supervisor or your commander. They won't be able to help if they aren't advised.

Read the results of other units' inspections; your supervisor should be able to get copies. These reports can tell you what the inspector looks at closely and what things denote an outstanding or excellent unit.

Get crossfeed information from supervisors in your chain of command, from your counterparts at other units (especially if they've been inspected recently), and from higher headquarters personnel who conduct staff assistance visits.

Think beyond your specialty. This is especially true for special-interest items and facility appearance. The way your shop looks is a reflection of the pride you take in your overall operation. There's an old IG saying: "I never saw a good unit that looked bad. I've seen a lot of bad units that looked good, but I never saw a good unit that looked bad."

During the inspection itself, there are some things you should do and some things you definitely should not do.

Dos

1. Do be positive and professional. It makes the inspector's job easier, and it demonstrates your knowledge and control of your area. At the same time, it's important to relax and be yourself. Everyone has a slightly different approach or style.

2. Do be open and honest. It shows you have nothing to hide and establishes your credibility.

3. Do ask questions to get feedback. Make sure that you fully understand the observations and recommendations of the inspection team.

4. Do expose working-level personnel. They're tomorrow's supervisors and leaders. Let them talk to the inspectors and explain what they do. This demonstrates your trust in them and helps build their confidence for the future.

5. Do update your supervisors at the end of each duty day. They may be able to shed more light on items that, on the surface, appear to be problems. You can pass this information on to the inspectors and eliminate some items that might otherwise wind up in the printed report.

Don'ts

1. Don't resent the inspectors' visit. Their sole reason for visiting your unit is to enhance the efficiency and effectiveness of the U.S. Air Force.

2. Don't try to use delaying tactics (war stories, excessive coffee breaks, scheduling conflicting appointments, "mislaying" important documents, and so forth). Inspectors are well aware of all the time-wasting tricks. They also have to analyze a lot of information in a very short time. If they see that you are trying to mislead them, they may think you have something to hide, and they'll usually look at your programs a lot closer to find out why.

3. Don't argue, philosophize, or rationalize. It's all right to disagree, but explain why—and be diplomatic. It's important to keep the focus on *what* is right, rather than *who* is right.

SOURCES OF ADDITIONAL INFORMATION

Air Force Recurring Periodical 90-1, *The Inspector General (TIG) Brief.*

Air Force Policy Directive 90-2, *Inspector General—The Inspection System.*

Air Force Instruction 90-201, *Inspector General Activities—The Inspection System.*

15

Promotion Systems

News travels fast when promotion time comes around. Sometimes it's good news:

"I got my promotion line number!"

"Congratulations!"

"The commander and first sergeant came around to give me my new set of stripes!"

"When's the party?"

Sometimes it's not so good:

"I got passed over again."

"It's the system, you know; it's just not fair."

"Bob's not saying very much; he must not have made it."

"The test asked questions about things I haven't even heard about in my career field."

Everyone wants to be promoted. There are many benefits, some big, some small. To many people promotion means a sense of self-satisfaction and achievements. To others it can mean increased opportunity or responsibility. And, of course, it also means extra dollars and cents, which can always be put to good use.

USAF PROMOTION POLICY

Promotions are conducted every year, based on the need to fill USAF requirements for specific grades within the ceilings. Promotions fill "grade vacancies" caused by changes in the status of other airmen, for reasons such as discharges, separations, retirements, demotions, deaths, and alterations to the annual grade ceilings. Promotions to the grades of senior airman through chief master sergeant are affected each fiscal year by monetary and statutory constraints. By law, the top two enlisted grades for chief master sergeant and senior master sergeant are limited to 1 and 2 percent, respectively, of the total number authorized for the enlisted force. Promotions to airman and airman first class are not limited by grade ceilings; personnel are promoted when they meet basic eligibility requirements.

With grade ceilings in mind, the Air Force determines how many airmen can be promoted each fiscal year. Then it's a matter of selecting those who have demonstrated outstanding performance and potential for handling increased responsibility. The selection process differs by grade. Selection for promotion to airman, airman first class, and senior airman is done on a fully qualified basis (completion of time-in-service or time-in-grade requirements, completion of training requirements, and recommendation by the airman's unit commander). Competition for promotion to staff sergeant, technical sergeant, and master sergeant falls under two different programs: the Weighted Airman Promotion System (WAPS) and the Stripes for Exceptional Performers (STEP) program. The promotion system for the top two enlisted grades, senior master sergeant and chief master sergeant, has two phases; the first is a review of weighted factors similar to the WAPS program, and the second is a score awarded by a central evaluation board at the Air Force Manpower Personnel Center after a review of the candidate's promotion folder.

PROMOTION TO AIRMAN AND AIRMAN FIRST CLASS
Air Force members are promoted to airman (Amn) and airman first class (A1C) on a noncompetitive basis as long as they are eligible, fully qualified, and recommended by their unit commander. As a general rule, an airman basic (AB) must have six months' time-in-grade (TIG) and time-in-service (TIS) to be eligible for promotion to airman. An airman must have ten months' time-in-grade to be eligible for promotion to airman first class. An exception occurs when a member's enlistment agreement guarantees a promotion to airman or airman first class; in this case the promotion becomes effective the day after graduation from basic military training.

PROMOTION TO SENIOR AIRMAN
Promotion to senior airman (SrA) depends on vacant positions caused by promotions, separations, discharges, and so on. AFMPC then computes the number of openings and establishes a promotion quota, then announces a date of rank (DOR) limit for all airmen first class. Those who meet the DOR cutoff are promoted on a fully qualified basis on the first day of the next month as long as they meet the following eligibility conditions: a 5 skill level (or a 3 level when no 5 level exists in their AFSC); either thirty-six months TIS and twenty months TIG or twenty-eight months TIG, whichever occurs first; and recommendation by the promotion authority.

An airman first class can also compete for early advancement to senior airman under the Below-the-Zone (BTZ) Promotion Program. This opportunity comes only once, usually six months before normal promotion time. To compete for a BTZ promotion, airmen must first meet all the eligibility criteria for normal promotion. They compete with other nominees in either a unit (if the unit has a large number of nominees) or a central base selection board (for smaller units with fewer numbers of nominees). In selecting those for BTZ promotion, commanders and board members will consider recommendations from supervisors, past performance reports, and supplementary data.

The emphasis will be on promoting top-quality personnel who have clearly demonstrated potential for assuming increased grade and responsibility. If the selection boards feel the quality is not there, they are not required to promote those nominated just to meet the full quota. In some cases, nominees are required to personally meet a formal selection board similar to that described in chapter 13, "Awards, Decorations, and Recognition Programs." This process is preferred by many selection board members because it permits personal observation and avoids the promoting of personnel sight unseen.

PROMOTIONS TO THE GRADES OF STAFF SERGEANT THROUGH MASTER SERGEANT

Airmen are promoted to the grades of staff sergeant (SSgt) through master sergeant (MSgt) under one of two programs: the Weighted Airman Promotion System (WAPS) or the Stripes for Exceptional Performers (STEP) program. Both programs evolved out of the need for an equitable, objective, and readily understood promotion system that provides feedback to those concerned. Minor criticisms of each system do circulate (usually by those who have not been selected for promotion), but the consensus is that they are vast improvements over the system that existed before 1970. In the old system, all those eligible for promotion had their promotion folders hand-carried en masse by a personnel specialist to their major command headquarters, where they were reviewed by a selection board. Promotion decisions were made, stripes were allocated, and back at the home base, everyone was told either yes or no, but never why.

Today's system tells everyone why. In the WAPS program, each eligible person receives a scorecard explaining how they fared in each weighted area. In the STEP program, only a very small number of nominees are selected for promotion. The authority to grant these stripes is restricted to senior Air Force officers who command large organizations. They base their decisions on recommendations forwarded through the chain of command. In every case those nominated must have clearly demonstrated that their performance was consistently outstanding and of a magnitude warranting immediate promotion to the next highest grade.

THE WEIGHTED AIRMAN PROMOTION SYSTEM (WAPS)

WAPS is the primary program used to select airmen for promotion to the grades of staff sergeant, technical sergeant, and master sergeant. The system gives credit and scores to six weighted factors:

TIS AND TIG REQUIREMENTS, PROMOTION ELIGIBILITY CUTOFF DATES, AND TEST CYCLES FOR PROMOTION TO AMN THROUGH CMSGT

	A	B	C	D	E
L I N E	**Grade**	**TIS**	**TIG**	**PECD**	**Test Cycle**
1	Amn	—	6 months	NA	NA
2	A1C	—	10 months	NA	NA
3	SrA	36 months	20 months or 28 months	NA	NA
4	SSgt	3 years	6 months	31 Mar	Apr–Jun
5	TSgt	5 years	23 months	31 Dec	Jan–Mar
6	MSgt	8 years	24 months	31 Dec	Jan–Mar
7	SMSgt	11 years	20 months	30 Sep	Oct
8	CMSgt	14 years	21 months	31 Jul	Aug

1. A Specialty Knowledge Test (SKT) for the career field.
2. A Promotion Fitness Examination (PFE), which tests general Air Force knowledge.
3. Credit for time-in-service (TIS).
4. Credit for time-in-grade (TIG).
5. Credit for decorations awarded.
6. A numerical score for the average ratings received on performance reports.

Analysis of these six weighted factors helps in selecting the airmen who have demonstrated potential for increased responsibility, consistent with grade ceilings and budget limitations.

The number of promotions to any grade is based on the total Air Force vacancies in that grade. You will compete for worldwide vacancies with all other airmen who have the same grade and Control Air Force Specialty Code (CAFSC). This ensures equitable consideration by career field, since each career field receives the same percentage promotion quota. For example, if 10 percent of all airmen can be promoted to the next higher grade, then at least 10 percent of the airmen eligible in every CAFSC will be promoted. If two thousand security police airmen are eligible and the promotion rate is 10 percent, then two hundred will be promoted. If it is a smaller career field of only one hundred eligible airmen (like radiologists from medical facilities), then ten airmen will be promoted.

Once the Air Force determines how many will be promoted in each career field, a promotion cutoff score is set. This is determined by the score of the last

MINIMUM ELIGIBILITY REQUIREMENTS FOR PROMOTION (NOTE 1)

	A	B	C	D	E	F
R U L E	If promotion is to the grade of (note 2)	and the PAFSC as of PECD is at the	and time in current grade computed on the first day of the month before the promotions are normally made in the cycle is	and the TAFMS on the first day of the last month of the promotion cycle is (note 3)	and the member has	then
1	SrA	3 level (note 4)	not applicable	1 year		the airman is eligible for promotion if recommended, in writing, by the promotion authority. He or she must serve on active duty in enlisted status as of the PECD, serve in continuous active duty until the effective date of promotion, and not in a condition listed in AFI 36-2502, table 1.1, *Determining Ineligibility for Promotion*, on or after the PECD. The individual must be in Promotion Eligibility Status (PES) code X on effective date of promotion (note 6)
2	SSgt	5 level (note 4)	6 months	3 years		
3	TSgt	7 level (note 4)	23 months effective Cycle 95A6	5 years		
4	MSgt	7 level	24 months	8 years		
5	SMSgt	7 level (note 4)	20 months	11 years	has 8 yrs cumulative enlisted service (TEMSD) creditable for basic pay (note 5)	
6	CMSgt	9 level (note 4)	21 months	14 years	has 10 yrs cumulative enlisted service (TEMSD) creditable for basic pay (note 5)	

NOTES:

1. Use this table to determine standard minimum eligibility requirements for promotion consideration. HQ USAF may announce additional eligibility requirements. The individual must serve on enlisted active duty and have continuous active duty as of promotion eligibility cut-off date (PECD).

2. The high year of tenure policy applicable as of PECD may affect promotion eligibility in grades SrA and above.

3. Use years of satisfactory service for retirement in place of TAFMSD to determine promotion eligibility for Air National Guard and Air Force Reserve airmen ordered to active duty under a mobilization. Mobilized airmen are eligible for any cycle that has a PECD at least 60 calendar days after mobilization. For promotion to SrA an airman must serve on active duty at least 60 calendar days before the effective date promotion incrementing starts for that cycle.

4. Airmen must meet skill-level requirements by the effective date of promotion for SrA. Airmen must meet skill-level requirements by the PECD for SSgt. SSgts test and compete for promotion to TSgt if they have a 5 skill level as of PECD; however, they must have a 7 skill level before promotion. MSgts and SMSgts must meet minimum skill-level requirements listed above. In some cases, commanders may waive this to allow them to compete for promotion.

5. Service in a commissioned, warrant, or flight officer status is creditable for pay. Such service does not count for this requirement (38 Comptroller General 598). You may consider a promotion for airmen who meet this requirement on the first day of the last month promotions are normally made in the cycle. Actual promotion does not occur earlier than the first day of the month following the month the airman completes the required enlisted service. This applies if the selectee had a sequence number in an earlier promotion increment; however, if the airman meets the required enlisted service on the first day of the month, the DOR and effective date is that date.

6. If a TDY student meets the requirements of this table but does not maintain satisfactory proficiency, the MPF that services the airman's TDY unit tells the MPF servicing the airman's unit of assignment.

promotee; for example, if two hundred security police personnel are selected for promotion, the top two hundred with the highest scores will be promoted and the score of the airman who placed two hundredth amongst the selectees will be used as a cutoff. In case of tie scores, everyone with the same cut-off score will be promoted, even if it means promoting slightly more than the selection percentage. When the promotion list is released, everyone (selectees and nonselectees) gets a score notice that explains strong and weak areas and relative standings (for example: total number eligible in your AFSC, two thousand; your standing among other selectees, two hundred).

How Will You Measure Up? The best way to start preparing for a WAPS testing cycle is to compute the weighted factors that you already know—your time-in-service (TIS), time-in-grade (TIG), decorations, and performance reports. Then you need to get the promotion cutoff score used for your AFSC's last promotion cycle. It can be obtained from one of your contemporaries who tested during the last cycle or from the promotion and testing branch of your Military Personnel Flight (MPF). Subtracting the four factors you already know from the cutoff score will give you the approximate total score you will need on your SKT and PFE tests. Divide this number by two, and you'll know approximately what scores to aim for on each test. Remember that promotion cutoff scores will change slightly from cycle to cycle, so the figures will not be absolute, but they will be close enough for now. Fill in the accompanying computation sheet to see how you stand.

WEIGHTED AIRMAN PROMOTION SYSTEM (WAPS) POINTS COMPUTATION SHEET

	Maximum points obtainable	Your projected score
Specialty Knowledge Test (SKT) score	100	_____
Promotion Fitness Examination (PFE) score	100	_____
Time-in-service (TIS) score (see note 1)	40	_____
Time-in-grade (TIG) score (see note 2)	60	_____
Decorations score (see note 3)	25	_____
Performance report score (see note 4)	135	_____
Maximum total score	460	_____

Note 1: Two points are awarded for each year of total active federal military service (TAFMS) up to twenty years. Your points are computed up to the last day of the promotion cycle. One-sixth of a point is credited for each month; fifteen days or more is counted as a month, fourteen days or less is not counted.

Note 2: One-half of a point is awarded for each month you have held your current grade, not to exceed ten years. Compute your score up to the first day of the last month of the promotion cycle. Fifteen days or more is counted as a month, fourteen days or less is not counted.

Note 3: Specific point values are assigned based on the decoration's order of precedence, as follows: fifteen points: Medal of Honor; eleven points: Air Force Cross, Navy Cross, and Distinguished Service Cross; nine points: Defense Distinguished Service Medal, Distinguished Service Medal, and Silver Star; seven points: Legion of Merit, Defense Superior Service Medal, and Distinguished Flying Cross; five points: Airman's Medal, Soldier's Medal, Navy-Marine Corps Medal, Coast Guard Medal, Bronze Star Medal, Defense Meritorious Service Medal, Meritorious Service Medal, and Purple Heart; three points: Air Medal, Air Force Commendation Medal, Army Commendation Medal, Navy Commendation Medal, Joint Service Commendation Medal, and Coast Guard Commendation Medal; one point: Navy Achievement Medal, Coast Guard Achievement Medal, and Air Force Achievement Medal.

Note 4: Due to the introduction of the new Enlisted Performance Report (EPR), the procedure for computing performance reports points under the WAPS program has changed. Computations are now based on a time-weighting system that places more emphasis on recent duty performance. Scores are based on performance reports that have closed out within five years preceding the promotion eligibility cutoff date (PECD). Not more than ten of the most recent reports may be used. The overall evaluation for each performance report is multiplied by one of ten time-weighting factors (the most recent report has a factor of 50, the second most recent report has a factor of 45, and so forth in descending order in increments of five points per report). The subtotal for each report is then multiplied by an EPR multiplier of 27 or an APR multiplier of 15. That product, in turn, results in an EPR or APR performance value. These performance values are added together and then divided by the total number of time weighting factors. The answer is the performance score. The highest attainable score is 135.

Computing Your Performance Report Score. The following is an example for a servicemember who had five performance reports considered.

EPR/APR Ratings (most recent first)	X	Time-Weighting Factor	=	Subtotal	X	EPR/APR Multiplier (EPR = 27) (APR = 15)	=	EPR/APR Performance Value
4 (EPR)	X	50	=	200	X	27	=	5,400
4 (EPR)	X	45	=	180	X	27	=	4,860
9 (APR)	X	40	=	360	X	15	=	5,400
9 (APR)	X	35	=	315	X	15	=	4,725
8 (APR)	X	30	=	240	X	15	=	3,600
—	X	25						
—	X	20						
—	X	15						
—	X	10						
—	X	5						
		200 *						23,985

(*Total only the time-weighting factors for the number of reports used.)

The total sum of performance values (23,985) divided by the total time weighting factors (200) equals a performance score of 119.91.

To compute your performance report score for WAPS, fill in the blanks on the following format.

EPR/APR Ratings (most recent first)	x	Time-Weighting Factor	=	Subtotal	x	EPR/APR Multiplier (EPR = 27) (APR = 15)	=	EPR/APR Performance Value
_____	x	50	=	_____	x	_____	=	_____
_____	x	45	=	_____	x	_____	=	_____
_____	x	40	=	_____	x	_____	=	_____
_____	x	35	=	_____	x	_____	=	_____
_____	x	30	=	_____	x	_____	=	_____
_____	x	25	=	_____	x	_____	=	_____
_____	x	20	=	_____	x	_____	=	_____
_____	x	15	=	_____	x	_____	=	_____
_____	x	10	=	_____	x	_____	=	_____
_____	x	5	=	_____	x	_____	=	_____
		_____						_____

The total sum of performance values (_____) divided by the total time weighting factors (_____) equals your WAPS performance score of _____.

Analyzing a Sample WAPS Computation Sheet. Let's imagine that SrA Jim E. Bent is getting ready to test for staff sergeant under the WAPS program. Jim would start listing the data he knows.

Time-in-service (TIS) score:
(7 years = 84 months x $\frac{1}{6}$ point per month)   14.00 points
Time-in-grade (TIG) score:
(3 years and 6 months = 42 months x $\frac{1}{2}$ point per month)   21.00
Decorations score:
(One Air Force Achievement Medal = 1 point)   1.00
Performance score:
(4–EPR, 4–EPR, 9–APR, 9–APR, 8–APR)   119.92

Jim's total score without the SKT and PFE: 155.92 points

Jim's next step is to find out the cutoff selection score for promotion to staff sergeant in his career field during the last promotion cycle. He reviews his shopmate's score notice and finds that the promotion cutoff was 297.50.

Now Jim subtracts his raw score of 155.92 from 297.50. This leaves 141.58, the approximate total score that Jim must try to achieve for his SKT and PFE tests together. Carrying this one step further, Jim can divide 141.58 by two tests and see that he needs to score at least a 70.79 on each. He can also see that if he gets a maximum score of 100 on one test, he will need a 41.58 score on the other.

Preparing for Your WAPS Test. As you prepare to take your WAPS test, there are six areas you need to concentrate your efforts on:

1. Know the criteria; learn how the WAPS program works and what will be covered on your PFE and SKT tests. The best way to start is to review Air Force Pamphlet 39-8, *Weighted Airman Promotion System (WAPS) Study Reference List,* which identifies the latest study references for every Specialty Knowledge Test (SKT). With it, you can quickly identify the Career Development Course (CDC), directives, and technical orders used to write your SKT. You can also eliminate items that will not appear on the test. The Promotion Fitness Examination (PFE) test is largely derived from Air Force Pamphlet 36-2241, Volume 1, *Promotion Fitness Examination Study Guide.*

2. Set up a study schedule. Have a specific time and place to study. Consider temperature, ventilation, lighting, table, desk, and chair; be organized; have all your study materials ready. Avoid distractions: TV, radio, stereo, and other interruptions such as people and pets.

Break the information down into smaller units; it will be easier to study. Establish a timetable based on your test date. Preparing properly usually takes a minimum of three months. You will need enough time to read all the material and plan an overall review. Allow at least one day to read each of the twenty chapters in the PFE study guide and each chapter in the CDCs. After this, you should allow at least two weeks for an overall review. Review the important areas, consolidate your notes, and get assistance for subjects that you do not fully understand. The week before you take the test should be a time to relax and program your memory. If you are still doing some of the initial reading during this final week, it's probably too late to score high.

3. Develop good reading habits. You have to be able to read for understanding. Moving your eyes over a written page is looking, not reading. Looking at the pages of a CDC book but thinking of something else won't raise your scores on the next test.

Skimming the content of a chapter before you read can be useful. It lets you know what to expect and keys you into interrelationships of ideas. As you read, look for facts (descriptions, events, systems, people) and work to integrate these facts into concepts, principles, and ideas. Remember, you won't be able to integrate concepts if you missed some of the facts. If you're not able to explain a concept in your own words, it may be a sign that you don't fully understand it.

Monitor what your read. Get into the habit of catching your mind as soon as it wanders off the material. Did you ever get to the bottom of a page, realize your mind was on something else, and say to yourself, "I don't remember a thing I read"? In cases like this, if you go on to the next page you're doing yourself a disservice. If you can't get into it, stop. There will be times when you are fatigued or preoccupied, and attempting to study further seems impossible. Take a break. But if you find yourself taking too many breaks or not sticking to your study schedule, ask yourself a very basic question: "Do I really want to get promoted this time?"

4. Designate what's important and program your memory. Plan for two levels: memorizing (the ability to recall facts) and understanding (grasping the meaning without necessarily recalling exact facts and definitions).

Recognize that memory is limited. Start programming your memory when you first start to study. Avoid cramming; don't go over material too quickly. If your mind isn't organized as the material goes in, it won't be organized when the material comes out (for the test). Form mental images to help remember key facts. Use key words or phrases, such as ROB—red, orange, blue—for parts of components or electrical wiring. Use numbers in larger units; 7642 may be easier to commit to memory as 76-42 than as 7-6-4-2).

Designate what's important during your reading by underlining or highlighting significant material. It's quick, easy to do, and will help reduce the amount of material to be restudied. Do it after you understand the passage you've read. Oftentimes key words or key phrases in a sentence will suffice. Don't overdo it; 20 to 50 percent is enough. Remember, you're trying to designate what's important. After you've read everything for the first time, go back and review the items you've underlined or highlighted. Identify what you know is of primary importance or requires more attention for concepts you may not fully understand with notes in margins, asterisks, and so on.

As a final step, take notes to reduce the amount of material to study for your final review. Use a spiral notebook (loose pages tend to get lost). Keep your notes simple, not more than a page per chapter, and only key words and phrases. These notes will be your key study material as you get closer to your test date.

5. Don't worry! Anxiety is basically a response to a perceived threat. The key to doing well is to know the material; "overlearn" it beyond the point at which you first feel you have mastered it. Before your testing date, do practice tests and volume review exercises (VREs), and study questions within your career development courses (CDCs) that come after each study module (001, 002, and so on). The night before the test, go over your review notes. Then hit the sack at the regular time. You've gone through a lot of careful preparation over the past few months. Get a good night's sleep so you will be rested and alert during the test.

6. Taking the test: First and foremost, make sure you are present to take the test at the time and date you've been scheduled for. If you are not, you could be identified as a "no-show" and rendered ineligible for consideration during the promotion cycle.

When you go in to take the test, it's normal to be a bit apprehensive and nervous. Forget about the other people in the room; relax and concentrate on the test. After all, you haven't crammed; you've studied and you know the material. Carefully follow the test officer's instructions. Resist the temptation to rush, but don't waste time.

Always read the full question carefully; look for the main point, principle, or theme. Look for the subject of the question and the basis for the decision (best, most, least). Then read all the answers. Several of the answers may sound partially right. You're looking for the *most correct* one. Watch out for key words like *succeeded, successor, preceded, predecessor* (what comes after or what comes before). Look for negatives (which of the following *never*) and positives (which of the following *always*). If you're having difficulty with a question, eliminate answers you know are wrong or reverse the question. "When is an NCO not in compliance with dress and appearance standards" can be changed to "When is an NCO always in compliance with dress and appearance standards?" Rearranging a question may help your memory jog the answer by thinking about it from a different perspective. Reduce the number of possible answers by working the answers backward. Find the worst answer and eliminate it; try to find the better of two answers, not the best of four.

Your first impression is usually your best bet. If you're unsure about your answer, avoid changing it. Ask NCO Academy graduates about their tests; ask how many of their answers would have been correct had they not changed their first impressions. If you cannot solve a question after a reasonable length of time, eliminate responses you know are wrong, mark an answer, and don't waste any more time. In advance, select one column for all guesses, such as column C. Don't vary; you'll get some right every test. If you wander about in your guessing, it's doubtful that you'll get many right.

During the test, constantly compare question numbers with answer numbers. You don't want to get out of sequence and transfer your answers to the incorrect space. When you finish the test, check to see that all the questions on the answer sheet have been marked. Random check a few to ensure they were answered in the correct sequence (question 74, answer sheet 74).

7. After you've completed the test, you can hand in your materials, breathe a sigh of relief, and depart. When you return to your duty section, do not discuss the content of either test. That is prohibited by regulation and could require an investigation for test compromise. It could also affect your selection because your contemporaries in your duty section may not have tested yet and they are some of your competition for the same stripes.

In summary, the WAPS is a very good program in many ways. The selection criteria are known to all concerned. The scoresheet provides feedback and lets you know which areas require improvement. Also, the testing process requires study. This has an added benefit of enhancing your knowledge of the Air Force and your proficiency in your career field. Each of these tests was written by a select group of senior noncommissioned officers drawn from the major commands and from almost every career field in the USAF.

The primary emphasis in this chapter has been on testing, since these results make up almost half the total WAPS score. Doing well on the tests is the prime factor in getting promoted rapidly. Those who do not study must wait for points to accrue in other areas, primarily time-in-service (two points a year) and time-in-grade (six points a year). That could delay promotions by several years.

THE STRIPES FOR EXCEPTIONAL PERFORMERS (STEP) PROGRAM

STEP is much smaller in scope than the WAPS program. It was established as a means to provide immediate on-the-spot promotion to the grades of staff sergeant, technical sergeant, and master sergeant. It allows major command commanders, commanders of separate operating agencies (SOAs), and senior Air Force officers in organizations with large enlisted populations to promote those whose performance has clearly been exceptional and of a magnitude that warrants immediate advancement to a position of increased grade and responsibility.

STEP promotions are made once or twice each year. Numerical quotas are allocated to each agency that has been delegated STEP selection authority by HQ USAF. These agencies establish their own selection criteria. In general, selections are based on a review of a recommendation from the nominee's supervisor or commander and the nominee's last five performance reports.

To be eligible for consideration, nominees must meet the following time-in-service requirements: for promotion to staff sergeant, three years; to technical sergeant, five years; to master sergeant, eight years. There are no time-in-grade requirements; however, the military member concerned can receive only one promotion under any promotion program within a twelve-month period.

PROMOTION TO SENIOR MASTER SERGEANT AND CHIEF MASTER SERGEANT

Promotion to the top two enlisted grades is very competitive; your performance over many years will be considered. It's a two-phase process. Phase 1 consists of a weighted score, computed like the WAPS score. The total score possible is 360 points. The six individual factors considered and the maximum scores for each are as follows:

1. The USAF Supervisory Examination (USAFSE): 100 points (based on the percent of correct answers).

2. Performance report score: 135 points (computed the same way as under the WAPS program).

3. Professional Military Education (PME): 15 points for the Command NCO Academy; the method of completion, whether in-residence or by correspondence, has no bearing on the point value. (*Note:* Beginning with the CMSgt 90S9 promotion cycle, the 20 points for the Senior NCO Academy have been deleted for both CMSgt and SMSgt promotions. The Senior NCO Academy will reflect on your selection brief, and the Central Selection Board will consider it.)

4. Decorations score: 25 points (based on the decoration's order of precedence, the same way as under the WAPS program).

5. Time-in-grade (TIG) score: 60 points (computed as one-half point for each month in current grade, based on the individual's date of rank, up to a period of 10 years, computed as of the first day of the last month of the promotion cycle).

6. Time-in-service (TIS) score: 25 points (based on one-twelfth point for each month of total active federal military service (TAFMS), up to 25 years, computed as of the last day of the promotion cycle).

Phase 2 is conducted by a Central Promotion Evaluation Board (CPEB) at the Air Force Personnel Center (AFPC). It entails scoring each member's promotion selection folder using the whole-person concept, which considers the member's performance over a period of years. The factors evaluated are duty performance, level of responsibility, breadth of experience, leadership, professional competence, awards and decorations, and education. The results of the Phase 1 board score (the weighted factors) are not reviewed as part of the Phase 2 evaluation.

All the airmen competing for promotion in a single Air Force Specialty Code (AFSC) or Special Duty Identifier (SDI) are considered by the same panel, which consists of two colonels and one chief master sergeant. Each member of the panel reviews every selection folder and evaluates each candidate's potential for increased grade and responsibility. Individually, they assign a numerical score using a rating scale of 6 through 10 in half-point increments. The three scores are added together and multiplied by 15, and the result is the candidate's Phase 2 board score. The highest possible board score for this phase is 450 points.

The final selection is based on the combined scores for Phase 1 and Phase 2 (the maximum number of points obtainable is 810). Candidates are rank-ordered in order of merit within each career field, and a promotion cutoff score is set based on the allocation quota. Candidates with the highest number of points are selected for promotion. As in the WAPS program, all airmen with a tie score at the cutoff point are selected for promotion.

After the promotion list is released, all master sergeants and senior master sergeants who were considered will receive a senior NCO promotion score notice showing their promotion status, points for weighted factors, total weighted score, board score, relative standing, and groupings by board scores of selectees and nonselectees. If errors are detected on the score notice, supplemental consideration may be requested.

ONE FINAL NOTE

Traditionally, the airmen who have obtained timely promotions have a record of outstanding performance and have made the effort to research requirements, ask questions, and seek out answers *before* the promotion cycle.

SOURCES OF ADDITIONAL INFORMATION

Air Force Instruction 36-2502, *Airman Promotion Program.*

Consult the promotion monitor in your unit orderly room or personnel representatives from the Promotion and Testing Branch of your Military Personnel Flight (MPF).

16

How to Get the "Right" Assignments

The word *assignments* is close to the hearts of almost everyone in the U.S. Air Force. Sometimes it brings smiles, sometimes frowns. It refers to the location (an Air Force base or station) and organization (wing, group, squadron, special activity) where you will live and perform your duties. To get the assignments you're interested in, it helps to understand how the system works.

After you've received your initial training in your designated career field, you will be awarded a skill level in your Air Force Specialty (AFS). Your assignment will then be determined based on the number of people in your specialty, by rank and skill level, needed to meet mission requirements at each base or operating location. That number is based on the assigned strengths (how many airmen are required to perform the mission). If there is a shortage of personnel, the assignments system identifies a vacancy and names an airman to fill that vacancy. When an airman is permanently assigned (or reassigned) to a new location, that is referred to as a permanent change of station (PCS) move.

The Air Force Personnel Center (AFPC) at Randolph AFB, Texas, is the agency responsible for determining PCS assignments. The major commands (MAJCOMs) can also initiate some types of assignments, with the review and approval of the AFPC. Computer programs help identify personnel to fill positions for assignments to and from overseas and from technical training schools. The balance of requirements are usually processed manually as requirements become known.

Many considerations are taken into account when an airman is selected for an assignment: an airman's status (volunteer or nonvolunteer), retainability (how much time remains on the term of enlistment), eligibility requirements, and past assignment history. Individual preferences are weighed against the mission requirements of the Air Force. Moving costs are scrutinized with a view toward meeting the manning needs of each organization in the most cost-effective manner. Humanitarian requests—to help a military member alleviate a serious personal problem or hardship—are reviewed on a case-by-case basis. Equal opportunity is also of prime concern. Air Force assignments are made without regard to color, race, religion, national origin, ethnic background, age, or sex, except where limitations are set by law, living facilities, or physical capabilities.

FORECASTING FOR YOUR ASSIGNMENTS

The Military Personnel Flight (MPF) is the focal point at base level for all assignment actions. Within the MPF, two offices can help you with questions concerning assignments. The customer service branch helps with general inquiries, and the assignments branch deals more with specific issues and provides personal counseling when required.

The key to your assignment future is Air Force Form 392, "Airman Assignment Preference Statement." It's used by all airmen, airman basic through senior master sergeant, to list their preferences for U.S., overseas, and AFPC-Controlled Special Duty Assignments. From this form, the places you would like to go are put into the Air Force personnel computer. Afterward, it's kept in your official personnel records until you change your preferences by completing another AF Form 392. The computer is used to match persons with places. So it's very important that you carefully review all your options and be as specific as possible when filling out this form.

Every new airman is required to fill out an AF Form 392 during basic military training. After that, you can change your assignment preferences or volunteer for overseas duty at almost any time. For the most part, the opportunity will be brought to your attention by the personnel specialists during annual record reviews, on arrival at a new duty station, or during overseas returnee counseling.

As you can see from the accompanying illustration, there are five major sections to the form. Filling out the form in the most advantageous way will help you get where you want to go—or close to it.

The introductory information is self-explanatory: name, grade, Social Security account number, organization, and duty telephone.

Section 1 is for listing your overseas preferences. If you do not wish to be an overseas volunteer, enter "none" in the first preference block. This is not your best option. By entering "none" you are telling the personnel system that you are a nonvolunteer for every overseas assignment (because you haven't listed any specific country that you have a preference for). If their list of volunteers has been exhausted, they will turn to the list of eligible people who are nonvolunteers. Bottom line: If you are eligible for an overseas assignment you can be sent almost anywhere, even if you did enter "none."

You can use all eight blocks listing individual countries or worldwide preferences. This is a good option if there are eight countries that you really want to be assigned to. But one very important point to remember is that the eight blocks do not represent first, second, and third choice; all preferences are considered equally for assignment purposes, in no specific order.

AIRMAN ASSIGNMENT PREFERENCE STATEMENT

AUTHORITY: 10 USC 8012; 44 USC 3101; and EO 9397.
PRINCIPAL PURPOSES: Allows airman to indicate geographic preferences for CONUS assignment, volunteer status for oversea duty, homebasing/follow-on volunteer status for special duty volunteer status.
ROUTINE USES: Used as a source document for data entered into the Advanced Personnel Data System. Data used in assignment selection at MAJCOMs and AFMPC. The SSAN is used for identification.
DISCLOSURE IS VOLUNTARY: If the information is not provided, assignment selections are made without regard to member's preferences.

I.

NAME *(Last, First, Middle Initial)*	GRADE	SSAN	ORGANIZATION	DUTY TELEPHONE
MARSHALL, JOHN, V.	SrA	000-00-0000	000 Headquarters Squadron	EXT: 1234

OVERSEA PREFERENCE

Enter up to eight country, or "worldwide" preferences in any combination. Enter separate status code from the list at right for each preference. If you do not wish to be an oversea volunteer, enter "none" in 1st preference block. See Note 1 on reverse.

OVERSEA VOLUNTEER STATUS CODES
A - COT to Long *(standard tour)*
B - COT to Long *(extended tour)*
C - COT to Short *(standard tour)*
N - Non-CONUS Resident to Home Area

1 - CONUS to Long *(standard tour)*
2 - CONUS to Long *(extended tour)*
3 - CONUS to Short *(standard tour)*

	1ST	2ND	3RD	4TH	5TH	6TH	7TH	8TH
COUNTRY	SPAIN	ENGLAND	ITALY	JAPAN	KOREA	PHILIP-PINES	AZORES	HAWAII
VOLUNTEER STATUS	2	1	1	1	3	1	1	N

II.

CONUS PREFERENCE

Enter up to eight bases, locales, states, or areas in any combination. If you have no preference, enter "None" in 1st preference block. See Note 2.

	1ST	2ND	3RD	4TH	5TH	6TH	7TH	8TH
BASE/LOCALE/STATE/AREA	Base BP	Base BT	Base CD	Base CN	State (CA) Code: 06	State (NV) Code: 32	Locale M6	Area 5

III.

AFPC-CONTROLLED SPECIAL DUTY ASSIGNMENT VOLUNTEER STATUS

If you wish to volunteer for an AFMPC-Controlled Special Duty Assignment, indicate the specific type of duty and up to three geographical preferences *(Oversea country, CONUS state, or "World-wide".)* Otherwise enter "None" in Type Duty block. See Note 3.

TYPE DUTY	GEOGRAPHICAL PREFERENCES		
	1ST	2ND	3RD
POSTAL SPECIALIST	SPAIN	ENGLAND	ITALY

IV.

CERTIFICATION

I have read and understand the applicable items on the front and back of this form. I am a volunteer for any oversea location listed in Section I and/or duty listed in Section III.

DATE	SIGNATURE OF AIRMAN	CBPO USE ONLY	
15 SEP 1988		DATE OF BLMPS UPDATE	INITIALS

V.

COMMANDER'S CERTIFICATION

(To be completed for members who volunteer for AFMPC-Controlled Special Duty Assignments)

I have personally interviewed the applicant for the type of assignment for which he or she has applied, considering his or her judgement, emotional stability, moral character financial encumbrances, and other pertinent information.

☒ RECOMMENDED
☐ NOT RECOMMENDED *(Justify and return to individual)*

DATE	SIGNATURE OF COMMANDER
1 OCT 1996	*James A. Doe*, Lt Colonel, USAF

AF FORM 392
OCT 82
PREVIOUS EDITION WILL BE USED.

GPO : 1986 O - 499-341

Air Force Form 392, Airman Assignment Preference Statement

Under each country you should put an overseas status code; codes help determine your position on the waiting list for each country. Codes 1, 2, and 3 are for people who want to go from the continental United States (CONUS) to an overseas tour (*long* or *short* refers to the length of a tour; long is eighteen months or more, short is less than eighteen months). Codes A, B, and C are for people who are presently overseas and would like to be assigned to another base overseas. This is known as a request for a consecutive overseas tour (COT). Code N may only be used by non-CONUS residents applying for assignment to their home of record. A non-CONUS resident is an airman whose official home of record is Alaska, Hawaii, the territories of the Virgin Islands, Guam, American Samoa, Trust Territory of the Pacific Islands, the Commonwealth of Puerto Rico, and the Canal Zone (for those who enlisted prior to 1 October 1979).

Or you can list only a few specific countries that you want to be assigned to and list your volunteer status codes under each preference. For example, you might put England in block 1, Germany in block 2, and then put "none" in blocks 3 through 8. This is a good option if you want to list a few countries but not overvolunteer.

In Section 2 you list your CONUS preferences. You can list codes for up to eight bases, locales, states, or areas. The codes are listed in Air Force Instruction 36-2110.

Base and *state* are self-explanatory. A *locale* is defined as a grouping of major installations and bases in the same general area. For example, the southern California locale is Locale Code M6. The places you could be assigned to under that code include Edwards AFB, El Centro NAS, Hawes CCM, Los Angeles AFB, March AFB, Ontario CTY, and Vandenberg AFB, in California; and Hawthorne RBS, Indian Springs AAF, Lake Mead Base AIN, Las Vegas CTY, Nellis AFB, and Pittman ADM in Nevada (a total of thirteen locations). An *area* consists of several states in the same general region. For example, Area 5 includes all the major installations and bases in Arizona, California, Colorado, Nevada, New Mexico, and Utah.

When you list your CONUS preferences, there are two major points to remember. Your preferences will be considered in the order you list them. Also, it's best to list choices from each category rather than to select only eight specific bases. For example, if you wanted to go to specific bases in southern California it would be best to list the bases in blocks 1 through 4, the states of California and Nevada in blocks 5 and 6, the code M6 for the southern California locale in block 7, and the code for Area 5 in block 8. That way, you will be considered against the requirements at all the bases named and within that locale or area. It means you've multiplied your options. Instead of limiting yourself to eight specific bases, you've established your preferences (in a priority sequence) for approximately sixty locations in a geographical area of your choice.

Section 3 is to be completed if you wish to volunteer for an AFPC-Controlled Special Duty Assignment. More information about this is provided later in this chapter. If you are interested in this type of duty, you will be considered a volunteer to serve only at the overseas country listed.

Section 4 is for your certification: date and signature.

Section 5 is for your commander's certification if you have volunteered for an AFPC-Controlled Special Duty Assignment. He or she will either recommend or not recommend approval.

On a final note, there is one major consideration that you should always remember when filling out your AF Form 392. Think about your Air Force Specialty, and make sure the place you want to go to has openings for your career field. For example, an air traffic controller would not want to select a small Air Force station without a runway, a mental health technician would not want to select a small base whose hospital did not have a mental health clinic, and an aircraft maintenance specialist who works on the F-16 would not want to volunteer for an assignment to a remote communications site that doesn't have any assigned aircraft. Bottom line: Make the most of your form; put a valid preference in each block.

YOUR FIRST ASSIGNMENT

Assignments for airmen from basic military training school and technical training school are based on the preferences made on their AF Form 392 and the manning needs of the Air Force at the time of their projected graduation date. If airmen do not successfully complete training courses, they are evaluated to see if they should be allowed to remain in the USAF. Some are discharged. Others are allowed to apply for retraining, in which case up to six Air Force Specialty Code (AFSC) preferences that these airmen are qualified for are sent through personnel channels. If retraining is approved, the airmen are sent either to another technical training school or on a directed duty assignment (DDA) straight to their first base, where they are entered into on-the-job training (OJT).

The Pipeline Student Airman Swap Program was established to let airmen exchange assignments with each other. To do so, they must have the same AFSC, be projected graduates of the same course, and be of similar rank. Swap requests must be submitted to the personnel office not later than three workdays after you are first advised of your initial assignment. You will be advised if there are other general criteria that must be met. Overall it's a very good program, especially for two airmen who want to have each other's assignments.

TEMPORARY DUTY ASSIGNMENTS

Temporary duty assignments (TDY) can be scheduled after you've been assigned to your permanent base. They are used primarily when a member's presence is required at another location for training purposes, exercises, or manning assistance. The length of time can vary; it's usually 30 days or less but can be scheduled for up to 179 days if no training is involved. TDY is based on military necessity balanced with a view toward keeping costs, personnel moves, and family separation at minimum levels.

OVERSEAS ASSIGNMENTS

Overseas assignments can be scheduled at any time during your career after you complete your initial training. Airmen are selected for these tours based on grade and skill level within each Air Force specialty. A lot also depends on what the Air Force calls your "vulnerability" for an overseas tour, which takes into account your volunteer status and past overseas assignment history. From this information, they place each airman in a priority list to ensure the equitable distribution of assignments. Basically, your last overseas return date, number of overseas tours, and the amount of time you have been on your present base are looked at in determining who is the most eligible to fill an overseas tour requirement. Ideally, everyone will go on at least one overseas tour (long or short) before someone is selected involuntarily to go on a second overseas tour.

The types of tours vary. There are long tours, served with or without dependents, ranging from eighteen to forty-eight months. There are short tours, less than eighteen months, usually served without dependents. At some locations, you are given the option to stay longer. This is called a voluntary extension of overseas tour. In many cases, this can be beneficial to both you and the Air Force. Many families enjoy life overseas; it affords the opportunity to travel, save money, pursue educational goals, and enjoy family life at one location. It's advantageous to the Air Force because fewer PCS moves are required, so costs are lowered, and because of the increased continuity of operation in the overseas unit. Requests for extensions are reviewed on a case-by-case basis, and recommendations for approval or disapproval are made by the member's immediate commander.

There is a wide range of overseas locations you may be eligible to be assigned to. Some of the countries with large contingents of U.S. armed forces include the Azores (Portugal), Germany, Guam, Iceland, Italy, Japan, Korea, Okinawa (Japan), Panama, Turkey, and the United Kingdom.

To find out how to apply for overseas duty, see "Forecasting for Your Assignment," above.

SPECIAL DUTY ASSIGNMENTS

Special Duty Assignments (SDAs) are one of the Air Force's best-kept secrets. They're not really secrets, actually; it's just that thousands of positions are available, but their existence and the procedures for applying for them are not common knowledge.

Why would you apply for SDAs? For the prestige and challenge, perhaps. You'll have the opportunity to be a member of an organization with a well-known and highly visible mission. You'll also be able to work with other high-caliber personnel.

SDAs also offer enhanced promotion opportunity. Positions such as these indicate that a person is capable of increased responsibility in a position of special trust and confidence. SDAs also mean a controlled tour of duty. Most assignments are for a specific period of time (two, three, or four years, sometimes with an option to stay longer), which offers stability. Your future becomes much more predictable and you can plan for other commitments (family, education, purchasing a home). And of course, they provide the opportunity to travel extensively, especially overseas, where some of the assignments are in major cities like London, Tokyo, Rome, or Paris.

The following pages will give examples of some of the Special Duty Assignments available. Each position has a list of eligibility and ineligibility criteria, all of which may not be listed here. Our primary concern for now is to bring this information to your attention and to stimulate some interest. If you're interested in applying for a Special Duty Assignment, you should visit your Military Personnel Flight (MPF) and ask to speak to someone who works in either the customer service branch or the assignments branch. All the criteria for applying for these positions are located in Air Force Instruction 36-2110, *Assignments.*

General Information. In general, the Air Force has a number of special positions that require uniquely qualified personnel. Those selected must have outstanding records of performance, and there must be no unfavorable comments about their personal qualities (conduct, working relations, job knowledge, or personal appearance). In most cases, these positions are filled by volunteers. They are selected in one of two ways.

Some Special Duty Assignments are controlled directly by the responsible organization or major command (such as Air Combat Command, Air Education and Training Command, or Air Mobility Command), which can select applicants from their own bases or ask the Air Force Personnel Center (HQ AFPC) for assistance if they do not have enough applicants on file.

The other category is AFPC-Controlled Special Duty Assignments. If you volunteer for this kind of duty, you can indicate the type of duty you want and two preferences for the country or state you'd like to be assigned to. Consideration will be given to these two preferences, but ultimately, military requirements will determine the activity to which you will be assigned.

Major Command and Organization-Controlled Special Duty Assignments

1. Air Mobility Command (AMC) Flight and Ground School Enlisted Instructors:

C-141 or C-5 instructor duty at Altus AFB, Oklahoma

Helicopter or C-130 instructor duty at Kirtland AFB, New Mexico

C-130 instructor duty at Little Rock AFB, Arkansas

2. Air Education and Training Command (AETC) Technical Instructor for Medical Training.

3. Air Education and Training Command (AETC) Military Training Instruc-

tors (MTI) and Student Training Advisors (STA): Applicants for MTI duty are assigned only to the Basic Military Training School at Lackland AFB, Texas. Applicants for STA duty must be sergeants or above with over four years of service. They may request assignment to training centers at the following bases: Keesler AFB, Mississippi; Lackland ABF, Texas; and Sheppard AFB, Texas.

4. NCO Professional Military Education (PME) Instructor Duty: Airmen in any AFSC may apply.

5. Air Education and Training Command (AETC) Survival Training Instructor: Career airmen and nonprior-service airmen attending Basic Military Training are eligible regardless of AFSC.

6. Air Force Reserve Officer Training Corps (AFROTC): Those selected are assigned to U.S. colleges and universities. They counsel cadets on personal and administrative matters, prepare personnel records for newly commissioned officers, serve as assistants to instructors, and assist on field trips and various other cadet activities.

7. Recruiting Duty: Airmen in grades sergeant (with four or more years' TAFMS and career-committed) through master sergeant (with sixteen years' TAFMS or less) may apply regardless of their AFSC. Waivers for lower grades can be considered on an individual basis. Those selected are assigned to recruiting stations in cities throughout the United States.

8. USAF Honor Guard: Personnel assigned to the honor guard represent the Air Force at public ceremonies. They are inspected by the President of the United States and other high-ranking dignitaries while performing duties at the U.S. Capitol, the White House, the Pentagon, the Tomb of the Unknowns, and other official locations. Airmen in grades airman basic through senior master sergeant are eligible to apply. Selection criteria are very stringent.

9. USAF Air Demonstration Squadron (the Thunderbirds): Airmen in over twenty maintenance and support specialties are eligible to apply. F-16 experience is desirable but not mandatory.

10. Orientation Group, USAF: The Orientation group, USAF, is the official Air Force exhibit unit. Its personnel conceive, design, plan, construct, maintain, and present exhibits, displays, aircraft, and other visual aids depicting Air Force progress, activities, missions, and personnel to the public. Since they interact extensively with the public, airmen of the highest caliber and skills are needed. They are stationed out of Wright-Patterson AFB, Ohio, and usually spend a great deal of time on the road in temporary duty status for thirty-five to forty-five days at a time.

11. Air Force Office of Special Investigations (OSI): Airmen in grades senior airman through technical sergeant, regardless of AFSC, are eligible to apply for investigative duties. Personnel with a background in electronics are encouraged to apply for investigative duties with the Technical Services Division. Positions for noninvestigative duty are also available for some AFSCs at HQ AFOSI and at detachments throughout the world.

12. Medical Research Duty: Airmen, grades airman through chief master sergeant, in more than a dozen medical and support career fields may be eligible to apply for research positions at the USAF School of Aerospace Medicine, Brooks AFB, Texas, or at the 6570 Aerospace Medical Research Laboratory, Wright-Patterson AFB, Ohio.

13. Pararescue Duty: Applicants are selected for duty with the Aerospace Rescue and Recovery Service (ARRS) and must be physically qualified for aircrew duty, parachutist duty, and marine diving duties. Male airmen, airman basic through senior master sergeant, who are not older than thirty-one are eligible to apply, regardless of AFSC.

14. Aerospace Guidance and Metrology Center: Selected applicants are assigned to duty at Newark AFS, Ohio. Airmen in grades staff sergeant through chief master sergeant are eligible to apply if they are highly qualified precision measurement equipment laboratory (PMEL) technicians, if they have experience in quality control and calibration procedures, and if they possess a 7 skill level Primary Air Force Specialty Code (PAFSC) in the PMEL career fields.

15. Community College of the Air Force (CCAF): There are positions for program administrators, grades staff sergeant through senior master sergeant, in twenty-eight career fields. In these positions, selectees use the expertise gained in their Air Force Specialty to help develop and administer the CCAF degree programs related to their career field and to advise students on ways and means of completing their CCAF degree requirements. There are also staff support positions for airmen in grades senior airman through master sergeant. Those selected work in areas such as management information systems, public affairs, admissions and records, institutional research, resource management, and executive support.

16. Auditor Duty: Airmen, grades staff sergeant and technical sergeant, with less than fourteen years' active military service may apply. They must be serving on a second or later enlistment and possess one or more of the following prerequisites: a Certified Public Accountant Certificate; a minimum of twelve college semester hours in accounting and auditing subjects; or at least three years' experience in responsible accounting positions that required the application of the principles and theory of accounting.

17. Air Education and Training Command (AETC) Non-Resident Career Development Course (CDC) Writers: Career airmen, in grades of staff sergeant and above, in all Air Force specialties may apply. They must be highly qualified within their specialties and must also have excellent writing talent. Their job is to develop and write career development courses that will be used for training other USAF airmen.

Remember, there are sixty-nine MAJCOM and organization-controlled Special Duty Assignments; we've described only seventeen. For additional information, consult Air Force Instruction 36-2110; it's well worth a look. Bear in mind that as Air Force requirements change, these assignments will change. Some may be added, some discontinued. Requirements for Air Force specialties may also change; this is especially true as some career fields are combined and the numerical designations are changed.

AFPC-Controlled Special Duty Assignments

1. Air Force Missions (Latin America): Assignments are limited to airmen in grade staff sergeant (or selectee) and above. The airman, dependents, and close living relatives must be U.S. citizens.

2. U.S. Military Training Missions to Saudi Arabia: The airman must be a U.S. citizen. The airman and dependents must be temperamentally and socially adaptable for duty that requires daily contact with the forces of allied nations.

3. Allied Command Europe (SHAPE, NATO, and HQ EUCOM): Positions are in Belgium and Germany.

4. Defense Attaché Offices: Positions are primarily overseas in major cities and capitals. Selection criteria are very stringent. Of particular importance is the role of the family members (the important part they play in these assignments and their ability to conduct themselves in a way that creates a favorable impression of the United States, especially in their associations with foreign nationals). All applicants must be career airmen. Airmen in any AFSC are eligible to apply.

5. United Nations Command and U.S. Forces (Korea).

6. Pacific Command—Joint Services Headquarters (Hawaii).

7. Joint U.S. Military Groups (JUSMAG), Advisory and Training (Greece and Turkey).

8. Inter-American Air Force Academy (Panama): Applicant must be fluent in Spanish.

9. Air Staff Duty: Assignments are primarily in Washington, D.C., in positions at HQ USAF, the Office of the Secretary of Defense (OSD), the Joint Chiefs of Staff (JCS), and the Defense Communications Agency (DCA).

10. Air Force Inspection Agency: Assignments are at Kirtland AFB, New Mexico.

11. USAF Academy: Assignments are for permanent-party airmen in a wide range of support specialties.

12. Defense Intelligence Agency (DIA): Assignment locations vary.

13. Air Force Personnel Center (AFPC): Assignment location is Randolph AFB, Texas. Most positions are for personnel and support career fields.

14. White House Communications Agency (WHCA): The WHCA mission is to provide worldwide communications for the President of the United States at all times. Also included for support are the Vice President, the U.S. Secret Service, and others as designated by the President. Duty involves some of the most sophisticated communications-electronics equipment in existence, extensive travel throughout the world, and a six-year controlled tour in the Washington, D.C., area. Applicants are selected from communications and support career fields. Selection criteria and the subsequent screening process are very stringent.

15. Postal Specialist: Requirements exist at virtually all overseas locations. Airmen in any AFSC, grades airman first class through chief master sergeant, may apply.

For information on Special Duty Assignments not listed here, consult Air Force Instruction 36-2110. Again, bear in mind that these assignments are always subject to change consistent with Air Force mission requirements.

RECENT PROGRAM ADDITIONS TO THE ASSIGNMENT PROCESS

The following four programs have recently been added to enhance your say in what type of job and location you are assigned to. You can obtain more information about these programs from your Military Personnel Flight (MPF). If you have a question they cannot answer, they can send a message to your MAJCOM or HQ AFPC for a response. Up-to-date information and guidance are also distributed by way of your base newspaper, bulletin, and *Airman Magazine*. The *Air Force Times* publishes EQUAL listings on a recurring basis.

Enlisted Quarterly Assignments Listing (EQUAL). The Enlisted Quarterly Assignments Listing system provides airmen with a listing of assignment requirements that are available for upcoming assignment cycles and tells you what is available, by AFSC and grade, at particular locations. It also allows you to make your AF Form 392, "Airman Assignment Preference Statement," a better means to align your assignment preferences to Air Force needs. Overall, the EQUAL system enhances your opportunity to get the assignments you want. It provides a clearer picture of what is available, so that you will know when and where the openings are, and it lets you prioritize those options in the sequence you desire.

EQUAL Plus. This system was developed to advertise unique assignments, such as special duties, joint/departmental requirements, and chief master sergeant assignments. It's also used to advertise rotational assignments that cannot be advertised under EQUAL because of time constraints. This system will show requirements currently available and any special requirements or qualifications needed.

Volunteer Enlisted CONUS Assignment Program (VECAP). This program allows airmen to volunteer for any CONUS base after completing six years on the current duty location. To qualify, you must be eligible for reassignment, not have an assignment selection date, and not be assigned to a base or unit that is scheduled for closure or deactivation. Your application for this program must be supported with your unit commander's approval.

The Voluntary Stabilized Base Assignment Program (VSAP). This program was designed to provide stability at Los Angeles AFB, California (including Fort McArthur); Grand Forks AFB, North Dakota; and Minot AFB, North Dakota, which have historically had high personnel turnover rates. This program offers a four-year stabilized tour at Los Angeles AFB and a five-year tour at Grand Forks and Minot. To qualify, you must not be a volunteer for an overseas assignment, have completed a tour, or have thirty-six months on station, and you must be able to obtain twenty-four months' retainability, be eligible for a PCS assignment, and be recommended by your unit commander.

SOURCES OF ADDITIONAL INFORMATION

Air Force instruction 36-2110, *Assignments.*

At the Military Personnel Flight (MPF), the customer service branch or the assignments branch can provide current information, answer questions, and help you process the paperwork necessary to apply for the duty desired.

Other airmen, especially your supervisor and experienced personnel in your career field, can provide information about duty locations and career progression opportunities. Most career airmen will advise you that preplanning is a must. The day you begin processing into your new base is a very good time to start thinking about your next assignment.

17

Commissioning Opportunities

While on active duty, airmen from the enlisted force have the opportunity to become commissioned officers through one of several commissioning programs. Competition for these programs is extremely keen and selection criteria are very high. Even so, it is an attainable goal, one that many enlisted personnel have achieved. It provides expanded opportunities for those who have demonstrated the potential to assume higher levels of responsibility. It also allows members to apply for a variety of specialized positions where being a commissioned officer is a prerequisite (such as rated positions for pilots and navigators).

PRIMARY OPPORTUNITIES
There are four commissioning routes that are most commonly pursued.

USAF Officer Training School (OTS). The OTS program provides an opportunity for enlisted members with a baccalaureate or higher degree from an accredited college or university, completed either before entry in active service or during off-duty education programs while serving on active duty. To be eligible, applicants must demonstrate outstanding potential for commissioning and be recommended by their commander; be a U.S. citizen; achieve favorable scores on the Air Force Officer Qualification test (AFOQT); be physically qualified; and be commissioned before the age of thirty for nonflying duties or twenty-seven and a half for flying training. There are no marital restrictions. For further information, contact the Military Personnel Flight (MPF) at your base.

Airmen Education and Commissioning Program (AECP). This program provides the opportunity for career-minded airmen with a college background to complete a baccalaureate degree in selected technical fields, such as engineering, meteorology, or computer sciences. To apply for the program, airmen must have completed at least forty-five semester hours including six in calculus and analytic geometry and, in some cases, one course in physics or chemistry (with laboratory experience). Those selected are allowed up to thirty-six months to complete their degree requirements while attending a civilian college or university; tuition costs are paid by the Air Force. After graduation, those selected are enrolled in Officer Training School. To be eligible, applicants must meet the criteria listed above; demonstrate outstanding potential for commissioning and be recommended by their commander; be a U.S. citizen; be physically qualified; achieve favorable scores on the Air Force Officer Qualification Test (AFOQT); have at least one year on active duty as an enlisted member (if serving at an overseas location, members must complete at least one-half of their overseas tour before being entered into this program); and meet age requirements similar to those for the OTS program. There are no marital restrictions.

Air Force Reserve Officer Training Corps (AFROTC). The Airman Scholarship and Commissioning Program (AFROTC-ASCP) establishes procedures for active-duty airmen to receive AFROTC scholarships and attend the college or university of their choice in a four-year AFROTC program. Those selected are subsequently discharged from active duty and enlisted in the Air Force Reserve. Upon completion of degree and AFROTC requirements, airmen are commissioned as officers in the Air Force, with active-duty service commitments of four years or longer, depending on the scholarship awarded and the career field they are entered into. To be eligible, airmen must meet the criteria noted above; demonstrate outstanding potential and be recommended by their commander; be a U.S. citizen; be physically qualified; achieve favorable scores on the Air Force Officer Qualification Test (AFOQT); have an academic eligibility letter from AFROTC; and be under age twenty-nine as of 30 June of the calendar year in which they would be eligible for appointment as a commissioned officer. There are no marital restrictions.

The Air Force Academy and Air Force Academy Preparatory School. These programs offer opportunities to attend the U.S. Air Force Academy in Colorado Springs, Colorado, graduate with a bachelor of science degree, and be commissioned as an officer in the Regular Air Force. Selection processes are extremely competitive and attract the highest caliber of candidates from every part of the nation.

Vacancies are available for airmen serving on active duty and for those serving in the Air Force Reserve and the Air National Guard. Prospective candidates must apply through their unit commander, who processes the application and forwards it to the Director of Cadet Admissions for a determination of eligibility. Before airmen apply, they must meet the following basic eligibility criteria: be at least seventeen years of age and not have passed their twenty-second birthday as of 1 July in their year of entry into the Academy program; meet physical requirements; be a U.S. citizen; be unmarried; and not have a legal obligation to support a child or children or any other person.

The Air Force Academy Preparatory School was established for those who require additional instruction to improve their performance on Academy entrance examinations and to help them prepare for Academy courses. It is open to civilian candidates as well as military personnel on active duty in the USAF and airmen serving in the Air Force Reserve and the Air National Guard.

Prospective candidates must apply through their unit commander, who will review the application and forward it along with a statement of recommendation to the Cadet Admissions Office at the Academy. Academic terms at the Preparatory School usually last for ten months; members are then enrolled as cadets in the formal Academy course. To apply, airmen must meet the following basic eligibility criteria: be at least seventeen years of age and not over twenty-one years old as of 1 July in the year they would be admitted to Preparatory School; meet physical requirements; be a U.S. citizen; be unmarried; and have no dependent children.

For additional information on the two programs, consult your base's Academy Project Officer, or write to the Cadet Admissions Office, U.S. Air Force Academy, Colorado Springs, CO 80840.

OTHER COMMISSIONING OPPORTUNITIES

Air Force Reserve Officer Training Corps (AFROTC). The AFROTC offers a Professional Officer Course (POC) Early Release Program for airmen on active duty. You must request voluntary separation to enter an AFROTC program at an accredited college or university. Those who apply must be able to complete all degree and commissioning requirements within two academic years. Normally, selectees must complete all requirements and be commissioned before they turn thirty. For outstanding and deserving airmen, the Air Force Personnel Center (AFPC) may extend this age restriction to thirty-five.

Leaders Encouraging Airman Development (LEAD). This program offers two avenues for commissioning for active-duty enlisted personnel. The first allows wing commanders to nominate airmen who are younger than twenty-one before 1 July to attend the Preparatory School at the USAF Academy. The second allows major command commanders to select airmen to receive two- to four-year scholarships at AFROTC-offering universities. This latter program is allowed to offer fifty scholarships annually.

Professional Officer Course Early Release Program (POCEAR). This program allows active-duty airmen to apply for early separation to enter the junior or senior year of AFROTC. They must be able to complete all requirements within two academic years. This is not a scholarship program, but ROTC students qualify for a $150 monthly stipend and may qualify for a $1,000 incentive grant each semester.

Medical Service Direct Appointment. In this program, qualified airmen can apply for direct appointments for duty as officers in the medical specialties.

Judge Advocate Direct Appointment. This program makes provisions for qualified airmen to apply for direct appointments for duty as officers in the legal fields.

ONE VERY IMPORTANT CONSIDERATION

One very important theme has a direct bearing on selection for a commissioning program—demonstration of outstanding potential to become an officer and the concurrence and recommendation by a commander. In a nutshell, this means that your performance, as reflected in your performance reports and your day-to-day efforts, must be outstanding and must clearly show that you have the proper aptitude, attitude, and motivation to succeed as an officer. When commanders make recommendations, they do so based on their personal observations, a review of your records, and the recommendations put forth by your supervisors. Their final decision will reflect the best interests of the Air Force; it's not always an automatic "yes, I concur."

I remember one young airman who talked with his commander about commissioning opportunities. The airman was very bright, enthusiastic, and very positive: "I've decided that I want to become an officer." He and the commander discussed several programs and options. After the airman left, the commander asked the first sergeant to contact the supervisors involved. Two days later, the supervisors (a senior master sergeant and a technical sergeant) came to see the commander. Their comments: "We think that Airman Smith is a bright and capable young man; however, we're concerned about his total commitment to the Air Force and his reasons for wanting to become an officer. He's qualified within his specialty, but he lacks initiative and sometimes imposes unfair workloads on his fellow airmen. This was reflected in his last performance report, which recommended improvements in several areas. In addition, he's told us that he wants a commission so he can be reassigned to another location."

The commander reviewed the airman's official personnel records and then discussed the situation with the airman. In summary, the commander said: "I know that you would like to become an officer, but after considering all factors, I have concluded it would be inappropriate for me to approve your request at this time. Approval may be appropriate at some future date if you can show improvement in the areas noted."

As you can see, the screening process considers many factors. Before candidates can be selected, they must first be recommended. So if you're seriously interested in a commissioning program, set your goals high and go for it, but don't neglect your duty performance in your present job. Your potential for future positions will always be assessed, in part, on your past record of performance.

SOURCES OF ADDITIONAL INFORMATION

The base education officer or the customer service branch of your Military Personnel Flight (MPF) can provide further information.

18

The Family in the
Air Force Community

Providing for the needs and well-being of a servicemember's family is recognized at every level as an essential factor in accomplishing the overall mission of the U.S. Air Force. Many family-oriented programs have evolved over a period of time; others have been implemented to keep pace with new developments and changes in force structure.

One point is commonly agreed upon at all levels: Long-term commitment to the USAF is strongly affected by the family's feelings of satisfaction with the Air Force way of life. The level of satisfaction usually has a strong and observable bearing on the military member's daily duty performance and ultimately on the decision to reenlist.

The composition and the needs of Air Force families have evolved and taken on many new dimensions over the past twenty years. Most of these changes can be traced to the shift from the draft to the all-volunteer force. In the past, the draft provided the personnel (mainly men) to meet the needs of the Air Force. With the coming of the all-volunteer force, personnel planners provided a wide range of new inducements to attract people to the USAF. As the range of new volunteers arrived, so did the range of needs, which were not previously provided for.

For example, the emergence of more single-parent families had a very definite effect on duty scheduling; prolonged periods of separation caused by temporary duty requirements were a particular problem. This also resulted in an increased need for child-care centers.

Also, as the number of dual-career families increased, more child-care centers were needed. Military reassignments meant the nonmilitary spouse had to stop working, resulting in partial loss of pay and benefits, an interruption in career progression within a profession, and loss of seniority. Even assignments when a husband and wife were both military members had to be considered more carefully.

In the "new" Air Force, more women were placed in nontraditional jobs, such as aircraft maintenance and security police. The full and effective use of trained female personnel was a slow process, sometimes accompanied by resistance to change. Women also brought a new dimension: the "dependent husband" in the USAF community.

This range of new needs made it necessary to expand existing family-related programs and to develop additional ones.

FAMILY SUPPORT CENTERS: THEIR ROLE AND THEIR SERVICES

We have always been proud of the idea that the Air Force takes care of its own. Family Support Centers are an important part of this.

—Gen. Charles A. Gabriel,
former Chief of Staff, U.S. Air Force

Family Support Centers (FSCs) have been expanded considerably at base level over the past few years. They are a result of the Air Force's recognition that family issues have a direct effect on the morale and productivity of Air Force members and on decisions for making the Air Force a career. They serve as a focal point for responding to family issues that affect the Air Force mission.

Their services include the following:

1. Information/referral center, where you can get information or specialized assistance.

2. Relocation assistance, for help when you're moving to another base.

3. Support during family separations.

4. Financial management programs.

5. Spouse employment programs, which offer information about job opportunities and programs on how to develop job-hunting skills.

6. Special-needs programs, such as single parents' groups.

7. Family skills, which offer programs on communication and enhancing a family's quality of life.

8. Private and professional assistance for personal crisis issues, marital, child-related, and so forth.

Family Support Centers provide something for everyone in the Air Force family, whether they are singles, couples, or families with children. The best way to see what they have to offer is to stop in and get acquainted. They may be able to help you. You may be able to help them if you have skills or experience that would be useful for programs they would like to offer.

SETTLING INTO A NEW COMMUNITY

The Air Force community offers many social, educational, and volunteer opportunities for men and women who are married to military members. Their role should not be one of isolationism, but one of actively seeking out and pursuing their interests.

Volunteer Work. Many important programs in the Air Force community are made possible through the efforts of volunteer workers. The concept isn't unique to the USAF. It's really a reflection of American community life where, for generations, people from all walks of life have reached out to help others. It's also a way to meet other people who share similar experiences and to get experience for future employment. Within the USAF, thousands of people offer their time to support community services, such as the thrift shops, family services programs, family support center programs, youth activities (such as sports and Scouts), and as Red Cross assistants in medical facilities. Some positions are full-time; others are part-time, sometimes for a few hours a week. Some volunteers also hold down a full-time job but still serve as Scout leaders or sports coaches. Many of these programs are not fully funded, so without volunteers they would have to be discontinued. If you are interested in volunteer work, it's best to contact the agency directly; they'll usually welcome you with open arms. Information is also available in the family support center and periodically in the base newspaper.

Employment Opportunities for Spouses. Employment opportunities for spouses vary, depending on location and occupation. Working off-base in a local community is common in the United States. If you'd like to work on-base, your first stop should be the Civilian Personnel Office. Job openings are posted here and applications are taken. They also provide standard information handouts that describe available employment opportunities. Other on-base options include the Army and Air Force Exchange Service (AAFES), the commissary, banks, and credit unions. Overseas areas include all these plus teaching and administrative positions in the Department of Defense Dependent Schools (DODDS) system. Opportunities to work off-base in overseas areas do exist, but they vary from country to country, based on the laws and customs of the host nation.

Dispelling Some Myths. When it comes to volunteer work and employment by spouses, two very popular myths always seem to circulate.

The myth: "What I do in the military community will have an effect on my spouse's career, especially when it comes to promotions."

The reality: Military success is determined by the servicemember's duty performance and adherence to Air Force standards. Support and encouragement from a spouse usually have a positive effect on that performance. Involvement in programs in the Air Force community is always recognized and appreciated, but this involvement is not directly linked to a member's potential for promotion. There are circumstances where a spouse's actions can indirectly have an adverse effect—instances of continued indebtedness, criminal acts, use of illegal drugs, and so forth—because of their potentially disrupting influence on the member's performance. When performance declines, career progression can be affected.

The myth: "I can't get a job because Air Force policy states that I have to support my husband's career."

The reality: According to Air Force policy statement of 18 March 1988, "It is Air Force policy that the choice of a spouse to pursue employment, to be a homemaker, to attend school, or to serve as a volunteer in the Air Force or local community activities is a private matter and solely the decision of the individual concerned. No commander, supervisor, or other Air Force official will directly or indirectly impede or otherwise interfere with this decision. Neither the decision of the spouse in this matter, nor the marital status of the military member will be a factor used to affect the evaluation, promotion or assignment of the military member, except under conditions specifically permitted by Air Force regulation (e.g., joint spouse assignments or personal hardship circumstances).

"Air Force spouses and members have a long tradition of service to their communities. Their individual and collective efforts have enhanced the quality of life in military and civilian communities around the world. This generous and willing participation in volunteer organizations, in clubs and in other support activities has contributed greatly to the morale and well being of the Air Force family. The Air Force welcomes and values this generosity of spirit. At the same time, the Air Force recognizes that voluntary service must be exactly that—voluntary, and must be so regarded by all Air Force members."

"I talked my wife into getting this job. It's part of my retirement program."

CHILDREN'S NEEDS

The life of a military child is a mix of new places, new people, and new routines. It's also a life of many opportunities. Because they are exposed to a variety of changing situations, children often mature much more quickly and become more self-reliant. As world travelers, they also have a much greater awareness of people and their cultures: similarities, differences, customs, history, and languages.

As children become older, each move usually becomes a little bit harder to make. New environments can pose a temporary threat. Children are very adaptable, however, and in most cases they tend to make the readjustment before parents do—sometimes before all the boxes are unpacked.

When you arrive at a new location, it's a good idea to provide your children with a miniorientation. At a minimum, they should know the following:

• Where mom or dad works (office, shop, or duty location) and how to get in touch with you (a duty telephone number).

• The telephone numbers of a relative or close friend in case they can't contact you.

• How to get in touch with the hospital, fire department, and security police.

• Some information about places you consider to be "no-go" areas: streets they shouldn't cross, off-limits areas such as active flightlines, and so forth.

A smooth transition to a new environment comes easier with exposure to community programs. Most of the ones that affect kids revolve around their neighborhood friends, the schools, and special youth activities, such as sports, Scouts, and other programs. The base newspaper and the family support center are excellent sources of information on what's happening locally. Your sponsor should be able to answer most general questions.

Any reference to community problems that affect children, such as vandalism or drugs, should be checked out through a reliable source. Each installation usually has a "rumor control" telephone number. Some stories may have substance; others may have been greatly exaggerated.

When it comes time for school enrollment, it's usually necessary to furnish documents such as your children's birth certificates, shot records, and latest report cards or transcripts. It's a good idea to hand-carry these items with you whenever you're reassigned.

Child-Development Centers. Most bases have child-development centers that offer full-day, part-day, and hourly care for children six months to eleven years of age. Some bases also provide infant programs for children of ages six weeks to six months. Most centers use theme programming to provide quality care and to encourage growth physically, emotionally, intellectually, and socially. As a service distinct and apart from child care, many bases offer structured preschool classes for two, three, or five days a week.

Youth Activity Centers. Youth Activity Centers offer a variety of specially supervised programs for children ages five through eighteen. Activities include a variety of sports programs and special activities, such as special interest clubs, dances, instructional classes (ballet, gymnastics, self-defense, and so on), and trips to local places of interest. Many youth centers feature game rooms, special interest rooms for teens, and snack bars.

Children with Special Needs. Some children may need additional attention, care, or teaching because they are affected by physical, learning, or emotional disabilities or speech and language impairments. The Air Force provides for these needs with the Children Have a Potential (CHAP) program. Under this program, an airman may receive an assignment or deferment from an assignment to establish a special-education or medical program for a handicapped child. Each request is reviewed on a case-by-case basis and reevaluated upon request each time a member is selected for reassignment.

Single-Parent Families. Single-parent families are commonly found (and accepted) throughout the Air Force. They exist when one parent is responsible for managing the affairs of a family without a partner or spouse. Military members in this category have "extended duty days" at home to fulfill the role of the absent partner. Sources of help and assistance include members of their extended families, coworkers, and neighbors; schools, child-care centers, and religious organizations; Family Support Centers, which often provide referral services; and single-parent support groups, for mutual support and assistance.

PLANNING FOR FAMILY SEPARATIONS DURING TEMPORARY DUTY ASSIGNMENTS

The USAF conducts missions around the world. To support these requirements, sometimes it is necessary for military personnel to go away for short periods on unaccompanied tours of duty. A little preplanning can eliminate a lot of potential problems. Be sure to discuss the following with your family or designated representative:

1. Departure and return dates.

2. The mailing address at the temporary duty location. If you are overseas, make sure your spouse knows the number and combination for your mailbox.

3. Important local addresses, points of contact, and telephone numbers for routine matters and in case of an emergency. At a minimum they should include your commander and first sergeant, hospital, fire department, security police, legal office, chaplain, the Family Support Center, and the Red Cross.

4. Dependent ID cards. Check them for expiration dates, and if necessary, get new ones from the customer service unit of the Military Personnel Flight. ID cards are issued to children when they reach ten years of age; exceptions can be made on a case-by-case base when required.

5. The use of power of attorney. If you already have one, make sure it is current and still meets your needs. Some provide full powers to act in your absence; some provide limited powers. If you are a single parent, make sure it allows for medical care of children. The same applies for wills; ensure they are

current. If in doubt, check with the base legal office. They can prepare both these documents for you at no expense.

6. Financial arrangements. For the military member: Have sufficient funds for expenses, but don't carry a lot of cash. Consider traveler's checks if you're going to leave your checkbook at home with your spouse. Pay known bills in advance, especially car insurance so it doesn't expire while you're away. For your family members: Make sure they have sufficient funds. If your paycheck does not go directly to the bank, ensure that your spouse has a current power of attorney to cash your government paycheck.

7. The family car. Check tires, oil, car insurance, and base-pass expiration dates. Let your spouse know whom to contact in case of problems.

8. Procedures for minor house repairs. If the house is rented, note the land-lord's telephone number. If you live in base housing, make a note of the service call number in case a repairman needs to be called out to check heating, plumbing, appliances, and so forth.

9. The children's needs. It's a good idea to talk to them candidly. Tell them why you're going, how long you'll be gone, and when you'll be back. This will help put them at ease and let them understand that it's just a temporary absence. Single parents may have special considerations to take into account under the dependent care program, particularly if a child's temporary guardian does not have military entitlements and privileges—arranging access to the base, commissary, exchange, medical facilities, and so forth. The best sources of information for questions are your supervisor, the unit orderly room, and your first sergeant.

Before you leave, make sure you have adequate clothing for the climate at the temporary duty location, leave high-value items at home, and complete any performance reports that may be due while you're away.

AIR FORCE SOCIAL FUNCTIONS
Social functions in the U.S. Air Force include formal and informal gatherings in base facilities, private living quarters, and at locations in the surrounding community. Most are attended by those who really want to be involved, who enjoy each other's company, and want to mix and have fun. Nowadays, when people mention gatherings for "mandatory fun" they usually speak in terms of sympathy for senior officials who have full calendars of engagements, sometimes four and five nights a week.

Social courtesies in military circles are very similar to commonly accepted courtesies in civilian circles. Invitations are usually sent out for formal functions. A written response should be provided when requested; it helps the host make the necessary plans and arrangements. For informal occasions, people are usually invited in personal conversation, but never in front of someone who is not being invited.

Writing home is a small gesture that can make a big impact.

Always ask your host before bringing other guests. Take children if it is a children's function (such as a Christmas or Halloween party), but not otherwise, unless they are specifically invited. Be punctual. Be yourself and go with the flow of the occasion.

At the social function, it's appropriate to rise when being introduced or when shaking hands, especially when the other individual is a woman, an older person, or a distinguished person. Formal terms of address for military personnel are noted in chapter 7, "Courtesies and Customs." Try to avoid too much shop talk. It's usually a common denominator in military circles and hard to steer clear of altogether. But it can be a real source of irritation, especially to a spouse, if it goes on throughout the evening.

Enjoy the occasion, but do not overindulge in booze. Everyone has different tolerance levels. Having an occasional soft drink with ice is a good way to pace yourself. There's nothing wrong with politely turning down offers for another drink ("No thanks, I already have one"). This can also pay dividends when it comes time to go home. Driving while drunk is not legal in the United States or overseas. Besides that, it can be very dangerous (even life-threatening) for you, your family, your friends, and other people on the roads. Don't overstay your welcome. And when it's time to leave, always remember to thank the host.

WRITING HOME

Some people are quite good at writing home regularly. Others may do so only once or twice a year. How often you decide to write is an individual decision, of course, but family members will be anxious and concerned if they don't hear from you for long periods, especially if you are a long way from home.

SOURCES OF ADDITIONAL INFORMATION

Air Force Instruction 36-3009, *Family Support Center (FSC) Program.*

Air Force Instruction 36-2110, *Assignments,* for information concerning Children Have a Potential (CHAP) programs.

You may also consult your supervisor, your first sergeant, or the Family Support Center.

19

Dollars and Sense

Money matters affect everyone—single, married, those embarking on a career, and those preparing to separate or retire. Here we'll take a look at some basic aspects of dollars and sense/cents in the military.

THE JOINT UNIFORM MILITARY PAY SYSTEM (JUMPS)

The Joint Uniform Military Pay System (JUMPS) is a computerized pay system that automatically computes your pay entitlements, deductions, and leave based on information from local Accounting and Finance Offices (AFOs), Military Personnel Flight (MPF), and the Air Force Personnel Center (AFPC).

When and How You Are Paid. Air Force members can choose to be paid either once or twice a month. Once-a-month pay is computed from the first to the last calendar day of each month. Twice-a-month pay is computed for two periods: the first through the fifteenth calendar day, and the sixteenth through the last day of the month.

Paydays are the fifteenth calendar day of each month and the first day of the following month. If a payday falls on a Saturday, a Sunday, or a holiday, the payday is moved up to the workday before the weekend or the holiday.

During 1989, direct deposit of paychecks became a condition of employment in the Air Force. Under the Direct Deposit program (previously referred to as the SURE-PAY program), you are required to establish a direct-deposit account when you report to your first permanent duty station. Payments are then made to your personal savings or checking account, which can be in any U.S. financial institution (such as a bank, a credit union, or a savings and loan association). This system helps you avoid waiting in lines on paydays. It's also useful when you are sent on temporary duty; it reduces the prospect of delayed payments when you are at one location and your check is at another.

Local payments, whereby your local Accounting and Finance Office pays you directly by cash or check, are authorized under two circumstances:
• When new personnel are assigned to Basic Military Training School, Officer Training School, or other initial training courses.
• When it is clearly in the best interest of the servicemember and the government; for example, a waiver of the Direct Deposit program might be granted

when an individual repeatedly demonstrates that he or she is incapable of handling a checking account.

What You Are Paid. The amount of money each member receives is computed as follows:

	Entitlements	Basic pay, allowances, and special and incentive pay
plus	**Miscellaneous payments**	Advances of pay or travel allowances, casual and partial payments, and sale of accrued leave
minus	**Deductions**	Taxes, life insurance, allotments
equals	**Net Pay**	The amount on your paycheck, also referred to as take-home pay

Payments. Let's look at some of the ingredients more closely. There are several sources of what are called entitlements.

• *Basic pay* is based on your grade and years in service.
• *Allowances* are nontaxable payments for your welfare and the welfare of your dependents. They include the following:

1. Basic Allowance for Subsistence (BAS): for enlisted members when government dining facilities are not available or when they are authorized to purchase meals outside government facilities. Most married personnel, personnel with dependents, and in some instances, single personnel draw BAS.

2. Basic Allowance for Quarters (BAQ): for housing. There are two rates, one for members with dependents and one for members without dependents. This allowance is not provided if you are assigned to government housing or quarters. Additional allowances may be paid for housing. In the United States, Variable Housing Allowances (VHAs) are paid for designated high-cost areas based on duty locations. In overseas areas, rates can be based on the fluctuation of foreign currency exchange rates and whether or not utilities are included as part of the rent.

3. Family Separation Allowances (FSA): for added housing expenses incurred when airmen are separated from their dependents as a result of official duty requirements. The allowances compensate for the costs of maintaining quarters in two places.

4. Clothing Allowances: for repair and maintenance of military uniforms. In certain cases, personnel are entitled to civilian clothing allowances if civilian clothing is required to perform official duties.

DAILY BASIC ALLOWANCE FOR SUBSISTENCE
(effective 1 January 1997)

Enlisted	E-1 under Four Months	All Others
When on leave or authorized to mess separately	$ 6.79	$ 7.36
When rations in kind are not available	7.65	8.30
When assigned to duty under emergency conditions where no government messing facilities are available	10.16	10.99

MONTHLY BASIC ALLOWANCE FOR QUARTERS
(effective 1 January 1997)

Pay Grade	Without Dependents Full	Partial	With Dependents
E-9	500.40	18.60	659.70
E-8	459.30	15.30	608.10
E-7	392.40	12.00	564.60
E-6	355.20	9.90	521.70
E-5	327.60	8.70	469.20
E-4	285.00	8.10	408.00
E-3	279.60	7.80	379.80
E-2	227.10	7.20	361.50
E-1	202.50	6.90	361.50

5. Station Allowances outside the United States: for extra costs incurred when an airman is reassigned on a permanent change of station to places outside the continental United States. They include allowances for cost-of-living adjustments and temporary lodging.
• *Special pay* is provided to airmen who use specialized skills or who are assigned to specified locations (for example, Foreign Duty Pay and Overseas Extension Pay).
• *Bonus or contract pay* is provided to stimulate enlistments and reenlistments. Examples include enlistment bonuses for critically manned specialties, reenlistment bonuses, and proficiency pay to attract and retain highly qualified personnel in a designated Special Duty Assignment.

AIR FORCE ACTIVE DUTY BASIC PAY RATES
(effective 1 January 1997)

Grade	Under 2	2	3	4	6	8	10	12	14	16	18	20	22	24	26
ENLISTED MEMBERS															
E-9	0.00	0.00	0.00	0.00	0.00	0.00	2701.80	2762.40	2824.80	2889.90	2954.70	3011.70	3169.80	3293.40	3478.50
E-8	0.00	0.00	0.00	0.00	0.00	2265.60	2330.70	2391.90	2454.00	2519.10	2576.40	2639.70	2794.80	2919.30	3106.50
E-7	1581.90	1707.90	1770.60	1833.00	1895.40	1955.70	2018.40	2081.40	2175.30	2237.10	2298.90	2329.20	2485.50	2609.10	2794.80
E-6	1360.80	1483.50	1545.00	1610.70	1671.30	1731.30	1794.90	1887.30	1946.70	2009.40	2040.00	2040.00	2040.00	2040.00	2040.00
E-5	1194.30	1299.90	1362.90	1422.30	1515.90	1577.70	1639.80	1700.40	1731.30	1731.30	1731.30	1731.30	1731.30	1731.30	1731.30
E-4	1113.60	1176.30	1245.60	1341.60	1394.70	1394.70	1394.70	1394.70	1394.70	1394.70	1394.70	1394.70	1394.70	1394.70	1394.70
E-3	1049.70	1107.00	1151.10	1196.70	1196.70	1196.70	1196.70	1196.70	1196.70	1196.70	1196.70	1196.70	1196.70	1196.70	1196.70
E-2	1010.10	1010.10	1010.10	1010.10	1010.10	1010.10	1010.10	1010.10	1010.10	1010.10	1010.10	1010.10	1010.10	1010.10	1010.10
E-1	900.90	900.90	900.90	900.90	900.90	900.90	900.90	900.90	900.90	900.90	900.90	900.90	900.90	900.90	900.90

E-1 with less than 4 months—$833.40

• *Incentive pay* is provided those who are required to perform certain hazardous duties. Examples include parachute duty, hazardous duty (flight) pay, demolition duty, hostile fire duty, experimental stress duty, toxic fuel handling, and lab work with live, dangerous viruses or bacteria.

• *Miscellaneous payments* are made for three purposes. Amounts vary based on individual circumstances.

1. Advances of pay or travel allowances are usually granted, on request, in conjunction with a permanent-change-of-station move. Up to three months of advance pay may be requested. Repayment is deducted from your future pay, usually spread over the following six-month period. For pay grades E-1 through E-4, the approval of your commander is required. If the desired payback period is greater than twelve months, then all members require the approval of their immediate commander. Advance travel allowances for permanent change of station and temporary duty assignments are also permitted.

2. Casual payments (to members away from their home stations) and partial payments (to personnel at their home stations) are made primarily under emergency situations. These payments are the exception rather than the rule. The amounts advanced are deducted from future paychecks.

3. Accrued leave pay compensates for leave earned but not taken. One day's basic pay is provided for each day of unused leave. Up to sixty days may be "sold back" during a military career. Amounts received are subject to federal and state taxes.

Deductions. There are two general categories of deductions: voluntary and involuntary. Involuntary deductions are automatically taken out. They include the following:

1. Federal Insurance Contributions Act (FICA) and medicare deductions, commonly referred to as Social Security tax.

2. Federal Income Tax Withholding (FITW).

3. State Income Tax Withholding (SITW).

4. U.S. Soldier's and Airmen's Home (USSAH) deductions, 50 cents per month for each enlisted member.

Other involuntary deductions include erroneous payments, loss or damage to government property, fines and forfeitures from disciplinary actions, court-ordered child support or alimony, charges for shipping excess household goods, and writing bad checks to the commissary, exchange, or nonappropriated fund activities (such as the NCO club).

Voluntary deductions are taken out with your consent. They include allotments made to others on your authorization. The Defense Accounting and Finance Center (DAFC) sends checks to the persons or organizations you have designated as recipients, such as charities, home loans, insurance programs, support of dependents, and personal savings and investment programs. You may authorize up to fifteen allotments.

DEFENSE FINANCE AND ACCOUNTING SERVICE MILITARY LEAVE AND EARNINGS STATEMENT

ID	NAME (LAST, FIRST, MI)	SOC. SEC. NO.	GRADE	PAY DATE	YRS SVC	ETS	BRANCH	ADSN/DSSN	PERIOD COVERED
	JONES, JOHN J.	123-45-6789	E7	780127	16	950902	AF	5250	1-31 AUG 94

ENTITLEMENTS

	TYPE	AMOUNT
A	BASE PAY	2067.30
B	BAQ	500.10
C	BAS	210.80
D	VHA	106.92
E		
F		
G		
H		
J		
K		
L		
M		
N		
O		
	TOTAL	2685.12

DEDUCTIONS

TYPE	AMOUNT
FEDERAL TAXES	247.22
FICA-SOC SECURITY	128.17
FICA-MEDICARE	29.98
SGLI FOR 200,000	18.00
AFRH (USSH)	.50
DENTAL	9.65
MID-MONTH-PAY	1222.66
TOTAL	1656.18

ALLOTMENTS

TYPE	AMOUNT

SUMMARY

+AMT FWD	.00
+ TOT ENT	2,885.12
- TOT DED	1,656.18
- TOT ALMT	.00
= NET AMT	1,228.94
- CR FWD	.00
= EOM PAY	1,228.94

LEAVE	BF BAL 28.0	ERND 27.5	USED 37	CR BAL 18.5	ETS BAL 49.0	LV LOST .0	LV PAID 30.0	USE/LOSE .0
FICA TAXES	WAGE PERIOD 2067.30	SOC WAGE YTD 16277.66	SOC TAX YTD 1009.20	MED WAGE YTD 16277.66	MED TAX YTD 236.06			
PAY DATA	BAQ TYPE W/DEP	BAQ DEPN SPOUSE	VHA ZIP 78150	RENT AMT 895.00	SHARE 1	STAT R	JFTR	DEPNS 0	2D JFTR	BAS TYPE REGULAR

	WAGE PERIOD	WAGE YTD	M/S	EX	ADD'L TAX	TAX YTD
FED TAXES	2067.30	16277.66	S	01	.00	1938.65
STATE TAXES TX	.00	.00	S	01	.00	.00

CHARITY YTD .00	TPC	PACIDN

REMARKS: YTD ENTITLE 22957.31   YTD DEDUCT 3397.11

| BANK: BANK OF AMERICA |
| ACCT #: 987654321-00 |

VHA BASED ON W/DEP, ZIP 78150

LOOKING FOR A CHALLENGING, REWARDING CAREER BROADENING ASSIGNMENT? INTERESTED IN EARNING UP TO $275/MONTH SPECIAL DUTY ASSIGNMENT PAY? THE AIR FORCE NEEDS TOP-NOTCH SSGTS AND TSGTS WITH AT LEAST 2 YEARS TIME ON STATION AND LESS THAN 16 YEARS TAFMS TO SERVE AS AIR FORCE RECRUITERS IN LOCATIONS NATIONWIDE. TO FIND OUT IF YOU QUALIFY, CONTACT YOUR LOCAL MILITARY PERSONNEL FLIGHT OR CALL THE RECRUIT-THE-RECRUITER TEAM AT DSN 487-2812.

FAS Form 702, May 92

Leave and Earnings Statement.

Premium payments for Servicemen's Group Life Insurance (SGLI) are also considered a voluntary deduction. SGLI is a low-cost, government-subsidized life insurance program. Each airman is entered into the program automatically but can discontinue coverage or request only partial coverage; either action must be requested in writing.

Keeping Track of Your Pay. Each military member is provided with a monthly copy of a Defense Finance and Accounting Service Military Leave and Earnings Statement, a personal account of your pay status. In specialized blocks, it shows details of your entitlements, allotments, deductions, payments, taxes, indebtedness, and net pay. It also has a remarks section to inform you of any changes specifically made during the month.

You should save these statements and keep them in a safe place. They're useful for tax purposes, for making inquiries at the Accounting and Finance Office (AFO), and for helping AFO personnel determine amounts of casual or partial payments.

If you are paid twice a month and use the Direct Deposit system (check sent directly to bank), the Accounting and Finance Center also sends an abbreviated pay notice during the middle of the month, telling how much was deposited to your account at that time.

AIR FORCE POLICIES CONCERNING LEAVE

Your leave status is also reflected on your Leave and Earnings Statement. The policy concerning its use is noted in Air Force Instruction 36-3003, *Military Leave Program.*

As a member of the armed forces, you accrue two and a half days of leave for each month of active duty. Leave is paid time off for thirty days each year. It can be taken all at once or at short intervals. Each request must be approved by your supervisor and, in some cases, by your commander; it is normally granted, except in cases where military necessity requires your presence. It's always important to watch your leave balance (number of days you have accrued and not used); as on the last day of September each year, any days in excess of sixty will be lost.

Types of Leave. *Ordinary Leave.* Leave the Air Force grants you upon your request at any time during a fiscal year to the extent of the leave that you may earn during that fiscal year, plus your leave credit from previous years.

Sick or Convalescent Leave. Leave the Air Force grants you for absence because of illness or convalescence upon recommendation of medical authority. It is not chargeable as leave.

Advance Leave. The Air Force may grant you advance leave in anticipation of the future accrual of leave. Such leave would apply in cases of emergency leave and leave used when making a permanent-change-of-station (PCS) move.

		SECTION I		

LEAVE REQUEST / AUTHORIZATION
(See Privacy Act Statement and General Instructions below)

TO: ACFP

1. DATE OF REQUEST	2. TYPE OF TRANSACTION (1–5) (AFO Use Only)
1 Nov 92	

3. SSN (6–14)	4. NAME (Last, First, Middle Initial) (15–19)	5. GRADE	6. CURRENT LV BALANCE	6a. DOS
123-45-6789	Doe, John D.	E-5	30	1 Dec 93

7. RECOMMEND CONVALESCENT LEAVE	8. TYPE OF LEAVE (Check one)		
FROM _____ TO _____	☐ Terminal (P) ☐ Emergency (D) ☒ Ordinary (A) ☐ Convalescent (F)	☐ Reenlistment (E) ☐ Graduation (J) ☐ Appellate Review (R) ☐ Special (H) ☐ Other (Specify) ☐ Permissive TDY (T)	PTDY Reason (AFR 35–26, Atch 1) _____

PROVIDER'S SIGNATURE & STAMP

REMARKS:

9. NO. DAYS REQUESTED (33–35)	10. LEAVE AUTH NO. (37–43)	11. FIRST DAY/TIME OF LV STATUS	12. FIRST DAY OF CHARGEABLE LV (47–52)	13. LAST DAY OF CHARGEABLE LV (53–58)
5	LX-1234	5 Nov 92/0001	5 Nov 92	9 Nov 92

14. LEAVE AREA (36)	15. EMERGENCY PHONE NO.	16. LEAVE ADDRESS (Street, City, State, Zip Code, and Phone No.)
☒ CONUS ☐ OS ☐ OS to CONUS	(512) 555-7878	711 Main St.

17. DUTY PHONE NO.	18. UNIT	19. DUTY SECTION	Anytown, MN 12345
7-5034	7110MS	OMP	512-555-7878

20. DUTY LOCATION
Randolph AFB TX

LEAVE REQUEST CERTIFICATION: *I acknowledge that the leave requested by me will be charged against my leave account unless otherwise cancelled or corrected through Part III of this form. In addition, if I cannot earn enough leave before separation to cover this request, I consent to withholding from current pay, final pay, or any other pay due me to satisfy this indebtedness. I understand that there is no actual debt until my final separation from the Air Force; however, I consent to this withholding of pay in anticipation of the indebtedness for the unearned portion of my leave balance. I further consent to such withholding at a rate sufficient to satisfy this indebtedness no later than my requested or projected separation date, and understand that this could result in the withholding of 100% of any current pay, final pay, or any other money due me. I have read the instructions on PART II.*

21. MEMBER'S SIGNATURE	22.		
John D. Doe	LEAVE IS ☒ APPROVED ☐ DISAPPROVED	DATE 1 Nov 92	

23. SUPERVISOR'S NAME AND GRADE (Print or Type)	24. DUTY PHONE NO.	25. SUPERVISOR'S SIGNATURE
JANE D. DOE, Major	7-5034	*Jane D. Doe*

SECTION II *(To be completed by supervisor/ unit commander to authorize advance or excess leave)*

26. LEAVE AVAILABLE TO ETS (From LES)	27. ADVANCE LEAVE REQUESTED (Block 9 minus 6)	28. EXCESS LEAVE REQUESTED (44–46) (Block 9 minus 26)	29. TOTAL LEAVE APPROVED

30. UNIT HEADQUARTERS	31. COMMANDER'S SIGNATURE / GRADE	32. AUTHORIZATION DATE	33. AUTHORITY FOR ADVANCE LEAVE OVER 30 DAYS

PRIVACY ACT STATEMENT

AUTHORITY: 10 U.S.C., Chapter 40; 37 U.S.C., Chapter 9; EO 9397, November 1943.
PRINCIPAL PURPOSES: To authorize military leave, document the start and stop of such leave; record address and telephone number where you may be contacted in case of emergency during leave; and certify leave days chargeable to you.
ROUTINE USES: Information may be disclosed to the Department of Justice, and to federal, state, local or foreign law enforcement authorities for investigating or prosecuting a violation or potential violation of law; the American Red Cross for information concerning the needs of the member or dependents and relatives in emergency situations.
DISCLOSURE: Disclosure of SSN is voluntary. However, this form will not be processed without your SSN, since the Air Force identifies members by SSN for pay or leave purposes.

GENERAL INSTRUCTIONS
(For emergency, reenlistment, convalescent, terminal, appellate review leave, and PTDY, see variations in AFM 177–373, Volume II, Ch 7.)
1. THIS FORM MUST BE TYPED OR COMPLETED IN INK.
2. BEFORE SEPARATING PARTS I, II, AND III, COMPLETE THE FOLLOWING BLOCKS:
  a. Blocks 1 thru 5, 9, 12 thru 21, and 23 thru 25 are self-explanatory.
  b. Block 6, Current Leave Balance. Verify that the member has enough leave balance to cover the period of leave requested. This may be done by checking the member's LES or the orderly room's leave balance listing. Complete 6a when member requests leave with a planned return date within 30 days of DOS.
  c. Block 7. This block will be completed, signed, and stamped by the appropriate medical authority if convalescent leave is recommended.
  d. Block 8. For PTDY, state the paragraph number of the applicable reason for PTDY as stated in AFR 35–26 and in Remarks area give abbreviated description of purpose of PTDY. (For example: base baseball team.)
  e. Block 10. Leave Authorization Number. Supervisor or designee obtains a leave authorization number from the unit orderly room immediately before signing a leave approval and forwarding Part I to AFO. Do not get leave number earlier than 14 days before effective date.
  f. Block 11. First Day/Time of Leave Status. This is the earliest time a member can depart or sign up for space available transportation. If planned departure is on a non-duty day, enter the non-duty date and 0001 hours. If planned departure is on a duty day without performing the majority (more than 50%) of scheduled day, enter the date and time when more than 50% of the scheduled duty will be completed. NOTE: Leave status is not necessarily chargeable leave. Date cannot be more than 1 day before the date in block 12. See also Part III, Instructions for Charging Leave.
  g. Block 22. For PTDY, use approval level required by AFR 35–26.
  h. Blocks 26–33. Complete only to authorize advance or excess leave. Blocks are self-explanatory except for blocks 27, 28, and 33.
  (1) Advance Leave (Block 27). If the requested leave exceeds the current balance but does not exceed the balance to ETS, the leave is advance leave. Complete Blocks 26–27 and forward the form (all parts) to the unit commander for approval. If a member requesting leave has a cumulative advance balance of 30 days, comply with AFR 35–9.
  (2) Excess Leave (Block 28). If the requested leave exceeds the balance to ETS, the leave is excess leave. Complete Blocks 26 and 28 and forward the form (all parts) to the unit commander for approval.
  (3) Authority for Advance Leave Over 30 Days (Block 33). Record message date/time group if approval was received by message.
3. AFTER INITIALLY COMPLETING THIS FORM:
  a. Separate Part I immediately after getting a leave authorization number and signing the form. Forward to the AFO using normal distribution unless the leave is terminal/separation or involves excess or advance leave. Forward these requests (all parts) to the unit for approval.
  b. Separate Part II and give to member.
  c. Hold Part III for completion after the member's return from leave. If member requests cancellation before any leave is taken, complete Section III of Part III and forward to your unit commander.
4. INSTRUCTIONS FOR COMPLETING AND PROCESSING PART III ARE PRINTED ON PART III.
5. GUIDELINES FOR CHARGING LEAVE AND INSTRUCTIONS FOR LEAVE ADJUSTMENTS ARE PRINTED ON PART III.

AF Form 988, SEP 91   *PREVIOUS EDITION WILL BE USED*   PART I — AFO COPY

Leave Request/Authorization

Emergency Leave. Leave the Air Force may grant you upon assurance that an emergency exists and that granting of such leave will contribute to the alleviation of the emergency. The total leave advanced, including emergency leave, may not exceed forty-five days. The Air Force charges it against present or future accrued leave.

Excess Leave. Leave of up to thirty days that the Air Force grants you that is in excess of the amount you have accrued, that is, except for such advance or ordinary leave as specifically authorized, without pay and allowances, and that you may take only under exceptional circumstances upon authority of commanders. Excess leave is charged against leave accrued in the future.

Prenatal and Postpartum Leave. Normally, a woman who becomes pregnant while on active duty goes into "sick in quarters" status about four weeks before delivery, as determined by the attending physician. Time spent in the hospital for delivery is duty time. Following completion of inpatient care, the servicemember receives convalescent leave until her medical condition permits her to return to duty, normally not more than six weeks after her release from the hospital.

Delays en Route in Executing Travel. The Air Force counts and charges as leave authorized delays stated in travel orders.

General Leave Policies. *Day of Departure; Day of Return on Duty Days.* The Air Force will charge you both the day of departure and the day of return as leave unless you were present for duty all or nearly all of the normal working day on either the day of commencement or termination of the leave period.

Day of Departure; Day of Return on Nonduty Days. When you sign out on a nonduty day, the Air Force will charge that day as leave. When you sign in on a nonduty day, the Air Force will not charge that day as leave.

Leave to Visit outside the United States. Air Force members may visit foreign countries as leave, either from the United States or from their overseas station. Such leaves are chargeable as ordinary leave.

To visit communist or communist-oriented countries, special procedures must be followed. Some specialties may be more affected than others, especially in cases where personnel have access to sensitive information. For information, contact your unit security manager, the customer service branch of the Military Personnel Flight (MPF), or your first sergeant.

Application for Leave. Use AF Form 988, "Leave Request/Authorization," to apply for leave. State the amount of leave desired and the amount of accumulated leave due. Generally, you must also give an address where the Air Force can reach you while you are on leave. Copies of the form may be obtained from your supervisor or the unit orderly room.

PERSONAL FINANCIAL MANAGEMENT PLANNING

In today's society, our quality of life in the present and sense of security in the future depend largely on our ability to manage our finances. And while money is a subject close to everyone's heart, few of us give serious forethought to financial planning. Some people live from paycheck to paycheck. Others believe they'll achieve financial comfort and security "someday," when they reach higher income levels. Neither of these approaches is realistic.

The first step in planning your financial future is to find out where you are today, by taking a close look at your net worth. Your net worth lets you know where you stand compared to your expectations. It is computed by adding up your assets (what you own or have saved) and subtracting your liabilities (what you owe). The accompanying worksheet includes items commonly considered; you may want to add or delete categories to suit your circumstances.

PERSONAL NET WORTH CALCULATION

Assets		**Liabilities**	
Funds available		Major loans	
Cash on hand	$ _____	Mortgage balance	$ _____
Savings accounts	_____	Car loan balance	_____
Checking accounts	_____	Cash loan balance	_____
U.S. savings bonds	_____		
Money lent to others (to be paid back)	_____	Money owed to others	_____
Investments		Unpaid bills	
Real estate	_____	Credit cards	_____
Stocks, bonds, etc.	_____	Charge accounts	_____
Life insurance (cash value)	_____	Insurance payments	_____
		Taxes	_____
		Education payments	_____
Property		Other items owed	
Value of home	_____		_____
Automobile	_____		_____
Furniture	_____		_____
Other items	_____		_____
Total assets	$ _____	Total liabilities	$ _____

	Total assets	$ _____
minus	**Total liabilities**	$ _____
equals	**Net worth**	$ _____

After you've computed your net worth you'll have a better idea of your financial strengths and weaknesses. This leads you to your second step: identifying your financial goals, where you'd like to be tomorrow. This phase is easy. Take a pencil and make a long list. Then put them in a priority sequence based on needs and wants (needs come first, wants come second). Try to further define each goal; make it specific and establish a target date for achieving it.

For example, if you'd like to have $10,000 cash at the end of a four-year enlistment, divide the sum by the number of pay periods available. If you just came in, you would have to save approximately $100 every two-week pay period to achieve this.

Money Management and Budgeting. After you've established your goals, it's time to take a look at your income and analyze your day-to-day spending habits. The best way to start is to keep a written record of your daily expenses for a couple of weeks or a month. This will tell you exactly where your money is going. People are frequently surprised at how rapidly these smaller expense accumulate. Consider the following:

- A $10 compact disk (CD) per week would equate to $520 a year.
- A $2 lunch every day would equate to $730 a year.
- Spending $3 a day at the bar would equate to $1,095 a year.

These are trivial examples, but they add up to $2,345 a year. Necessary expenses? Perhaps. But there are more inexpensive options. The important point is that you need to develop an awareness of where your money is going and why. As you reduce the amounts spent for unnecessary items, you'll have more of your income left for the goals that you have established.

The next step is establishing a monthly budget. Write down your total income. Then figure out and write down your fixed expenses (food, lodging, transportation, and bills). Try to economize where possible. Then look at your flexible expenses (clothing, entertainment, impulse buying habits, and so forth). This is the area to economize in. One good way to start a savings program is to "pay yourself first," identifying a specified dollar amount as a fixed expense. Reevaluate your budget after a month or two. Look at the figures and review your goals to see if you are achieving them. Make adjustments where necessary.

While you're reviewing the document you used to develop your budget, it's a good idea to think about establishing a record-keeping system. It doesn't have to be anything fancy; maybe just a cardboard box with some file folders and envelopes. Contents can include items such as Leave and Earnings statements, savings and checking statements, bills (those paid and those to be paid), receipts for major purchases, and copies of tax forms filed during previous years. By doing this, you can assure that all your important documents will be together and easy to find when you need them.

Moonlighting. *Moonlighting* means working a second job, often at night. Current policy allows Air Force members to have second jobs as long as they don't interfere with duties or create a conflict of interest with other members of the armed forces, the Department of Defense, or the U.S. government.

Financial Institutions. Financial institutions whose services you may require include banks, credit unions, and savings and loan associations. The type you choose to do business with will usually depend on its location, services, and service charges.

Almost everyone uses savings and checking accounts. The status of these accounts is usually sent to each customer with a written statement each month. The statement lists all the transactions—deposits, withdrawals, and interest or dividends credited—made during the period. It's important to check this statement for accuracy. Then check it against your checkbook balance; that will help you avoid writing checks when funds aren't available.

Balancing a checking account is a simple three-step process: (1) Write down the current dollar balance from your bank statement, (2) add any deposits you've made that are not reflected on the statement, and (3) subtract the total of outstanding checks. Your account is reconciled when the balance amount on your statement and the balance amount in your checkbook are the same. If the figures don't agree, double-check your computations and make sure you've included all deposits and withdrawals. If they still don't agree, discuss it with a customer service representative at the financial institution. Banks, too, can make mistakes from time to time.

Credit and loan services allow you to buy items that you may not have sufficient funds for. Associated costs include interest payments, loan fees, insurance fees, and late charges. Use of these services is commonplace, especially for large purchases like a car or home. The best way to approach credit is make sure that you use it, not that it uses you. Shop around and compare costs. Get the items that you need, but don't overextend yourself financially.

Cosigning for a Loan. There may come a time when you will be asked by a friend or relative to be a cosigner on a loan agreement. Cosigners are usually required when a lending institution such as a bank or credit union considers the borrower (the person requesting the loan) a bad risk. When you cosign for another person's loan, your credit is added to the borrower's to reduce the risk. If the loan is then approved, you have a legal responsibility to repay the loan if the borrower defaults. Technically, you could be liable for missed payments, late fees, and demands for payment of any balance due. As you can see, cosigning for a loan can mean taking on a heavy responsibility. So before you agree, give it some careful thought.

Take a close look at why your friend needs the loan. Your friend may be a very junior airman who is considered a bad risk because of low earnings, not necessarily because of misused credit in the past. If your friend seems to be responsible, and if the loan is for a small amount, and if he or she can pay it back before reassignment, then it might be all right (but that's a lot of "ifs"). On the other hand, if your friend seems to be perpetually in debt, if the size of the loan is large, and if he or she may be reassigned soon, it's probably not a good idea to cosign.

Consider becoming a guarantor instead of a cosigner. This will make you only secondarily liable. If you are a guarantor, the lending institution can't ask you to repay the loan without first trying to have the borrower pay. In either case, read the small print of any agreement very carefully before you sign; seek an opinion from the Base Legal Office if necessary.

Buying a House. Buying a house is a major step in a person's life. In some cases it can yield many benefits and be a dream come true. In others, it can become a burden and turn into a financial nightmare. The decision to buy requires careful consideration of the circumstances.

A home purchase can be to your advantage when there are major income tax benefits, the house's value will appreciate significantly during the time you own it, or you are planning to keep the house for a long time, perhaps to live in when you retire.

A purchase may *not* be to your advantage if the payments are beyond your means, the mortgage has an adjustable interest rate and is subject to periodic increases, you may be reassigned in the near future, and the prospects do not look good for reselling the house at an increased price or finding a reliable tenant.

The Personal Financial Management Program. The Personal Financial Management Program (PFMP) was developed by the Air Force to help all Air Force people successfully manage their finances. It provides help in three primary ways:

1. Educational instruction courses on good money management in basic training and at permanent duty stations.

2. Counseling to meet individual needs or problems.

3. Information through different media such as base newspapers and handouts. Special pamphlets also explain a range of financial subjects such as buying with credit, buying a car, insurance, and estate planning. They use a commonsense approach and provide practical advice. These pamphlets are free and can usually be obtained from Family Support Centers, Personal Affairs Offices, and some Accounting and Finance Offices.

SOURCES OF ADDITIONAL INFORMATION

Consult the Air Force directives and pamphlets referred to in this chapter or your supervisor, first sergeant, or unit commander.

For questions on your pay, allowances, or deductions, consult the Accounting and Finance Office, or the *Military Money Guide,* published by Stackpole Books, 5067 Ritter Road, Mechanicsburg, PA 17055.

For questions on managing personal finances, consult the Family Support Center. The Base Legal Office or Staff Judge Advocate can answer questions on the legal aspects of financial responsibility.

For a thorough discussion of managing your personal finances, consult *Armed Forces Guide to Personal Financial Planning,* published by Stackpole Books, 5067 Ritter Road, Mechanicsburg, PA 17055.

20

Where to Go for Information, Assistance, or "Help!"

The U.S. Air Force has a broad system of customer service oriented agencies that respond to the needs of its personnel and their families. Some are staffed by active-duty servicemembers and civilian employees, others by volunteers: family members, retirees, and people from the local community.

The agencies provide a wide range of services—from meeting physical needs to career aspirations; from helping people resettle at a new base to helping someone in financial difficulty; from ensuring equal opportunity and treatment to ensuring national security. Despite the variety in the end product, there's a common thread that runs through every organization: service to the individual and the Air Force community.

AIR FORCE AID SOCIETY (AFAS)
Administered by the Personal Affairs Office, which is assigned to the Military Personnel Flight (MPF), the Air Force Aid Society (AFAS) was established to provide assistance for unforeseen financial emergencies. Each case is reviewed individually, and where aid is appropriate, it can be given as either a noninterest loan or an outright grant. For example, full or limited financial assistance may be provided to meet costs of rent, utilities, food, transportation, off-duty education, and funeral expenses.

AREA DEFENSE COUNSELS (ADCs)
Located at every major base, Air Defense Counsels (ADCs) are Air Force lawyers whose primary responsibility is to act as defense counsel for military personnel undergoing courts-martial. They also are available to advise personnel who have been administered Article 15 punishment or recommended for administrative discharge, and when a suspect in a criminal investigation asks to see a lawyer.

THE CIVILIAN PERSONNEL OFFICE

As manager of the personnel system for the civilian workforce, the Civilian Personnel Office implements programs, classifies applicants according to their qualifications, places personnel in positions, and provides overall program management—training, appraisal, equal opportunity, labor relations, performance awards, pay, travel, leave, promotions, and so on.

THE MILITARY PERSONNEL FLIGHT (MPF)

The Military Personnel Flight (MPF) is the office of primary responsibility for all base-level personnel actions involving military members and their dependents. The customer service branch is the focal point for all general inquiries. In most cases they will be able to act on and complete your requests. If not, they will refer you to a personnel representative from one of the following four sections:

1. The Customer Assistance Section, which includes the customer service branch, the records center, and personal affairs.

2. The Personnel Utilization Section, which includes assignments, manning control, and personnel readiness.

3. The Career Progression Section, which includes promotion and testing, classification and training, and on-the-job training.

4. The Quality Force Section, which includes separations and reenlistments, performance reports, maintenance of all unfavorable information files (UIFs), and all records of special disciplinary actions.

THE EDUCATION OFFICE

The Education Office provides information about a wide range of educational opportunities, primarily at the college level. For more information, see chapter 11, "Training and Education."

EDUCATION PROGRAMS/SCHOOLING FOR DEPENDENT CHILDREN

In the United States, some schools may be located on bases; however, most children attend schools in surrounding civilian communities. In overseas areas, the Department of Defense Dependent Schools (DODDS) network provides elementary and secondary education for children in kindergarten through twelfth grade. Their schools are staffed with American teachers, and the curriculum and standards are comparable with those in the United States. If DODDS facilities are not available, children may attend private or locally operated schools; when this is approved, costs are paid for by the government. Students who wish to continue their education can attend a university of their choice or participate in college-level courses offered on their sponsor's base on a space-available basis. In these cases, all costs are absorbed by the sponsor or dependent. Information about student grants and loans, from federal and Air Force sources, is usually available at base education centers.

FAMILY SERVICES
Family Services is a people-oriented program administered by volunteers from Air Force families, both active-duty and retired. Primarily they provide assistance to personnel arriving and departing from a base. Of special note is their "loan-out" program: You can check out, free of charge, household items you need to keep you going until your items arrive or after your things have been shipped when you're being reassigned. Items range from small kitchen accessories to baby furniture to linens. Some offices maintain brochures with information about other bases. They also arrange emergency services when possible, such as baby-sitting and transportation.

FAMILY SUPPORT CENTERS (FSCs)
Family Support Centers (FSCs) are designed to help provide support and assistance to military members (single or married) and their immediate families. They serve as one-stop centers for reliable information, courses, and services. Sometimes they help by encouraging people to see other referral agencies that can provide more specialized assistance or counseling. The following are some examples of normal services:

1. Personal Financial Management Program courses in the following areas:
• Basic budgeting, addressing the need for and techniques of developing a personal or family budget. Topics include goal development, spending plans, savings plans, estate planning, and retirement planning.
• Checkbook maintenance, giving instruction on how to open and maintain a checking account.
• Personal financial planning, including the need for long-term planning and the probable results of successful planning versus the results of failing to plan for the future.
• Smart car buying, giving instruction on purchasing or leasing a new or used vehicle, including prepurchase research, advertising gimmicks, price negotiations, and trade-in decisions and negotiations.
• Social Security registration, in which representatives from the Social Security Administration provide guidance and assistance in completing applications for new or replacement Social Security numbers. This reduces the stress of lines at the agency's offices and offers convenient service to base personnel.

2. The Transition Assistance Management Program equips separating or retiring members and their families with the skills and knowledge required to make a smooth, successful transition to another career or retirement.

3. Employee Resource Programs offer workshops and other assistance:

• An interview workshop provides job seekers with information and practical experience in conducting an effective job interview.

• A job search workshop takes participants through the entire job-search process, from initial preparation to interviewing.

• A mini employment workshop has representatives from the local community explain the essentials of an effective job search.

• A positive image workshop has representatives from the local community outline tips for successful dressing for interviews and appropriate ways of presenting yourself to the business world.

• A résumé workshop provides job seekers with current information and firsthand experience in developing résumés and cover letters.

• An SF-171 workshop provides information on how to complete the form, federal service hiring procedures, employment opportunities, and veterans benefits.

• A state employment workshop covers details of obtaining employment at the state level.

• A temp workshop offers information from various temporary employment agency representatives, who discuss how they fill job openings, some of which can become permanent positions.

• Additionally, there is a Resource Area that contains tools and resources to ease job hunting. It may include job vacancy listings; pamphlets and books on employment subjects; videos on careers, résumé writing, and interviewing techniques; educational opportunities; employment trends and projections; and word-processing programs to prepare cover letters, résumés, and job applications.

4. Training in Marriage Enrichment (TIME) teaches couples how to make marriage more effective, rewarding, and satisfying.

5. Parenting programs offer assistance in the following areas:

• Systematic Training for Effective Parenting (STEP) offers three programs: STEP (Early Childhood) gives parents a better understanding of children under six years old and presents factors that influence their behavior and development. STEP (6–12 years) helps parents relate to children in this age group through discussion and practice. STEP (Teens) offers a down-to-earth way to meet the challenges of raising teenagers. Topics include peer pressure, education and career plans, sexuality, using the family car, and drinking and drug use.

• Siblings without Rivalry teaches parents how to help children resolve conflicts and get along better with brothers and sisters. The courses identify what causes hostility between children and what kinds of attitudes and language you should use to decrease hostile actions.

• Strengthening Stepfamilies offers information, skills, and practical advice for successful living when two families are united as one.

• Single Parents' Support Groups offer an opportunity for single parents to share their experiences raising children without the aid of a partner while coping with the stresses of military life.

6. The Airman's Attic program offers donated clothes, furniture, and household goods for staff sergeants and below at no charge. (This program is usually through the Family Support Center, but at some locations it is aligned under other base activities.)

7. Relocation service, helping new families settle in and helping those preparing for a move.

8. Services for special-need families (single parents, special-education requirements, and cultural orientation programs for non-English-speaking family members).

9. Referral and aid for families in crisis.

10. Spouse employment training, consultation, and job information (career planning, writing a résumé, preparing for a job interview).

11. Support during separation, when the military member is going away on temporary duty or on a remote tour.

12. Information about overseas areas, such as language courses, customs requirements, cultural differences and sensitivities, and what items to ship and what not to ship. Brochures, guides, and some videos are available on bases worldwide.

HOUSING OFFICES

Housing offices handle the assignment and maintenance of on-base housing, priority for which is based on your grade, date of arrival, number of dependents, and units available. They maintain lists of available off-base housing or rental agents. They also help mediate in cases of landlord-tenant disputes. At some locations, they provide information on the purchase of a home (what's available, veterans benefits, and financing).

LEGAL ASSISTANCE

Legal assistance is provided by the Staff Judge Advocate's Office, also referred to as the Base Legal Office. Active-duty members and their dependents are eligible to receive assistance, as are retires and sometimes civil service employees, when time permits. Assistance is restricted to matters of a personal nature (not for businesses) or a civil nature (not criminal matters; they are referred to the Area Defense Counsel). Each Judge Advocate (lawyer) is a graduate of an accredited law school and has been admitted to the bar (authorized to practice law) in at least one state or territory. Because of their duty status in the USAF (usually as a commissioned officer), they are not allowed to represent military clients in any state or federal court. However, they can, with your permission, provide advice and assistance (such as writing letters or contacting other people on your behalf). Primary services provided by the Legal Office are help with financial claims, consumer matters, wills and powers of attorney, taxes, insurance, separation and divorce, and military justice issues. Walk-in service is provided for common needs; appointments are given for more complex issues.

MEDICAL AND DENTAL CARE
Medical and dental care is provided to all active-duty members. Dependents are provided full medical care in military and civilian hospitals under the Uniformed Services Health Benefit Program (USHBP). Under this program, care is available anywhere in the world in a uniformed service medical facility (Air Force, Army, Navy, and certain public health facilities) subject to the availability of space and facilities and type of specialized care required. Dependents are also eligible for care under the Civilian Health and Medical Program of the Uniformed Services (CHAMPUS), a cost-sharing program in which the government pays for most of the allowable charges.

Air Force medical facilities vary in size. There are small facilities, such as medical aid stations and dispensaries. There are larger facilities, such as clinics, hospitals, and regional medical centers. One special aspect of the medical system is the air evacuation program. It operates worldwide through the use of specially modified aircraft. Its purpose is to bring patients to medical centers that provide specialized treatment when care is not available locally.

Full dental care is provided to active-duty members. Dependents receive limited care. In the United States, supplementary insurance is offered to cover most needs. In overseas areas, dependents are usually provided with an annual examination during their sponsor's birth month. If follow-up work is needed, appointments are made on a space-available basis.

THE AIR FORCE OFFICE OF SPECIAL INVESTIGATIONS (OSI)
The Air Force Office of Special Investigations (OSI) usually has a detachment office at each major installation. It is responsible for the following:
1. Investigations of espionage, sabotage, and subversion.
2. Counterintelligence.
3. Major criminal matters.
4. Liaison and assistance to other United States and foreign government agencies, when requested.
5. Protection of senior distinguished visitors and dignitaries, both foreign and domestic, when requested by proper authority.
6. Internal security investigations.

PERSONAL AFFAIRS OFFICES
Personal Affairs Offices are located in the Military Personnel Flight (MFP). They provide a variety of information and assistance in matters concerning government and personal passports, visas, the Air Force Aid Society, casualty assistance, veterans benefits, and travel in foreign countries.

POSTAL SERVICES

Postal services are provided by the U.S. Postal Service at most bases in the United States. At overseas installations, services are provided at Air Force Post Offices (APOs), operated by USAF airmen. The scope of service includes delivery of mail to individually assigned post office boxes, parcel post, stamp sales, postal insurance, and money orders. Delivery of first-class mail to overseas areas usually takes four to seven days. Larger packages and newspaper or magazine subscriptions can take a while longer, depending on how they are sent. Air mail comes quickly. Boat mail comes slowly.

PUBLIC AFFAIRS OFFICES (PAs)

Public Affairs Offices provide information in three different forums:

1. The internal information program to inform members of the Air Force and their dependents about current developments.

2. The public information program to give the public unclassified information about the Air Force: stories, statements, interviews, speeches.

3. The community relations program to obtain support for the unit's mission in the local community.

RED CROSS

Representatives of the Red Cross are available at all major overseas bases twenty-four hours a day. In the United States, representatives are available either on base or in the local civilian community. They can provide military members and their dependents with financial aid for emergency situations (such as for food, clothing, or shelter); verification of doctors' reports on family members who are ill; travel and maintenance loans or grants for military personnel on emergency leave; and counseling assistance on related problems.

RELIGIOUS PROGRAMS

Religious programs are provided through a network of base chapels and chaplains representing many denominations. Chaplains are accredited clergymen and women who serve on active duty as commissioned officers. Their programs include worship services and masses, religious education for adults and children, weddings, baptisms, confirmations, spiritual retreats, choirs, Bible study groups, youth and young adult fellowships, women's groups, and special conferences. They interact with and provide humanitarian support and guidance to other agencies such as the hospital, the Red Cross, and Family Support Centers. They also provide confidential counseling and referral services.

SECURITY POLICE

The security police has two primary segments: security and law enforcement. The security branch is committed to safeguarding operational resources (such as aircraft). The law enforcement branch acts as a community police force, conducting investigations, responding to inquiries, implementing crime prevention programs, manning gate guard positions, monitoring traffic control, and so forth. Most bases provide a special telephone number for assistance.

SOCIAL ACTIONS OFFICES
Social Actions Offices serve as a focal point for programs and counseling related to drug and alcohol abuse control, human relations education, and equal opportunity and treatment.

THRIFT SHOPS
Staffed by volunteers, usually from the Noncommissioned Officers' Wives Club and the Officers' Wives Club, thrift shops provide a community service by selling—at very reasonable prices—articles no longer needed by military members and their dependents: clothing, furniture, small appliances, toys, and other miscellaneous items. A small commission charge (usually 15 percent of the purchase price) for each sale is put back into charities in the local Air Force community.

SOURCES OF ADDITIONAL INFORMATION
Consult the organization listed. If you're unsure where it's located, look in the base telephone directory, which usually lists telephone numbers and building numbers.

Consult the Family Support Center, your supervisor, or your unit's first sergeant or commander. Each is familiar with the referral agencies and can probably help you select the one that best meets your needs.

21

Off-Duty Pursuits

When people think about the armed forces they usually think in general terms about the on-duty aspects and the tangible conditions such as pay, job security, medical care, education, and retirement benefits. Yet one of the major benefits, not always recognized as such, is a package of off-duty pursuits and benefits that can't be matched by many major corporations in the world. This package includes a worldwide system of shopping facilities; a full range of morale, welfare, and recreation programs; optional membership in private associations and clubs; and the opportunity to travel extensively in the United States and overseas. The extent of these programs varies from base to base and is usually governed by the size of the installation. To gain access to these facilities and programs, all you need is a current military identification (ID) card.

SHOPPING FACILITIES
Shopping facilities are provided worldwide under the control of the Army and Air Force Exchange Service (AAFES) and the Air Force Commissary Service (AFCOMS). Their mission is to supply and control retail outlets whose size, inventory, and services are consistent with the size of the population served. Merchandise provided varies from necessity to convenience items. Everything is competitively priced and, in most cases, is less expensive than similar products off base. Some of their primary outlets, services, and facilities include the following:

Base Exchanges (also referred to as the BX or the Main Exchange). Normally the largest shopping facility on each base. Merchandise available includes most of the items you would find in any large department store off base: clothing, appliances, jewelry, health and beauty aids, stationery, toys, greeting cards, candy, and so forth. Customer service sections offer mail-order services, gift wrapping, and other services.

Commissaries. Large grocery stores with selections comparable to their stateside equivalents. In overseas areas, most packaged, frozen, and canned goods come from U.S. sources; some of the meat, poultry, dairy, and produce items are acquired from local areas. All goods must pass rigid inspections and health controls.

Exchange Concessions. Smaller individual outlets that offer specialized services: laundromats, service stations, barber and beauty shops, dry cleaning, photo processing, tailor, repair shops (electrical, watch, shoe), and television and video rentals. At some overseas locations, facilities are available for souvenir and gift shops and approved agents who sell new U.S. cars.

Foodlands or Shopettes. Small, quick-service convenience stores with smaller inventories: food, beverages, health and beauty aids, and stationery.

Furniture Centers, Garden Centers, and Sports Centers. Specialized outlets that carry a specific range of merchandise. Furniture outlets, in particular, are usually found in overseas areas.

Military Clothing Sales Stores. Sell military uniforms, insignia, badges, devices, and related items.

Package Liquor Stores. Primarily found in overseas locations, where they are referred to as Class VI Stores. Excellent selections of American and foreign liquors and wines are sold at very low prices. Purchases and quantities are controlled under a ration card system. Since most of the items are sold on a tax-free basis, rules and procedures vary from country to country.

Stars and Stripes Bookstores. Found primarily in overseas locations. They offer a wide selection of reading material, including newspapers, magazines, and hard- and softcover books. In addition, they are usually the place to buy college textbooks for off-duty education programs.

AIR FORCE SERVICES

The Air Force Services programs have evolved over the years and are considered to be an integral part of the Air Force way of life. They represent an assortment of self-supporting activities that provide services to enhance the morale of military members and their families. They do this at minimum expense to the Air Force community and "reinvest" their earnings to improve and operate their respective programs. Examples of programs include the following:

Aero Clubs. Offer safe, low-cost flying in light aircraft. Local instructors are usually available to provide courses for personnel who wish to obtain a private pilot's license for this type of aircraft.

Audio/Photo Clubs. Very popular in overseas areas. They offer a comprehensive range of stereo equipment, televisions and video equipment, cameras, and in some cases, computer equipment.

Base Theaters. Show a wide range of popular motion pictures at reduced rates. The facilities are also used for visiting shows and large briefings, such as commander's calls.

Bowling Lanes. Vary in size based on location. Some small, remote Air Force stations have two-lane alleys. Larger installations have facilities comparable with some of the best in the civilian community. Often included are automatic pinspotters, foul lights, and overhead score projectors. Snack bars and pro shops offering bowling accessories are usually available in the large facilities. Both organized leagues and open bowling are scheduled.

Child-Care Centers. Offer services for full- or part-day care, including nursery, preschool, and play-school programs. With the increase in the number of single-parent families, these centers have received additional emphasis during recent years. Many new facilities have been built, and high standards have been set to assure the best quality of care. Types of programs and ages accepted may vary based on size of the staff and facility.

Gymnasiums and Sports Centers. Provide coed facilities for varsity, intramural, and individual endeavors. Scope of services is normally determined by the size of the installation. May include basketball courts, exercise and weight rooms, steam and sauna rooms, handball and squash courts, tennis courts, swimming pools, and outdoor tracks, football, softball, and soccer fields. Schedules are adjusted seasonally. Opportunities also exist for varsity competitions (base teams) to participate with other local and interservice teams.

Golf Courses. Available on some installations. They range from standard nine-hole and eighteen-hole courses down to miniature courses. Pro shops and snack bars are commonly found.

Hobby Shops. Organized either individually or collectively in a complex. Popular examples include craft and ceramics shops, photo shops (for rental of cameras and use of a lab to process and develop film), wood hobby shops, and auto hobby shops (operated by experienced personnel, with an extensive range of tools for checkout on the premises and facilities ranging from work bays with hydraulic lifts to wash racks and paint booths).

Libraries. Contain a wide variety of books, magazines, newspapers, recordings, and other media that can be used for pleasure or self-improvement. Many have recently acquired video and computer equipment, with software, to complement education programs.

Open Mess Facilities (NCO and Airmen's Clubs). Facilities provided for members usually include a main lounge, a dining room, a casual bar, and a game room. Services may include floor shows, dances, take-out food, and support for special events such as awards banquets and squadron parties. Also included are check-cashing facilities and foreign currency exchange at overseas installations. At some locations, separate facilities such as "The Top Three Club" may exist for senior noncommissioned officers.

Recreation Centers or Community Activities Centers. Offer a wide range of activities and entertainment. Depending on the size of the installation, they usually have three main areas: a large room with a stage (suitable for conferences or large functions), a game room (pool tables, Ping-Pong tables, musical instruments, records, CDs, tapes, and cards), and a television lounge. The "Rec Center" is usually the primary location for special programs such as shows, plays, tournaments, coin and stamp clubs, chess clubs, square dancing, and so forth. Local tours to surrounding areas are frequently organized and offered. Overseas centers normally provide reimbursable telephone services for personnel who want to make calls to the United States. Free refreshments or concession snack bar facilities are commonly available.

Recreation Supply. Issues, stores, and maintains all athletic equipment and supplies for teams or individuals. Also provides equipment you can check out for a small fee, usually for seventy-two hours, including softball and baseball equipment, camping equipment (tents, sleeping bags, stoves, and coolers), tennis rackets, horseshoe sets, fishing equipment, and golf clubs. Sometimes gardening equipment such as lawn mowers and weed eaters are available.

Rod and Gun Clubs. Offer facilities for skeet and trap shooting, and make arrangements for fishing and hunting excursions in surrounding areas. These clubs usually offer a sports equipment shop and snack bar or restaurant.

Youth Centers. Provide facilities for leisure activities for base youths between ages six and eighteen. Activities offered usually include sports and social programs, dances, arts and crafts, and Scouting programs.

CLUBS AND PRIVATE ASSOCIATIONS

Each installation has a number of self-supporting private community-service groups that cater to sports, religious, fraternal, and special interest groups. Examples include the following:

Air Force Association Chapters
Air Force Sergeants Association Chapters
Alcoholics Anonymous
American Legion Chapters
Barbershop Groups (singing)
Booster Clubs (for sports activities)
Bowling Associations
Chess Clubs
Choirs and Singing Groups
Coin and Stamp Clubs
Computer User Clubs
Darts Teams
Drama Clubs
Little League
Marriage Encounter Groups

Martial Arts Clubs
Masonic Lodges
Model Airplane Clubs
Motorcycle Clubs
NCO Association Chapters
Parent Teacher Associations
Scouting Programs: Cubs through
  Explorers, Brownies through
  Girl Scouts
Square Dancing Clubs
Swim Clubs
Wives' Clubs: NCO Wives' Clubs,
  Enlisted Wives' Clubs,
  Airmen's Wives' Clubs,
  Protestant Women of the Chapel,
  Council of Catholic Wives

The list of private associations lengthens or shortens from time to time, depending on the needs of the local population. Where similar interests exist, people are encouraged to join together and start an organization.

OVERSEAS ACTIVITIES

American communities overseas traditionally offer a wider range of leisure activities than stateside bases. Two very special pluses about being overseas are opportunities to travel and to make friends with people of other cultures.

To enjoy an overseas tour, try to achieve a balance among duty commitments, touring and traveling, and getting involved in local base or community life. Try to avoid becoming a "barracks rat," staying in your dormitory room or house and never going anywhere. People who do this miss a lot of great opportunities. Their tours of duty drag out and they often find themselves counting the day until their return to the United States.

One of the best ways to get acquainted with an overseas country is to go to the Recreation Center and sign up for one of the newcomers' tours. They're inexpensive and are geared for both singles and families. Some are day trips; others take advantage of long weekends. Trips are usually organized around the following:

1. Local attractions.

2. A specific theme, such as shopping for antiques, visiting ancient churches or castles, going to live entertainment shows, eating out at traditional restaurants, stopping at local pubs or taverns or visiting a local McDonald's or Pizza Hut.

3. Sporting events, either watching or participating, ranging from skiing in the Alps or deep-sea fishing to international events such as the Olympics or World Cup soccer matches.

You can watch for upcoming events by reading the base newspaper or contacting the base's Community Relations Advisor. These positions are sometimes created by the host government to help personnel and their families settle in. They can advise on shopping, transportation, traveling, education, and many other aspects of local life. They can also introduce you to local clubs and organizations and provide information on facilities where you can pursue your hobbies and recreational interests while you are stationed there.

For the more adventurous, you can consult local travel agents or even plan your own itineraries. Many countries have national tourist offices, which routinely provide free literature, such as maps and brochures, and will do their best to answer your travel questions. The following are some of the most frequently used offices:

British Tourist Authority, 40 West 57th Street, New York, NY 10019
French Government Tourist Office, 610 Fifth Avenue, New York, NY 10020
Irish Tourist Board, 757 Third Avenue, New York, NY 10017
Italian Government Tourist Office, 630 Fifth Avenue, New York, NY 10020

German National Tourist Office, 747 Third Avenue, New York, NY 10017
Netherlands Board of Tourism, 355 Lexington Avenue, New York, NY 10017
Spanish National Tourist Office, 665 Fifth Avenue, New York, NY 10022
Swiss National Tourist Office, 608 Fifth Avenue, New York, NY 10020

Another common way to enjoy travel overseas is to plan your itinerary so that you can take advantage of facilities at other U.S. military installations. This is commonly referred to as base-hopping. It's especially useful if you're traveling by car and have a periodic need to convert dollars to the local currency, want to service the car, or take advantage of exchange or medical entitlements. Billeting can sometimes be arranged on a space-available basis. Some overseas activities and installations that offer special recreational facilities or that are located close to major cities are noted below. Use the telephone numbers listed to contact the base operator or a billeting office.

England
RAF Lakenheath, 48th Tactical Fighter Wing, APO AE 09464, commercial
     phone Eriswell, 3131, DSN 226-1110 or 3131. Located north of Newmar-
     ket, about seventy miles north of London.

Germany
Germany has a U.S. Armed Forces Recreation Area with extensive recreational programs and facilities. It is located in the beautiful surroundings of the Bavarian Alps, south of Munich by the Austrian border. Activities for all seasons are planned for singles, couples, and families with children. A full range of support activities is also available (exchanges, commissaries, medical, child-care centers, and so forth). For additional information write to Garmisch-Partenkirchen, Armed Forces Recreation Center, APO AE 09053-5000.

Hawaii
Bellows Air Force Stations, HI 96853, commercial phone (808) 259-7271.
     Recreation area with 104 furnished beach cottages, located on the eastern
     coast of the island of Oahu.
Hale Koa Hotel, Fort DeRussy, HI 96815, commercial phone (808) 955-0555,
     toll-free (800) 367-6027. Located on Waikiki Beach, by Honolulu.
Hickam AFB, 15th ABW, Honolulu, HI 96853, commercial phone (808) 449-
     2603, DSN 430-0111. Located next to the Honolulu International Airport.
Kilauea Armed Forces Recreation Camp, Hawaii Volcanoes National Park, HI
     96718, commercial phone (808) 543-2658, DSN R1 1101-00. Located on
     the island of Hawaii, the "Big Island."

Waianae Army Recreation Center, Waianae, HI 96792, commercial phone (808) 696-2494 or -2883. Located on the northeast coast of the island of Oahu.

Italy
Camp Darby, 8th Support Group, APO AE 09613-5000, commercial phone (0586) 93001, DSN 633-8371. Located in northwestern Italy, by the city of Pisa.
Naples, Naval Support Activity, FPO AE 09619-5000, commercial phone (081) 724-4379, DSN 621-1100. Located in Naples, south of Rome; recreation center located in Carney Park, three miles from base.
Vincenza, Hq USA/SETAF, APO AE 09630-5000, commercial phone (0444) 500333, DSN 634-1000. Located between the cities of Venice and Milan.

Japan
Sanno Joint Services Transient Billeting Facility, APO AP 96337-0110, commercial phone 581-6741. Located in the Akasaka district of downtown Tokyo.
Yokota Air Base, 374 MSS, APO AP 96328-5123, commercial phone 0425-52-2511, DSN 248-1101. Located approximately thirty miles from Tokyo.

Korea
Naija Hotel and R&R Center, U.S. Army Garrison, Korea, APO AP 96205-0427, commercial phone, Seoul: 73-5580. Located in downtown Seoul, close to the capitol building.
U.S. Army Garrison, Yongson, Hq U.S. 8th Army, U.S. Forces, Korea, and United Nations Command, APO AP 96205-0177, commercial phone 293-0-4448, DSN 315 262-1101. Located in the Yongson district of Seoul.

Scotland
U.S. Naval Security Group Activity, FPO AE 09419-1200, commercial phone Edzell, 431, DSN 229-1110. Located near the town of Edzell in the Scottish highlands (limited facilities).

Spain
Rota, U.S. Naval Station, FPO AE 09645-5500, commercial phone 862780, DSN 727-1110. Located south of Seville on Spain's southern coast.

FURLOUGH FARES AND SPACE AVAILABLE TRAVEL

For those of you who would rather not travel by car, there are two other special options to pursue. Active-duty personnel and their dependents are eligible to ask for furlough fares. These are special discounted travel rates offered by major airlines, bus companies, railways, rental car agencies, and hotel chains. The amount of discount can vary from company to company, anywhere from 10 to 60 percent of the standard rate. A valid ID card and your leave authorization slip are usually required to obtain the special rates.

The second option is space-available travel, often referred to as "Space-A" or "catching a hop." This system lets military members and their families travel on government aircraft when there are extra seats available. Base Operations and Air Mobility Command (AMC) Passenger Terminals are your primary points of contact for this kind of travel. They can provide information about frequency of flights, destinations, and travel requirements.

There are some basic guidelines for Space-A travel. Space is always subject to mission requirements. There's a priority system for passengers, based on urgency of need and duty status. Those on emergency leave are normally processed first, then passengers in a duty status, passengers in a leave status, and retirees. Members may sign up in advance to get priority within their category. To do so, they must present an ID card and either special orders or a copy of their leave authorization form. In some instances, passports, visas, and shot records may also be required. Military members can travel on a space-available basis in the Untied States; dependents cannot. However, they can accompany a military member who is traveling to, from, or within an overseas area. When traveling, active-duty personnel must travel in uniform.

These rules may seem somewhat restrictive at first glance, but they are necessary to provide some general controls and ensure the smooth and equitable operation of the system. Thousands of people travel this way every week. And in the long run, almost everyone's in agreement about one thing: People who can fly from California to Japan or from New Jersey to England at no cost don't really mind a little bit of red tape.

SOURCES OF ADDITIONAL INFORMATION

Contact the shopping facilities and Air Force Services programs referred to in this chapter.

Contact the Air Mobility Command (AMC) passenger service terminal or base operations for information on space-available travel on government aircraft.

For overseas travel, contact the Base Recreation Center or the Personal Affairs Branch of the Military Personnel Flight (MPF).

A good source of information on temporary military lodging and Space-A air opportunities is Military Living Publications. For information on their publications, write to Military Living Publications, P.O. Box 2347, Falls

Church, VA 22042, or call (703) 237-0203. Military Living will send a free welcome kit to anyone on orders to the Washington, D.C., area.

For a thorough discussion of installations in the continental United States and overseas, consult *Guide to Military Installations,* published by Stackpole Books, 5067 Ritter Road, Mechanicsburg, PA 17055.

22

Veterans Benefits

There comes a time in every career, be it long or short, to consider other career options. Some changes are pursued by choice. Others may be necessitated by conditions that are beyond any one individual's ability to control.

Events such as the dissolution of the Soviet Union, the emergence of small regional conflicts, advances in technology, and reductions in federal funding levels resulted in the need to restructure the U.S. armed forces and make significant reductions in the number of personnel who serve. In order to draw down the numbers of active-duty personnel, the services developed a wide range of voluntary and involuntary separation programs that offer special benefits and incentives in order to ease the transition from military to civilian life. In addition to the programs offered by the armed forces, there are various benefits available to veterans and their dependents that are administered by local, state, and federal government agencies and private organizations.

This chapter provides an overview into some of the primary benefit programs and sources of support available to eligible veterans.

THE TRANSITION ASSISTANCE PROGRAM

The Labor Department has established the Transition Assistance Program (TAP) to assist servicemembers who are scheduled for separation from active duty. The program establishes a partnership with the Department of Defense, Department of Veterans Affairs, and Labor Department to provide employment and training information to servicemembers within 180 days of separation. Three-day workshops to assist in civilian employment are conducted at military installations. Additional counseling is available to disabled veterans. For additional information, contact VETS, Department of Labor, 200 Constitution Ave., NW, Room S1313, Washington, DC 20210, or call (202) 219-5573.

REEMPLOYMENT RIGHTS

Under the Veterans' Reemployment Rights (VRR) law, as noted in chapter 43 of Title 38, U.S. Code, a person who left a civilian job to enter active duty in the armed forces, either voluntarily or involuntarily, may be entitled to return to his or her civilian job after discharge or release from active duty. Four requirements must be met in order for a veteran to pursue employment rights:

1. The person must have been employed in other than a temporary civilian job.

2. The person must have left the civilian job for the purpose of entering military service.

3. The person must not remain on active duty longer than four years, unless the period beyond four years is at the request and for the convenience of the federal government and the military discharge form carries this statement. (In some cases, the limitation may be extended to six years.)

4. The person must be discharged or released from active duty under honorable conditions.

Under this law, returning veterans are to be placed in the job as if they had remained continuously employed instead of going on active duty. This means that the person may be entitled to benefits that are generally based on seniority (such as pay increases, pensions, missed promotions, and missed transfers). The law also protects a veteran from discharge without just cause for one year from the date of reemployment.

A veteran must apply to the preservice employer within ninety days following separation from active duty. If the veteran is hospitalized or recuperating when discharged, the ninety-day application period begins upon release from the hospital or completion of recuperation, which may last up to one year. Applications for reemployment should be given verbally or in writing to a person who is authorized to represent the company for hiring purposes. A record should be kept of when and to whom the application was given.

Questions on the VRR law, or requests for assistance in attaining reemployment if there are problems with private employers or state or local governments, should be directed to the Department of Labor's director for Veterans Employment and Training (DVET) for the state in which the employer is located. For additional information, consult telephone directories under U.S. Department of Labor or call (800) 442-2838 for the appropriate DVET telephone number.

JOB-FINDING ASSISTANCE

Assistance in finding jobs is provided to veterans through state employment offices throughout the country. These offices have special veterans offices that provide veterans with free job counseling, testing, training referral, and placement services, as well as information about unemployment compensation, job marts, and on-the-job and apprenticeship training opportunities.

EMPLOYMENT IN THE FEDERAL GOVERNMENT

The federal government has over 2 million civilian positions representing approximately nine hundred different occupations. Annual salary levels range from $12,000 for entry-level positions to $80,000 for more senior positions.

These positions are located in the major federal agencies: the Legislative branch, Judiciary, Executive Office of the President, Department of Agriculture, Department of Commerce, Department of Defense, Department of Education, Department of Energy, Department of Health and Human Services, Social Security, Department of Housing and Urban Development, Department of the Interior, Department of Justice, Department of Labor, Department of State, Department of Transportation, Department of the Treasury, Department of Veterans Affairs, Environmental Protection Agency, General Services Administration, National Aeronautics and Space Administration, Office of Personnel Management, Small Business Administration, Central Intelligence Agency, and Federal Bureau of Investigation.

There are two primary programs that provide veterans with special access to federal employment opportunities:

1. The Vietnam-Era Veterans Readjustment Assistance Act of 1974 enacted into law the *Veterans Readjustment Appointment (VRA) authority,* which provides for the U.S. policy of promoting maximum job opportunities within the federal government for qualified disabled veterans. The VRA authority allows agencies to make noncompetitive appointments, at their discretion, to federal jobs for Vietnam-Era and post-Vietnam-Era veterans. These appointments lead to conversion to career or career-conditional employment upon satisfactory completion of two years' service. Veterans seeking VRA appointments should apply directly to the federal agency where they are seeking employment.

2. The *Disabled Veterans Affirmative Action Program (DVAAP)* is administered by the Office of Personnel Management. All federal agencies and departments are required to establish action plans to facilitate the recruitment, employment, and advancement of disabled veterans. Eligible veterans may receive veterans preference in federal employment, which provides for additional points added to passing scores in examinations, first consideration for certain jobs, and preference for retention in reduction-in-force actions.

If you are interested in these benefits or other federal employment opportunities, contact the personnel offices of the federal agencies in which you wish to be employed. Information may also be obtained by contacting the Federal Employment Information Centers of the U.S. Office of Personnel Management. The centers are listed in the telephone books under U.S. Government. Veterans may also obtain a nationwide listing of the Federal Employment Information Centers by writing to the U.S. Office of Personnel Management, Federal Employment Information Center, 1900 E Street, NW, Washington, DC 20415.

AFFIRMATIVE ACTION PROGRAM

Employers with federal contracts or subcontracts of $10,000 or more are required to take affirmative action to employ and advance Vietnam-Era and special disabled veterans. Legislative requirements are administered by the U.S. Department of Labor's Office of Federal Contract Compliance Programs (OFCCP).

SMALL BUSINESS ADMINISTRATION
Ever thought about starting your own business? The Small Business Administration (SBA) has a number of programs designed to help foster and encourage small business enterprises, including businesses owned or operated by veterans. The SBA provides business training, conferences, one-on-one counseling, advocacy, surety bonding, government procurement, and financial management assistance. In each SBA field office there is a veterans affairs officer who is designated as the contact person to assist veterans in dealings with the SBA. Information on SBA programs is available without charge from any of the approximately one hundred field offices. For the address of the nearest SBA office, check the U.S. Government section of your local telephone directory, or use the agency's national toll-free number, (800) 827-5722.

UNEMPLOYMENT COMPENSATION
Unemployment compensation is available for ex-servicemembers to provide a weekly income for a limited period of time to help them meet basic needs while searching for employment. The amount and duration of payments are governed by state laws, which vary considerably. Benefits are paid from federal funds. Ex-servicemembers should apply at their nearest state employment office immediately after leaving military service. Copies of military discharge forms (DD Form 214) are required to help determine eligibility for programs.

DEPARTMENT OF VETERANS AFFAIRS (VA) BENEFITS
The Department of Veterans Affairs (VA) is a federal agency whose primary role is providing benefits to those who have served their country in the active military, naval, or air service and to their dependents.

Eligibility for most VA benefits is based on the type of discharge from active military service and, in some cases, minimum periods of time served as specified by law. Honorable and general discharges qualify veterans for most VA benefits. Dishonorable and some bad-conduct discharges issued by general courts-martial bar VA benefits. Those who enlisted in the military after 7 September 1980 and officers commissioned or who entered active military service after 16 October 1981 must have completed two years of active duty or the full period of their initial service obligation to be eligible for most VA benefits. Veterans with service-connected disabilities or those discharged for disability or hardship near the end of their service obligation are not held to this provision.

You can file a claim for VA benefits in person, through a veterans service organization, or through the mail. In order to file a claim with the VA, you must submit a copy of your service discharge form (a DD Form 214), which documents service dates and type of discharge, or provide your full name, military service number, branch of service, and dates of service. Once a claim is filed, the VA will set up a file number (Social Security numbers are presently used for this purpose) to track all of your future claims actions. This file number is often referred to as a C number.

Types of VA Benefits. The VA offers an extensive range of benefits, some of which must be applied for within a specified period of time. The following are the most frequently sought after:

• *Disability compensation.* Disability compensation is monetary benefits paid to veterans who are disabled by injury or disease incurred or aggravated during active military service in the line of duty. This compensation is paid in monthly payments based on the degree of a veteran's disability. Expressed as a percent, they run from 0 to 100 percent in 10 percent increments. Current rates range from $91 for a 10 percent disability to $1,870 for a 100 percent disability rating. The dollar amounts of these benefits, which are not subject to federal or state income tax, are usually changed each year by the Congress. Higher amounts may be awarded to veterans who have suffered certain specific, severe disabilities. These are granted on a case-by-case basis. Federal law prohibits the award of VA disability compensation that can be received when a veteran receives military retirement pay, except to the extent that an equal amount of military retirement pay is waived. Special entitlements can be granted to certain disabled veterans. These include the following:

1. Special allowances such as specialty adapted housing grants, housing insurance, adaptive equipment for automobiles or other conveyances, and clothing allowances for veterans who use prosthetic or orthopedic appliances.

2. Allowances for dependents are granted for service-connected disabled veterans who are rated at 30 percent or more.

3. Former prisoners of war who were incarcerated for at least thirty days are entitled to a presumption of service connection for disabilities resulting from certain diseases or ailments if manifested to a degree of 10 percent at any time after active service.

• *Non-service-connected (NSC) disability pensions.* Monetary benefits can be paid, in some instances, to veterans who have ninety days or more of wartime service; were separated from such service for a service-connected disability and became permanently and totally disabled from reasons not traceable to military service; or are over sixty-five years old. NSC pensions are not paid when a veteran's income and estate and that of his or her spouse and dependent children is so large that it is reasonable that some of it could be used for living expenses or when their income exceeds the applicable limit under federal law.

• *Medical care.* Medical care is provided to veterans on either a mandatory or a discretionary basis. Mandatory care is provided to those who have adjudicated service-connected medical or dental conditions. Discretionary care is provided to other categories of veterans with non-service-connected disabilities if space and facilities are available after providing care to service-connected veterans. Non-service-connected veterans can be charged for discretionary care based on their level of income, which is determined by a review of a VA Form 10-10f, "Financial Worksheet," filled out at the time care is requested. The VA has the authority to compare income information provided by veterans with information obtained from the Department of Health and Human Services and the Internal Revenue Service. The types of services available at VA medical facilities include, but are not limited to, inpatient and outpatient medical, surgical, and psychiatric care; dental care; nursing home; domiciliary; pharmacy; prosthetics; blind aids and services; drug/alcohol treatment; beneficiary travel; and special physical examinations for Agent Orange, ionizing radiation, and/or problems incurred in the Persian Gulf.

• *Medical Care for Dependents and Survivors.* The Civilian Health and Medical Program of the Department of Veterans Affairs (CHAMPVA) helps pay for medical services and supplies obtained from civilian sources by eligible dependents and survivors of certain veterans. The following are eligible for CHAMPVA benefits, provided they are not eligible for care under CHAMPUS (the Civilian Health and Medical Programs of the Uniformed Services) or Medicare:

1. The spouse or child of a veteran who has a permanent and total service-connected disability.

2. The surviving spouse or child of a veteran who died as a result of a service-connected condition or who at the time of death was permanently and totally disabled from a service-connected condition.

3. The surviving spouse or child of a person who died while on active military service in the line of duty.

4. A surviving spouse who remarries may qualify for care after the subsequent marriage is terminated.

Care under the CHAMPVA program is not normally provided in VA medical facilities. For additional information, apply to the CHAMPVA Center, 4500 Cherry Creek Drive South, Denver, CO 80222, or call (800) 733-8387.

• *Education and training programs* that include counseling and funding are available for veterans, servicemembers and eligible dependents. See chapter 11, "Training and Education," for an overview of GI Bill programs and benefits. The Vocational Rehabilitation Program provides training and rehabilitation services to veterans who have a compensable service-connected disability and a need for such services in order to overcome an employment handicap. Under this program, up to forty-eight months or more may be authorized in colleges, universities, vocational schools, on-farm, on-job, or apprenticeship programs, as well as special rehabilitation facilities. The VA will pay for tuition, books, fees, supplies, and equipment and will also provide employment assistance following completion of the program.

• *Guaranteed loans* for the purchase and refinancing of homes, condominiums, and manufactured homes may be obtained by eligible veterans and unmarried surviving spouses. The VA guarantees part of the total loan so a veteran may obtain a mortgage with a competitive interest rate—without a down payment, if the lender agrees.

Points of Contact within the Department of Veterans Affairs. The type of benefit you are interested in obtaining will determine whom you should contact to obtain additional information. In general, the VA has four primary sources:

1. *Vet centers* are located throughout the country. They provide veterans with counseling to assist in readjusting to civilian life. Assistance includes group, individual, and family counseling; community outreach; and education. Vet center staff can also help veterans find services from the VA and non-VA sources if needed.

2. *VA Regional Offices (VAROs)* process claims for VA benefits and administer those benefits, which include disability compensation, pension, home loan guaranty, life insurance, education, vocational training for disabled veterans, burial benefits, and survivor's compensation, pension, and education.

3. *VA Medical Centers (VAMCs)* are the immediate sources for obtaining information regarding medical care. Through a national network, they provide all types of medical care. Many of the VA Medical Centers also operate smaller outpatient clinics at separate geographical locations. These smaller clinics can make referrals for a wider range of care in the larger VA Medical Centers.

4. *VA national cemeteries* can provide information about eligibility of veterans and dependents for burial benefits.

Veterans and dependents from throughout the country may obtain information on VA benefits from regional offices by calling a toll-free number, (800) 827-1000. Callers are then automatically connected to the closest VA regional office, where a veterans benefits advisor (VBA) will direct the caller to an appropriate program manager. Other toll-free VA telephone services available in all states include the following:

CHAMPVA: (800) 733-8387
Debt Management Center: (800) 827-0648
Education loan: (800) 326-8276
Life insurance: (800) 669-8477
Prisoner of War (POW) Hotline: (800) 821-8139. (Calls are received in a twenty-four-hour service center in Washington, D.C., which in turn coordinates with local VA medical centers and regional offices in arranging benefits assistance and resolving differences.)
Radiation Helpline: (800) 827-0365
Telecommunication Device for the Deaf (TDD): (800) 829-4833

You can also use your local telephone directory, which lists the addresses and commercial telephone numbers of all VA facilities in your area, under Department of Veterans Affairs in the Federal or U.S. Government section.

Many states also offer benefits to veterans. These are independent of federal benefits and may differ from state to state. Eligibility for state benefits usually requires that the state be a veteran's place of residence or home of record at the time of enlistment. For further information, consult your local telephone directory under the state government listing section.

Department of Veterans Affairs Regional Office (VAROs) and VA Medical Centers (VAMCs) that can provide you with assistance include the following:

Alabama:	Birmingham (VAMC); Montgomery (VARO and VAMC); Tuscaloosa (VAMC).
Alaska:	Anchorage (VARO).
Arizona:	Phoenix (VARO and VAMC); Prescott (VAMC); Tucson (VAMC).
Arkansas:	Fayetteville (VAMC); Little Rock (VARO and VAMC).
California:	Fresno (VAMC); Livermore (VAMC); Loma Linda (VAMC); Long Beach (VAMC); Los Angeles (VARO); Los Angeles/Brentwood (VAMC); Los Angeles/Wadsworth (VAMC); Martinez (VAMC); Palo Alto (VAMC); San Diego (VARO and VAMC); San Francisco (VARO and VAMC); Sepulveda (VAMC).
Colorado:	Denver (VARO and VAMC); Fort Lyon (VAMC); Grand Junction (VAMC).
Connecticut:	Hartford (VARO); Newington (VAMC); West Haven (VAMC).
Delaware:	Wilmington (VARO and VAMC).
District of Columbia:	(VARO and VAMC). (*Note:* Benefits to veterans residing in foreign countries not included in this listing are under the jurisdiction of the VARO and VAMC in Washington, D.C.)
Florida:	Bay Pines (VAMC); Gainesville (VAMC); Jacksonville (VA Office); Lake City (VAMC); Miami (VA Office and VAMC); St. Petersburg (VARO); Tampa (VAMC).
Georgia:	Atlanta (VARO and VAMC); Augusta (VAMC); Dublin (VAMC).

Hawaii:	Honolulu (VARO). (*Note:* Jurisdiction includes American Samoa, Guam, Wake, Midway, and the Trust Territory of the Pacific Islands.)
Idaho:	Boise (VARO and VAMC).
Illinois:	Chicago (VARO); Chicago–Lakeside (VAMC); Chicago–North Chicago (VAMC); Chicago–West Side (VAMC); Danville (VAMC); Hines (VAMC); Marion (VAMC).
Indiana:	Indianapolis (VARO and VAMC); Fort Wayne (VAMC); Marion (VAMC).
Iowa:	Des Moines (VARO and VAMC); Iowa City (VAMC); Knoxville (VAMC).
Kansas:	Wichita (VARO and VAMC); Leavenworth (VAMC); Topeka (VAMC).
Kentucky:	Lexington (VAMC); Louisville (VARO and VAMC).
Louisiana:	Alexandria (VAMC); New Orleans (VARO and VAMC); Shreveport (VAMC and VA Office).
Maine:	Portland (VA Office); Togus (VARO and VAMC).
Maryland:	Baltimore (VARO and VAMC); Fort Howard (VAMC); Perry Point (VAMC).
Massachusetts:	Bedford (VAMC); Boston (VARO and VAMC); Brockton (VAMC); Northampton (VAMC); Springfield (VA Office); West Roxbury (VAMC).
Mexico:	Benefits to veterans residing in Mexico are under the jurisdiction of the VA Regional Office in Houston, Texas.
Michigan:	Allen Park (VAMC); Ann Arbor (VAMC); Battle Creek (VAMC); Detroit (VARO); Iron Mountain (VAMC); Saginaw (VAMC).
Minnesota:	Minneapolis (VAMC); St. Cloud (VAMC); St. Paul (VARO).
Mississippi:	Biloxi (VAMC); Jackson (VARO and VAMC).
Missouri:	Columbia (VAMC); Kansas City (VA Office and VAMC); Poplar Bluff (VAMC); St. Louis (VARO and VAMC).
Montana:	Fort Harrison (VARO and VAMC); Miles City (VAMC).
Nebraska:	Grand Island (VAMC); Lincoln (VARO and VAMC); Omaha (VAMC).
Nevada:	Reno (VARO and VAMC).
New Hampshire:	Manchester (VARO and VAMC).
New Jersey:	East Orange (VAMC); Lyons (VAMC); Newark (VARO).

New Mexico: Albuquerque (VARO and VAMC).
New York: Albany (VA Office and VAMC); Batavia (VAMC);
                       Bath (VAMC); Bronx (VAMC); Brooklyn (VAMC);
                       Buffalo (VARO and VAMC); Canandaigua (VAMC);
                       Castle Point (VAMC); Montrose (VAMC); New York
                       City (VARO and VAMC); Northport (VAMC);
                       Rochester (VA Office); Syracuse (VA Office and
                       VAMC).
North Carolina: Asheville (VAMC); Durham (VAMC); Fayettesville
                       (VAMC); Salisbury (VAMC); Winston-Salem
                       (VARO).
North Dakota: Fargo (VARO and VAMC).
Ohio: Chillicothe (VAMC); Cincinnati (VA Office and
                       VAMC); Cleveland (VARO and VAMC); Columbus
                       (VA Office); Dayton (VAMC).
Oklahoma: Muskogee (VARO and VAMC); Oklahoma City (VA
                       Office and VAMC).
Oregon: Portland (VARO and VAMC); Roseburg (VAMC).
Pennsylvania: Altoona (VAMC); Butler (VAMC); Coatesville
                       (VAMC); Erie (VAMC); Lebanon (VAMC); Philadel-
                       phia (VARO and VAMC); Pittsburgh (VARO and
                       VAMC); Wilkes-Barre (VA Office and VAMC).
Philippines: Manila (VARO).
Puerto Rico,   San Juan (VARO and VAMC).
  Commonwealth: (*Note:* Jurisdiction includes the Virgin Islands.)
Rhode Island: Providence (VARO and VAMC).
South Carolina: Charleston (VAMC); Columbia (VARO and VAMC).
South Dakota: Fort Meade (VAMC); Hot Springs (VAMC); Sioux
                       Falls (VARO and VAMC).
Tennessee: Memphis (VAMC); Mountain Home (VAMC);
                       Murfreesboro (VAMC); Nashville (VARO and
                       VAMC).
Texas: Amarillo (VAMC); Big Spring (VAMC); Bonham
                       (VAMC); Dallas (VA Office and VAMC); Houston
                       (VARO and VAMC); Kerville (VAMC); Lubbock
                       (VA Office); Marlin (VAMC); San Antonio (VA
                       Office and VAMC); Temple (VAMC); Waco (VARO
                       and VAMC).
Utah: Salt Lake City (VARO and VAMC).
Vermont: White River Junction (VARO and VAMC).
Virginia: Hampton (VAMC); Richmond (VAMC); Roanoake
                       (VARO); Salem (VAMC).

Washington:	Seattle (VARO and VAMC); Spokane (VAMC); Tacoma (VAMC); Walla Walla (VAMC).
West Virginia:	Beckley (VAMC); Clarksburg (VAMC); Huntington (VARO and VAMC); Martinsburg (VAMC).
Wisconsin:	Madison (VAMC); Milwaukee (VARO); Tomah (VAMC).
Wyoming:	Cheyenne (VARO and VAMC); Sheridan (VAMC).

OBTAINING VA ASSISTANCE WHILE OVERSEAS

Virtually all VA monetary benefits (compensation, pension, educational assistance, and burial allowances) are payable regardless of place of residence or nationality. Beneficiaries residing in foreign countries should contact the nearest American embassy or consulate for information and claims assistance. In Canada, the local office of Veterans Affairs Canada should be contacted.

There are some program limitations in foreign jurisdictions that you should be aware of. These include the following:

• Reimbursed fee-basis medical care, including prosthetic services, is available to veterans outside of the United States for treatment of adjudicated, service-connected disabilities and conditions related to those disabilities. Prior to treatment, an authorization must be obtained from the nearest American embassy or consulate. In emergency situations, treatment should be reported within seventy-two hours.

• Nursing-home care is not available in foreign jurisdictions.

• Home loan guarantees are available only in the United States and selected territories and possessions.

• Educational benefits are limited to approved degree-granting programs in institutions of higher learning.

VETERANS SERVICE ORGANIZATIONS

Veterans service organizations (VSOs) provide a wide range of services to help veterans obtain the benefits they are entitled to. The states maintain state veterans service agencies that provide assistance, and there are also over thirty national organizations. The following are some of the larger organizations that have national service offices throughout the country:

• American Legion (AL). Membership: 3,000,000. National headquarters: P.O. Box 1055, Indianapolis, IN 46206, telephone (317) 635-8411. Washington headquarters: 1608 K Street, NW, Washington, DC 20006, telephone (202) 861-2711.

• Disabled American Veterans (DAV). Membership: 1,051,000. National headquarters: 3725 Alexandria Pike, Cold Springs, KY 41076, telephone (606) 441-7300. Washington headquarters: 807 Maine Avenue, SW, Washington, DC 20024, telephone (202) 554-3506.

VETERANS BENEFITS TIMETABLE

Time	Benefits	Where to apply
90 days	REEMPLOYMENT	Former employer
Limited time	UNEMPLOYMENT COMPENSATION: The amount of benefit and payment period vary among states. Apply soon after separation.	State employment service
120 Days or up to one year if totally disabled	INSURANCE: SGLI (Servicemen's Group Life Insurance), a five-year nonrenewable term policy, may be converted to VGLI (Veterans Group Life Insurance).	Servicemen's Group Life Insurance, 213 Washington St., Newark, N.J. 07102-9990
Two years (from date of notice of VA disability rating)	GI INSURANCE: Life insurance (up to $10,000) is available for veterans with service-connected disabilities. Veterans who are totally disabled may apply for a waiver of premiums on these policies.	Any VA office
One year (from date of notice of eligibility for premium waiver)	SUPPLEMENTAL INSURANCE: An additional $20,000 policy is available for those veterans who are under age sixty-five, eligible for waiver of premiums, and have Service Disabled Veterans Insurance. However, no waiver can be granted on the additional insurance.	Any VA office
Ten years from release	EDUCATION: Educational assistance depends upon period of service.	Any VA office
Twelve years (generally from date of discharge)	VOCATIONAL REHABILITATION: For disabled vets, VA will pay tuition, fees, and the cost of books, tools, and other program expenses, as well as provide a monthly living allowance. Upon completion of the vocational rehabilitation program, VA will assist in finding employment.	Any VA office
No time limit	GI HOME LOANS: VA will guarantee a loan for the purchase of a home, farm with a residence, manufactured home, or condominium.	Any VA office

- Non-Commissioned Officers Association (NCOA). Membership: 160,000. National headquarters: 10635 IH 35 North, San Antonio, TX 78233, telephone (512) 653-6161. Washington headquarters: 225 N. Washington Street, Alexandria, VA 22314, telephone (703) 549-0311.
- Paralyzed Veterans of America (PVA). Membership: 14,500. This organization serves the special needs of veterans of military service who have catastrophic paralysis caused by spinal cord injury or disease. National headquarters: 801 18th Street, NW, Washington, DC 20006, telephone (202) 872-1300.
- Veterans of Foreign Wars of the United States (VFW). Membership: 2,300,000. National headquarters: 406 West 34th Street, Kansas City, MO 64111, telephone (816) 756-3390. Washington headquarters: 200 Maryland Avenue, NE, Washington, DC 20002, telephone (202) 543-2239.
- Vietnam Veterans of America, Inc. (VVA). Membership: 40,100. National headquarters: 2001 S Street, NW, Suite 700, Washington, DC 20009, telephone: (202) 265-8019.

SOURCES OF ADDITIONAL INFORMATION

Consult with the Military Personnel Flight (MPF) or the Family Support Center at your present active-duty location concerning transition programs.

Contact the local, state, or national government or private veterans organizations as referenced in this chapter.

For a thorough discussion of veterans benefits, consult *Veteran's Guide to Benefits,* Stackpole Books, 5067 Ritter Road, Mechanicsburg, PA 17055.

23

Answers to
25 Commonly Asked Questions

1. What is the policy on taking leave?

As a member of the armed forces, you get credit for two and a half days' leave for each month of active duty under honorable conditions. This equates to thirty days a year, which can be taken at one time or broken up into smaller amounts throughout the year. Requests must be approved by your supervisor and, in some cases, your commander. They are normally granted for the period of time requested except when military necessity requires your presence. Most supervisors have a projected leave schedule based on information from their personnel. The best way to secure the days you would like is to provide your supervisor with plenty of advance notice. The best way to be disappointed is to wait until the last moment, when the workload is heavy and several other people from your duty section are on leave or in a temporary duty status at other locations.

2. What should I do if I'm experiencing pay problems?

Errors do not occur very often. Those that do happen are usually temporary delays caused by a change in a person's status, the date the change was brought to the attention of Accounting and Finance personnel, and the time required for processing the change in the automated computer pay system. Once corrected, payments are usually made within the following thirty days. If you're experiencing pay problems, you should contact the military pay branch at your local Accounting and Finance Office. Take your most recent Leave and Earnings Statement (LES); it can help identify potential problems and expedite their correction.

3. What's the best way for my parents or family to contact me in case of an emergency?

Tell them to contact their local Red Cross. There are almost thirty-three hundred offices in chapters or on military installations all over the world. They will verify the situation and rapidly transmit a message to you through the local Red Cross representative at your base.

4. It's hard for me to get up in the morning. What should I do to make sure I get to work on time?

If possible, ask a friend to stop by on the way to work. If not, take a look at the clocks you're using. Heavy sleepers tend to go back to sleep after they let the alarms on mechanical wind-up clocks unwind. Electric alarm clocks and clock radios with alarms are the best bet. Place them a good distance from the bed, so you have to get up to turn them off. If you seem to be waking up late on a regular basis, it might be because you're staying up too late the night before. If so, try hitting the sack a little bit earlier.

5. What should I do if I have problems getting along with my coworkers or my supervisor?

If the problem is a minor or one-time occurrence, it's probably nothing to be seriously concerned about. If problems recur and seem to center around major disagreements or conflicts, then you need to think about your actions and ask yourself to what degree you may be causing the problem; think of the possible solutions and talk openly and honestly with your supervisor or those concerned, or discuss the situation with someone else in your chain of command. Your unit's first sergeant is in a good position to provide insight and help resolve these kinds of issues.

6. Why do Air Force personnel have to work long hours?

In the Air Force environment, exercises, unforeseen workloads, and unprogrammed personnel losses can result in situations where unit commanders and supervisors are compelled to extend standard workdays or workweeks to meet mission requirements. When this happens for an extended period of time, higher headquarters is usually contacted to reevaluate requirements or provide manning assistance.

7. How should I get ready for the movers when I'm being reassigned to another base? What should I do if my furniture or personal possessions are damaged en route?

At base level, the Transportation Management Office (TMO) will schedule your move and provide you with specific information about procedures. You can start to make formal arrangements once you've received printed copies of your reassignment orders. Weight allowances are established based on grade and in some cases the location you are being reassigned to. Your possessions will usually be sent two ways—one for household goods (furniture and other possessions) and another for unaccompanied baggage (also referred to as hold baggage), which includes smaller possessions and items that you will need shortly after arrival to initially set up a household.

Before the movers come, have your belongings organized based on the way you want them shipped. For example, put the items you want to be shipped in unaccompanied baggage in one room, put the clothing and documents you intend to hand-carry in suitcases or a briefcase in another area, and so forth. Safeguard items of high value (jewelry, cash). Make sure everything is properly identified and recorded on the mover's inventory sheet, with its condition correctly annotated (scratched, worn, broken). Get a copy of the inventory before the movers leave. If you are asked to sign additional forms, read them carefully, and ask the movers to provide you with a personal copy if possible.

When your shipment is delivered, know where you want each item placed. Check off each item on the inventory to assure everything is accounted for. Assure that the movers make note of any damaged or missing articles.

Loss and damage claims should be filed as soon as possible after delivery of the shipment. Specific instructions will be provided by the Transportation Management Office. In general, you may be expected to provide estimates and receipts for repairs and replacements; keep anything that's been damaged until the claim has been resolved or awarded.

Note: Some bases refer to their Traffic Management Offices (TMO) as Personal Property Shipping Offices (PPSO) or Joint Personal Property Shipping Offices (JPPSO) in cases where multiple locations or joint forces are supported.

8. How are military couples assigned?

Military couples are assigned in accordance with the policy outlined in Air Force Instruction 36-2110, *Assignments*. The general policy is to assign military couples where possible to locations in the Continental United States (CONUS) and overseas, where they can maintain a joint residence. When it is not possible, each member is considered to be serving in his or her own right and must fulfill the obligations inherent to all Air Force members. One important step is to complete Air Force Form 1048, "Military Spouse Information," which advises personnel planners of a military couple's status and the fact that they want to be considered for a joint assignment. A primary factor governing joint assignments is the need at a location for both members' Air Force specialties.

9. How can I get reassigned or released from an assignment if I have a problem that needs to be taken care of?

Requests for a humanitarian reassignment are outlined in Air Force Instruction 36-2110, *Assignments*. They are considered on a case-by-case basis. Some cases may be incompatible with continued military service, and a hardship discharge, rather than reassignment or deferment, may be more appropriate.

A humanitarian or permissive humanitarian application may be approved in situations such as the recent death of spouse or child, when spouse or child has a disease and prolonged hospital or outpatient treatment has begun or is scheduled (for example, certain orthopedic and tuberculosis cases), terminal illness of a family member where death is imminent (within two years), and when reassignment or deferment is considered essential to an effective child advocacy program.

Normally, applications are disapproved in cases of threatened separation, divorce action, or action to pursue child custody; when climatic conditions or geographic areas adversely affect health of family member if the problem is of a recurring nature (for example, asthma or allergies); a housing shortage or home ownership problem; a financial or management problem related to off-duty employment, spouse's employment, private business activities, or settling of estates; and parents or parents-in-law suffering chronic disease or disability (problems of this nature are commonly encountered).

Requests are processed through the Military Personnel Flight (MPF) and forwarded to the Air Force Personnel Center (AFPC). Personnel seeking reassignment under such conditions should seek initial counsel from the customer service branch at the MPF or from their supervisor or their unit's first sergeant or commander.

10. What is overseas culture shock?

Overseas culture shock isn't always easy to recognize, because it affects different people in different ways. In general, it's an uncomfortable disorienting experience caused by living in a foreign country. Some people don't experience it at all. Others can have symptoms ranging from homesickness, irritability, and resentment to bitterness, hostility, and depression. Cultural adaptation usually has four phases:

Phase 1: Initial euphoria. Most people begin their new overseas assignment with great expectations and a positive outlook.

Phase 2: Irritation and hostility. During this phase, big and little differences that exist in the foreign country's culture become sources of frustration. Some people can feel uncomfortable, isolated, and even helpless.

Phase 3: Gradual adjustment. This comes as people become more familiar and at ease with local customs.

Phase 4: Adaptation. People accept and enjoy doing things in the host country. This can include travel, eating out, enjoying local customs, and even communicating in the foreign language. People in this phase, both military members and their families, feel right at home and actually miss certain aspects of the foreign culture when they're reassigned.

Most people move rapidly to the third and fourth phases. In overseas areas, many Family Support Centers and Recreation Centers offer programs to make cultural adaptation an easy and enjoyable experience.

11. What's Air Force policy if my spouse wants to work?

The Air Force fully supports the work aspirations of spouses, whether that work is in the home or in a commercial enterprise. Family Support Centers offer a wide range of programs to support these aspirations, including information about local job and career opportunities, job-hunting skills, and résumé preparation.

12. I've been thinking about reenlisting, but I can't make up my mind. What should I do?

It's a decision that, in some ways, only you can make. First, you should talk with your unit career advisor. He or she can tell you if you are eligible to reenlist; some people are not, based on their past performance and the Air Force's quality force program. They can also tell you what career fields and job opportunities are available. Then it's a matter of weighing the pros and cons of staying in, and talking it over with close friends and family members.

The Air Force offers a lot in terms of challenge, career progression, education and training, travel, and benefits for members and their families. It also requires involvement, commitment, and some degree of personal sacrifice. Most first-term airmen decide to reenlist during their last six months. Sometimes it helps to visit home (or wherever you plan to live after you get out). Places can change, as can opportunities. Your personal outlook has also evolved over the past few years. Your original plans may not seem so attractive now. Weigh all the factors concerned and you'll be in a much better position to make a final decision.

13. What are some of the benefits of military retirement?

Some of the most commonly cited benefits are as follows: Retirement pay, which ranges from 40 to 75 percent of your base pay for your grade at the time of retirement. Medical care. Unlimited exchange, commissary, and theater privileges in the United States and overseas, where not limited by Status of Forces Agreements. Federal benefits administered by the Department of Veterans Affairs. The Survivor Benefit Plan. Membership privileges in open messes. Worldwide space-available travel on Department of Defense aircraft. Air Force Aid Society assistance.

14. Can I volunteer to help with youth activities such as sports and Scouting programs if I'm single?

Yes. There are no limitations based on grade or marital status. Many single airmen have skills and experience in such programs and find that their involvement with children is personally rewarding and greatly appreciated by those in the Air Force community.

15. What's Air Force policy for time off from duty to participate in Air Force-related sports programs?

The Air Force supports participation in regularly sponsored sports programs. The mission comes first, but supervisors are encouraged to adjust duty schedules for men and women when possible. Highly skilled athletes may also be selected to participate in specialized training programs to prepare for inter-service, national, and international competitions such as the Olympics and the Pan American Games. At base level, the focal point for details on Air Force sports programs is the base gymnasium.

16. How can I exercise my right to vote when I'm in the service?

If you reside in your home state where your are registered to vote, you would vote in the normal way. If you reside elsewhere, you would vote by using an absentee ballot. Each commander appoints a voting officer who helps personnel, their spouses, and dependents register with the state they are eligible to vote in. Registration is done by submitting a Standard Form (SF) 76, "Post Card Registration and Absentee Ballot Request." This is mailed to the state you are eligible to vote in; in turn, you will be sent a ballot through the mail.

17. What should I do if I'm approached by someone who wants access to classified or sensitive information?

Verify his or her right to have access. It must be based on an official need to know and possession of a security clearance for the level of classified information involved. It is not automatically granted because of the requestor's position or rank. If the request is made from outside official channels (by another American citizen or from a citizen of a foreign country), you should immediately inform your supervisor, commander, or the nearest Air Force Office of Special Investigation (AFOSI).

18. Should I write my representative in Congress if I have a complaint?

Every citizen has a right to write to elected representatives and should be encouraged to do so. But it's also important to focus on the reason for writing. Many times a complaint, if surfaced, can be resolved much more quickly at the unit level. The Air Force has established programs locally to help solve real or perceived problems that affect the morale and welfare of assigned personnel and their dependents. They are usually handled by a senior officer or senior noncommissioned officer on each base who is designated as the Inspector General. When contacted, he or she looks into all the facts of a given situation and calls other affected agencies or personnel if required. Where issues can be resolved, they usually are. When congressional complaints are filed, the base will provide a written response to the congressional representative based on a review of the facts and the options available.

19. What is a chain of command?

The chain of command is a system designed to resolve problems at the lowest possible level. Each link in the chain of command is a level of responsibility and authority, extending from the President, as Commander-in-Chief, down to each supervisory level in the Air Force. Each level in the chain is responsible for a lower level and accountable to a higher level. The chain of command is used for performing official duties in support of the mission and also to help resolve problems and issues of concern to individual members. At the unit level, your upward chain starts with your immediate supervisor and goes through the unit's first sergeant to the commander. Most of the questions and concerns are resolved at this level.

20. Can I contest a performance report that I think is inaccurate and might be unfair, unjust, and prejudicial to my career?

Yes. Appeals and requests for changes to reports can be made after the reports have been entered into the personnel system and have been made a matter of record. Procedures are outlined in Air Force Instruction 36-2603, *Air Force Board for Correction of Military Records,* and Air Force Instruction 36-2401, *Correcting Officer and Enlisted Evaluation Reports.* Each request is considered on its own merits. The customer service branch in the Military Personnel Flight (MPF) is the focal point for initial information and assistance.

21. What's Air Force policy on the use of alcohol?

The use of alcohol is acceptable, when it is not restricted by public law or military directives. The Air Force does not investigate private drinking habits unless they affect public behavior, duty performance, or physical or mental health. Driving while intoxicated (DWI) is not tolerated. Violators are subject to apprehension and punishment under the Uniform Code of Military Justice (UCMJ). Programs are available through the Social Actions Office to help personnel resolve alcohol-related problems.

22. What does it mean if I've been counseled?

It depends on the purpose. Counseling is conducted to provide feedback on performance and career opportunities, to assure that Air Force standards are understood and maintained, and to advise personnel about other sources of help if they need specialized assistance. Some examples include the orientation of new personnel, training evaluations, and disciplinary problems. Counseling can be done orally or in writing.

Written counselings usually record specific facts or a problem, the cause of the problem (if known), the outcome (actions being taken or planned), and the signatures of the counselor and the individual being counseled. The overall intent is to provide help. Supervisors are specifically encouraged to conduct written counseling in cases where adverse trends (such as disciplinary problems or failure to meet Air Force standards) continue over a period of time. When appropriate, they may be forwarded to a unit's first sergeant or commander.

23. What is a letter of reprimand?

A letter of reprimand is a formal act of censure that rebukes an offender for misconduct. It is primarily given by commanders in cases not serious enough to warrant Uniform Code of Military Justice (UCMJ) action or for conduct that is not technically criminal but is, in the commander's opinion, not conducive to the effective performance of the mission. It's also a way to deal with people on first offenses (inexperienced personnel or those with good past behavior). In this method, a member is formally advised in writing of the mistakes of judgment and warned of the future consequences if there is a recurrence. If a pattern of irresponsibility continues, a commander may consider other actions, such as an Article 15.

The actual letter contains narrative statements, the commander's signature, and a place for the member's signature, referred to as the acknowledgment indorsement. The acknowledgment indorsement does not mean agreement by the member, but only receipt and understanding of the contents of the letter.

24. What is an Article 15?

Article 15 of the Uniform Code of Military Justice (UCMJ) is a procedure used by military commanders to impose punishment for minor offenses on military members under their command. It's often referred to as nonjudicial punishment because the punishment is not imposed by a court of justice. In the Air Force, any member from the grade of airman basic to general officer can be punished under the provisions of this article.

The purpose of Article 15 is to give commanders a means for maintaining morale, discipline, and efficiency within their units, as well as the flexibility to punish members for offenses not serious enough to warrant court-martial proceedings. Under this system, the primary objective is the rehabilitation of the offender, but in cases where the offender is beyond rehabilitation the punishment may be intended to be punitive or to serve as a deterrent to others.

The types of punishment that can be given are proscribed based on the grade of the commander. Examples range from forfeiture of pay, reduction in grade, and imposition of additional duties, to restriction and placement in correctional custody. Commanders also have the authority to suspend, mitigate, and set aside punishments.

When a commander contemplates giving an Article 15, he or she considers the nature of the offense, the age and prior service record of the accused, and the recommendations of key personnel (supervisors, first sergeants, and representatives from the legal office). Airmen who receive an Article 15 will not automatically be discharged from the service or denied reenlistment. Those decisions are based on performance over a period of time.

25. What happens to Air Force members who are caught using illegal drugs?

When drug use is substantiated, the outcome is determined on a case-by-case basis. Nonjudicial punishment (an Article 15) can be administered. A court-martial may be requested. Fines can be levied. Stripes can be taken. Administrative discharges under other than honorable conditions may be requested. Confinement may be considered for possession. Prison terms for dealing drugs normally range from fifteen months to three years. Local rehabilitation programs are available and must be successfully completed before reenlistment is considered. In most cases, retention in the service is not favorably considered.

Why is the outcome so rough? The Air Force has a heavy responsibility to the nation and the American people. The use of drugs by any member compromises that responsibility. To condone their use could result in dangerous consequences.

Supervisors and commanders won't have much sympathy for those who are caught. Excuses that won't fly: "I made a mistake, but I have an outstanding record." "I don't know how it got there." "I didn't use it while I was on duty." "I was only using it off base." "It's only his word against mine."

Substantiated drug abuse may also have spinoff effects after the Air Force: on future employment, existing marital relationships, and child custody proceedings.

Appendix A

Major USAF Installations

With permission of the Air Force Association, the following guide to USAF bases in the United States is reprinted from *Air Force Magazine*.

Note: A major installation is an Air Force Base, Air Base, Air Guard Base, or Air Reserve Base that serves as a self-supporting center for Air Force combat, combat support, or training operations. Active-duty, Air National Guard, or Air Force Reserve units of wing size or larger operate the installation with all land, facilities, and support needed to accomplish the unit mission. There must be real property accountability through ownership of all real estate and facilities. Agreements with foreign governments that give the Air Force jurisdiction over real property meet this requirement. Shared-use agreements (as opposed to joint-use agreements where the Air Force owns the runway) do not meet the major installation criteria.

Altus AFB, Okla. 73523-5000; within Altus city limits. Phone (405) 482-8100; DSN 866-1110. AETC base. 97th Air Mobility Wing. Operates AETC's strategic airlift and aerial flying training schools. Maintains and supports C-5, KC-135, C-141, and C-17 aircraft. Base activated in Jan. 1943; inactivated in May 1945; reactivated in Jan. 1953. Area 4,095 acres, plus 818 leased and 1,069 easement/right-of-way. Runways 13,440 ft., with an additional 9,000-ft. parallel runway and 3,500-ft. assault strip. Altitude 1,376 ft. Military 3,500; civilians 550; approx. 400 TDY students (officer and enlisted) in training per month. Payroll $137.7 million. Housing: 148 officer, 652 NCO, 368 VAQ, 14 TLF. 15-bed hospital.

Andersen AFB, Guam, APO AP 96543-5000; 2 mi. N of Yigo. Phone (commercial, from CONUS) 011-671-366-1110; DSN 366-1110. PACAF base. Hq. 13th Air Force. Host unit: 36th Air Base Wing. No USAF aircraft assigned. Associate organizations: 634th Air Mobility Support Sqdn. (AMC); 44th Aerial Port Sqdn. (AFRES); 254th Air Base Gp. (ANG); Det. 5, 750th Space Gp.; Det. 602, Air Force Office of Special Investigations (AFOSI). Navy HC-5 Helicopter Combat Support Sqdn., H-46D Sea Knight operations. Andersen is the Pacific center for power projection, regional cooperation, and multinational training. It serves as a logistic support and staging base for aircraft operating in

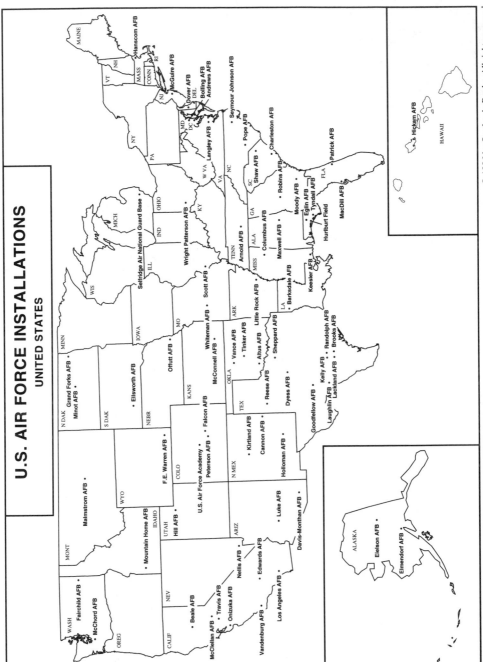

U.S. AIR FORCE INSTALLATIONS
UNITED STATES

MAINE

Hanscom AFB

NH

VT

MASS

CONN RI

McGuire AFB

NY

MD
DC
DEL

Bolling AFB
Dover AFB
Andrews AFB

Langley AFB

Seymour Johnson AFB

PA

Pope AFB

Charleston AFB

W VA

VA

Patrick AFB

Shaw AFB

NC

SC

Robins AFB

FLA

MICH

OHIO

KY

Wright Patterson AFB

GA

Moody AFB
Eglin AFB
Tyndall AFB

MacDill AFB

IND

ILL

Selfridge Air National Guard Base

TENN

ALA

Columbus AFB

Hurlburt Field

WIS

MISS

Arnold AFB

Maxwell AFB

Keesler AFB

Barksdale AFB

LA

IOWA

MO

Scott AFB

ARK

Little Rock AFB

Whiteman AFB

Vance AFB

Sheppard AFB

MINN

Grand Forks AFB

McConnell AFB

Tinker AFB

Randolph AFB
Brooks AFB

N DAK

Minot AFB

KANS

OKLA

Altus AFB

Kelly AFB

Ellsworth AFB

Offutt AFB

TEX

Goodfellow AFB

S DAK

NEBR

Dyess AFB

Laughlin AFB
Lackland AFB

Reese AFB

F.E. Warren AFB

COLO

U.S. Air Force Academy
Peterson AFB
Falcon AFB

N MEX

Kirtland AFB
Cannon AFB

Holloman AFB

WYO

Malmstrom AFB

IDAHO

UTAH

Hill AFB

ARIZ

Luke AFB

Davis-Monthan AFB

MONT

Mountain Home AFB

NEV

Nellis AFB

Edwards AFB

Los Angeles AFB

WASH

Fairchild AFB

McChord AFB

OREG

CALIF

Beale AFB

Travis AFB

Onizuka AFB

McClellan AFB

Vandenburg AFB

HAWAII

Hickam AFB

ALASKA

Eielson AFB

Elmendorf AFB

the Pacific and Indian Oceans. Base activated in late 1944; named for Gen. James Roy Andersen, lost at sea between Kwajalein and Hawaii Feb. 26, 1946. General Andersen was Chief of Staff, Hq. AAF, Pacific Ocean Areas. Area: 20,504 acres. Runways (north) 10,555 ft. and (south) 11,182 ft. Altitude 612 ft. Military 2,163; civilians 677. Payroll $105 million. Housing: 248 officer, 1,508 enlisted. Transient housing: 53 VOQ, 115 VAQ, 18 TLF. One USAF clinic and one Navy hospital.

Andrews AFB, Md. 20762-5000; 10 mi. SE of Washington, D.C. Phone (301) 981-1110; DSN 858-1110. AMC base. Gateway to the nation's capital and home of Air Force One. Host wing: 89th Airlift Wing. Responsible for presidential support and base operations; supports all branches of the armed services, several major commands, and federal agencies. The wing also hosts Det. 302, AFOSI; Hq. Air Force Flight Standards Agency; AFOSI Academy; Air National Guard Readiness Center; 113th Fighter Wing (D. C. ANG); 459th Airlift Wing (AFRES); Naval Air Facility; Marine Aircraft Gp. 49, Det. A; Hq. Air Force Review Boards Agency. Base activated May 1943; named for Lt. Gen. Frank M. Andrews, military air pioneer and WWII commander of the European theater, killed in aircraft accident May 3, 1943, in Iceland. Area 7,550 acres (including easements). Runways 9,300 ft. and 9,755 ft. Altitude 281 ft. Military 7,400; civilians 3060. Payroll NA. Housing: 325 officer, 1,753 NCO, 414 off-base units, 974 UEQ, 325 transient (including 68 temporary living quarters for incoming personnel, 21 DV suites, 180 VOQ, 56 VAQ). 185-bed hospital.

Arnold AFB, Tenn., 37389; approx. 7 mi. SE of Manchester. Phone (615) 454-3000; DSN 340-5011. AFMC base. Arnold Engineering Development Center, the world's largest complex of wind tunnels, jet and rocket engine test cells, space simulation chambers, and hyperballstic ranges. AEDC supports the acquisition of new aerospace systems by conducting research, development, and evaluation testing for DOD, other government agencies, and commercial aerospace firms. Base dedicated June 25, 1951; named for Gen. of the Army H. H. "Hap" Arnold, wartime Chief of the AAF. Area 40, 118 acres. Inactive 6,000-ft. runway. Altitude 1,100 ft. Military 123; civilians 201; NAF 46; contract employees 2,900. Payroll $128.3 million. Housing: 23 officer, 17 NCO, 45 transient. Medical aid station and small VA clinic.

Aviano AB, Italy, APO AE 09601; adjacent to Aviano, 50 mi. N of Venice. Phone (commercial, from CONUS) 011-39-434-667111; DSN 632-1110. USAFE base. Hq. 16th Air Force. 31st Fighter Wing, the only permanent U.S. NATO fighter wing in southern Europe, and 616th Regional Support Gp. 31st FW maintains two LANTIRN-equipped F-16 fighter squadrons, the 555th and the 510th, capable of conducting offensive and defensive air combat operations, and the 603d Air Control Sqdn. One of the oldest Italian air bases, dating to 1911; USAF began operations in 1954. Area 1,140 acres. Runway 8,596 ft. Altitude 413 ft. Military 3,163; civilians 572. Payroll $67.3 million, $265.5 million economic impact. Housing: 850 govt.-leased units, 32 billeting spaces, 498 dorm bed spaces, approx. 1,000 contracted hotel spaces. Clinic.

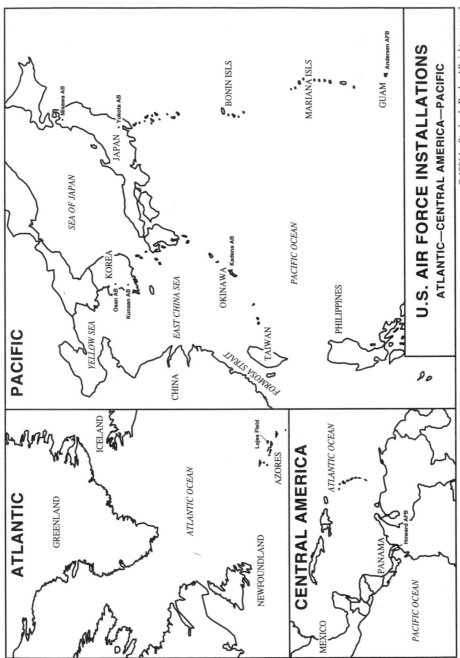

U.S. AIR FORCE INSTALLATIONS
ATLANTIC—CENTRAL AMERICA—PACIFIC

Barksdale AFB, La. 71110-5000; in Bossier City. Phone (318) 456-2252; DSN 781-1110. ACC base. Hq. 8th Air Force; 2d Bomb Wing, B-52H operations; 49th Test Sqdn.; 917th Wing (AFRES), B-52 and A-10 operations; Det. 1, 307th Civil Engineering Sqdn. RED HORSE; 8th Air Force Museum. Base activated Feb. 2, 1933; named for Lt. Eugene H. Barksdale, WWI airman killed in Aug. 1926 crash near Wright Field, Ohio. Area 22,000 acres (18,000 acres reserved for recreation). Runway 11,756 ft. Altitude 166 ft. Military 5,799; civilians 649. Payroll $227.2 million. Housing: 105 officer, 324 enlisted, 1,488 UEQ, 534 transient (94 VOQ, 416 VAQ, 24 TLF). 40-bed hospital.

Beale AFB, Calif. 95903-5000; 13 mi. E of Marysville. Phone (916) 634-3000; DSN 368-1110. ACC base. 9th Reconnaissance Wing; Det. 1, 612th Air Operations Gp. (ACC); 7th Space Warning Sqdn. (AFSPC). Aircraft include U-2 reconnaissance aircraft and T-38 Talon trainers. Originally U.S. Army's Camp Beale. Became Air Force installation in Apr. 1948; became AFB in Nov. 1951; named for Brig. Gen. E. F. Beale, Indian agent in California prior to Civil War. Area 22,944 acres. Runway 12,000 ft. Altitude 113 ft. Military 3,078; civilians 492. Payroll $55.8 million. Housing: 191 officer, 1,518 enlisted, 823 UEQ, 6 UOQ, 159 transient (53 VOQ, 89 VAQ, 17 TLF). 9-bed hospital

Bolling AFB, D. C. 20332-5000; 3 mi. S of U.S. capitol. Phone (703) 545-6700; DSN 227-0101. 11th Wing; U.S. Air Force Honor Guard; U.S. Air Force Band; Air Force Office of Scientific Research (AFMC); Air Force Chief of Chaplains; Air Force Surgeon General; Hq. Air Force History Support Office; Hq. Air Force Office of Special Investigations; Air Force Real Estate Agency; Air Force Medical Operations Agency; Defense Intelligence Agency; Air Force Legal Services Agency. Activated in Oct. 1917; named for Col. Raynal C. Bolling, first high-ranking Air Service officer killed in WWI. Area 604 acres. No runway. Military 1,572; civilians 810. Payroll $90 million. (Personnel and payroll figures apply to 11th Wing only.) Housing: 275 officer, 209 transient. Clinic.

Brooks AFB, Tex. 78235; in SE San Antonio. Phone (210) 536-1110; DSN 240-1110. AFMC base. Human Systems Center; USAF School of Aerospace Medicine (AFMC); Armstrong Laboratory, Human Systems Program Office; 70th Air Base Gp. Associate units include 70th School Sqdn. (Systems Acquisition School); Air Force Medical Support Agency; 68th Intelligence Sqdn.; Air Force Center for Environmental Excellence; Medical Systems Implementation and Training Element. Base activated Dec. 8, 1917; named for Cadet Sidney J. Brooks, Jr., killed Nov. 13, 1917, on his commissioning flight. Area 1,310 acres. Runway length NA. Altitude 600 ft. Military 2,098; civilians 2,307. Payroll $128 million. Housing: 70 officer, 100 NCO. Clinic.

Cannon AFB, N. M. 88103-5000; 7 mi. W of Clovis. Phone (505) 784-3311; DSN 681-1110. ACC base. 27th Fighter Wing, F-16 operations, and the only USAF base with EF-111A and F-111F fighter operations. (Beginning May 1995, and continuing through fall 1996, the 27th FW is retiring the F-111F.)

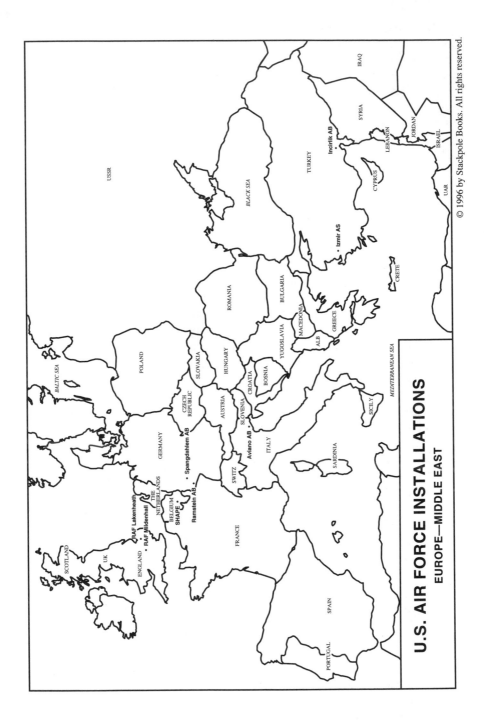

U.S. AIR FORCE INSTALLATIONS
EUROPE—MIDDLE EAST

Base activated in Aug. 1942; named for Gen. John K. Cannon, WWII commander of all Allied air forces in the Mediterranean theater and former commander, Tactical Air Command. Area 25,663 acres. Runways 10,400 ft. and 8,000 ft. Altitude 4,295 ft. Military 4,889; civilians 588. Payroll $181.6 million. Housing: 173 officer, 1,549 enlisted, 1,051 dorm bed spaces, 6 DVQ, 45 TLF. 20-bed hospital.

Charleston AFB, S. C. 29404-5000; in North Charleston, 10 mi. from downtown Charleston. Phone (803) 566-6000; DSN 673-2100. AMC base. Joint-use airfield. 437th Airlift Wing; 315th AW (AFRES Assoc.); Det. 1, 158th Fighter Wing (Vermont ANG); Det. 17, Site Activation Task Force; Field Training Det. 317; Det. 719, AFOSI; 1st Combat Camera Sqdn. Base activated in Oct. 1942; inactivated in Mar. 1946; reactivated in Aug. 1953. Area 6,235 acres (including auxiliary airfield). Runway 9,000 ft. Altitude 45 ft. Military 7,352 (including AFRES); civilians 1,295. Payroll $190 million. Housing: 127 officer, 850 NCO, 1,636 dorm spaces, 75 trailer spaces, 535 transient (7 DV suites, 128 VOQ, 400 VAQ). Clinic.

Columbus AFB, Miss. 39710-1000; 10 mi. NW of Columbus. Phone (601) 434-7322; DSN 742-1110. AETC base. 14th Flying Training Wing, undergraduate pilot training and Introduction to Fighter Fundamentals. Base activated in 1941 for pilot training. Area 6,015 acres. Runways 6,300 ft., 8,000 ft., and 12,000 ft. Altitude 214 ft. Military 1,541; civilians 1,346. Payroll $99 million. Housing: 272 officer, 494 enlisted, 27 VAQ, 72 VOQ, 26 TLF/TLH. 4-bed hospital.

Davis-Monthan AFB, Ariz. 85707-5000; within Tucson city limits. Phone (602) 750-3900; DSN 361-1110. ACC base. 355th Wing; Hq. 12th Air Force; A-10 combat crew training; OA-10 and FAC training and operations; 41st, 42d, and 43d Electronic Combat Sqdns., EC-130E/H electronic operations; 305th Rescue Sqdn. (AFRES), MH-60G Pave Hawk helicopter operations; Det. 1, 120th Fighter Wing (Montana ANG), F-16 air defense operations. Also site of AFMC's Aerospace Maintenance and Regeneration Center, storage location for excess DOD aerospace vehicles. Base activated in 1927; named for two local early aviators: 1st Lt. Samuel H. Davis, killed Dec. 28, 1921, and 2d Lt. Oscar Monthan, killed Mar. 27, 1924. Area 11,000 acres. Runway 13,645 ft. Altitude 2,620 ft. Military 5,957; civilians 744. Payroll $175.8 million. Housing: 132 officer, 1,107 enlisted, 482 transient (298 VAQ, 168 VOQ, 16 TLF). 3335-bed hospital.

Dover AFB, Del.19902-7219; 3 mi. SE of Dover. Phone (302) 677-3000; DSN 445-3000. AMC base. 436th Airlift Wing; 512th AW (AFRES Assoc.) Dover operates the largest aerial post facility on the East Coast. Base activated Dec. 1941; inactivated in 1946; reactivated Feb. 1951. Area 3,908 acres. Runway 12,900 ft. Altitude 28 ft. Military 7,213; civilians 1,120. Payroll $140 million. Housing: 108 officer, 1,441 enlisted, 634 transient (512 VAQ, 108 VOQ, 14 TLF). 20-bed hospital.

Dyess AFB, Tex. 79607-1980; WSW border of Abilene, Phone (915) 696-0212; DSN 461-1110. ACC base. 7th Wing, two B-1B squadrons (one operational, one training); two C-130 squadrons. First base to activate an operational B-1B wing. Conducts all B-1 combat crew training for the Air Force. First B-1B arrived in June 1985; wing met initial operational capability in Oct. 1986. Base activated in Apr. 1942; deactivated in Dec. 1945; reactivated as Abilene AFB Sept. 1955. In Dec. 1956, renamed for Lt. Col. William E. Dyess, WWII fighter pilot who escaped from a Japanese prison camp, killed in P-38 crash at Burbank, Calif., in Dec. 1943. Area 6,437 acres (including off-base sites). Runway 13,500 ft. Altitude 1,789 ft. Military 4,907; civilians 426. Payroll $165.3 million. Housing: 142 officer, 4 senior enlisted, 848 enlisted, 52 VAQ, 70 VOQ, 9 DVQ, 39 TLF. 15-bed hospital.

Edwards AFB, Calif. 93524; 20 mi. E of Rosamond. Phone (805) 277-1110; DSN 527-1110. AFMC base. Site of Air Force Flight Test Center (AFFTC), which conducts developmental and follow-on testing and evaluation of manned and unmanned aircraft and related avionics, flight-control, and weapon systems. AFFTC also operates the USAF Test Pilot School, which trains test pilots, flight-test engineers, and flight-test navigators. Also site of Phillips Laboratory's Astronautics Directorate, NASA's Ames Dryden Flight Research Facility, and secondary landing site for space shuttle missions. Det. 2, 9th Reconnaissance Wing, SR-71 operations (ACC). Base activities began in Sept. 1933. Originally Muroc AAF; renamed for Capt. Glen W. Edwards, killed June 5, 1948, in crash of a YB-49 "Flying Wing." Area 301,000 acres. 21 runways from 4,000 to 39,000 ft. Altitude 2,302 ft. Military 4,283 (including associate units); government and contract civilians 7,400 (not including 557 NAF employees). Payroll $570 million (including associate units and contractors). Housing: 657 officer (including BOQ), 2,348 enlisted (including 765 dormitory spaces and 191 BNCOQ), 161 transient (49 VAQ, 42 VOQ, 9 SNCOQ, 10 VIP/VOQ, 51 TLF), 189 trailer spaces. 10-bed hospital.

Eglin AFB, Fla. 32542; 2 mi. SW of the twin cities of Niceville and Valparaiso; 7 mi. NE of Fort Walton Beach. Phone (904) 882-1110; DSN 872-1110. AFMC base. Eglin is the nation's largest Air Force base in terms of acreage, covering an area roughly two-thirds the size of Rhode Island. Host unit: Air Force Development Test Center. Associate units: Aeronautical Systems Center. Associate units: Aeronautical Systems Center, Eglin, and Armament Directorate of Wright Laboratory (AFMC); 33d Fighter Wing; 53d Wing (ACC); 96th Air Base Wing; 46th Test Wing; 919th Special Operations Wing (AFRES); 20th Space Surveillance Sqdn. (AFSPC); 9th Special Operations Sqdn.; 728th Tactical Control Sqdn.; a U.S. Army Ranger Training Battalion; a U.S. Navy Explosive Ordnance Disposal School; Air Force Armament Museum. Base activated in 1935; named for Lt. Col. Frederick I. Eglin, WWI flyer killed in aircraft accident Jan. 1, 1937. Area 463,452 acres. Runways 10,000 ft. and 12,000 ft. Altitude 85 ft. Military 8,484; civilians 4,303 (excluding Hurlburt

Field). Payroll $444.2 million (excluding Hurlburt Field). Housing: 263 officer, 2,071 enlisted, 1,200 unaccompanied enlisted units (dorm rooms), 226 trailer spaces (officer and enlisted), 88 family transient. 125-bed USAF regional hospital. AFMC clinic at Hurlburt Field.

Eielson AFB, Alaska 99702-5000; 26 mi. SE of Fairbanks. Phone (907) 377-1178; DSN (317) 377-1110. PACAF base. Host unit: 354th Fighter Wing, F-16C/D, A-10, and OA-10 operations. Base hosts recurring Cope Thunder exercises, which provide realistic combat training. Associate organizations include the Arctic Survival School (AETC); 168th Air Refueling Wing (ANG); Det. 460, Air Force Technical Applications Center. Base activated Oct. 1944; named for Carl Ben Eielson, Arctic aviation pioneer who died in an Arctic rescue mission in Nov. 1929. Area 19,790 acres (including 16 remote sites, 63,195 acres). Runway 14,500 ft. Altitude 534 ft. Military 2,741; full-time civilians (NAF, AAFES, Civil Service) 882 (includes ANG civil service technicians) and 529 traditional and full-time ANG members. Payroll $137.2 million. Housing: 151 officer, 1,409 enlisted. Unaccompanied housing: 8 officer units, 422 rooms, 746 bed spaces (includes NCOQ), 212 VOQ, 240 bed spaces (179 rooms) VAQ, 6 enlisted and 6 officer DVQ.

Ellsworth AFB, S. D. 57706-5000; 12 mi. ENE of Rapid City. Phone (605) 385-1000; DSN 675-1000. ACC base. Host unit: 28th Bomb Wing, one B-1B squadron. Associate units: 366th Wing's (Mountain Home AFB, Idaho) geographically separated 34th Bomb Sqdn., B-1B; South Dakota Air and Space Museum. Base activated in July 1942 as Rapid City AAB; renamed June 13, 1953, for Brig. Gen. Richard E. Ellsworth, killed Mar. 18, 1953, in crash of RB-36 in Newfoundland, Canada. Area 10,632 acres. Runway 13,497 ft. Altitude 3,286 ft. Military 3,724; civilians 463. Payroll $114.8 million. Housing: 202 officer, 1,882 enlisted, 218 transient units (57 VAQ, 125 VOQ, 6 DVQ, 30 TLF). 15-bed hospital.

Elmendorf AFB, Alaska 99506-5000; bordering Anchorage. Phone (907) 552-1110; DSN (317) 552-1110. PACAF base. Largest composite wing in PACAF; hub for air traffic to and from the Far East. Hq. Alaskan Command; Hq. 11th Air Force (PACAF); Hq. Alaska NORAD Region. Host unit: 3d Wing, F-15/F-15E fighter and C-130 and C-12 airlift operations, E-3 airborne air control operations, and 3d Medical Gp. Associate units: 11th Rescue Coordination Center (ANG); 381st Intelligence Sqdn.; 632d Air Mobility Support Sqdn. (AMC); various U.S. Army, Navy, and Marine activities. Base activated in July 1940; named for Capt. Hugh Elmendorf, killed Jan. 13, 1933, at Wright Field, Ohio, while flight-testing a new pursuit plane. Area 13,130 acres. Runways 7,500 ft. and 10,000 ft. Altitude 213 ft. Military 6,565; civilians 997. Payroll $275.9 million. Housing: 1,628 family units, 197 VOQ, 879 VAQ, 1,316 UEQ. 60-bed hospital.

Fairchild AFB, Wash. 99011-5000; 12 mi. WSW of Spokane. Phone (509) 247-1212; DSN 657-1212. AMC base. Air refueling hub for the western US.

Host unit: 92d Air Refueling Wing (KC-135R, KC-135T). Tenant units: 366th Crew Training Gp. (Survival School, AETC); 141st Air Refueling Wing (ANG, KC-135E); 2d Support Sqdn. (ACC). Base activated in Jan. 1942; named for Gen. Muir S. Fairchild, USAF Vice Chief of Staff at his death in 1950. Area 4,543 acres. Runway 13,901 ft. Altitude 2,426 ft. Military 4,316; civilians 931. Payroll $122.3 million. Housing: 176 officer, 1,247 NCO, 18 TLF, 154 BAQ/VAQ, 149 VOQ. 30-bed hospital.

Falcon AFB, Colo. 80912-5000; 10 mi. E of Colorado Springs. Phone (719) 567-1110; DSN 560-1110. AFSPC base. Host unit: 50th Space Wing. Tenant units: 76th Space Operations Sqdn.; National Test Facility; Space Warfare Center. Base activated in Oct. 1985. Area 3,840 acres. No runway. Altitude 6,267 ft. Military active-duty 2,365; civilians 435; contractors 2,000. No housing or transient quarters. Medical aid station and dental clinic.

Francis E. Warren AFB, Wyo. 82005-5000; adjacent to Cheyenne. Phone (307) 775-1110; DSN 481-1110. AFSPC base. Hq. 20th Air Force. Host unit: 90th Missile Wing, 50 Peacekeeper and 150 Minuteman III missiles, UH-1 helicopters; 37th Air Rescue Flight. Base activated as Fort D. A. Russell July 4, 1867; under Army jurisdiction until 1947, when reassigned to USAF. Base renamed in 1930 for Francis Emory Warren, Wyoming senator and first state governor. Area 5,866 acres, missile site area covering more than 12,600 sq. mi. in Wyoming, Colorado, and Nebraska. No runway. Altitude 6,142 ft. Military 3,655; civilians 602. Payroll $130.7 million. Housing: 831 family units. 35-bed hospital. Air Force ICBM Museum.

Goodfellow AFB, Tex. 76908-5000; 2 mi. SE of San Angelo. Phone (915) 654-3217; DSN 477-3217. AETC base. The 17th Training Wing provides technical training for all Air Force members entering intelligence career fields; provides cryptologic training for members of the other military services, civilian intelligence agencies, and foreign military services; trains all U.S. Air Force, Army, and Marine Corps personnel in fire protection and rescue and conducts Air Force special instruments training. Major units include Goodfellow NCO Academy; 344th Military Intelligence Battalion (U.S. Army); Naval Technical Training Center Detachment; U.S. Marine Corps Detachment. Base activated in Jan. 1941; named for Lt. John J. Goodfellow, Jr., WWI fighter pilot killed in combat Sept. 14, 1918. Area 1,136 acres. No runway. Altitude 1,877 ft. Military 3,098; civilians 751. Payroll $143 million. Housing: 19 officer, 280 NCO, 1,000 transient (867 VAQ, 106 VOQ, 27 TLF). Clinic.

Grand Forks AFB, N. D. 58205-5000; 16 mi. W of Grand Forks. Phone (701) 747-3000; DSN 362-1110. AMC base. 319th Air Refueling Wing (KC-135R); 321st Missile Gp. (AFSPC, Minuteman III, HH-1H), inactivates in Sept. 1998. Home of the first of AMC's core air refueling wings. Base activated in 1956; named after the town of Grand Forks, whose citizens bought the property for the Air Force. Area 5,418 acres. Missile complex covers an additional 7,500 sq. mi. Runway 12,350 ft. Altitude 911 ft. Military 5,146; DOD civilians

501. Payroll $208.1 million. Housing: 332 officer, 1,886 enlisted, 1,000 dormitory, 137 transient. 15-bed hospital.

Gunter AFB, (see Maxwell AFB, Gunter Annex).

Hanscom AFB, Mass. 01731-5000; 17 mi. NW of Boston. Phone (617) 377-4441; DSN 478-5980. AFMC base. Hq. Electronic Systems Center (AFMC) manages development and acquisition of C⁴1 systems; Geophysics Directorate of Phillips Laboratory (AFMC), center for research and exploratory development in the terrestrial, atmospheric, and space environments; five divisions of Rome Laboratory's Directorate of Electromagnetics and Reliability. Base has no flying mission; transient USAF aircraft use runways of Laurence G. Hanscom Field, state-operated airfield adjoining the base. Base named for Laurence G. Hanscom, a pre-WWII advocate of private aviation, killed in a light plane accident in 1941. Area 846 acres. Runway length NA. Altitude 133 ft. Military 2,149; civilians 1,933. Payroll $186 million. Housing: 386 officer, 472 NCO, 35-unit TLF, 754 BOQ/VOQ. Clinic.

Hickam AFB, Hawaii 96853-5000; 9 mi. W of Honolulu. Phone (808) 471-7110 (Oahu military operator); DSN 471-7110. PACAF base. Hq. Pacific Air Forces. Host unit: 15th Air Base Wing, supporting Air Force units and installations in Hawaii and throughout the Pacific. Major tenant units include 154th Wing (ANG); 201st Combat Communications Gp.; 615th Air Mobility Support Gp. (AMC). Base activated in Sept. 1938; named for Lt. Col. Horace M. Hickam, air pioneer killed in crash Nov. 5. 1934, at Fort Crockett, Tex. Area 2,761 acres. Runway 12,300 ft. (joint use with Honolulu IAP). Altitude sea level. Military 3,657; civilians 1,280. Payroll $254.2 million. Housing: 566 officer, 2,103 enlisted. Unaccompanied housing: 810 enlisted, 200 VOQ, 200 VAQ. Clinic.

Hill AFB, Utah 84056-5990; 8 mi. S of Ogden. Phone (801) 777-7221; DSN 777-1110. AFMC base. Hq. Ogden Air Logistics Center. Provides Integrated Weapon System Management and logistics support for silo-based ICBMs (Minuteman and Peacekeeper); F-16 and C-130 aircraft; conventional munitions, including Maverick air-to-ground missiles and laser, infrared, and electro-optical guided bombs; and other aerospace components, such as landing gear, photographic and reconnaissance equipment, and training devices. Technology center for software and photonics. Other units include 412th Test Wing (AFMC), which manages the Utah Test and Training Range; 388th Fighter Wing (ACC); 419th Fighter Wing (AFRES); Defense Megacenter Ogden (DISA); Hill Aerospace Museum. Base activated in Nov. 1940; named for Maj. Ployer P. Hill, killed Oct. 30, 1935, while test-flying the first B-17. Area 6,698 acres; manages 962,076 acres. Runway 13,500 ft. Altitude 4,788 ft. Military 4,609; civilians 9,532. Payroll $482 million. Housing: 179 officer, 966 NCO, 40 transient. 25-bed hospital.

Holloman AFB, N. M. 88330-5000; 8 mi. SW of Alamogordo. Phone (505) 475-6511; DSN 867-1110. ACC base. 49th Fighter Wing, F-117 operations (7th, 8th, and 9th Fighter Sqdns.); F-4E aircrew training (20th Fighter Sqdn. and 1st German Air Force Training Sqdn.); AT-38B aircrew training (435th Fighter Sqdn.); HH-60 helicopters (48th Rescue Sqdn.). Twelve German Tornado aircraft and 350 German personnel arrived in early 1996 and are permanently assigned to the wing. Associate units are the 46th Test Gp. (AFMC); 4th Space Warning Sqdn. (AFSPC); Det. 1, 82d Aerial Target Sqdn. (QF-106 drone operations). Base activated in 1942; named for Col. George Holloman, guided-missile pioneer. Area 59,000 acres. Runways 10,575 ft., 12,131 ft., and 8,054 ft. with 7,044 ft. overrun. Altitude 4,093 ft. Military 4,134; civilians 717. Payroll $160.4 million. Housing: 191 officer, 1,359 enlisted, 403 transient (145 VAQ, 208 VOQ, 50 TLF). 8-bed hospital.

Howard AFB/Albrook AFS, Panama, APO AA 34001-5000. DSN 284-9805. ACC base. With headquarters at Howard, 24th Wing represents USAF in operations throughout Latin America. 24th Wing is an ACC unit reporting to 12th Air Force, Davis-Monthan AFB, Ariz. Major tenants: 640th Air Mobility Support Sqdn. (AMC); 33d Intelligence Sqdn. Established in 1928 as Bruja Point Military Reservation; later named for Maj. Charles Harold Howard. Military 1,661, civilians 519. Payroll $43.6 million. Housing: 238 officer, 933 enlisted, 680 transient (554 VAQ, 120 VOQ, 6 TLF).

Hurlburt Field, Fla. 32544-5000; 5 mi. W of Fort Walton Beach. Phone (904) 882-1110; DSN 579-1110. AFSOC base. Hq. Air Force Special Operations Command. Host unit: 16th Special Operations Wing, equipped with MC-130E Combat Talon Is, MC-130H Combat Talon IIs, AC-130H/U Spectre Gunships, MH-53J Pave Lows, MH-60G Pave Hawks, and MC-130P Combat Shadows (located at Eglin AFB), and C-130Es. Major tenants include 505th Command and Control Evaluation Gp., including the USAF Air Ground Operations School, USAF Battle Staff Training School (Blue Flag); 720th Special Tactics GP.; 23d Special Tactics Sqdn.; Joint Warfare Center; USAF Special Operations School; 18th Flight Test Sqdn.; 823d Civil Engineering Sqdn. RED HORSE; Det. 1,335th Technical Training Sqdn.; Det. 4, Air Weather Service; Field Training Det. 327; and Det. 309, AFOSI. Base activated in 1943; named for Lt. Donald W. Hurlburt, WWII pilot killed Oct. 1, 1943, in a crash at nearby Eglin Field Military Reservation. Area 6,600 acres. Runway 6,900 ft. Altitude 38 ft. Military 7,292; civilians 758. Payroll $411.1 million. Housing: 48 officer, 632 enlisted, 258 VOQ/VAQ, 24 TLF. Medical clinic at Hurlburt, 125-bed hospital at Eglin AFB, 12 mi. away.

Incirlik AB, Turkey, APO AE 09824; 10 mi. E of Adana. Phone (commercial, from CONUS) 011-90-322-316-1110; DSN 676-1110. USAFE base. Host unit: 39th Wing, supports Operation Provide Comfort and rotational weapons training deployments for USAFE fighter aircraft. Combined Task Force assets include Turkish F-16s, F-4s, KC-135s, British Tornados, VC-10s, French Jaguars, and U.S. F-16s, F-15s, KC-135s, EC-3s, and UH-60 helicopters. Also home for 628th Air Mobility Support Sqdn. (AMC), which provides a full aerial port operation. Base activated in May 1954; present unit began operations in Mar. 1966. Incirlik, in Turkish, means fig orchard. Area 3,400 acres. Runway 10,000 ft. Altitude 240 ft. Military 2,473 (including 337 GSUs), OPC Tent City 2,000 TDY personnel; civilians 2,776. Payroll $76 million. Housing: 950 units, 205 govt.-leased, 60 BOQ, 80 TLF, 592 VAQ, 259 VOQ, 628 dorm rooms, 30-bed regional hospital, expandable to 250 beds.

Kadena AB, Japan, APO AP 96368-5000; 15 mi. N of Naha, Okinawa, Japan. Phone (commercial, from CONUS) 011-81-98938-1111; DSN 630-1110. PACAF base. Host organization: 18th Wing (12th, 44th, and 67th Fighter Sqdns.), F-15C/D operations; 909th Air Refueling Sqdn., KC-135 operations; 961st Airborne Air Control Sqdn., E-3 operations; 33d Rescue Sqdn., HH-60 operations. Major associate units: Support Center Pacific (AFMC), 353d Special Operations Group (AFSOC), and Training Det. 911 (AETC). Base named for city of Kadena, Okinawa, Japan. Area 15,000 acres. Runway length NA. Military 7,300; appropriated-fund civilians 2,934 (U.S. and local nationals); USAF nonappropriated-fund civilians 1,334 (U.S. and local nationals); local nationals 434; contractors 3,000 (monthly average). Payroll $146 million. Housing: 899 officer, 3,073 enlisted, 124 temporary lodging units. Unaccompanied housing: 139 officer/civilian, 2,473 enlisted dormitory rooms, 276 VOQ, 274 VAQ. Clinic. U.S. Naval Hospital at Camp Lester.

Keesler AFB, Miss. 39534-5000; located in Biloxi. Phone (601) 377-1110; DSN 597-1110. AETC base. Hq. 2d Air Force. 81st Training Wing (avionics, communications, electronics, radar systems, computer and command-and-control systems, weather, precision equipment, physician residencies, specialized nurse training, and medical technicians); Keesler Medical Center; 403d Wing (AFRES); AFMC engineering installation squadron; AETC NCO Academy—Keesler. Base activated June 12, 1941; named for 2d Lt. Samuel R. Keesler, Jr., a native Mississippian and WWI aerial observer killed in action Oct. 9, 1918, near Verdun, France. Area 3,546 acres. Runway 5,600 ft. Altitude 26 ft. Military 8,300; civilians 4,236. Payroll $275 million. Housing: 287 officer, 1,666 NCO, 49 trailer spaces, 2,122 transient (366 VOQ, 1,756 VAQ;). 250-bed hospital.

Kelly AFB, Tex. 78241-5000; 5 mi. SW of San Antonio. Phone (210) 925-1110; DSN 945-1110. AFMC base. Hq. San Antonio Air Logistics Center provides logistics management, procurement, and systems support for such Defense Department aircraft as the C-5AB, C-17, C-9, T-37, and T-38 and for such foreign-operated aircraft as the OV-10, A-37, F-5, and C-47. As a specialized repair activity, San Antonio ALC modernizes and performs heavy depot maintenance on the entire fleet of C-5s. It also overhauls F100, TF39, and T58 engines and manages more than seventy-five percent of the USAF engine inventory, fuel and lubricants used by the Air Force and NASA, and nuclear weapons. Other major units on base: Hq. Air Intelligence Agency; Air Force Information Warfare Center; Joint Command and Control Warfare Center; Air

Force News Agency; Defense Commissary Agency; 433d Airlift Wing (AFRES); 149th Fighter Wing (ANG); Defense Reutilization and Marketing Office; Air Force Audit Agency Defense Distribution Depot; Defense Information Systems Agency. Dating from Nov. 21, 1916, Kelly AFB is the oldest continuously active air base in the U.S. Named for Lt. George E. M. Kelly, first Army pilot to lose his life flying a military aircraft, killed May 10, 1911. Area 4,660 acres. Runway 11,550 ft. Altitude 689 ft. Military 4,581; civilians 14,397. Payroll $669 million. Housing: 57 officer 374 NCO. Clinic.

Kirtland AFB, N. M. 87117-5606 SE quadrant of Albuquerque. Phone (505) 846-0011; DSN 2460011. AFMC base. Hq. 377th Air Base Wing. Major agencies and units include 58th Special Operations Wing (AETC); Air Force Operational Test and Evaluation Center; Phillips Laboratory; 150th Fighter Wing (ANG); Field Command's Defense Nuclear Agency; Sandia National Laboratories; Department of Energy's Albuquerque Operations Office; Kirtland NCO Academy; 898th Munitions Sqdn.; Air Force Security Police Agency; Defense Nuclear Weapons School; Air Force Inspection Agency; Air Force Safety Center. These agencies furnish nuclear, advanced weapons, and space research, development, and testing; advanced helicopter training and search-and-rescue operations; pararescue training; and operational test and evaluation. Other units: Albuquerque Seismological Laboratory; University of New Mexico Civil Engineering Research Facility. Base activated in Jan. 1941; named for Col. Roy C. Kirtland, air pioneer and commandant of Langley Field in the 1930s, who died May 2, 1941. Area 52,678 acres. Runway 19, 375 ft. Altitude 5,352 ft. Military 5,875; civilians 13,9346. Payroll $1 billion. Housing: 2,122 homes. VAQ/VOQ: 130 officer, 180 enlisted. Air Force/Veterans Administration joint medical center located outside base gates.

Kunsan AB, Republic of Korea, APO AP 96264-5000; 8 mi. SW of Kunsan City. Phone (commercial, from CONUS) 011-82-654-470-1110; DSN 782-1110. PACAF base. Host unit: 8th Fighter Wing, F-16C/D operations, home of the "Wolf Pack." The 8th FW converted to the F-16 in Sept. 1981, making it the first active overseas F-16 wing. Associate units include the U.S. Army's 143d Air Defense Artillery, 1st Battalion, Echo and Foxtrot Batteries; U.S. Army Contracting Command Korea. Base built by Japanese in 1938. Area 2,556 acres. Runway length 9,000 ft. Altitude 29 ft. Military 2,270; U.S. civilians 17; local nationals 364. Payroll $100.6 million. Unaccompanied housing: 247 officer, 3,940 enlisted, 9 VIP, 28 VOQ, 60 VAQ. 6-bed hospital.

Lackland AFB, Tex.78236-5000; 8 mi. SW of San Antonio. Phone (210) 671-1110; DSN 473-1110. AETC base. The 37th Training Wing is the largest training wing in the Air Force. Its four primary training functions graduate more than 65,000 students annually. The 737th Training Gp. provides basic military training for about 33,000 enlisted people entering the Air Force, Air Force Reserve, and Air National Guard annually. The 37th Training Gp. conducts more than 250 technical training courses in base support functions for more than 30,000 people annually from all military services. The Defense Language Institute English Language Center conducts English language training for 2,400 international and U.S. military students annually. The Inter-American Air Forces Academy conducts professional, technical, and management training in Spanish to military forces and government agencies from Latin American and Caribbean nations for about 660 students per year. The 59th Medical Wing (Wilford Hall USAF Medical Center) is the Air Force's largest medical facility with 592 beds. Base activated in 1941; named for Brig. Gen. Frank D. Lackland, early commandant of Kelly Field flying school, who died in 1943. Area 6,725 acres (including 3,973 acres at Lackland Training Annex). No runway. Altitude 745 ft. Military 6,357, civilians 6,202; students 8,682. Payroll $552.6 million. Housing: 109 officer, 611 NCO, 2,363 transient (1,831 VAQ, 374 VOQ, 158 TLF).

Lajes Field, Azores, Portugal, APO AE 09720-5000; Terceira Island, 900 mi. W of Portugal. Phone (commercial, from CONUS) 011-351-95-530100-1110; DSN from U.S. 535-1110, from Europe 245-1110. ACC base. Host unit: 65th Air Base Wing. Tenants: U.S. Forces Azores; Army 1324th Medium Port Command Azores; 629th Air Mobility Support Sqdn. (AMC); Det. 6, Air Force Broadcasting Service. U.S. operations began at Lajes Field in 1946. Area 1,148 acres. Runway 10,865 ft. Altitude 180 ft. Military 833; civilians 571. Payroll $24.9 million. Housing: 80 officer, 404 enlisted, 30 TLF, 184 VOQ, 532 VAQ, 6 DVQ, 4 SNCO. 7-bed hospital.

Langley AFB, Va. 23665-5000; 3 mi. N of Hampton. Phone (804) 764-1110; DSN 574-1110. ACC base. Hq. Air Combat Command. Host unit: 1st Fighter Wing, F-15 fighter operations. Associate units: Air Operations Sqdn. (ACC); Training Support Sqdn. (ACC); Computer Systems Sqdn. (ACC); ACC Heritage of America Band; U.S. Army TRADOC Flight Det.; Army/USAF Center for Low-Intensity Conflict; Air Force Doctrine Center. Base activated Dec. 30, 1916. Langley is one of the oldest continuously active air bases in the US. Named for aviation pioneer and scientist Samuel Pierpont Langley, who died in 1906. NASA's Langley Research Center is adjacent to the base. Area 3,216 acres. Runway 10,000 ft. Altitude 10 ft. Military 7,988; civilians 1,102. Payroll $250 million. Housing: 384 officer, 1,074 NCO, 416 transient (215 VAQ, 101 VOQ, 100 TLF). 50-bed hospital.

Laughlin AFB, Tex. 78843-5000; 6 mi. E of Del Rio. Phone (210)298-3511; DSN 732-1110. AETC base. 47th Flying Training Wing, specialized undergraduate pilot training. Base activated in July 1942; named for 1st Lt. Jack Thomas Laughlin, Del Rio native, B-17 pilot killed over Java Jan. 29, 1942. Area 5,228 acres. Runways 6,246 ft. 8,310 ft., and 8,850 ft. Altitude 1,082 ft. Military 1,223; civilians 1,016. Payroll $73.9 million. Housing: 600 units, 54 trailer spaces, 58 transient, 22 TLF. Hospital.

Laurence G. Hanscom AFB (see Hanscom AFB).

Little Rock AFB, Ark. 72099-5000; 17 mi. NE of Little Rock. Phone (501) 988-3131; DSN 731-1110. ACC base. 314th Airlift Wing, only C-130 training base in DOD, training crew members from all branches of military service and some foreign countries. Tenants include 189th Airlift Wing (ANG); 96th Mobile Aerial Port Sqdn.; 348th USAF Recruiting Sqdn.; Det. 251, AFOSI; Det. 310, 373d Field Training Sqdn.; Det. 234, Air Force Audit Agency; Combat Aerial Delivery School (ACC); Hq. Arkansas ANG. Base activated in 1955. Area 11,373 acres. Runway 12,000 ft. Altitude 310 ft. Military 4,450; civilians 589. Payroll $179.8 million. Housing: 140 officer, 1,395 enlisted, 11 single-occupancy dormitories housing 836, 341 transient (140 VAQ, 201 VOQ). 25-bed hospital.

Los Angeles AFB, Calif. 90245-4687; in El Segundo, 3 mi. SE of Los Angeles IAP; base housing and support facilities 18 mi. S of the main base, in San Pedro. Phone (310) 363-1110; DSN 833-1110. AFMC base. Hq. of AFMC's Space and Missile Systems Center, responsible for research, development, acquisition, on-orbit testing, and sustainment of military space and missile systems. Support unit is 61st Air Base Gp. Area 112 acres at Los Angeles AFB and 127 acres at Fort MacArthur Annex. No runway. Altitude 95 ft. Military 1,540; civilians 1,046. Payroll $150 million. Housing at Fort MacArthur Annex: 574 townhouses. Clinics, base exchanges, and child development centers at main base and Fort MacArthur; commissary and Family Support Center at main base.

Luke AFB, Ariz. 85309-5000; 20 mi. WNW of downtown Phoenix. Phone (602) 856-7411; DSN 896-1110. AETC base. 56th Fighter Wing, F-16 operations; 944th Fighter Wing (AFRES), F-16 operations; 607th Air Control Sqdn., forward air control operations. Luke, the largest fighter training base in the world, conducts USAF and allied aircrew training in the F-16. Base activated in 1941; named for 2d Lt. Frank Luke, Jr., observation balloon busting ace of WWI and first American aviator to receive the Medal of Honor, killed in action Sept. 29, 1918, near Murvaux, France. Area 4,197 acres, plus 2.7 million-acre range at Gila Bend, Ariz. Runways 10,000 ft. and 9,910 ft. Altitude 1,090 ft. Military 6,374; civilians 1,092. Payroll $161.2 million. Housing: 95 officer, 679 enlisted, 256 transient (132 VOQ, 84 VAQ, 40 TLF). 30-bed hospital.

MacDill AFB, Fla. 33621-5000; located on the Interbay Peninsula in southern Tampa. Phone (813) 828-1110; DSN 968-1110. ACC base. 6th Air Base Wing; Hq. U.S. Special Operations Command; Hq. U.S. Central Command; Joint Communications Support Element; NOAA Aircraft Operations Center; 610th Aeromedical Evacuation Sqdn.; 290th Joint Communications Support Sqdn. The 6th ABW's mission is to operate the air base for U.S. warfighting commands. Base activated Apr. 15, 1941; named for Col. Leslie MacDill, killed in aircraft accident Nov. 8, 1938, near Washington, D.C. Area 5,600 acres. Runways 11,480 ft. (active) and 7,167 ft. (inactive). Altitude 6 ft. Military 1,956; civilians 465. Payroll $47.7 million. Housing: 109 officer, 571 enlisted, 23 DVQ, 62 VAQ housing 124 personnel, 137 VOQ, 24 TLF. 50-bed hospital.

Malmstrom AFB, Mont. 59402-5000; 1.5 mi. E of Great Falls. Phone (406) 731-1110; DSN 632-1110. AFSPC base. Host unit: 341st Missile Wing (Minuteman III). Tenant unit: 43d Air Refueling Gp. (AMC), KC-135. Base activated Dec. 15, 1942; named for Col. Einar A. Malmstrom, WWII fighter commander killed in air accident Aug. 21, 1954. Site of SAC's first Minuteman wing. Area 4,137 acres, plus about 24,000 sq. mi. of missile complex. Runway length NA. Altitude 3,525 ft. Military 4,350; civilians 428. Payroll $178 million. Housing: 258 officer, 1,148 enlisted, 105 transient. Clinic.

Maxwell AFB, Ala. 36112-5000; 1 mi. WNW of Montgomery. Phone (334) 953-1110; DSN 493-1110. AETC base. 42d Air Base Wing; Hq. Air University; Air War College; Air Command and Staff College; Air Force Quality Institute; Air University Library; College of Aerospace Doctrine, Research, and Education; Air Force Reserve Officers Training Corps; Officer Training School; Ira C. Eaker College for Professional Development; Hq. Community College of the Air Force; Hq. Civil Air Patrol—USAF; Squadron Officer School; Air Force Institute of Technology (at Wright-Patterson AFB, Ohio). Associate units: 908th Airlift Wing (AFRES); Air Force Historical Research Agency. Air University conducts professional military, graduate, and professional continuing education for precommissioned and commissioned officers, enlisted personnel, and civilians to prepare them for command, staff, leadership, and management responsibilities. Base activated in 1918; named for 2d Lt. William C. Maxwell, killed in air accident Aug. 12, 1920, in the Philippines. Area 2,524 acres. Runway 7,000 ft. Altitude 168 ft. Military 3,729; civilians 2,986. Payroll $276.7 million. Housing: 268 officer, 22 senior enlisted, 348 junior enlisted, 1,211 transient (1,116 VOQ, 65 VAQ, 30 TLF). 30-bed hospital.

Maxwell AFB, Gunter Annex, Ala. 36114; 4 mi. NE of Montgomery. Phone (334) 416-1110; DSN 596-1110. AETC base. Under Hq. Air University: College for Enlisted Professional Military Education (includes USAF Senior NCO Academy); Extension Course Institute; Standard Systems Group (AFMC); Air Force Logistics Management Agency. Activated Aug. 27, 1940; named for William A. Gunter, longtime mayor of Montgomery and airpower advocate who died in 1940. Area 368 acres. No runway. Altitude 220 ft. Military and civilian populations and payroll data included in Maxwell entry. Housing: 104 officer, 90 senior enlisted, 130 junior enlisted, 617 transient (274 VOQ, 340 VAQ, 3 TLF).

McChord AFB, Wash. 98438-5000; 10 mi. S of Tacoma. Phone (206) 984-1910; DSN 984-1110. AMC base. Host unit: 62d Airlift Wing. Major tenants include: 446th Airlift Wing (AFRES); Western Air Defense Sector (ANG). The 62d AW operates the C-141 Starlifter but is scheduled to receive the C-17 Globemaster III as the C-141 fleet retires. The base is responsible for strategic airlift of personnel and cargo worldwide, on short notice, in support of national objectives. Base is adjacent to Fort Lewis, its primary customer. Base activated May 5, 1938; named for Col. William C. McChord, killed Aug. 18, 1937, while attempting a forced landing at Maidens, Va. Area 4,616 acres. Runway 10,100 ft. Altitude 323 ft. Military 4,125; civilians 1,339. Payroll $253.6 million. Housing: 98 officer, 883 NCO, 760 dorm rooms, 289 VAQ, 71 VOQ, 12 TLF. Dispensary. Madigan Army Medical Center is located 4 mi. SE, with 414 beds (expandable to 622 in an emergency).

McClellan AFB, Calif. 95652-5000; 9 mi. NE of Sacramento. Phone (916) 643-2111; DSN 633-1110. AFMC base. Hq. Sacramento Air Logistics Center provides logistics management, procurement, maintenance, and distribution support for F/EF-111 and A-10 and, as a second source, for the F-15 and KC-135 weapon systems. The ALC is also program manager for the F-117A stealth fighter and will be the support center for the F-22. Other responsibilities include more than 200 electronic systems and programs and eight space systems; technology centers for very-high-speed integrated circuits, fiber optics, and advanced composites. The ALC has unique capability for robotic nondestructive inspection using X-ray and neutron radiography of F-111-sized aircraft. Other major units include Defense Depot—McClellan; Defense Information Systems Organization—McClellan; 938th Engineering Installation Sqdn.; Technical Operations Division, Air Force Technical Applications Center; 4th Air Force (AFRES); U.S. Coast Guard Air Station, Sacramento (DOT). Named for Maj. Hezekiah McClellan, pioneer in Arctic aeronautical experiments, killed in a crash May 25, 1936. Area 3,763 acres. Runway 10,600 ft. Military 3,000; civilians 10,300. Payroll $497 million. Housing: 100 officer, 564 enlisted, 19 transient. 77th Medical Gp. Clinic and 77th Medical Gp. Hospital located at the former Mather AFB.

McConnell AFB, Kan. 67221-5000; SE corner of Wichita. Phone (316) 652-6100; DSN 743-1110. AMC base. 22d Air Refueling Wing; 931st Air Refueling Gp. (AFRES Assoc.); 184th Bomb Wing (ANG). Base activated June 5, 1951; named for Capt. Fred J. McConnell, WWII B-24 pilot who died in a crash of a private plane Oct. 25, 1945, and for his brother, 2d Lt. Thomas L. McConnell, also a WWII B-24 pilot, killed July 10, 1943, during an attack on Bougainville. Area 3,113 acres. Two 12,000-ft. runways. Altitude 1,371 ft. Military 2,984; DOD civilians 423. Payroll $104 million. Housing: 76 officer, 437 enlisted, 95 transient (49 VOQ, 26 VAQ, 20 temporary units off base).

McGuire AFB, N. J. 08641-5000; 18 mi. SE of Trenton. Phone (609) 724-1100; DSN 440-1100. AMC base. 305th Air Mobility Wing; Hq. 21st Air Force; 621st Air Mobility Operations Gp.; Air Mobility Warfare Center, Fort Dix, N. J.; N. J. ANG; N. J. Civil Air Patrol; 108th Air Refueling Wing (ANG); 514th Air Mobility Wing (AFRES Assoc.); McGuire NCO Academy (AETC). Base adjoins Army's Fort Dix; formerly Fort Dix AFB. Activated as AFB 1949; named for Maj. Thomas B. McGuire, Jr., P-38 pilot, second leading U.S. ace of WW II, recipient of Medal of Honor, killed in action Jan. 7, 1945, in the Philippines. Area 3,597 acres. Runways 7,124, ft. and 10,000 ft. Altitude 133 ft. Military 10,512 (including AFRES and ANG); civilians 1,604. Payroll NA. Housing: 186 officer, 1,568 NCO, 403 transient (144 VOQ, 229 VAQ, 30 TLF).

Minot AFB, N. D. 58705-5000; 13 mi. N of Minot. Phone (701) 723-1110; DSN 453-1110. ACC base. 5th Bomb Wing (B-52H); 91st Missile Wing (AFSPC), Minuteman III operations; CPT Flight/23d Bomb Sqdn.; 54th Rescue Flight (UH-1N). Base activated in Jan. 1957; named after the city of Minot, whose citizens donated $50,000 toward purchase of the land for the Air Force. Area 5,049 acres, plus additional 8,500 acres for missile sites. Runway 13,200 ft. Altitude 1,668 ft. Military 3,768; civilians 567. Payroll $139.8 million. Housing: 394 officer, 2,047 enlisted, 22 UOQ, 1,302 dormitory spaces, 32 VAQ, 39 VOQ, 39 TLF. 45-bed hospital.

Misawa AB, Japan, APR AP 96319-5000; within Misawa city limits. Phone (commercial, from CONUS) Direct:011-81-3117-66-1111. Switchboard: 011-81-176-53-5181; DSN 94-315-226-1110. PACAF base; joint-service base. Host unit: 35th Fighter Wing, F-16C/D fighter operations. Tenant units: 3d Space Surveillance Sqdn. (AFSPC); 301st Intelligence Sqdn. (AIA); Naval Air Facility; Naval Security Gp. Activity; U.S. Army field station; Company E, U.S. Marine Support Battalion. Base occupied by U.S. forces in Sept. 1945. Area 3,865 acres. Runway 10,000 ft. Altitude 119 ft. Military 4,653 (total U.S. forces); U.S. civilians 160; local nationals 939. Payroll $168 million. Housing: 11 senior office, 113 field-grade officer, 211 company-grade officer, 1,835 enlisted. Unaccompanied housing: 120 officer, 871 enlisted, 166 transient (40 VAQ, 80 VOQ, 46 TLF). Unaccompanied Navy housing: 108 officer (transient), 356 enlisted (196 permanent party, 160 transient). 15-bed hospital, expandable to 65 for contingencies.

Moody AFB, Ga. 31699-5000; 10 mi. NNE of Valdosta. Phone (912) 333-4211; DSN 460-1110. ACC base. 347th Wing, F-16C/D (LANTIRN-equipped), C-130E, A/OA-10; 71st Air Control Sqdn. Tenant units: 336th USAF Recruiting Sqdn.; Det. 717, AFOSI; 332d Training Det. Base activated in June 1941; named for Maj. George P. Moody, killed May 5, 1941, while test-flying a Beech AT-10. Area 6,050 acres. Runway 8,000 ft. Altitude 233 ft. Military 3,752; civilians 408. Payroll $145.9 million. Housing: 32 officer, 270 enlisted, 18 VAQ, 32 VOQ, 12 TLF, 39 trailer spaces. 10-bed hospital with Acute Care Clinic.

Mountain Home AFB, Idaho 83648-5000; 10 mi. SW of Mountain Home. Phone (208) 828-2111; DSN 728-2111. ACC base. 366th Wing, USAF's first and only air-intervention composite wing, with F-16C attack, F-15E interdiction, F-15C air superiority, and KC-135R air refueling aircraft prepared to deploy rapidly worldwide and perform composite air-intervention operations. Base activated in Aug. 1943. Area 9,112 acres. Runway 13,500 ft. Altitude 3,000 ft. Military 3,635; civilians 416. Payroll $174.2 million. Housing: 246 officer, 1,275 enlisted, 178 VAQ, 16 VOQ, 65 TLF. 50-bed hospital

Nellis AFB, Nev. 89191-5000; 8 mi. NE of Las Vegas. Phone (702) 652-1110; DSN 682-1110. ACC base. Host unit: Air Warfare Center. Operational elements: 57th Wing; 99th Air Base Wing; 53d Wing (Eglin AFB, Fla.). Major units within 57th Wing include the USAF Weapons School, USAF Air

Demonstration Sqdn. (Thunderbirds), 57th Operations Gp., 57th Test Gp. (including 422nd Test and Evaluation Sqdn.), and 57th Logistics Gp. Aircraft assigned to Nellis: A-10, F-15E, F-16, and HH-60G. Other Nellis units include the 414th Combat Training Sqdn. (Red Flag), 549th Combat Training Sqdn. (Air Warrior), 547th Intelligence Sqdn., 99th Range Gp., 820th Civil Engineering Sqdn. RED HORSE, 896th Munitions Sqdn. (AFMC), 11th Reconnaissance Sqdn. (UAV), and the 66th Rescue Sqdn. (Pave Hawks). Base activated in July 1941 as AAF Flexible Gunnery School; closed in 1947; reopened in 1949 and named for 1st Lt. William H. Nellis, WWII P-47 fighter pilot, killed Dec. 27, 1944, in Europe. Main base is 11,000 acres with a range restricted area of 3.5 million acres, plus 12,000 sq. mi. of airspace over the range and the military operating area. Runways 10,051 ft. and 10,119 ft. Altitude 1,868 ft. Military 7,009; civilian 942. Payroll $302.7 million. Housing: 90 officer, 1,142 enlisted, 267 VAQ, 153 VOQ, 60 TLF. 119-bed Nellis Federal Hospital, a joint Air Force-Veterans Administration venture assigned to the 99th Medical Gp.

Newark AFB, Ohio 43057-5990; 1 mi. SW of Newark. Phone (614) 522-2171; DSN 346-7000. AFMC base. Aerospace Guidance and Metrology Center. Repairs inertial guidance and navigation systems for most Air Force missiles and aircraft as well as a variety of inertial systems for other branches of the armed forces. Also manages the Air Force's worldwide measurement and calibration program, providing the link between the National Institutes of Science and Technology and the Air Force's 180 precision measurement equipment laboratories at bases around the world. Four tenant units. Activated as an Air Force station Nov. 7, 1962. Area 70 acres. No runway. Military 60; civilians 1,400. Payroll $70 million. Base was scheduled for closure Oct. 1, 1996.

Offutt AFB, Neb. 68113-5000; 8 mi. S of Omaha. Phone (402) 294-1110; DSN 271-1110. ACC base. Hq. U.S. Strategic Command. 55th Wing; Strategic Joint Intelligence Center; Hq. Strategic Communications-Computer Center; Air Force Global Weather Central; 6th Space Operations Sqdn. (AFSPC); National Airborne Operations Center (NAOC); Air Combat Command Heartland of America Band. Base activated in 1896 as Army's Fort Crook; landing field named for 1st Lt. Jarvis J. Offutt, WWI pilot who died Aug. 13, 1918, from injuries received at Valheureux, France. Area 4,056 acres (including housing area and off-base sites). Runway 11,700 ft. Altitude 1,048 Ft. Military 9,340; civilians 1,592. Payroll $351.9 million. Housing: 337 officer, 2,293 enlisted, 69 VAQ, 102 VOQ, 60 TLF. 60-bed hospital.

Osan AB, Republic of Korea, APO AP 96278-5000; 38 mi. S of Seoul. Phone (commercial, from CONUS) 011-82-333-661-1110; DSN 784-4110. PACAF base. Hq. 7th Air Force. Host unit: 51st Fighter Wing, F-16C/D, C-12F, A-10, and OA-10A operations. Tenant units: 303d Intelligence Sqdn.; 631st Air Mobility Support Sqdn. (AMC); 5th Reconnaissance Sqdn.; 31st Special Operations Sqdn.; Det. 1, 4th Space Surveillance Sqdn. (AFSPC). Originally designated K-55; runway opened in Dec. 1952; renamed Osan AB in 1956 for nearby town that was the scene of first fighting between U.S. and North Korean forces in July 1950. Area 1,674 acres. Runway 9,000 ft. Altitude 38 ft. Military 5,538, U.S. civilians 130; local nationals 617. Payroll NA. Housing: 75 officer, 212 enlisted. Unaccompanied housing: 602 officer and senior NCO, 2,750 enlisted, 120 VOQ. 140 VAQ. 30-bed hospital.

Patrick AFB, Fla. 32925-3237; 2 mi. S of Cocoa Beach. Phone (407) 494-1110; DSN 854-1110. AFSPC base. Operated by the 45th Space Wing in support of DOD, NASA, and other agency and commercial missile and space programs. Major tenants: Defense Equal Opportunity Management Institute; Air Force Technical Applications Center; 1st Rescue Gp., 41st Rescue Sqdn.; 71st Rescue Sqdn.; 301st Rescue Sqdn. (AFRES); 741st Consolidated Aircraft Maintenance Sqdn.; Joint Task Force for Joint STARS at Melbourne Regional Airport, Fla. Besides host responsibilities for Patrick AFB and Cape Canaveral AS, 45th SPW also oversees operations at tracking stations on Antigua and Ascension Islands. Patrick has supported more than 3,000 space launches from Cape Canaveral since 1950. Base activated in 1940; named for Maj. Gen. Mason M. Patrick, Chief of AEF's Air Service in WWI and Chief of the Air Service/Air Corps, 1921–27. Area 2,341 acres. Runway 9,000 ft. Altitude 9 ft. Military 2,700; civilians 1,900. Payroll $155 million (military, civilian). Housing: 136 officer, 1,230 NCO. 15-bed hospital.

Peterson AFB, Colo. 80914-5000; at eastern edge of Colorado Springs. Phone (719) 556-7321; DSN 834-7011. AFSPC base. Hq. Air Force Space Command. Host unit: 21st Space Wing (AFSPC). Provides support to Hq. North American Aerospace Defense Command; Hq. U.S. Space Command; Hq. Army Space Command; 302d Airlift Wing (AFRES). Edward J. Peterson Air & Space Museum. Base activated in 1942; named for 1st Lt. Edward J. Peterson, killed Aug. 8, 1942, in an aircraft crash at the base. Area 1,277 acres. Runway shared with city. Altitude 6,200 ft. Military active-duty 4,299; reserves 1,260; civilians 3,065. Payroll $227.3 million. Housing: 107 officer, 384 NCO, 210 transient (72 VOQ, 98 VAQ, 40 TLF). Clinic.

Pope AFB, N. C. 28308-5000; 12 mil. NNW of Fayetteville. Phone (910) 394-0001; DSN 486-1110. ACC base. 23d Wing. 624th Air Mobility Support Gp. (AMC); 23d Aeromedical Evacuation Sqdn.; 23d Combat Control Sqdn.; 3d Aerial Port Sqdn. (AMC); Det. 3, MACOS (Combat Control School); 18th Air Support Operations Gp.; 24th Special Tactics Sqdn. (AFSOC). Base adjoins Army's Fort Bragg and provides intratheater airlift and close air support for airborne forces and other personnel, equipment, and supplies. Base activated in 1919; named after 1st Lt. Harley H. Pope, WWI flyer, killed Jan. 7, 1917, when his JN-4 "Jenny" crashed into the Cape Fear River near Fayetteville. Area 1,750 acres. Runway 7,500 ft. Altitude 218 ft. Military 4,052; civilians 434. Payroll $97.7 million. Housing: 89 officer, 370 enlisted, 1,208 dormitory spaces, 153 VOQ, 111 VAQ, 8 TLF. Clinic.

RAF Lakenheath, United Kingdom, APO AE 09464-5000; 70 mi. NE of London; 25 mi. from Cambridge. Phone (commercial, from CONUS) 011-44-1638-52-3000; DSN 226-1110. Royal Air Force base. 48th Fighter Wing

(USAFE) flies the F-15E and the F-15C and trains for and conducts air operations in support of NATO. Base activated in 1941; 48th FW began operations at RAF Lakenheath in Jan. 1960. Named after nearby village. Area 2,226 acres. Runway 9,000 ft. Altitude 32 ft. Military 5,200; civilians 2,300. Payroll $230 million. Housing: 1,424 units, 1,093 govt.-leased housing, 326 billeting spaces. Regional medical center.

RAF Mildenhall, United Kingdom, APO AE 09459-5000; 30 mi. NE of Cambridge. Phone (commercial, from CONUS) 011-44-1638-54-3000; DSN 238-3000. Royal Air Force base. Hq. 3d Air Force (USAFE). 100th Air Refueling Wing (USAFE), KC-135R and European Tanker Task Force operations, regional logistics support. Associate units include 352d Special Operations Gp. (AFSOC); 627th Air Mobility Support Sqdn. (AMC); 95th Reconnaissance Sqdn. (ACC); 488th Intelligence Sqdn. (AIA); Naval Air Facility. Base activated in 1934; U.S. presence began in July 1950; named after nearby town. Area 1,121 acres. Runway length NA. Altitude 33 ft. Military 4,765; civilians 765. Payroll $134 million. Housing: 42 officer, 116 enlisted; U.S. govt.-leased housing shared with RAF Lakenheath; 421 transient (40 TLF, 212 VOQ, 169 VAQ). Medical Annex.

Ramstein AB, Germany, APO AE 09094-0385: adjacent to Ramstein; 10 mi. W of Kaiserslautern. Phone (commercial, from CONUS) 011-49-6371-47-113; DSN 480-1110. Hq. USAFE and Hq. Allied Air Forces Central Europe (NATO) base. Host unit: 86th Airlift Wing. The 86th AW has a broad mission; the 37th Airlift Sqdn. flies the C-130E Hercules, the 75th Airlift Squadron flies the C-9 Nightingale, and the 76th Airlift squadron flies the C-20 Gulfstream, C-21 Learjet, and CT-43. Ramstein provides inter- and intratheater operational airlift, intratheater aeromedical evacuation, and CONUS staging and aeromedical evacuation. The wing commander also serves as commander of the Kaiserslautern Military Community, the largest concentration of U.S. citizens (49,300) outside the U.S. The KMC encompasses more than 1,000 sq. mi. and 12 USAF and Army military installations. Base activated and U.S. presence began in 1953. Area 10,261 acres. Runway 8,030 ft. Altitude 782 ft. Military 8,733; civilians 4,908. Payroll $149.5 million. Housing: 1,797; 9 govt.-leased units; 1,078 billeting units. Clinic on base, and the Landstuhl Regional Medical Center is nearby.

Randolph AFB, Tex. 78150-5000; 17 mi. ENE of San Antonio. Phone (210) 652-1110; DSN 487-1110. AETC base. Hq. Air Education and Training Command; Hq. 19th Air Force; 12th Flying Training Wing; T-37, T-38, and T-1A pilot instructor training; T-43 undergraduate navigator training, C-21A airlift, and T-3 flight screening at Hondo, Tex., and the U.S. Air Force Academy; Hq. Air Force Personnel Center; Hq. Air Force Management Engineering Agency; Hq. Air Force Services Agency; USAF Occupational Measurement Sqdn.; Hq. Air Force Recruiting Service. Base activated in June 1930; named for Capt. William M. Randolph, killed Feb. 17, 1928, when his AT-4 crashed on takeoff at Groman, Tex. Area 5,011 acres. Two 8,350-ft. runways. Altitude 761 ft. Military 5,607; civilians 3,940. Payroll $384 million. Housing: 254 officer, 765 NCO, 210 VAQ, 480 VOQ, 348 UEQ, 200 UOQ, 30 TLF. Clinic.

Reese AFB, Tex. 79489-5000; adjacent to Lubbock. Phone (806) 885-4511; DSN 838-1110. AETC base. 64th Flying Training Wing, specialized undergraduate pilot training. Base activated in 1942; names for 1st Lt. Augustus F. Reese, Jr., P-38 fighter pilot killed during a train-strafing mission at Cagliari, Sardinia, May 14, 1943. Area 3,953 acres. Runways 6,500 ft, 10,500 ft., and 10,500 ft. Altitude 3,338 ft. Military 1,326; civilians and contractors 1,166. Payroll $50 million. Housing: 153 officer, 243 NCO, 83 transient (8 suites, 25 TLF, 34 VOQ, 16 VAQ). Clinic.

Robins AFB, Ga. 31098; 15 mi. SSE of Macon at Warner Robins. Phone (912) 926-1110; DSN 468-1110. AFMC base. Hq. Warner Robins Air Logistics Center provides worldwide logistics management for the F-15 air-superiority fighter, C-130 and C-141 cargo aircraft. helicopters, missiles, and remotely piloted vehicles. Other management responsibilities include the LANTIRN system, JTIDS, avionics, most Air Force airborne electronic warfare equipment, airborne communications equipment, airborne bomb- and gun-directing systems, fire-fighting equipment, general-purpose vehicles, and the Worldwide Military Command and Control System. 93d Air Control Wing (ACC), activated January 1996, will eventually have 2,500 personnel and 20 E-8C Joint STARS aircraft assigned. Other major units include Hq. Air Force Reserve (AFRES); 116th Bomb Win (ANG), B-1B; 78th Air Base Wing (AFMC); 19th ARW will be downsizing to a group, transferring all but 13 KC-135R and two EC-135 aircraft; 5th Combat Communications Gp. (ACC); 78th Communications-Computer Systems Gp. (AFMC). Base activated in Mar. 1942; named for Brig. Gen. Augustine Warner Robins, an early chief of the Materiel Division of the Air Corps, who died June 16, 1940. Area more than 8,700 acres. Runway 12,000 ft. Altitude 294 ft. Military 4,613; civilians 12,409. Payroll $740.7 million. Housing: 245 officer, 1,149 NCO, 40 TLF, 137 VOQ, 20-bed hospital.

Scott AFB, Ill. 62225-5000; 6 mi. ENE of Belleville. Phone (618) 256-1110; DSN 576-1110. AMC base. 375th Airlift Wing; Hq. Air Mobility Command; Hq. Air Force C4 Agency; Hq. U.S. Transportation Command; Hq. Air Weather Service; Combat Climatology Center; 932d Airlift Wing (AFRES Assoc.). Base activated June 14, 1917; named for Cpl. Frank S. Scott, the first enlisted man to die in an aircraft accident, killed Sept. 28, 1912, in a Wright B Flyer at College Park, Md. Area 3,230 acres. Runway 7,061 ft. Altitude 453 ft. Military 6,100; civilians 3,550. Payroll $466 million. Housing: 304 officer, 1,394 NCO, plus 96 spaces for privately owned trailers, 300 transient. 55-bed hospital; 82-bed aeromedical staging facility.

Seymour Johnson AFB, N.C. 27531-5000; within city limits of Goldsboro. Phone (919) 736-5400; DSN 488-1110. ACC base. 4th Fighter Wing,

F-15E operations; 916th Air Refueling Wing (AFRES), KC-135 operations. Base activated June 12, 1942; named for Navy Lt. Seymour A. Johnson, Goldsboro native, killed Mar. 5, 1941, in aircraft accident in Maryland. Area 3,233 acres. Runway 11,758 ft. Altitude 110 ft. Military 4,602; civilians 659. Payroll $185.7 million. Housing: 154 officer, 1,544 enlisted, 7 dorms housing 504 personnel, 7 DVQ, 6 SNCOQ, 46 VOQ, 64 VAQ, 27 TLF. 15-bed hospital.

Shaw AFB, S. C. 29152-5000; 10 mi. WNW of Sumter. Phone (803) 668-8110; DSN 965-1110. ACC base. 20th Fighter Wing, F-16 fighter operations and A/OA-10 close air support/forward air control operations; Hq. 9th Air Force. Base activated Aug. 30, 1941; named for 2d Lt. Ervin D. Shaw, one of the first Americans to see air action in WWI, killed in France July 9, 1918, when his Bristol fighter was shot down during a reconnaissance mission. Area 3,363 acres; supports another 13,000 acres. Runways 10,000 ft. and 8,000 ft. Altitude 244 ft. Military 5,462; civilians 553. Payroll $108.7 million. Housing: 170 officer, 1,534 enlisted, 897 UEQ, 180 transient (44 VAQ, 96 VOQ, 40 TLF). 25-bed hospital.

Sheppard AFB, Tex. 76311-5000; 4 mi. N of Wichita Falls. Phone (817) 676-7441; DSN 736-7441. AETC base. The 82d Training Wing includes the 82d and 782d Training Gps., which conduct courses in financial management, communications, electronics, aircraft maintenance, munitions, aerospace ground equipment, transportation, civil engineering skills, and education/training career fields; 882d Training Gp., which provides training in biomedical sciences, dentistry, health service administration, medical readiness, medicine, nursing, and the Physician Assistant Training Program; 982d Training Gp., which provides weapon system training at training detachments and operating locations worldwide; 82d Support Gp.; 82d Medical Gp., 82d Logistics Gp. The 80th Flying Training Wing (AETC) conducts T-37 and T-38 undergraduate pilot training and instructor pilot training in the Euro-NATO Joint Jet Pilot Training program. The 80th FTW also conducts the Introduction to Fighter Fundamentals course with AT-38 aircraft. Base activated June 14, 1941; named for U.S. Sen. Morris E. Sheppard of Texas, who died Apr. 9, 1941. Area 6,100 acres. Runways 6,000 ft., 7,000 ft., 10,000 ft., and 13,100 ft. Altitude 1,015 ft. Military 8,922; civilians 3,828. Payroll $257 million. Housing: 171 officer, 1,058 NCO, 7,563 transient (1,772 VAQ, 4,698 UPH, 564 UEPH, 58 TLF, 103 UOQ, 368 VOQ). 90-bed hospital.

Spangdahlem AB, Germany, APO AE 09126-5000; 9 mi. E of Bitburg; 20 mi. NE of Trier. Phone (commercial, from CONUS) 011-49-6565-61-1110; DSN 452-1110. USAFE base. 52d Fighter Wing flies A/OA-10s, F-15s, and F-16s. Base activated and U.S. presence began in 1953; named after local town. Area 1,282 acres. Runway 10,000 ft. Altitude 1,196 ft. Military 5,808 (including 1,387 GSUs); civilians 798 (including 63 GSUs). Payroll $175 million. Housing: 157 officer, 2,039 enlisted, 499 govt.-leased units, 157 billeting spaces. 20-bed hospital at Bitburg Annex.

Tinker AFB, Okla. 73145-3010; 8 mi. SE of Oklahoma City. Phone (405) 732-7321; DSN 884-1110. AFMC base. Hq. Oklahoma City Air Logistics Center manages and provides logistics support and depot maintenance for more than 850 aircraft including the B-1B, B-2, B-52, and KC-135. Tinker is home to eight major DOD, Air Force, and Navy activities, including the 552d Air Control Wing (ACC); 507th Air Refueling Wing (AFRES), Oklahoma's only Air Force Reserve flying unit; Navy Strategic Communications Wing One. Also at Tinker are the Defense Logistics Agency's Defense Distribution Depot Oklahoma City; the 3d Combat Communications Gp.; Air Force Electronic Systems Center's 38th Engineering Installation Wing; and the Oklahoma City Megacenter (DIS), which manages Tinker's computer systems and services 110 other bases in 46 states. Base activated in Mar. 1942; named for Maj. Gen. Clarence L. Tinker, whose LB-30 (an early model B-24) went down at sea southwest of Midway Island June 7, 1942. Area 5,000 acres. Runways 10,000 ft. and 11,100 ft. Altitude 1,291 ft. Military 8,425; civilians 12,858. Payroll $765 million. Housing: 108 officer, 622 NCO. 22-bed hospital.

Travis AFB, Calif. 94535-5000; 50 mi. NE of San Francisco at Fairfield. Phone (707) 424-5000; DSN 837-1110. AMC base. Hq. 15th Air Force; 60th Air Mobility Wing; 615th Air Mobility Operations Gp.; 349th Air Mobility Wing (AFRES Assoc.); David Grant Medical Center; America's Band of the Golden West; Air Museum. Base activated May 17, 1943; named for Brig. Gen. Robert F. Travis, killed Aug. 5, 1950, in a B-29 accident. Area 6,258 acres. Two runways, each approximately 11,000 ft. Altitude 62 ft. Military 12,238; civilians 2,083. Payroll $618 million. Housing: 370 officer, 2,092 enlisted, 1,259 enlisted dormitory spaces, 924 transient (79 TLF, 201 VOQ, 644 VAQ). 298-bed hospital (acute care), 75 aeromedical staging flight beds, 52 dental treatment rooms.

Tyndall AFB, Fla. 32403-5000; 12 mi. E of Panama City. Phone (904) 283-1113; DSN 523-1113. AETC base. 325th Fighter Wing, F-15 operations. The 325th FW provides training for all USAF F-15 air-to-air pilots and maintains readiness for 77 aircraft and assigned operations and support personnel for combat units worldwide. Associate units include Hq. 1st Air Force; Southeast Air Defense Sector (ANG); 475th Weapons Evaluation Gp. (ACC); Air Force Civil Engineer Support Agency; 325th training Sqdn. Base activated Dec. 7, 1941; named for 1st Lt. Frank B. Tyndall, WWI fighter pilot killed July 15, 1930, in a P-1 crash. Area 29,115 acres. Runways 10,000 ft., 8.075 ft., and 7,065 ft. Altitude 18 ft. Military 5,237; civilians 1,109. Payroll $181 million. Housing: 1,069 family units. 35-bed hospital.

U.S. Air Force Academy, Colo. 80840-5025; N of Colorado Springs. Phone (719) 472-1818; DSN 259-3110. Direct reporting unit. Established Apr. 1, 1954. Moved to permanent location in Aug. 1958. Aircraft flown: 95, consisting of T-3A aerobatics trainers; TR-41D basic trainers; TG-3, TG-4, and TG-10 gliders; TG-7A and TG-11A motorized gliders; ASK-21 and 126E sailplanes; UV-18 jump planes; Cessna 150s. Tenant: Air Force Band of the Rockies (AFSPC). Area 18,325 acres. Runways 2,300 ft., 3,500 ft., and 4,500 ft. Altitude 7,200 ft. Military 2,402; cadets 4,000; civilians 1,861. Payroll $197.7 million. Housing: 619 officer, 609 enlisted, 78 VOQ, 25 TLF. 55-bed hospital.

Vance AFB, Okla. 73705-5000; 3 mi. SSW of Enid. Phone (405) 237-2121; DSN 940-2121. AETC base. 71st Flying Training Wing, undergraduate pilot training. Base activated in Nov. 1941; named for Lt. Col. Leon R. Vance, Jr., Enid native, 1939 West Point graduate, and Medal of Honor recipient, killed July 26, 1944, when airevac plane returning to the U.S. went down in the Atlantic near Iceland. Area 4,394 acres. Runways 5,000 ft., 9,200 ft., and 9,200 ft. Altitude 1,007 ft. Military 854; civilians 1,410 (approx. 1,200 contract employees). Payroll $69.5 million. Housing: 130 officer, 80 enlisted, 48 transient, 10 TLF. Clinic.

Vandenberg AFB, Calif. 93437-5000; 8 mi. NNW of Lompoc. Phone (805) 734-8252 (ext. 6-1611); DSN 276-1110. AFSPC base. Hq. 14th Air Force. Host unit: 30th Space Wing, conducts polar-orbiting space launches and supports research and development tests for DOD, USAF, and NASA space, ballistic missile, and aeronautical systems. It also has UH-1H helicopter assets. The 30th SPW furnishes facilities and essential services to more than 60 aerospace contractors on base. Originally Army's Camp Cooke. Activated in Oct. 1941. Base taken over by USAF June 7, 1957; renamed for Gen. Hoyt S. Vandenberg, USAF's second Chief of Staff. Area 98,400 acres. Runway length NA. Altitude 400 ft. Military 3,255; civilians 1,387; civilian contractors 3,835. Payroll $103 million (military and civilians). Housing: 494 officer, 1,499 NCO, 172 trailer spaces, 400 transient. 45-bed hospital.

Warren AFB (see Francis E. Warren AFB).

Whiteman AFB, Mo. 65305-5000; 2 mi. S of Knob Noster. Phone (816) 687-1110; DSN 975-6123. ACC base. Host unit: 509th Bomb Wing, activated Apr. 1, 1993. It received its first of 20 B-2 bombers Dec. 17, 1993. 442d Fighter Wing (AFRES). Base activated in 1942; named for Sedalia resident 2d Lt. George A. Whiteman, first pilot to die in aerial combat during the attack on Pearl Harbor. Area 4,627 acres. Runway 12,400 ft. Altitude 869 ft. Military 3,038; civilians 570. Payroll $121.9 million. Housing: 96 officer, 893 enlisted, 77 VAQ, 49 VOQ, 31 TLF. 30-bed hospital.

Wright-Patterson AFB, Ohio 45433; 10 mi. ENE of Dayton. Phone (513) 257-1110; DSN 787-1110. AFMC base. Hq. Air Force Materiel Command; Hq. Aeronautical Systems Center (AFMC); Wright Laboratory; Air Force Institute of Technology (AETC); Wright-Patterson Medical Center; 88th Air Base Wing (AFMC); 445th Airlift Wing (AFRES); approximately 70 other DOD activities and government agencies. Originally separate, Wright Field and Patterson Field were merged and redesignated Wright-Patterson AFB Jan. 13, 1948. Named for aviation pioneers Orville and Wilbur Wright and for 1st Lt. Frank S. Patterson, killed June 19, 1918, in the crash of a DH-4. The Wright brothers did much of their early flying on Huffman Prairie, now in Area C of present base. The prairie is part of the Dayton Aviation Heritage National Historical Park and is open to the public. Area 8,145 acres. Runway 19,600 ft. Altitude 824 ft. Military 8,505; civilians 14,628. Payroll (FY 1994) $879 million. Housing: 744 officer, 1,589 NCO. 301-bed hospital.

Yokota AB, Japan, APO AP 96328-5000; approx. 28 mi. W of Tokyo. Phone (commercial, from CONUS) 011-81-0425-2511, ext. 7020; DSN 225-7020. PACAF base. Hq. U.S. Forces, Japan; Hq. 5th Air Force, 630th Air Mobility Support Sqdn. (AMC). Host unit: 374th Airlift Wing (PACAF), C-130, UH-1N, C-9, and C-21 operations. Primary aerial port in Japan. Base opened as Tama AAF by Japanese in 1939. Area 1,750 acres. Runway 11,000 ft. Altitude 457 ft. Military 4,135; U.S. civilians 2,563; local nationals 1,359. Payroll $125 million. Housing: 644 officer, 1,942 enlisted, 56 TLF. Unaccompanied housing: 184 officer, 1,330 enlisted, 59 SNCOQ, 86 VOQ, 58 VAQ. 30-bed hospital.

Appendix B

Professional Reading Guide

A very important part of professional development is acquired through self-paced reading. The following pages note works that provide insight into the international military arena, the history of the USAF, and career development. Most of these titles can be obtained from your base library (either directly or through an inter-library loan), your base exchange, a Stars and Stripes bookstore, or the publisher. The letters in parentheses indicate reading ease: E = easy; A = average; D= difficult.

Air Power Journal. Professional journal of the United States Air Force. Published bimonthly by Government Printing Office, Washington, DC. A journal designed to stimulate professional thought concerning aerospace doctrine, strategy, tactics, and related matters.

Armitage. M. J. and R. A. Mason. *Air Power in the Nuclear Age.* Urbana, IL: University of Illinois Press, 1983. A discussion of the potential limits of airpower in the age of possible nuclear war, conventional or traditional conflicts, and unconditional warfare. (A)

Atkinson, Rick. *Crusade: The Untold Story of The Persian Gulf War.* New York: Houghton Mifflin Company, 1993. Balanced and well-written journalistic account of Operation Desert Storm. (E)

Baker, David. *The Shape of Wars to Come.* New York: Stein and Day, 1982. The author is a technical information consultant to NASA and has been deeply involved in future mission planning. He describes the work presently going on in antisatellite techniques, discusses the possibilities of lasers and charged-particle-beam weapons, and speculates on the ultimate threats from space. (A)

Blainey, Geoffrey. *The Causes of War.* New York: Free Press, 1988. An interesting account of the causes of war, blending history with international relations. (A)

Boettcher, Thomas D. *Vietnam: The Valor and the Sorrow.* Boston: Little, Brown and Company, 1985. The author has written a highly readable account of the American involvement in Vietnam. Beginning with the North Vietnamese struggle against French imperialism, Boettcher leads the reader through an analysis of the key events and major participants involved in America's struggle in Southeast Asia. Superb illustrations complement a comprehensive and even-handed account of the Vietnam Conflict. (E)

Brodie, Bernard, and Fawn Brodie. *From Crossbow to H-Bomb.* Bloomington: Indiana University Press, 1973. A historical survey of the role of science and technology in war. The Brodies present information on the major weapons that have affected war since ancient times. The book provides insight into the relationship among technology, tactics, and strategy. (A)

Brodie, Bernard. *War and Politics.* New York: The MacMillan Company, 1973. Brodie addresses an idea put forth by Clausewitz that the question of why we fight must dominate any consideration of means. Brodie first provides a general history of WWI, WWII, Korea, and Vietnam. He then discusses changing attitudes toward war and provides some theories on the causes of war. (D)

Builder, Carl H. *The Icarus Syndrome.* New Brunswick, NJ: Transaction Publishers, 1993. A provocative and critical look at the role of airpower in theory in the development of the U.S. Air Force. (A)

Builder, Carl H. *The Mask of War.* Baltimore, MD: The John Hopkins University Press, 1989. A provocative study arguing that institutional personalities determine how the services approach strategy and planning. (A)

Burrows, William E. *Deep Black: Space Espionage and National Security.* New York: Random House, 1987. Controversial and unverifiable look at space-based intelligence operations. (A)

Clausewitz, Karl Von. *On War.* Edited and translated by Michael Howard and Peter Paret. Princeton, NJ: Princeton University Press, 1976. The military classic on the art of waging war and the foundation of modern strategic science in warfare. (D)

Copp, DeWitt S. *A Few Great Captains.* New York: Doubleday, 1980. Written under the auspices of the Air Force Historical Foundation, this is a history of pre-WWII U.S. airpower that catches the drama and excitement of that early era. (A)

Copp, DeWitt S. *Forged in Fire.* New York: Doubleday, 1982. This sequel to *A Few Great Captains* covers WWII. It looks at the men who developed American airpower, surveys strategic bombing in Europe, and relates the quest for an independent Air Force. (A)

Douglass, Joseph D., Jr., and Amoretta M. Hoeber. *Soviet Strategy for Nuclear War.* Stanford, CA: Hoover Institution Press, 1979. This book is based on Soviet military literature available in the West. It reveals how the Soviet Union is using and planning to use its growing military power, both conventional and strategic, as an instrument of imperial expansion. (A)

Douhet, Guilio. *The Command of the Air.* Translated by Dino Ferrari. Washington, DC: Office of Air Force History, 1983 (1942). The first and most passionate exposition of a comprehensive air warfare theory. (A)

Hackett, John Winthrop. *The Profession of Arms.* London: Times Publishing Co., 1963. Traces the development, meaning, and implications of our military traditions while offering perceptive observations on training, discipline, and professionalism. (A)

Hallion, Richard P. *Storm over Iraq: Air Power and the Gulf War.* Washington, DC: Smithsonian Institution Press, 1992. This book argues that the Gulf War air campaign marked a revolution in military conflict: the ascendancy of airpower in warfare. (A)

LaQueur, Walter. *Guerrilla.* Boston: Little, Brown and Company, 1976. A critical interpretation of guerrilla and terrorist theory and practice throughout history. Rather than presenting a universal theory, the author uses a comparative approach to reveal common patterns. (D)

Newman, Aubrey S. *Follow Me: The Human Element in Leadership.* Novato, CA: Presidio Press, 1981. This book is basic to the better understanding of military life and leadership. The author, a seasoned combat veteran, draws upon a long and rich experience, flavored with humor, to illustrate practical lessons of leadership. (E)

Osgood, Robert E. *Limited War Revisited.* Boulder, CO: Westview Press, 1979. The author examines the development of limited way strategy since the end of WWII. In particular, he focuses on the impact of that strategy on the Vietnam Conflict and a limited war scenario in Central Europe. He also offers a comprehensive discussion on the types of conflict most likely to occur in the future. (A)

Preston, Richard A., Sidney F. Wise, and Alex Roland. *Men in Arms: A History of Warfare and Its Interrelationships with Western Society.* Fort Worth: Holt, Rhinehart and Winston, 1991. Sets military history in the broad spectrum of social, economic, political, and technological change in world history. (A)

Puryear, Edgar F. *Stars in Flight.* Novato, CA: Presidio Press, 1981. The biographer of *Nineteen Stars* addresses Air Force leadership, and his subjects are the first five Air Force Chiefs: Arnold, Spaatz, Vanderberg, Twining, and White. Similarities and differences among these individuals are examined as well as the differences between air command and ground command. The questions considered are, How did they get to the top; how did they lead while on the way to the top; and how did they run the show when they reached the top? (E)

Smith, Perry M. *Assignment Pentagon: The Insider's Guide to the Potomac Puzzle Palace.* Elmsford, NY: Pergamon Press, Inc., 1989. This book is a "must read" for personnel at all levels who are or will be working in the Pentagon. It's also of value for anyone who will be assigned to an intermediate headquarters. Content stresses effective staff work and communication. Of special note is the chapter titled "Rules of Thumb: Helpful Hints on How to Get Ready to Work, Survive, and Thrive." (E)

Smith, Perry. M. *Taking Charge: Making the Right Choices.* Garden City, NY: Avery Publishing Group, 1988. This book by Major General Smith provides exceptional insight into leadership roles in large and complex organizations. The content is well organized and presented in an easy-to-read format. Of special note are the segments on decision making and communication. (E)

Summers, Harry G., Jr. *On Strategy: The Vietnam War in Context.* Novato, CA: Presidio Press, 1982. A look at strategy in Vietnam. Why did we win all the battles yet lose the war? He explores Clausewitz's Balance Trinity of War—the People, the Government, and the Army. Special emphasis is placed on the role of public support in strategic planning and the role of the military in strategic thought. (A)

Sun Tzu Wu. *The Art of War.* New York: Oxford University Press, 1971. This short military treatise written in the sixth century B.C. lays down a set of basic military principles dealing with strategy, tactics, communications, supply, etc. The basic nature of Sun Tzu's tenets gives them a lasting relevance. (E)

Taylor, Robert L., and William E. Rosenback. *Military Leadership—In Pursuit of Excellence.* Boulder, CO: Westview Press, 1984. This book of writings by noted military and civilian authors covers the concept of leadership, the dilemma of leadership and management, leadership in transition, and military leadership as a challenge and an opportunity. The readings are well chosen to reflect traditional and contemporary leadership thoughts and practices. (E)

United States Air Force. *AFM 1-1, Volumes I and II: Basic Aerospace Doctrine of the United State Air Force.* Washington, DC: Government Printing Office, March 1992. Volume I contains the current definitive statement of U.S. Air Force basic doctrine. Volume II contains a set of background essays explaining and supporting current Air Force basic doctrine. (A)

Warden, John A. III. *The Air Campaign: Planning for Combat.* Washington, DC: Pergamon-Brassey's, 1989. An important book that proposes a theory of air warfare and links that theory to practical application at the operational (theater) level of warfare. (A)

Watts, Barry. *The Foundations of U.S. Air Doctrine: The Problem of Friction in War.* Maxwell Air Force Base, AL: Air University Press, 1984. A careful review of the development of Air Force doctrine and its application in World War II and Korea. Watts is especially concerned with the "friction" in war and argues for a less mechanistic approach to doctrine and strategy. The author is currently on active duty with the U.S. Air Force. (A)

Weigley, Russell F. *The American Way of War.* Bloomington, IN: IU Press, 1977. This is probably the most readable military history of the United States. The Weigley thesis divides our strategic thought into two categories. The first, annihilation as practiced by Grant and Eisenhower in the broad-front, weardown of the enemy, is cited as "the American way." The second strategy is that of attrition, as practiced by George Washington, Winfield Scott, and Geronimo. This strategy is not "the American way" in Weigley's view but deserves more attention that it gets. (A)

Whiting, Kenneth R. *The Development of the Soviet Armed Forces, 1917–1977.* Maxwell AFB, AL: Air University Printing Plant, 1977. After providing an introduction to Russian military heritage from medieval Russia through World War I, Dr. Whiting traces the development of the Soviet armed forces from a "ragged group of Red Guards" in 1917 to one of the mightiest armed forces in history. The book concludes with chapters that detail the organization and deployment of Soviet forces and provides a projection of Soviet military power. (A)

CAREER DEVELOPMENT GUIDES AND MILITARY/USAF–RELATED PUBLICATIONS FROM STACKPOLE BOOKS:

Benton, Col. Jeffrey C. (USAF, Ret.) *The Air Force Officer's Guide,* 31st Edition. Provides Air Force officers and those on their way to joining the officer corps the facts they need to get ahead.

Budahn, P. J., *Military Money Guide* (1st Edition). A complete guide to all types of military pay and entitlements.

Cline, Lydia Sloan. *Today's Military Wife: Meeting the Challenges of Service Life.* 2nd Edition. A down-to-earth sourcebook with practical advice on how to get the most out of military life.

Cragg, SGM Dan (USA, Ret.). *Guide to Military Installations,* 5th Edition. Comprehensive guide to the location, facilities, housing, climate, and customs of major military installations in the United States and overseas.

McIntosh, William A. *Guide to Effective Military Writing.* A handbook for getting things written quickly, correctly, and easily.

Meese, Maj. Michael (USA) *Armed Forces Guide to Personal Financial Planning,* 4th Edition. Strategies for managing your budget, savings, insurance, taxes, and investments.

Rhea, John. *SDI: What Could Happen.* Eight possible Star Wars scenarios.

Roots of Strategy: The 5 Greatest Military Classics of All Time. Edited by BG T. R. Phillips.

Roots of Strategy Book 2. Three classics in one volume by du Picq, Clausewitz, and Jomini.

Roots of Strategy Book 3. Three more recent classics on *Defense,* the *Power of Personality* and *Surprise.*

Tomes, LTC Jonathan P. (USA). *The Servicemember's Legal Guide,* 3d Edition. Everything you and your family need to know about the law.

Index

About the Author

Wayne A. Valey served in the United States Air Force in the grades of airman through technical sergeant in the Aerospace Defense Command, the United States Air Forces in Europe, and the Military Airlift Command. Following his commissioning at the USAF Officer Training School, he served as an executive officer for the Deputy Commander for Air Defense, Headquarters Tactical Air Command, as an inspector for major command inspector general teams, Chief of Base Level Information Management Services, and as a section commander for a USAF aircraft maintenance squadron that supported F-4D Phantom and F-16 Falcon fighter aircraft.

He is a graduate of the USAF Security Service Noncommissioned Officer Academy and the USAF Squadron Officer School at Air University. Valey retired from the USAF in the grade of captain and is a member of the Colorado Authors League and has presided on the Board of Directors for the National Writers Club and the Associated Business Writers of America. He and his family reside in Boulder, Colorado. He is presently employed with the United States Department of Veterans Affairs.